The Impact of the Holocaust
on Jewish Theology

The Impact of the Holocaust on Jewish Theology

EDITED BY

Steven T. Katz

New York University Press

NEW YORK AND LONDON

NEW YORK UNIVERSITY PRESS
New York and London
www.nyupress.org

Library of Congress Cataloging-in-Publication Data
The impact of the Holocaust on Jewish theology / edited by Steven T. Katz.
p.   cm.
Contains papers presented at 2 conferences entitled "Jewish thought after
the Holocaust," held in Ashkelon, Israel, in 1999 and 2001.
Includes bibliographical references and index.
ISBN 0-8147-4784-1 (cloth : alk. paper)
1. Holocaust (Jewish theology)—Congresses. 2. Holocaust, Jewish
(1939–1945)—Influence—Congresses. 3. Israel—History—Religious
aspects—Judaism—Congresses.   I. Katz, Steven T., 1944–
BM645.H6I45 2005
296.3'1174—dc22   2004027686

New York University Press books are printed on acid-free paper,
and their binding materials are chosen for strength and durability.

Manufactured in the United States of America

10 9 8 7 6 5 4 3 2 1

Contents

Editor's Introduction

In the 1960s and '70s the issue of post-Holocaust theology received a burst of attention. Among the seminal Jewish works on this subject produced in this period were Richard Rubenstein's *After Auschwitz* (Indianapolis, 1966) and *The Cunning of History* (New York, 1975); Emil Fackenheim's most important contributions, *God's Presence in History* (New York, 1970) and the essays collected together in his *Jewish Return into History* (New York, 1980); Ignaz Maybaum's *The Face of God after Auschwitz* (Amsterdam, 1965); Eliezer Berkovits's thoughtful *Faith after the Holocaust* (New York, 1973), and his interesting but less influential works, *Crisis and Faith* (New York, 1976) and *With God in Hell* (New York, 1979); and three major essays by Yitz Greenberg.[1] Taken altogether, these studies produced a body of serious and sustained reflection on this fundamental subject.

In turn, these original theological contributions also provoked significant critical responses by a number of Jewish thinkers.[2] Over the past twenty-five years, however, interest in this subject, judged by the absence of new ways of considering this basic theological issue, has waned. Jewish thinkers have simply been unable to find original and creative ways to address—to confront—the profound challenges raised by this subject.

Given the abiding importance of this topic for Jewish thought—and for Judaism as a living religion—this intellectual gridlock is, at least in the opinion of many reflective individuals, highly problematic. Recognizing this, and with the hope of encouraging new approaches to the subject, the Memorial Foundation for Jewish Culture funded and organized two conferences on "Jewish Thought after the Holocaust." The first of these was held in Ashkelon, Israel, in 1999, and the second was held at the same place in 2001. The present volume contains the majority of the papers presented at these conferences.[3]

As the co-organizer of these conferences (along with Professor Eliezer Schweid of the Hebrew University) I do not want to exaggerate the results they achieved. The key theological problems facing any Jewish (or other) thinker when trying to respond to the Holocaust remain monumental. At the same time, however, the original and erudite essays that make up this collection do help to clarify and advance the fundamental discussion in meaningful ways. They do represent significant contributions on key themes that all students of the subject will benefit from reading, especially because they are not only philosophically and theologically informed but also because many reflect, and draw on, deep Jewish learning not always evident in this area of scholarly concern. Given their many virtues, these essays, considered individually and taken as a whole, deserve a wide and thoughtful readership.

It is a pleasure for me to thank the Memorial Foundation and its thoughtful and innovative director, Dr. Jerry Hochbaum, for their material and spiritual assistance. The subject matter of this collection was a controversial one for the foundation to take on, but Dr. Hochbaum never flinched in his support. Financial help was also provided by the Conference on Material Claims against Germany, and we thank the leadership of the Claims Conference most sincerely for this support.

Sincere thanks are also owed to Jennifer Hammer, religion editor at New York University Press, whose generous help and support made this publication possible.

Closer to home, thanks are due to Ms. Pagiel Czoka, administrative assistant at the Elie Wiesel Center for Judaic Studies at Boston University, who helped in numerous ways with the work that first went into the two Ashkelon conferences and subsequently with the present publication.

NOTES

1. "Cloud of Smoke, Pillar of Fire: Judaism, Christianity, Modernity after the Holocaust," in E. Fleischner (ed.), *Auschwitz: Beginning of a New Era?* (New York, 1977), 1–55; "Judaism and History: Historical Events and Religious Change," in Jerry V. Dillen (ed.), *Ancient Roots and Modern Meanings* (New York, 1978), 43–63; and "New Revelations and New Patterns in the Relationship of Judaism and Christianity," *Journal of Ecumenical Studies* (Spring, 1979), 249–67.

2. Included in this group were, among others, Michael Wyschograd, Robert Gordis, Arthur Green, Jacob Neusner, Arthur A. Cohen, Michael Meyer, and myself.

3. A second volume drawn from the papers given at these conferences centers around the issue of "The Holocaust and Education." The work is being edited by Professor Jonathan Cohen of the Hebrew University of Jerusalem and is scheduled for publication in the near future.

Part I

The Holocaust

Chapter 1

Is There a Religious Meaning to the Idea of a Chosen People after the Shoah?

Eliezer Schweid

I prefer the above formulation of the problem of Jewish self-understanding after the Shoah because it emphasizes the emotional and intellectual difficulties that are involved in it. The idea of a chosen people established the self-consciousness of the Jewish people from its inception in the Babylonian exile to its second return to Zion. It seems that the Jewish people cannot recognize itself as the same people in any other image, but after the Shoah, the idea of a people created to fulfill a universal mission for humanity became for the majority of Jews a meaningless pretense.

Putting the question whether Jews still think of their people in terms of chosenness on the level of ritual and dogma, the answer would be positive with regard to the religious movements, both Orthodox and non-Orthodox, and negative with regard to secular movements. But, going down to the level of the individual, especially of the young generation, it seems that the question whether the individual's Jewishness endows him or her with a sense of universal mission will be answered with great embarrassment. Indeed, one should refrain from such politically incorrect questions, but on the other hand, one must admit that avoiding the question means covertly avoiding the concept that has given continuity to Jewish self-understanding throughout the ages.

I therefore believe that the task of integrating the memory of the Shoah into the comprehensive historical memory of the Jewish people obligates us to assume the burden of facing the problem, at least by clarifying the intellectual and emotional difficulties inherent in it.

The questions that should be asked preliminarily are as follows. First, what are the profound causes of the unwillingness to relate to the problem philosophically? Second, what does the will of the Jewish people "to hide its face" mean from the point of view of Jewish solidarity in the near future? And finally, is there a possibility that the Jewish people will reclaim a universal message that makes the continuity of its existence important to humanity? Is there a possibility that individual Jews who succeeded in reintegrating themselves socially and nationally into the normal life prevailing in the Western culture of our age will prefer being Jewish to any other form of self-identification that is open for them and that seems much more convenient in terms of normality?

I must first summarize very briefly the situation of the problem before the Shoah. Elsewhere[1] I have described the background of relations among Judaism, Christianity, and Islam and the fatal role that the Jewish people had to play in the formation of the new collective identities of secular nations and societies of the twentieth century. Here I will state only briefly that after the Enlightenment the Jewish people became the main challenger of a traumatic conflict in the self-understanding of Western nations and societies, thus placing itself in an unbearable position both for itself and for its sociocultural environment.

Trying to get out of the trap, the Jewish people was divided into two parts with regard to emancipation, one of which rejected the idea of Jewish chosenness and internalized the Christian, and afterwards the secular, anti-Semitic view that chosenness indicates a shameful depravity. The other part responded with reaffirmation of chosenness in its traditional halakic meaning, declaring that it means absolute separation, requiring Jews to remain uninvolved in the social, cultural, and political life of the surrounding secular culture. But the dialectics of the conflict eventually brought each of the groups, in its own way, to reclaim the idea of chosenness in new humanistic interpretations.

First to re-adopt chosenness through reinterpretation of its traditional meaning was the Reform movement. Against the refusal of the surrounding Christian society to accept the Jews as equals as long as they remained Jewish in any sense, Reform Judaism reinterpreted assimilation as a mission to teach humanity the values of humanism, and the right way to implement them in reality. The engagement with the idea of chosenness became even more profound for Reform Judaism in Germany after the last two decades of the nineteenth century, when it became clear that the success that many individual Jews had in assimilating into secular culture was so great that the vision of emancipation for the whole Jewish people was heading towards a catastrophic failure. The hatred against them motivated already assimilated Jews to turn with hurt pride back to their own original Jewish selves, research their Jewish roots, and reclaim chosenness because of the evidence that Judaism and the Jewish people are the only hope for humanism in Western culture.

Second to re-adopt the idea of a chosen people were the secular Zionist movements that headed first towards normalization in terms of European nationalism. The cause of the dramatic change was a combination of two factors. First, being engaged in the realization of the Zionist program made it evident that the idea of normalizing an exiled people is indeed abnormal. It needed many more resources than an impoverished, dispersed, and unorganized people possessed, while help from the outside was scarce. One could of course draw for strength upon necessity and lack of choice. Still, to achieve a significant start, Zionism needed the motivation of self-sacrificial idealism. Second, being engaged in the realization of the Zionist program required one to redefine the meaning of being normal. Does it mean to become exactly like the surrounding nations? If so, are they normal in their own terms? The anti-Semitism that motivated the Jewish return to normality was the indication of a deep crisis that followed the era of emancipation, both of nationalities and of societies in Europe. This meant that for the sake of truly becoming normal, the Jewish people must solve for itself not only its specific problem but also those cultural-political problems that modern Western civilization still failed to solve. Thus it became incumbent upon the Zionist movement to make the Jewish people like all the other nations, through a heroic universal undertaking that at one and the same time would normalize the Jewish people and would make it "a light unto all the nations."

This may explain the fact that on the brink of the Second World War almost all the movements within the Jewish people adopted the idea of chosenness, each in its own interpretation. In the Shoah they came even closer to each other. The common experience convinced them that Hitler declared his war specifically and mainly against the Jewish people because it symbolized for him the universal humanism that he rejected. The chosen people incarnated all that Hitler hated in the name of German racist superiority. The Shoah was, then, in the eyes of the victimized Jews, the struggle between Jewish moral chosenness and German racist monstrosity. Thus the final victory was also considered to be the success of the Jewish people to withstand its trial, to resist absolute wickedness, as the representative of true humanity created in the image of God.

But, what was the impact of this unifying consensus on Jewish self-understanding after the war and after the establishment of Israel as a main response to the Shoah? One impact was the natural feeling that Jewish solidarity must become the main life-restoring value and that it should be implemented by the unification of the Jewish people in its effort to build and strengthen Israel as a stronghold against any second threat of genocide. As a result, the idea of political Zionism—the most radical understanding of the will to normalize the Jewish people as a nation like all other nations—became the basis for Jewish solidarity after the Shoah. The Jewish people redefined itself through Zionism as the people that has survived. This redefinition was indeed a renewal of the ancient covenant as a "covenant of destiny," and its first commandment was to become a normal people that can defend itself effectively. Let us remember that the danger of a second Shoah was still ahead. The threat of Arab and Communist countries was too real to be ignored. Thus the memory of the Shoah and the task of economic, political, and military normalization became the common denominators defining Jewish unity despite the divisions and the antagonisms that still prevailed.

After the Six-Day War Emil Fackenheim defined this Zionist unifying consensus in the theological terms of chosenness. It was for him the 614th commandment "not to let Hitler have victory after his death," which positively meant making a second Shoah an impossibility. One should emphasize that Fackenheim understood this commandment not only in terms of the particularistic Jewish right to survive. The Jewish people still symbolized for him true humanity and its universal ethical values. The commandment to make a second Shoah impossible was for him a commandment to all humanity "to mend the world." But asking the practical question of how humanity should achieve this goal, taking into account all the lessons that should be drawn from the Second World War, Fackenheim pointed to the fact that the Shoah was an "unprecedented event," namely, an event that could be thought about and then executed only against the Jewish people, because of its specific condition in exile and its specific moral-theological mission to humanity. The implication was then that, practically, "to mend the world" means normalizing the conditions of the Jewish people by accepting it into the family of nations as a nation in its own right, then helping it to become strong enough to resist and protect itself efficiently against any threat.

It should be reemphasized that Fackenheim's impressive philosophical formulation of the idea of Jewish mission after the Six-Day War was already the pragmatic understanding that unified the Jewish people right after the War of Independence. This became also the main message of Jewish education, and, what is most important, it became the basic assumption that shaped Jewish policies both in Israel and in the Diaspora. All the efforts were concentrated around the undertaking of strengthening Israel in absorbing *aliyah,* in colonizing the land, in achieving economic independence, in integrating Israeli society, and last but not least, in building and fortifying its military power.

I believe that interpreting the mission of the Jewish people after the Shoah in these terms of normalization provides the profound explanation of the embarrassment surrounding the problem of chosenness today. The generation that matured after the Shoah, both in Israel and in the Diaspora, experienced the process of restoring the life of their people in terms of normalization, internalizing for that sake gradually also the new ethics of postmodernistic egoistical individualism. Thus it did not experience either in its Jewish education nor in its Jewish activities a sense of the universal message that Judaism is about. The only universal message this generation did experience was, as stated above, the lesson that after the Shoah a nation must rely for its well-being and safety only on itself, not on any idealistic vision, not on any belief in the progress of humanity, not on divine providence. Even for Orthodox Jews, both Zionists and *haredi,* the messiah that they believe in is a messiah that has already started to arrive, and their messianism is a matter of striving for power, safety, and happiness in the here and now of worldly achievements. Against this background, mending the world is interpreted in terms of developing balances of power among individuals, parties, societies, and nations that will make cooperation among them more beneficial than rivalry, enmity, and war.

Fackenheim emphasized this understanding of his 614th commandment when he protested against claims that a Jewish state should keep a higher standard of morality than other nations, even when fighting against enemies that try to destroy it. His response was similar to that of political Zionism before the Second World War: in the past this was the cause of Jewish weakness and therefore the Jewish people was victimized. After the Shoah we should know better. Weakness tempts enemies to implement their murderous wishes, so the ethical commandment should be, Thou shalt not be weak! If you chose to be weak, you are morally condemned! Which means that after the Shoah the Jewish people should defend itself in ways that will make its enemies think twice before they attack it. This is the way every normal group of people defends itself. Why should a Jewish state behave differently? Which nation has the right to demand that a Jewish state should behave differently?

I am not trying to contest this view. I am also a Zionist, and I think that in the context of a war for existence this attitude is fully justified. It seems to me that it is also justified in Jewish halakic terms. But when this political program also becomes the essence of mending the world as a Jewish message to humanity, the whole idea of chosenness becomes a farce. Let me illustrate what I mean with one example.

During the period of building the land before the establishment of the state, and even in the first decades after its establishment, Israel was proud of its idealistic socialistic achievements and proclaimed them to be its universal message to humanity. But the moshavim and the kibbutzim collapsed under the economic capitalistic success of Israel. After being normalized economically, Israel then took as its pride in spectacular achievements in agriculture, namely, its success in transforming the desert into a source of abundance. For several years this was Israel's contribution to some poor countries, especially in Africa, and it was considered to be its universal message to humanity. But agriculture too became an economic burden due to capitalistic economic normalization, so now the pride of Israel is the IDF as the strongest military power in the Middle East and as a leading power in the use of high-tech armaments. The IDF is surely very important for safety, wealth, and peace with neighbors, but naturally one can hardly interpret it as a redeeming message to humanity, though Israel indeed became distinguished in the world as a producer and deliverer of sophisticated arms. But should we consider this capacity to be the ultimate universal message of normalization?

Naturally, during the period of struggle for survival, when the threat of a second Shoah was real, one could not realize that such an outcome would be the impact of the 614th commandment. But is was precisely after the Six-Day War that caused Fackenheim to formulate his commandment that Jews started to have more and more reason to believe they had already restored their people to normal parameters of safety, personal freedom, higher education, economic success, a high standard of living, and strong political status, both in Israel and in the western Diaspora, and this, of course, made a revolutionary difference.

It suddenly became obvious that once normalization has been achieved, this state cannot be morally conceived of as an end in itself, nor can it be appreciated as an act of mending the world, even if it becomes a place where genocides and other national and social wrongs and injustices are unthinkable. On the contrary, it means participating as one power among other powers in being responsible for a world full of injustices and terror, in which attempted genocides occur quite regularly and in which, eventually, in the process of restoring itself to power, Israel itself may become a cause of injustice done to another people.

What then are the implications of the normalization that has already been achieved when it is understood not as a tool of working for higher ideals but as an end in itself? What does normalization in the sense of being "like all other nations" mean for a people that is still different structurally and historically from all other nations in terms of religion, ethics, culture, political establishments, and ways of communicating among its different parts and its different environments? The irony of the present situation may be summed up in the following sentence: Being normal "like all other nations" (By the way, is there even one nation that is normal in such universal terms?) seems to be definitely abnormal for the Jewish people. Through normalization the Jewish people become a conglomerate of antagonistic identities, and the war between its parts and parties makes it act as its own enemy.

As my space is limited, I will try not to prove my verdict through an analytical description of the present: the Kultur Kampf in Israel, the growing assimilation in the Diaspora, and the growing estrangement between Israel and the Diaspora. I assume these phenomena are known to everyone as they are known to me. My conclusion is that unless the Jewish people is restored to its real self as a people engaged in the realization of a redeeming principle for itself and for humanity, it will become a stranger to itself, will bring itself to the brink of another catastrophe, as it has already done several times during its long history.

The final question that I must try to answer is therefore this: can we find a meaning to the idea of a chosen people after the Shoah, not only in terms of ritual and dogma but also in terms of values, ideals, and commandments? I will try to answer this question very briefly, in fact "on one foot" like our old sage Hillel. As I have said in the beginning of my paper, I think that the Orthodox understanding of the idea of a chosen people became meaningless for the majority of the Jewish people after the Shoah, and I do not believe that it can be recovered or reinterpreted in a convincing way, but the idea of a chosen people may become meaningful again, and indeed redeeming, if interpreted in terms of the ancient prophetic covenant that obligated the Jewish people to the ethics of responsibility to build a different society and a different statehood, based on freedom and justice. By "ethics" I mean those that interpret human freedom and dignity not in terms of individual rights, which eventually create formal obligations towards the other and the collective, but in terms of obligations towards the other and the collective, which become the sound basis for realized individual rights. I believe that the morality of the covenant is the only way to reunite the Jewish people, to root it in its sources and in its historical memory, and at the same time to respond to the challenge of egoistical individualism that has now become the essence of paganism in our era and is the biggest moral threat to the future of humanity. The commandment to "mend the world" should be interpreted in the terms of the covenant.

Let me conclude my paper by reminding readers that the covenant has been renewed only yesterday, immediately after the Shoah, with the establishment of the state of Israel. In its Scroll of Independence Israel has taken upon itself the obligation to become a Jewish state: Jewish in its responsibility to all the people and to its history and Jewish in its statutes, laws, and policies, which must strive to realize the eternal prophetic values of Judaism and thus redeem the Jewish people spiritually as well as materially, and contribute to the redemption of humanity. The sources of this covenant were according to the Scroll of Independence, "the Eternal Book of Books," the history of the Jewish people, the history of the Zionist enterprise, and the universal Scroll of Human Rights. On this basis the founders of Israel took it upon themselves to build a state that "will be based on the foundations of freedom, justice and peace in the light of the prophets of Israel." Indeed, all this was stated in the scroll in too general terms, but the cited sources made the scroll a basis for a concrete conception of a society and a state that will become the spiritual center for the Jewish people and the source of a universal message to humanity.

NOTE

1. Eliezer Schweid, "The Holocaust as a Challenge to Jewish Thought on Ultimate Reality and Meaning," in *Ultimate Reality and Meaning*, vol. 14, no. 3 (September, 1991).

Chapter 2

The Issue of Confirmation and Disconfirmation in Jewish Thought after the Shoah

Steven T. Katz

Karl Popper, in particular, has taught modern thinkers that in assessing the truth of a proposition it is necessary to state the conditions under which the proposition would not be true. Since Popper's initial work on this issue, it has become clear that the matter is not as straightforward as he, with his specific philosophical, logical, and scientific assumptions, thought—and that there are deep problems connected with establishing the truth of a proposition by recourse to the conditions that would disconfirm it. However, the Popperian legacy in this regard, if I might so refer to it, is not without importance, especially in relationship to theological discourse in what I will broadly call the analysis of theodicy. That is, theologians and philosophers of religion need to pay close attention to the logical matters of confirmation and disconfirmation when they attempt to answer questions regarding divine justice—and this nowhere more so than when Jewish thinkers attend to the issue of theodicy after Auschwitz.

In this essay I would like to critically review some of the efforts that have been made in this arena as a first step towards trying to think through to a more substantial, defensible Jewish theological response to the Shoah.

To make clear what is at stake in this discussion, I will begin by reconstructing the position of the well-known Jewish "Death of God" theologian Richard Rubenstein. Rubenstein has been criticized severely within the Jewish intellectual community, but his effort raises elementary theological and metaphysical questions with clarity and directness. Rubenstein's position can be summed up in three words: "God is dead." The logic that has driven him to utter these three extraordinarily powerful words can be put in the following syllogism: (1) God, as He is conceived of in the Jewish tradition, could not have allowed the Holocaust to happen; (2) the Holocaust did happen. Therefore, (3) God as he conceived of in the Jewish tradition does not exist.

This seemingly straightforward argument is the basis upon which Rubenstein has felt compelled to reject the God of history and hence the God of Jewish tradition. The radical negation represented by this position is of the utmost seriousness for modern Jewish (and non-Jewish) thought, even if one finally dismisses it as out of place in a Jewish context, as some naïve critics have done.[1] It does raise a real, if frightening, possibility about the "meaning of Auschwitz," i.e., that there is no meaning to history, for history is a random, arbitrary series of events that are unrelated either to a transcendental order or to a context of absolute meaning or value. In *After Auschwitz*,[2] Rubenstein stated this contention articulately:

> When I say we live in the time of the death of God, I mean that the thread uniting God and man, heaven and earth has been broken. We stand in a cold, silent, unfeeling cosmos, unaided by any purposeful power beyond our own resources. After Auschwitz what else can a Jew say about God? . . . I see no other way than the "death of God" position of expressing the void that confronts man where once God stood.[3]

Philosophically this challenge to belief, generated from the consideration of the implications of Auschwitz, is both interesting and more problematic than it at first appears. Let me note, specifically, before saying anything else, that rather than accept Israel's sinfulness as the justification for the Holocaust or see it as some inscrutable act of divine wrath or fiat, the vision of which appears to blaspheme against the loving God of the Jewish tradition and the entire meaning of Jewish covenantal existence, the radical theologian takes the difficult step of denying both poles of the divine-human dialectic, thereby destroying the traditional theological encounter altogether. There is no God and there is no covenant with Israel:

> If I believe in God as the omnipotent author of the historical drama and Israel as His chosen People, I had to accept [the] . . . conclusion that it was God's will that Hitler committed six million Jews to slaughter. I could not possibly believe in such a God nor could I believe Israel is the chosen people of God after Auschwitz.[4]

The second element emerging out of, as well as essential to, the "Death of God" view putatively grounded in the Holocaust experience is equally fundamental. It concerns nothing less than the way one views Jewish history, its continuities and discontinuities, its "causal connectedness" and interdependencies. By raising the issue of how one evaluates Jewish history and what hermeneutic of historic meaning one need adopt, I mean to bring into focus the fact—and it is a fact—that the radical theologian sees Jewish history too narrowly, i.e., focused solely in and through the Holocaust. He takes the decisive event of Jewish history to be the death camps. But this is a distorted image of Jewish experience, for there is a pre-Holocaust and post-Holocaust Jewish reality that must be considered in dealing with the questions raised by the Nazi epoch. These questions extend beyond 1933–1945 and touch the present Jewish situation as well as the whole of the Jewish past. One cannot make the events of 1933–1945 intelligible in isolation. To think, moreover, that one can excise this block of time from the flow of Jewish history and then, by concentrating on it, extract the "meaning" of *all* Jewish existence is more than uncertain,[5] no matter how momentous or demonic this time may have been.

Jews went to Auschwitz and suffered and died at Auschwitz through no specific fault of their own: their crime was their Jewishness. The Nuremberg laws extracted from the 1933–1945 generation the price of their parents', grandparents', and great-grandparents' decision to have Jewish children. This, if nothing else, forces us to widen our historic perspective when we try to comprehend what happened in Nazi Germany. When one tries to understand the "grandparents" of the death camp generation one will find that their actions are likewise unintelligible without following the historic chain that leads backwards into the Jewish millennial past. The same rule also applies in trying to fathom the historic reality of the murderers and their inheritance. The events of 1933–1945 were the product of the German and Jewish past; to decode this present we must enter into that past.

This recognition of a pre-Holocaust and post-Holocaust Israel forces two considerations upon us. The first is the very survival of the Jewish people despite their "sojourn among the nations." As both Fredrick the Great and Karl Barth are reported to have said, "the best proof of God's existence is the continued existence of the Jewish people." Without entering into a discussion of the metaphysics of history, let this point just stand for further reflection, i.e., that the Jews survived Hitler and Jewish history did not end at Auschwitz. Secondly, and equally if not more directly significant, is the recreation after Auschwitz of a Jewish state, the Third Jewish Commonwealth in the land of Israel.[6] This event, too, is remarkable in the course of Jewish existence. Logic and conceptual adequacy require that if in our discussion of the relation of God and history we want to give theological weight to the Holocaust, then we *must* also be willing to attribute *theological* significance to the state of Israel. Just what weight one assigns to each of these events, and then again to events in general, in constructing a theological reading of history is an extraordinarily complex theoretical issue, about which there is need for much discussion, and which allows for much difference of view. Still, it is clear that any final rendering of the "meaning of Jewish history" that values in its equation only the negative factors of the Nazi Holocaust or it and previous holocausts is, at best, arbitrary. If one wants to make statements about God's presence (or in this case absence) in Jewish history as a consequence of Auschwitz then one must also, in all theological and existential seriousness, consider the meaning of His presence (or absence) in Jewish history as played out in Jerusalem. If it makes sense to talk theologically at all—an open question—about God's presence and absence, His existence and nonexistence, and to judge these matters on the basis of what happened to the Jews of Europe in some sort of negative natural theology, then it is equally meaningful and logically—*and theologically—necessary* to consider what the events in *Eretz Yisroel* since 1945 tell us about His reality and ours.

To his credit, Rubenstein does appreciate that the state of Israel is of consequence, even momentous consequence, but he insists on treating it as *theologically* independent from Auschwitz so that no positive linkage in some larger rendering of Jewish experience is possible; nor can we posit what in traditional idiom would be termed "redemptive" significance to this national rebirth. Rather, the renaissance of Jewish life in its ancestral homeland is seen by Rubenstein, consistent with his own procedure, as the clearest manifestation of the post-1945 rejection of the God of history by Jews and their return to a natural, land-related, nontheistic life.

However, despite Rubenstein's interesting working through of this event in his own terms, his interpretation of the situation will not do, for it is clear that from a logical point of view it is methodologically improper to construct a phenomenology of historical reality that gives weight only to the negative significance of "evil" without any attempt to balance it against the positive significance of the "good" we encounter in history. History is too variegated to be understood only as good or evil; the alternating rhythms of actual life reveal the two forces as interlocked and inseparable. For our present concerns, the hermeneutical value of this recognition is that one comes to see that Jewish history is neither conclusive proof of the existence of God (because of the possible counterevidence of Auschwitz) nor, conversely, is it proof of the nonexistence of God (because of the possible counterevidence of the state of Israel as well as the whole three-thousand-year historic Jewish experience). Rubenstein's narrow focus on Auschwitz reflects an already decided theological choice based on certain normative presuppositions and a compelling desire to justify certain conclusions. It is not a value-free phenomenological description of Jewish history.

Before I leave this argument it should be made absolutely clear that it is not being asserted that the state of Israel is compensation for Auschwitz, nor that Auschwitz is the "cause," in a theological or metaphysical sense, of the creation of the Jewish state, as many simplistic historical and theological accounts, offered for all kinds of mixed reasons, have asserted. Whatever relation does exist between Holocaust Europe and the state of Israel is far more ambiguous and many sided than a simple causal or compensatory schema would explain. The argument as presented, however, is a reminder that the state of Israel is an event—one might, I think, even legitimately say a "miracle," if that term means anything at all—at least equal to if not more important than Auschwitz in Jewish theological terms; it must be respected as such.

There is an unspoken but implied, highly influential premise in Rubenstein's argument concerning the relation of God and history. This hidden premise relates to what is well known as the "empiricist theory of meaning" made famous by A. J. Ayer in *Language, Truth and Logic* and then given a more particularly significant theological twist by Anthony Flew in his "falsifiability challenge." This was first expressed in the widely discussed "University Discussion" reprinted in *New Essays in Philosophical Theology*.[7] Space prohibits an extended review of this most aggressive challenge to religious belief, which in any case is familiar enough if not always completely understood, but its implicit use in the "Death of God" argument must at least be called into the open, for it is the employment of this thesis that provides much of the initial rigor of the radical theologian's challenge. I am not sure whether Rubenstein's employment of this notion is intentional or indirect, but its presence and significance for Rubenstein is nonetheless real. He at least tacitly accepts the basic premise of the "empiricist falsifiability thesis," i.e.,[8] that propositions about God are to be straightforwardly confirmed or disconfirmed by appeal to empirical events in the world. It is only the result of the at-least-implicit adoption of this empirical principle, or something very close to it, that allows Rubenstein to judge that "God is dead," for it is only on the basis of some such norm that the conditions of the Holocaust can become the empirical test case for the existence or nonexistence of God. In effect Rubenstein argues as follows: if there is too much evil in the world (putting aside the problem of how one would measure this for the moment and recognizing that this subject is never dealt with by Rubenstein), then God, as conceived in the Jewish tradition, cannot exist. At Auschwitz there was such evil and God did not step in to stop it; thus God does not exist. Hence the traditional theological notions based upon such a belief in God are decisively falsified by an appeal to this empirical evidence.

Respecting this challenge as an important one that is often too lightly dismissed by theologians, and respecting Rubenstein's employment of it as an authentic existential response to an overwhelming reality, I nonetheless would point out that the empirical falsifiability challenge is not definitive one way or the other in theological matters and thus cannot provide Rubenstein (or others) with an unimpeachable criterion for making the negative theological judgments that he seeks to advance regarding the nonexistence of God. The falsifiability thesis allows one *decisively* neither to affirm nor to disaffirm God's presence in history, for history provides evidence both for and against the nonexistence of God on empirical verificationist grounds, i.e., there is both good and bad in history. Moreover, the very value of the empirical criteria turns on the one hand on what one considers to be empirical verificationist evidence, i.e., on what one counts as empirical or experiential, and on the other, on whether the empirical verificationist principle is, in itself, philosophically coherent, which it appears not to be. Again, here too the state of Israel is a crucial "datum" (and solidly empirical) for the radical theologian to consider when framing his falsifiability equation, for the Jew (or others) might challenge the critic with this counterclaim: "Yes, the assertion of God's existence does depend on what happens in history. Among the events of history is not only Auschwitz but also the creation of the state of Israel. Whereas the former event is evidence against the 'God hypothesis,' the latter is evidence in its favor." Neither position is decisively provable—but both are equally meaningful,[9] as well as equally unprovable.

Again, the Jew (or a Christian like Barth) might respond to the falsifiability challenge by returning to the first historical argument discussed above—i.e., Auschwitz is not decisive evidence for or against God's existence—and meet the empiricist critic head on by rephrasing the nature of the empiricist challenge itself. That is, he could argue that he accepts the challenge in general terms but offers different specific empirical conditions by which to decide the matter one way or the other. For example, he stipulates as the decisive falsifying condition the complete elimination of Jews from history, which was, in fact, Hitler's goal through his "Final Solution." Here we have a straightforward, if theologically enormous, claim: the existence of God is inseparably related to the existence of the Jewish people (a claim not too distant from that actually made in at least some classical Jewish sources). If the Jewish people are destroyed then we will agree that God does not exist. This is certainly a falsifiable proposition, or at least, it is hoped, only an *in principle* falsifiable thesis, i.e., the Jewish people *logically* are removable from history. What happens to the empiricist challenge at this point? This question seems especially challenging given that the hypothetical argument constructed can be construed, at least according to a certain quite respectable theological ideology, as a close analog to what actually transpired in twentieth-century Europe.

What this second counterexample, as well as the argument advanced above, suggests is that Rubenstein has too easily accepted some form of the empiricist theory of meaning and verification. Though this theory is obscure at best and probably ultimately philosophically indefensible, Rubenstein has made this, or something like it, a foundation stone of his entire enterprise without a sufficient degree of epistemological self-consciousness regarding its philosophical accuracy or logical adequacy. In his invocation of this procedure, he has sought to adopt a clear and indisputable method of reaching theological conclusions, the appeal of such clarity and decisiveness being obvious. But the seductiveness of this stratagem is more illusory than real, for the empirical verificationist criterion achieves its putative precision and rigor only by illegitimately reducing the complex to the simple and the ambiguous to the transparent. Thus its results are a caricature of the situation.

Before I move on, it should be registered that despite my criticism of Rubenstein's formulation of the empiricist issue as logically inadequate, his intentions are well directed, namely, he wants to find nonapologetic, nonhomiletical, nonsubjective ways to talk meaningfully about covenantal existence or, rather, its nonexistence, after the Holocaust and in light of what the Holocaust has to teach us. But, alternatively, what also needs to be recognized is that his frontal assault on the questions involved, which

uses various forms of empiricist verificationist instruments, is not successful; other ways to get at the root of the problem need to be found.

At the other theological extreme from Rubenstein's work stands the well-
known theological efforts of Emil Fackenheim. To sketch the salient features of his position is not too difficult. It has its roots, on the one hand, in
a desire to do two radically opposite things, and, on the other, it emerges
out of a need to hold two radically alternative possibilities in dialectical
tension, wishing to surrender neither. The two radically opposite things he
wants to maintain are that (1) the Holocaust is unique; but (2) it does not
lead to a denial of the existence of God à la Rubenstein. The dialectic he
wishes to affirm is that (1) the Holocaust is without "meaning"; and yet (2)
out of Auschwitz the commanding voice of the Living God of Israel is
heard. This complex structure is necessitated by the concern not to do
injustice to the martyrs of the death camps nor to speak against God. It
recognizes, indeed insists upon, the awesome nature of the Holocaust and
its "unique" significance for theology, yet it also demands that this event
be located within the structures of theistic belief rather than be allowed to
break these structures apart in an irreparable manner that would mark the
end of religion in any traditional sense.

Fackenheim, like Richard Rubenstein and most other "Holocaust theologians," rejects categorically any attempt to give a *causal* explanation of
the Holocaust in terms of any "answer" borrowed from traditional theodicy. Auschwitz is *not* punishment for sin; it is *not* divine judgment; it is *not*
moral education à la Job: "Behold, happy is the man whom God reproves.
. . . He delivers the afflicted by their affliction, and opens their ear by
adversity" (Job 5:17; 36:15). As Franklin Sherman has correctly noted,
the Jobean view has merit but only up to a point, for "when [a man's]
humanity begins to be destroyed, as was the case in the concentration
camps, then it is fruitless to talk of the ennoblement of character."[10] The
Holocaust is also inconceivable as an "affliction of love" (*yissurin shel
ahavahl*)[11] and unjustifiable on the grounds of any doctrine of progress or
of a Spinozalike dictum of *sub specie aeternitatis*. In short, no good reason
can be advanced to explain or defend Auschwitz. No theodicy seems able
to vindicate the time-honored normative view of God's absolute goodness
in the face of the Holocaust. Thus, as a consequence, as Fackenheim honestly acknowledges, God Himself is called into question, nothing less.

Yet, unlike those who at this crucial juncture try God and find Him
wanting, thus concluding His nonexistence, Fackenheim insists that God

does exist and that He is still present in history despite the crematoriums. Though it is enormously difficult to believe in God after the Kingdom of Night, it is precisely continued belief that must be the response to the challenge of Auschwitz. Though we cannot, and this is an absolute "cannot," fathom why God allowed Auschwitz and why He did not intervene to end the Holocaust, we must affirm that He was present even there, even at Auschwitz, and that He continues to be present still as the Lord of History.

This demand is first and foremost made as an affirmation of faith, of faith in the Kierkegaardian sense of holding fast to that which is objectively uncertain. Indeed, this stance owes much to Kierkegaard, the patriarch of modern religious existentialism. The conceptual link connecting Kierkegaard and Fackenheim is primarily the dialogical teaching of Martin Buber. To the extent that metaphysics or theology is employed in support of his account, Fackenheim draws heavily on Buber's philosophy of I-Thou. This dependence on Buber is clearly seen, for example, in Fackenheim's most sustained attempt to respond to the Holocaust, the lectures published in *God's Presence in History*. In this monograph he accepts, in its general specifications, the Buberian doctrine of I-Thou as the model for Jewish openness to the reality of the living God and thus for his own attempt to construct a post-Holocaust Jewish theology. Thus, he eschews all proofs for the existence of God, beginning instead with the presumption that God does exist. He accepts the Buberian dictum that God cannot be proven, He can only be met. Consequently, he argues that only from within the circle of faith can one "hear" the Eternal Thou (Buber's terminology for God) and respond accordingly. Developing this claim, Fackenheim, like Buber, insists that God reveals Himself in history in personal encounters with the Jews and Israel, but this revelation of Divine Presence, though it can happen everywhere and at all times, is not subject to external criteria of verification or objectivity.[12] God does not show Himself decisively to those who would not "hear" the Voice. The I-Thou encounter has its own rhythm and any attempt to force it into improper objective categories (I-It language, to use Buber's terminology) destroys its character and silences its message. Thus, the Fackenheim who hears "a commanding voice from Auschwitz" is the Fackenheim who already stands *within* the covenantal affirmation.[13]

Working from this base, Fackenheim asserts that we witness God's presence in history in the continued experience of the people of Israel throughout its existence, and this in two ways. The first of these ways Fackenheim calls the "root experiences"[14] of the people of Israel; the second he describes as "epoch making events."[15] The former are creative, extraordinary, historical happenings that are of a decisive and formative character such that they continue to influence all future "presents" of the Jewish people. These events are of such a magnitude that they continue to legislate as normative occasions to every future generation of the nation. Thus, for example, the Exodus is an historical movement that is relived every Passover and whose power affects each subsequent generation, continually revealing through this yearly reenactment the saving activity of God.[16] In this way these past "root experiences" are lived through as "present reality" and the Jew of every age is "assured that the past saving God saves still."[17] In contrast, "epoch making events" are not formative for Jewry's collective consciousness; rather, they are historical occasions that challenge the "root experiences" to answer to new and often unprecedented conditions. The destruction of the First and Second Temples are, for example, such events. These occurrences test the foundations of Jewish life, i.e., the saving and commanding God of the Exodus and Sinai, but do not shatter them, as the continued existence of the Jewish people testifies. This traditional interpretive pattern has heretofore always shown enough elasticity and resiliency to absorb and survive any and all catastrophes that threatened its fundamental structure.

But what of Auschwitz? Can it be assimilated to this older midrashic model? To this question Fackenheim answers an unreserved yes. Even Auschwitz does not destroy the "root experiences" of Israel's faith; God is present even in the Kingdom of Night, commanding Israel still from within the very eye of the Holocaust itself. This extreme reply to the unprecedented circumstances of Auschwitz is the essential response of Fackenheim and those who would follow his lead. The Jew cannot, dare not, must not reject God. Auschwitz itself is revelatory, commanding, and we must learn to sense what God would reveal to us even there.

What is the commanding word, which Fackenheim, in a now-famous phrase, has called the 614th commandment, which is heard at Auschwitz? "Jews are forbidden to hand Hitler posthumous victories!"[18] After Auschwitz Jews are under a sacred obligation to survive; Jewish existence is itself a holy act; Jews are under a duty to remember the martyrs; Jews are, as Jews, forbidden to despair of redemption, or to become cynical about the world and humanity, for to submit to cynicism is to abdicate responsibility for the here and now and to deliver the future into the hands of the forces of evil. And above all, Jews are "forbidden to despair of the God of Israel, lest Judaism perish."[19] Hitler's demonic passion was to eradicate

Israel from history. For the Jew to despair of the God of Israel as a result of Hitler's monstrous actions would be, ironically, to do Hitler's work and to aid in the accomplishments of Hitler's goal. The voice that speaks from Auschwitz demands above all that Hitler win no posthumous victories, that no Jew do what Hitler could not do. The Jewish will for survival is natural enough, but Fackenheim invests it with transcendental significance. Precisely because others would eradicate Jews from the earth, Jews are commanded to resist annihilation. Paradoxically, Hitler makes Judaism after Auschwitz a necessity. To say no to Hitler is to say yes to the God of Sinai; to say no to the God of Sinai is to say yes to Hitler.

Since 1945 every person who has remained a Jew has, from Fackenheim's perspective, responded affirmatively to the commanding voice of Auschwitz.

Yet this is only half of the traditional ideology of Judaism, for the God of biblical faith is *both* a commanding and a saving God. The crossing of the Red Sea is as much a part of Jewish history as is the revelation at Sinai: both are "root experiences." Fackenheim has made much of the commanding presence of Auschwitz, but where is the saving God of the Exodus? Without the crossing of the Red Sea there can be no Sinai. Fackenheim knows this. He is also aware that to talk of a God of deliverance, no matter how softly, no matter how tentatively, after the Holocaust is problematical when God did not work His kindness there and then. To even whisper about salvation after Treblinka and Maidenek is already to speak as a person of faith, not as a seeker, and even then one can only whisper. The continued existence of the people of Israel, however, and most specifically the establishment and maintenance of the state of Israel, forces Fackenheim to risk speaking of hope and the possibility of redemption. The destruction of European Jewry and the state of Israel are, for him, inseparably tied together; what the former seems to deny the latter, at least tentatively, affirms. For Fackenheim, the state of Israel is living testimony to God's continued presence in history. Through it the modern Jew witnesses a reaffirmation of the "root experience" of salvation essential to the survival of Jewish faith.[20]

Fackenheim argues for Jewish survival first and foremost on the positive basis of the presence of God in Jewish history and the ever contemporary possibility of I-Thou encounter between God and humanity. Only from this absolute ontological presupposition, which he borrows totally from Martin Buber, do the other corollaries of Fackenheim's account, including that of not giving Hitler a "posthumous victory," flow. To ignore this elemental feature of his thought, i.e., his dialogical ontology, or to read him differently is to misread him altogether.

This essential clarification of Fackenheim's view is, however, not a vindication of it. A serious difficulty remains; to phrase it differently, this schema needs to be criticized for the right reasons. Perhaps foremost among these is the largely uncritical acceptance of Buber's dialogical affirmations. Buber's metaphysical structure—indeed, his entire account of I-Thou relation and the nature and meaning of revelation—involves philosophical deficiencies that ultimately render it of little, if any, help in constructing a significant and viable metaphysics of history. His position is quite simply unworkable as the basis of an intelligible account of God's relation to humanity and history. Its weakness is that it provides intuitions where serious and well-formed conceptual articulation is required.[21] Thus, whereas Buber's teachings are called in to provide the broad schematic metaphysical basis for the "614th commandment," its own internal lacunae will not allow it to adequately fill this role.

Buber's dialogical thinking is incapable of dealing in any meaningful and sustainable fashion with real history, the presence of evil in the world, or the category of revelation, the very philosophical-cum-theological categories particularly relevant here. Fackenheim's considerable insight into history, and more particularly the nuances of the philosophy of history, in fact, comes more from his in-depth study of Hegel[22] than his discipleship in the school of dialogue. The difficulty is that Hegel and Buber do not easily mix; they are certainly not integratable. Buber was, in large part, reacting to Hegel's historicism; in his flight from Hegel he seems to have run away from history, despite his best intentions and disclaimers,[23] altogether.

Related to this flight from history, though grounded in independent metaphysical presuppositions, was Buber's inability to deal with evil. His feeble, bewildered response to the Holocaust is testimony to this. One is struck by the very paucity even of attempts to deal with what had happened to Jews in his generation, an event in which up to 1938 he had played so dramatic and heroic a role.[24] One can well appreciate Buber's silence, but this silence must be allowed to count against the adequacy of dialogical thought as a way of meeting the problem of evil more generally[25] and of the Holocaust in particular. "The Eclipse of God," the title of Buber's volume of essays[26] written, in part, as a response to Auschwitz, is a metaphor that itself needs to be explained, that cries out for, demands, explication and content. In and of itself it hides more than it reveals; it evades more than it illumines. Yet Buber had no real illumination to offer in these matters nor will he assist others—e.g., Fackenheim—just here where the theological going is roughest.

Lastly, Buber's prescription for contentless revelation, while setting out to protect revelation from its modern critics, turns back upon itself and devours its own substance. I-Thou encounter is in the end an incoherent model for the revelatory moment. As such it *cannot* serve as the theoretical model for Fackenheim's own attempt to reconstruct a viable analysis of revelation, certainly not of a meaningful, content-full revelation like his 614th commandment. The lapses in Buber's redescription of revelation are logically insuperable; they deny the very possibility of coherence to all who rely upon it—Fackenheim, unfortunately, included.[27]

A further word about the connection, or rather, impossibility of a connection, between Buber's dialogical, contentless revelation and Fackenheim's 614th commandment is required. How does one get from the former to the latter? On Buber's *I and Thou* account, the 614th commandment could only be a "human response" to the Divine Presence, *not*—and this negation is nonnegotiable in Buber's thinking—the imperative of the divine. If this is so, however, what universal status does it have? Buber's personalist summary of what he takes revelation to be, in part 3 of *I and Thou,* specifically rules out anything issuing from revelation that "can be held above all men's heads." Only the "I" partner of the encounter is commanded, if "commanded" is still even a meaningful concept in this setting, especially given Buber's acceptance of a Kantian embargo on heteronomous norms. This being so, however, how can this personalist, nonuniversalist model become the *urgrund* for a 614th commandment of any kind, particularly as from Buber's perspective the original 613 commandments have lost their commanding resonance?[28]

Discussion of the content of revelation brings us back to Fackenheim's sketch of the 614th commandment with the requirement that we put several additional questions to it. Passing over, for the present, the contradiction of there being any content to revelation on Buberian grounds, we must ask, what exactly does Fackenheim mean by the term "commandment"? In the older, traditional theological vocabulary of Judaism, it meant something God actually "spoke" through Moses, and through the sages in elaboration thereon, to the people of Israel. Fackenheim, however, would reject this literal meaning in line with his dialogical premises. But then what does "commanded" here mean? It would seem the word has only an analogical or metaphorical sense in this case, but if so, what urgency and compelling power does it retain? Fackenheim would, correctly, reject the just-mentioned option of analogy or metaphor, but if these are rejected, and the literal meaning is denied, what, we ask again, remains?

There emerges a curious "double think" in this position. On the one hand, the word "commandment" (and like terms, e.g., "revelation," "salvation," "redemption") are used because they have a content we all know from the biblical account. On the other hand, the literalness of the biblical witness is denied, leaving the intelligibility of these terms, both in their original biblical and in their modern employments, obscure. This, in turn, leads to two corollaries. The first of these relates back to a line of thought mentioned briefly above. When I ask Professor Fackenheim whether his 614th commandment is revelation as the Torah was believed to be revelation—i.e., *Halachah l'Moshe m'Sinai,* in the traditional formula—the answer must, I believe, be no. God did not "speak these things." They are, rather, a human response to Auschwitz, but a human awakening, even be it to Auschwitz, is religious anthropology rather than revelation as this term has heretofore been understood. Alternatively, to redefine the term "revelation" dialogically merely achieves similar, unsatisfactory results by a slightly different route. That is to say, is the 614th commandment revelation or only our talk *about* revelation?

At this juncture I would also stand one of our major objections to Richard Rubenstein[29] on its head and apply the inverted critique to Fackenheim. Whereas the radical theologians seem naively to rely on an empiricist criterion of falsifiability and meaning, Fackenheim seems to go to the other extreme, avoiding direct confrontation with empirical evidence to such an extent that all discussion and evaluation becomes irrelevant. Though Fackenheim does not state his doctrine in these terms, his demand that one must stand within the faith circle in order to understand the propositions of the religious person leads inexorably to this conclusion. This final cul-de-sac is arrived at partly consciously and partly as a legacy of his Buberian, and more generally existentialist, inheritance. The particularly significant implication of this stance is to make it difficult to see what would be allowed to count against the 614th commandment by its advocates. Under what circumstances would they admit either that "God is Dead" or, less extremely, that at least He had broken His covenant with Israel, thereby rendering Jewish belief either irrelevant or foolish after Auschwitz?

In his essay "Elijah and the Empiricists,"[30] Fackenheim attempts to respond to this challenge by engaging and overcoming the empiricist polemic presented in the well-known "University Discussion" and earlier by A. J. Ayer.[31] He notes that Judaism and Christianity must be treated differently in terms of this issue, the former being, in his view, more open to history and hence disconfirmation. He, in fact, goes so far as to offer this significant counterclaim:

> Unlike the Christian eschatological expectation, the Jewish is at least in part falsifiable by future history.
>
> Sophisticated philosophers have overlooked this possibility at a time when even ordinary Jewish believers are unable to overlook it. After Auschwitz, it is a major question whether the Messianic faith is not already falsified—whether a Messiah who could come, and yet did not come, has become a religious impossibility.
>
> Falsification is not, in any case, unimaginable.[32]

In support of this bold assertion he then, in good philosophical fashion, constructs the following example to indicate the conditions under which Jewish belief would be falsified. "Imagine," he writes,

> a small band of Jewish believers as the sole survivors of a nuclear holocaust. Imagine them to be totally certain that no human beings have survived anywhere else, and that they themselves and their children are inexorably doomed. They are not faced with a repetition of Noah's flood but rather with the end of history. Of the destiny of individual souls, the whole picture is not yet in sight. But the whole picture of history is already seen, and it refutes the Jewish eschatological hope concerning it. The suffering of individuals as such may still be given its point. But the suffering to which Jews have exposed themselves by remaining a people is already seen to have been pointless. (This is true at least of suffering radical enough to have remained pointless in pre-Messianic history.) Precisely insofar as it holds fast to history, Jewish faith risks falsification by history.[33]

This case appears to go a long way towards actually setting forth an at least *in principle*[34] situation in which Jewish faith, Fackenheim's faith, would be decisively disproven. It is true that the case is implausible and hence loses some of its force as a consequence, but, essentially, Fackenheim is attempting to meet the conceptual challenge with a philosophical response. But now he hedges and all that has been gained is lost. Seemingly worried by the possibility of falsification that has been allowed into the discussion, he feels constrained to add,

> Let us return to the example of the survivors of the nuclear catastrophe. Exactly what part of their faith is refuted? That God exists? No. That He loves us? To the extent to which it holds fast to actual history, Jewish faith has in any case long qualified any such sweeping and simplistic affirmation. Some evils in history may be only apparent, such as deserved punishment. Not all historical evils are apparent—history is unredeemed. Jewish faith cannot say why history is unredeemed, why God "hides His face," or is, as it were, temporarily without power, and in any case restrains the Messiah from coming. This does not, however, either refute Jewish faith nor deprive it of content, so long as the promised coming of the Messiah can still be expected. It is this promise, and it alone, that would be falsified by a catastrophic end of human history.[35]

This exposition is full of interest, for it now appears that, in contradistinction to the possibility of falsifying Jewish belief, i.e., the existence of the Jewish God, this is not the case. God's reality is untouched even by this hypothetical worst-case scenario, as is also, it seems, the more particular doctrine of God's love for us. Both are not, we are instructed, disconfirmed.

What then is disconfirmed? Only the Jewish Messianic doctrine. And what implications flow from this?

> How would a Jewish believer respond to this falsification? He could of course at long last surrender his age old stubbornness, and accept his faith as having been, all along, a mere hypothesis, now falsified. But then he should have let go of his stubbornness long ago, for the hypothesis had, after all, always been most improbable. The authentic Jewish believer would take a different course. He has in any case spent his life *working* for the coming of the divine kingdom, as well as waiting for it. He would now cite the divine commandment to do this work against God Himself, would refuse to abandon what God either chose to abandon or could not help abandoning and spend his last hours on earth beating swords into plowshares.
>
> It is a telling proof of anti-Judaic bias that contemporary empiricists treating the subject of the falsifiability of religious faith have wholly overlooked the possibility of citing God against God Himself. This possibility appears even in the New Testament, for Jesus asks why God has forsaken

him. In the Jewish Bible the theme is everywhere. Abraham cites God against God. So does Job. So do most of the prophets. Elijah at Mount Carmel would have done likewise had the necessity arisen. What if the heavenly fire had devoured the sacrifice of the priests of Baal, rather than his own? We have already seen what Elijah would not have done: accept the "hypothesis" that Baal "control[s] the physical world." It has now emerged what he *would* have done. He would have lamented that, already forsaken by men, he was now forsaken by *Adonai* as well—and continued to do His work, alone.[36]

In the final reckoning even the imagined catastrophe makes no real difference to Jewish belief. The Jew in Fackenheim's formulation continues, as it were, as if nothing had occurred. The recommended course of action— "citing God against God"—is particularly odd, for it is the very presence of God that is at stake. Whence comes the certitude about God's existence, *in the face of tragedy,* that allows such dispute, such dialogue, to continue? The only answer is that, in the last accounting, *nothing is* allowed to count against God's being there. Despite appearances, the falsification challenge has not been met; it has, rather, been sidestepped. All is in the end as it was in the beginning.

As a consequence, though Fackenheim is sincerely concerned to do more justice to the concatenations of Jewish history than he believes his rivals do, going so far as to assert that "authentic Jewish theology cannot possess the immunity I once gave it, *for its price is an essential indifference* to all history between Sinai and the messianic days,"[37] he seems finally to replace an authentic encounter with temporal events with a transhistorical faith that is impervious to the actual happenings of the world historical. Neither history nor logic in the end seem able, by definition, to provide possible counterevidence to the Fackenheimian thesis. This does not make the thesis false, but it does make it a special type of metaphysical claim that is less interesting, certainly less rigorous and probing, than it at first appears to be.

Consider now the very traditional theological position of Eliezer Berkovits.

One could pick at the edges of Berkovits's position at length, but the center of his argument turns on his advocacy of a traditional free will theodicy. Therefore one can cut to the heart of the matter by turning directly to a scrutiny of his presentation of this defense. Taking his cue from the biblical doctrine of *hester panim* ("the Hiding Face of God"),

Berkovits claims that God's hiddenness is required for the human being to be a moral creature. God's hiddenness brings into being the possibility for ethically valent human action, for by "absenting" Himself from history He creates the reality of human freedom that is necessary for moral behavior. For human good and human evil to be real possibilities God has to respect the decisions of humankind and be bound by them. Among the necessary corollaries of this ethical autonomy is that God has to abstain from reacting immediately to immoral deeds, and certainly from acting in advance to suppress them. But it is just here that the fundamental paradox emerges: for a moral humanity to exist freedom must exist, yet it is the nature of freedom that it is always open to the possibility of abuse.

The corollary of this, as Berkovits understands the situation, is that "while He [God] shows forbearance with the wicked, He must turn a deaf ear to the anguished cries of the violated."[38] Consequently, the paradoxical reality that flows from this divine circumstance is that humanity is impossible if God is strictly just, while if God is loving beyond the requirements of strict justice there will be human suffering and evil: "One may call it the divine dilemma that God's *erek apayim,* His patiently waiting countenance to some is, of necessity, identical with His *hester panim,* His hiding of the countenance, to others."[39] Auschwitz is a paradigmatic instantiation of this truth.

What is one to say to this argument? The first thing is, I think, that in the face of the Shoah this millennia-old theodicy is as coherent as any of those, new or old, that has been proposed, even if not fully convincing. The second thing is that Berkovits reveals his mature theological intuition by opting for this gambit as his "response." The third is that the many dramatic, intensely moving, examples of Jewish heroism in the face of Nazism that Berkovits cites in his studies do help advance a case for the existence of evil as a possibility that must be allowed by God in order for there to be true human freedom—and also for the reality of evil as an ingredient in the generation of certain "goods," for example, love and compassion, fidelity and courage. Granting all this, however, two pressing difficulties remain. With regard to human autonomy and while recognizing its two-sidedness, all the more because of Berkovits's discussion of Jewish heroism in the camps and elsewhere, an ancient enquiry reasserts itself: "Could not God, possessed of omniscience, omnipotence, and absolute goodness, have created a world in which there was human freedom but no evil?" And secondly, "Even if certain 'goods' are generated by overcoming or in response to evil, couldn't God either have allowed the production of these goods without so much evil, or, more radically still, wouldn't it be preferable if there were no such goods given the evil (and suffering) needed to produce them?" Let us examine each of these questions in turn.

The issue as to whether God could have created a world in which people always freely choose to do good has been given a particularly tight formulation by J. L. Mackie. In a well-known article in *Mind* he commented,

> I should query the assumption that second order evils are logically necessary accompaniments of freedom. I should ask this: if God has made men such that in their free choices they sometimes prefer what is good and sometimes what is evil, why could he not have made men such that they always freely choose the good? If there is no logical impossibility in a man's freely choosing the good on one, or on several, occasions, there cannot be a logical impossibility in his freely choosing the good on every occasion. God was not, then, faced with a choice between making innocent automata and making beings who, in acting freely, would sometimes go wrong: there was open to him the obviously better possibility of making beings who would act freely but always go right. Clearly, his failure to avail himself of this possibility is inconsistent with his being both omnipotent and wholly good.[40]

Many theologians and philosophers have replied to Mackie's challenge, the most cogent counter being Alvin Plantinga's. For our present purposes, I am prepared to admit his general conclusion, which I cite at length.

The Free Will Defense Vindicated

Put formally, the Free Will Defender's project is to show that
    (1) God is omniscient, omnipotent, and wholly good
is consistent with
    (2) There is evil.
What we have seen (in a previous argument) is that
    (3) It was not within God's power to create a world containing moral good but no moral evil
is possible and consistent with God's omnipotence and omniscience. But then it is clearly consistent with (1). So we can use it to show that (1) is consistent with (2). For consider
    (1) God is omnipotent, omniscient, and wholly good
    (3) It was not within God's power to create a world containing moral good without creating one containing moral evil; and

(4) God created a world containing moral good.

These propositions are evidently consistent—i.e., their conjunction is a possible proposition. But taken together they entail

(2) There is evil.

For (4) says that God created a world containing moral good; this together with (3) entails that He created one containing moral evil. But if it contains moral evil, then it contains evil. So (1), (3), and (4) are jointly consistent and entail (2); hence (1) is consistent with (2); hence set A is consistent. Remember: to serve in this argument (3) and (4) need not be known to be true, or likely on our evidence, or anything of the sort; they need only be consistent with (1). Since they are, there is no contradiction in set A; so the Free Will Defense appears to be successful.[41]

Berkovits provides nothing logically comparable to Plantinga's reasoning, but I am willing[42] to allow Plantinga's analysis to stand in defense of Berkovits's championing of the free will position, recognizing that Berkovits would endorse both Plantinga's procedure and his conclusion.

However, this vindication pushes us another step, and here I demur from Plantinga's and Berkovits's position. For the problem now becomes, "Could not God have created a world in which there was human freedom but less evil (as compared to no evil)?" Again Plantinga (and by inference Berkovits) answers "no" to this question[43] for, according to his analysis of the Free Will Defense, given genuine freedom, God cannot control the amount of evil in the world. But this "no" is not convincing, for the quantity of sheer gratuitous evil manifest during the Holocaust goes beyond anything that seems logically or metaphysically necessary for the existence of human freedom and beyond the bounds of "toleration" for an omnipotent, omniscient, and just God. One has only to recognize that given the belief in miracles, which Berkovits shares,[44] one miracle, even a "small" one, could have reduced some of the tragedy of the Shoah without canceling the moral autonomy of the murderers. Thus it is logically conceivable and requires no great feat of the imagination to imagine a world in which there was less evil.

As to the second question, it increasingly seems to me that it would have been preferable, morally preferable, to have a world in which "evil" did not exist, at least not in the magnitude witnessed during the Shoah, even if this meant doing without certain heroic moral attributes or accomplishments. That is to say, for example, though feeding and caring for the sick or hungry is a great virtue, it would be far better if there were no sickness or hunger and hence no need for such care. The price is just too high. This is true even for the much-exalted value of freedom itself. For we recognize the need to limit freedom where evil consequences are concerned, for example, we allow convicts to be incarcerated so that they will not cause further evil, we limit the right to cry "fire" in a crowded theater, we curtail the right to molest children, and the list goes on. That is to say, we recognize, as these examples indicate, that freedom is properly subordinated to the prevention of suffering and other undesirable consequences. In respect of the Shoah such a limitation on freedom would have clearly been preferable to the results of freedom run riot, whatever limited instances of good the evil of Auschwitz engendered.

At this juncture some might want to object that my refutation of the Free Will Defense and its attendant call to limit freedom in the face of the death camps has not confronted the truly radical implication of my own contention regarding autonomy and its restraints. This is because to suggest controlling free will would mean not only overriding the rights of individuals to do certain particular things, as in the examples just given, but also overcoming the basis for freedom altogether. This clarification rightly recognizes that free will is not equivalent to liberty of action, being more fundamental and at the same time a necessary condition of morality. In reply, however, it seems cogent to advance the reservations introduced above, if with modification. Better to introduce limits, even limits on that freedom of the will requisite to moral choice, than to allow Auschwitz. Here it is salient to recognize that free will is not, despite a widespread tendency to so understand it, all of one piece. One can limit free will in certain aspects, that is, with respect, for example, to specific types of circumstances, just as one constrains action in particular ways. For example, a person can have a phobia about X that does not impair that person's unrestrained power of decision in regard to Y. Such a case reveals that the call to limit free will does not necessarily mean its total elimination but rather its powerful curtailment by, in our present context, a Divine Intelligence under conditions such as those that reigned supreme during the Holocaust. Consider, too, that God could have created a humankind that, while possessing free will, nonetheless also had a proportionately stronger inclination for the good and a correspondingly weaker inclination to evil. He could also have endowed us with a greater capacity for moral education. Neither of these alterations in the scheme of things would have obviated the reality of free will, though they would have appreciably improved humankind's moral record, perhaps even to the point of significantly reducing the moral evil done to the innocent by a Hitler.

Much of my disquiet with this whole line of defense lies in my somewhat different mode of reasoning about morality. In contradistinction to the habitual way of conceiving the problem of freedom's relation to morality—that is, no volitional autonomy, no morality—one can and should turn the issue around and argue that if one has no, or smaller amounts of, evil to contend with, free will is less necessary because those virtues generated through its exercise, e.g., concern, love, etc., are not required in the same way. Macrocosmically, morality is a good not least because it helps us make our way in an evil world; eliminate or lessen the evil we encounter and the need for morality declines correspondingly.

From this angle of vision it becomes clear that the Jobean thesis usually developed in this connection, that is, the view that suffering creates higher goods and in addition trains one's character, requires another look. It has been asserted that

> the value judgment that is implicitly being invoked here [in the Jobean thesis] is that one who has attained to goodness by meeting and eventually mastering temptations, and thus by rightly making responsible choices in concrete situations, is good in a richer and more valuable sense than would be one created *ab initio* in a state either of innocence or of virtue. In the former case, which is that of the actual moral achievements of mankind, the individual's goodness has within it the strength of temptations overcome, a stability based upon an accumulation of right choices, and a positive and responsible character that comes from the investment of costly personal effort.[45]

This contention is not without interest as long as Job stays alive. But as a response to Auschwitz Job is not the right model, for unlike Job of old, the Jews in the death camps were not protected from destruction. Therefore, the Jobean defense of tragedy, of suffering as the occasion for growth and overcoming, has little relevance to the Holocaust.

The incremental conception is simply too naive, too optimistic. It emphasizes the positive value of evil as an aid to the growth and manifestation of goodness, but it ignores altogether the more telling fact that wickedness of the magnitude and quality unloosed by Nazism not only, or even primarily, increased our opportunities to display courage and love but even more—and essentially—destroyed forever such possibilities for six million Jews, including the all too many Jewish children whose youthful potential was never to be realized. Still more, the logic of this incremental thesis leads, if followed to its end, to an untenable conclusion. It suggests that good comes from, or in response to, evil, and that without evil there would be no heroism, no forgiveness, no love. The greater the malevolence, the greater the heroism. The significance of Berkovits's constant invocation of instances of truly extraordinary moral heroism in the face of Nazi brutality turns on this contention. Yet the irony here is this: if an increase in the diabolic is defended by recourse to the greater good it produces, i.e., more heroism is generated by Nazism than by a lesser plague, then the proper goal to be desired is a still greater Holocaust (God forbid) that would, by this line of reasoning, make for still more courage and fortitude. Thus if killing six million Jews caused a corresponding amount and kind of virtue, killing twelve million will produce, say, twice the amount and a still higher quality of moral nobility. But surely this is all wrong. The recognition of its absurdity forces us to acknowledge the inherent deficiency of the incremental thesis as exposed by the reality of the Shoah.

There is still another moral objection to this incremental line of reasoning. One can contend that selfless love or forgiveness, or faith and fortitude, are unavailable without that corruption to which they are a reaction, but even if one makes this case, which in itself is not an easy case to make, it does not justify the evil per se. To argue the contrary is to suggest that the Nazis were helping Jews be virtuous, and were assisting Jews in their ethical development. Likewise, is it morally acceptable to suggest that Jewish children should suffer disease and starvation, death by fire and by gas, so that others might have an opportunity to care for or comfort them? As to the children themselves, what sort of standard is involved? What moral improvement was achieved when Janus Korczak's orphans, and countless others like them, died in the ghettos and crematoriums? Their deaths contradicted that very freedom and moral autonomy that are at the base of the Free Will Defense. God's goodness is also impugned in the face of such barbarities. He, so the position contends, gave humankind freedom because He is gracious and compassionate, loving and concerned, but here His care for Nazis and for their freedom meant a total absence of solicitude for their victims.

The Free Will Defense becomes still more difficult to maintain when employed as a Jewish theodicy. The reason for this increase in complexity is the necessity of relating the Free Will Defense, as drawn in a more general philosophical way, with the God idea of Judaism, i.e., the God of the Bible who is known to perform miracles in the face of overwhelming evil. Thus, it is a case not only of trying to decipher, in some theologically neutral sense, the world God set out to create but rather of understanding Jewishly why, given the exaggeratedly high cost of human freedom, God did not once again, as He had in the past, step into the flow of events and say, "Enough."

Berkovits is theologian enough to be aware that this is a serious objection and he tries to meet it:

> Man can only exist because God renounces the use of his power on him. This, of course, means that God cannot be present in history through manifest material power. Such presence would destroy history. History is the arena for human responsibility and its product. When God intervenes in the affairs of men by physical might as, for instance, in the story of Exodus, we speak of a miracle. But the miracle is outside of history; in it history is at a standstill.[46]

But this is an evasion, for the critical challenge simply needs to be rephrased: why, if God performed a miracle and entered history at the Exodus, did He show such great self-restraint at Auschwitz? Wasn't Auschwitz far worse than Egypt, Pharaoh far more humane than Hitler? Given that history did not end because of the miracles connected with the Exodus, why would a miracle at Auschwitz now "destroy history"? Given Berkovits's biblically rooted faith this line of defense is not plausible.

Then, too, if God did not intervene in the Shoah, even if one might still thereafter be able to defend His power by recourse to a Berkovitslike argument regarding divine self-restraint, what happens in such an equation to God's love? Is a God who allows such total freedom, who does not act when human freedom takes on an apocalyptic character of frenzied sadism, still worthy of respect and admiration? Of being worshipped? In aid of the Free Will Defense Berkovits might be able to argue with cogency that "God cannot as a rule intervene whenever man's use of freedom displeases him."[47] But surely Auschwitz is not a mere "whenever"; it was a time that demanded just such interference.

A further corollary of Berkovits's teaching is also worthy of mention. He recognizes that for all its logical suggestiveness the Free Will Defense is not convincing.[48] Thus he feels compelled to add, "all this does not exonerate God for all the suffering of the innocent in history . . . there must be a dimension beyond history in which all suffering finds its redemption through God. This is essential to the faith of a Jew."[49] This well-worked proposal is tantamount to a confession that human freedom extorts too high a price; thus the traditional "crutch" of an afterlife is introduced without any justification to bolster the classical metaphysical and moral structure under pressure.

This otherworldly appeal, however, is less than adequate to the task. Besides the elemental difficulty of the absence of any legitimation being given for this belief in the hereafter, the fact is that what this suggestion translates into is an appeal for compensation. God wrongs humankind and then tries to make up to it for the unjustifiable evil done. But just as we reject such compensatory actions as lesser goods in human relations, how much more so does it seem unworthy of God. It is this moral disquiet that makes the conclusion of the Book of Job so unsatisfactory and that makes it more unsatisfactory still in the case of victims of the Shoah. God may "redeem" the suffering, but it seems morally preferable that there should be no evil to redeem. Berkovits is right; this argument does not exonerate God.

There is also a deep irony in all this relating to the heart of the free will thesis. If there is a heaven where one resides in bliss without the tensions and difficulties caused by freedom of choice, why did God not create such an earth without freedom of choice and all of its terrible consequences? That is, if heaven is better than earth with or without human autonomy, why wouldn't a similarly structured earth, one in which Auschwitz would be impossible, be likewise good? And if so, i.e., if this is a legitimate question to ask, the whole Free Will Defense falls.[50]

Berkovits's theodicy rests on the thesis, integral to the free will position, that God's "absence" is the real proof of His "presence"[51]—that in His "self-control" we are "introduced to a concept of Divine mightiness that consists in self restraint."[52] Thus, God's presence in history must be sensed as hiddenness and His hiddenness must be read as the sign of His presence. God reveals His power in the world by curbing His power so that humanity, too, might be powerful.

That man may be, God must absent himself; that man may not perish in the tragic absurdity of his own making, God must remain present. The God of history must be absent and present concurrently. He hides his presence. He is present without being indubitably manifest; he is absent without being hopelessly inaccessible. Thus, many find him even in his "absence"; many miss him even in his presence. Because of the necessity of his absence, there is the "Hiding of the Face" and suffering of the innocent; because of the necessity of his presence, evil will not ultimately triumph; because of it, there is hope for man.[53]

This suggestion is neither original nor without its fascination. However, in light of the Holocaust it becomes necessary not only to advocate this thesis but also to ask anew, how and when is God's restraint of His omnipotence to be interpreted differently from His lack of omnipotence? How in fact and in logic do we know there really is an omnipotent God who is exercising self-restraint at a staggering human cost rather than allowing this evidence of "self-restraint" to be construed as data for either the nonexistence of God or at least God's nonomnipotence as advocated, for example, by a platonic Whiteheadian "process" theism?

If the nonpresence, nonpower, noninvolvement of God proves His presence, His power, and His involvement, then by a similar demonstration we could "prove" all sorts of entities and attributes into existence.

There is, however, another aspect to Berkovits's presentation of this theme that is more intriguing and that in fairness must be taken up. For he does not merely refer to God's "hiddenness" and "presence" in the abstract but rather gives these notions flesh by tying them to a seminal, traditional, Jewish theological claim relating to God's involvement with the Jewish people. According to this account the true and enduring witness to God's ultimate power over history is the Jewish people. In Israel's history we see both God's "presence" and His "hiddenness." The continued existence of Israel despite its long record of suffering—"if God is powerless, God's people will be powerless"[54]—is the greatest single testimony, the most impressive proof that God is active in history despite his "hiddenness."[55] The Nazis, according to Berkovits, recognized this, and their slaughter of Jews was an attempt to slaughter the God of history. They intuited, even as Israel sometimes fails to, that God's reality in our world is necessarily linked to the fate of the Jewish people.

> That the Jewish people has withstood all the barbarous attacks upon it, that it has been able to maintain itself in the midst of deadly enemies, bespeaks the presence of another kind of power, invisibly playing its part in the history of men. The survival of the Jew, his capacity for revival after catastrophes such as had eliminated mighty nations and empires, indicate the

mysterious intrusion of a spiritual dimension into the history of man. The more radical the rebellion against the world of the spirit, the greater the hatred against the Jew. The Final Solution was not only to eliminate the Jewish people from history, but through the destruction of Israel it was meant to finalize the defeat of that mysterious spiritual force against which the rebellion was directed. The Nazis were quite correct in believing that if they did not succeed in the elimination of the "Jewish influence" upon world history, they would also fail in their plans for world conquest. No matter what they said in their official propaganda, they sensed the mysterious nature of that influence, the presence of a hiding God in history.[56]

As such, Jewish existence per se stands as prophetic testimony against the moral degeneracy of people and nations: it is a mocking proclamation in the face of all human idolatry and witnesses to the final judgment of history by a moral God.

For myself, I find much in this analysis suggestive, for, like Berkovits, I too wonder at Israel's continued existence. Jewish history defies all theories, usually being the "exception" that cracks open all generalizations put forward as historical laws. This much I feel able to say with philosophical probity. To say more than this is to speak in the language of faith, which, even if one shares it, or rather, precisely because one shares it, one can only witness to and not argue about. I see no way of convincing anyone that Israel is God's people or that, as Judah Halevi described it over a thousand years ago, Israel is the "heart" of the nations. Thus, while I, like Berkovits, find Israel's very survival[57] *the* strongest evidence both of its transhistorical vocation and the existence of divine providence, this affirmation, once offered, cannot be demonstrated.

The same judgment applies to the two additional themes of importance educed by Berkovits from God's "powerlessness." The first is that the Jewish people manifest a qualitatively different type of historical existence than other nations, that Israel lives in "faith history," the nations in "power history."[58] The second is that the state of Israel reveals God's "saving Presence."

For the Jew, for whom Jewish history neither begins with Auschwitz nor ends with it, Jewish survival through the ages and the ingathering of the exiles into the land of their fathers after the Holocaust proclaim God's holy presence at the very heart of his inscrutable hiddenness. We recognized in it the hand of divine providence because it was exactly what, after the

Holocaust, the Jewish people needed in order to survive. Broken and shattered in spirit even more than in body, we could not have been able to continue on our Jewish way through history without some vindication of our faith that the "Guardian of Israel neither slumbers nor sleeps." The state of Israel came at a moment in history when nothing else could have saved Israel from extinction through hopelessness. It is our lifeline to the future.[59]

Of course, Berkovits recognizes that this "lifeline" does not answer the agonizing questions of theodicy with logical decisiveness,[60] but he believes it gives hope to those who would share in such hope that they will be answered in God's future redemptive acts.

I accept Berkovits's contention that each of these themes reveals an authentic insight—yet each can be embraced, if embraced at all, only with one's critical eyes wide open. By this I mean that both of these are metaphysical claims that depend primarily on "faith" and are not subject—nor has Berkovits produced any evidence to the contrary—to either logical demonstration or verification of any stringent sort. This is not to say that they are false; indeed, I do not see how one could adjudicate whether they are "false" in a simple true/false sense. Rather, it is to indicate what type of propositions these are. Once it is recognized what sort of metaphysical statements they are, one also comes to recognize that one could not produce any argument or data that would disconfirm them, nor can I imagine under what circumstances Berkovits would reject any or all of them. Contrariwise, it is not evident how Berkovits, having stated his theological credo, could do anything to persuade a sceptic. Certainly he could not charge the sceptic with any logical error or self-contradiction for failing to give his consent to any of these claims, nor could the sceptic be indicted for holding fast to what is demonstrably an inadequate metaphysical structure per se, for neither of these corollaries necessarily flow from rejecting Berkovits's claims. Conversely, the sceptic cannot charge Berkovits with logical or metaphysical error—his propositions are well formed, intelligible, and Jewishly fertile, even if they are not confirmable.[61] This "stalemate" is, of course, if properly understood, to Berkovits's credit in that he has formulated several important theological theses that, even if they are "faith" statements, are suggestive in a Jewish theological context after Auschwitz. One can claim neither more nor less for them.

Having deciphered Berkovits's account, let me briefly take up the position of Arthur A. Cohen as set out in his book *The Tremendum*. I do so here because like Berkovits he endorses a version of the Free Will Defense, though in a totally different, very radical, metaphysical context. Cohen now situates his Free Will Defense in what is essentially a Whiteheadian process position that argues for what Cohen calls a "dipolar" account of God.

The subtle intention that lies behind this transformative redescription of God is twofold. On the one hand it seeks to assure the reality of human freedom and hence to facilitate a simultaneous reemployment of a sophisticated version of a free will theodicy. On the other hand, and reciprocally, it redefines the transcendent nature of God's being such that He is not directly responsible for the discrete events of human history and hence cannot be held responsible for the Shoah or other acts of human evil. This is a very intriguing two-sided ontological strategy. Our question therefore must be, does Cohen defend it adequately? If so, at what theological price?

Let us explore these questions by deciphering first Cohen's second thesis as to God's redefined role in history. The clearest statement of Cohen's revised God idea in respect of divine accountability for the Shoah comes in his discussion of God's putative silence and what Cohen takes to be the mistaken tradition-based expectation of miraculous intervention.

> The most penetrating of *post-tremendum assaults* upon God has been the attack upon divine silence. Silence is surely in such a usage a metaphor for inaction: passivity, affectlessness, indeed, at its worst and most extreme, indifference and ultimate malignity. Only a malign God would be silent when speech would terrify and stay the fall of the uplifted arm. And if God spoke once (or many times as scripture avers), why has he not spoken since? What is it with a God who speaks only to the ears of the earliest and the oldest and for millennia thereafter keeps silence and speaks not? In all this there is concealed a variety of assumptions about the nature and efficacy of divine speech that needs to be examined. The first is that the divine speech of old is to be construed literally, that is, God actually spoke in the language of man, adapting speech to the styles of the Patriarchs and the Prophets, and was heard speaking and was transmitted as having spoken. God's speech was accompanied by the racket of the heavens so that even if the speech was not heard by more than the prophetic ear, the marks and signals of divine immensity were observed. As well, there is the interpretive conviction that God's speech is action, that God's words act. Lastly, and most relevantly to the matter before us, God's speech enacts and therefore confutes the projects of murderers and tyrants. He saves Israel, he ransoms Jews, he

is forbearing and loving. God's speech is thus consequential to the historical cause of justice and mercy. Evidently, then, divine silence is reproof and punishment, the reversal of his works of speech, and hence God's silence is divine acquiescence in the work of murder and destruction.[62]

As opposed to this older view, Cohen recommends an alternative:

> Can it not be argued no less persuasively that what is taken as God's speech is really always man's hearing, that God is not the strategist of our particularities or of our historical condition, but rather the mystery of our futurity, always our posse, never our acts. If we can begin to see God less as the interferer whose insertion is welcome (when it accords with our needs) and more as the immensity whose reality is our prefiguration, whose speech and silence are metaphors for our language and distortion, whose plenitude and unfolding are the hope of our futurity, we shall have won a sense of God whom we may love and honor, but whom we no longer fear and from whom we no longer demand.[63]

In response to this reconstruction of the God idea, four critical observations are in order. First, it need not be belabored that there *is* truth in the proposition that "what is taken as God's speech is really always man's hearing."[64] But at the same time, it is only a half-truth as stated. For our hearing the word of revelation does not create "God's speech"—this would be illusion and self-projection. Certainly we can *mis*hear God, or not hear at all what there is to hear—but these qualifications do not erase the dialogical nature of divine speech, i.e., the requirement that there be a speaker as well as a hearer. And if revelation requires this two-sidedness, then we have to reject Cohen's revisionism because it fails to address the full circumstance of the reality of revelation and God's role in it. Alternatively, if Cohen's description is taken at face value, revelation as such disappears, in any meaningful sense, from the theological vocabulary, for what content can we ultimately give to "man's hearing" as revelation? And specifically from a Jewish point of view, anything recognizable as Torah and mitzvot would be negated altogether.

Secondly, this deconstruction of classical theism and its substitution by theological dipolarity fails to deal with the problem of divine attributes. Is God still God if He is no longer the providential agency in history? Is God still God if He lacks the power to enter history vertically to perform the miraculous? Is such a dipolar absolute still the God to whom one prays, the God of salvation? Put the other way round, Cohen's divinity is certainly not the God of the covenant,[65] nor again the God of Exodus Sinai, nor yet again the God of the Prophets and the *Churban Bayit Rishon* (Destruction of the First Temple) and the *Churban Bayit Sbeni* (Destruction of the Second Temple). Now, none of these objections, which point to Cohen's failure to account for the very building blocks of Jewish theology, count *logically* against Cohen's theism as an independent speculative exercise. However, they do suggest that Cohen's God is *not* the God of the Bible and Jewish tradition and that if Cohen is right—indeed, particularly if Cohen is right—there is no real meaning left to Judaism and to the God idea of Jewish tradition. Cohen's deconstruction in this particular area is so radical that it sweeps away the biblical and rabbinic ground of Jewish faith and allows the biblical and other classical evidence to count not at all against his own speculative metaphysical hypotheses.

The dipolar ontological schema is certainly logically neater and sharper than its "normative" biblical and rabbinic predecessor, but one questions whether this precision has not been purchased at the price of adequacy, i.e., at the price of an inadequate grappling with the multiple evidences and variegated problems that need to be addressed in any attempt, however bold, to fashion a defensible definition and description of God and His relations to humankind. Logical precision must not be achieved here too easily, nor given too high a priority, in the sifting and sorting, the phenomenological decipherment and rearranging, of God's reality and our own.

Third, is the dipolar, noninterfering God "whom we no longer fear and from whom we no longer demand" yet worthy of our "love and honor?"[66] This God seems closer, say, to Plato's *Demiurgos* or perhaps closer still to the innocuous and irrelevant God of the Deists. Such a God does not count in how we act, nor in how history devolves or transpires. After all "God is not," Cohen asserts, "the strategist of our particularities or of our historical condition." But if this is so, if God is indeed so absent from our life and the historical record, what difference is there for us between this God and no God at all? Again, is such a God, who remains uninvolved while Auschwitz is generating its corpses, any more worthy of being called a "God whom we may love," especially if this is His metaphysical essence, than the God of tradition?[67] A God who we can only see as the "immensity whose reality is our prefiguration," while rhetorically provocative, will not advance the theological discussion, for it provides negations and evasions just where substantive analysis is required.

Lastly, this proposed metaphysical reconstruction is not founded upon any direct phenomenological procedure per se. Though fashioned in response to the Shoah, belief in such a dipolar God requires just as great a "leap of faith," maybe an even greater one, as it lacks the support of the Jewish past—as do the theistic affirmations of the tradition. Phenomenologically, it is difficult to discern why one would move in the direction of dipolar theism, given the negativity of the Shoah, unless one were committed at a minimum to theism, if not dipolar theism, to start with. Cohen is correct that both Schelling and Rosenzweig begin "by *assuming* that human natures are created and therefore dependent upon the operative analogue of divine nature."[68] But why should we, or he, begin with this assumption—especially given his negation of much of the theistic inheritance that both Schelling and Rosenzweig retained, even if not always consciously? It is surely not enough to introduce this as an argument from authority, i.e., to hold this view on the claimed authority of Schelling and Rosenzweig; some better reason(s) for even introducing the dipolar God into the present conversation is required but remains always absent.

The second major aspect of Cohen's account turns on what I have called his revised free will theodicy. He advances the familiar thesis that God gave humankind freedom as an integral part of creation and, of necessity, this freedom can be variously misused, ergo the *tremendum*.

> The bridge that I have, not casually but I fear insubstantially, cast over the abyss is one that sinks its pylons into the deep soil of human freedom and rationality, recognizing no less candidly now than before that freedom without the containment of reason returns to caprice and reason without the imagination of freedom is supineness and passivity.[69]

In response to this proposal two reservations must be entered. The first is evoked by the particular form that the reconstructed Cohenian version of this classic theodicy takes. The second concerns itself with the "Free Will Defense in its generality.

It is not clear why we need dipolar theism to produce the Free Will Defense, or that the defense is any more or any less sound in a dipolar than a traditional theistic context. That is, given Cohen's metaphysical dependence on Kabbalah and Schelling it is hard to see why or how their thinking makes any effective difference to the correctness, or otherwise, of the free will position. Cohen, in attempting to justify recourse to these sources in this context, i.e., in relation to the reality of authentic human freedom, criticizes traditional theism, what he chooses to call "fundamental theism," for holding that "God [is] respondent to extremity, the greater the human need the greater the certainty of his assistance, with the result that human life denies its essential freedom returning to ethical passivity and quietism in which everything is compelled to be God's direct work."[70] But this criticism is inaccurate and establishes a "straw man" to be demolished by Cohenian dipolarity. "Fundamentalist" theologians have championed the Free Will Defense as vigorously and as "successfully" as Cohen; see, for example, Eliezer Berkovits's cogent theological response to the Holocaust.[71] Contra Cohen, the pressing, gnawing problematic for the "fundamentalist" does not arise from the side of human freedom but rather from the belief in a Saving God, a belief radically challenged by the Holocaust. That is to say, the "fundamentalist" knows the evil of humankind to be a striking challenge to its elemental doctrine(s) regarding the character of the Creator. In comparison, Cohen's position is specifically structured in such a way as to avoid having to grapple with this extreme difficulty. Indeed, this is the very reason for his particular theological reconstruction, i.e., the world's evil does not, cannot, impinge in a dipolar system upon God's being or status. But while this metaphysical redescription succeeds in solving, or dissolving, certain tensions—not allowing the evil of the world to count against God—it raises others of equal or greater force, especially regarding the divine attributes, in particular, those relating to the categories of omnipotence and omniscience. Of course, Cohen wants to redefine these cardinal attributes; this is, if I understand his call for a renewal of a kabbalistic Schelling model of Creation-Revelation aright, exactly what he intends. But in the process, does his dipolar God still remain Godlike? Or has Cohen actually capitulated to those critics who deny God's meaningful reality, by whatever name, while attempting to make a virtue of this covert capitulation?

Then, too, the moral dimension of theodicy remains to be dealt with even after Cohen's ontological reconstructions, if for something of a new reason. For the moral or, rather, amoral corollary of the dipolar schematization of God is deeply disquieting. Cohen's dipolar God appears, of necessity, morally indifferent to human suffering and historical acts of evil,[72] factors of no small consequence, for, in the end, the most sensitive as well as the most telling objections to theodicy arise from the side of the ethical.

I have already analyzed the logical weaknesses inherent in attempting to meet the theological problems raised by the Shoah through recourse to the free will argument. Though this analysis needs to be modified in certain specific respects given the total construction of Cohen's theodicy, the general negative conclusion there argued that this defense is inadequate to the immense task at hand applies in the case of *The Tremendum* as well.

Here I would also add another word about Cohen's view of the connection between God and history. That is, Cohen recognizes that his programmatic reconstruction impacts upon the fundamental question of God's relation to history. In explicating his understanding of this vexing relationship he writes, "God and the life of God exist neither in conjunction with nor disjunction from the historical, but rather in continuous community and nexus. God is neither a function nor a cause of the historical nor wholly other and indifferent to the historical.[73] If God then is unrelated to the historical in any of these more usual ways, as "neither a function nor a cause," how then is He present, i.e., not "wholly other and indifferent," and what difference does He make in this redefined and not wholly unambiguous role? Cohen tells us,

> I understand divine life to be rather a filament within the historical, but never the filament that we can identify and ignite according to our requirements, for in this and all other respects God remains God. As filament, the divine element of the historical is a precarious conductor always intimately linked to the historical, its presence securing the implicative and exponential significance of the historical and always separate from it, since the historical is the domain of human freedom.[74]

But this advocacy of an "implicit" but noncausal nexus will not do.

In the final reckoning, this impressionistic articulation of the problem must collapse in upon itself, for at some level of analysis the reciprocal notions of "causality" and "function" cannot be avoided. One can talk lyrically of God as a "filament" and a "conductor" in history as if these were not causal or connective concepts, but upon deeper probing it will be revealed that they are. For talk of God as "filament" and "conductor" to retain its coherence—for it not to evaporate into empty metaphor—we have to know what it means to refer to God as a "filament, as a "conductor," no matter how precarious the theological reconstruction. To rescue these instrumental concepts from complete intellectual dissolution we need also to know something of how God is present in the world in these ways. What evidence can we point to in defense of these images?[75] For example, and deserving of a concrete answer, is the question, what of God is conducted? His love? Grace? Salvation? And if so, how? Wherein, against the darkness of the *tremendum,* do we experience His love, His grace, His salvation? To anticipate this objection as well as to attempt to deflect it by arguing that God is a "filament" but "never the filament that we can identify"[76] is a recourse to "mystery"[77] in the obfuscatory rather than the explanatory sense. For as explanation it means simply, "I claim God is somehow present or related to history but don't ask me how." Alternatively, to come at this thesis from the other side, the analogies of "filament" and "conductor" are disquieting as analogs of the relation of God and history because they so strongly suggest passivity and inertness. If they are the proper analogs for God's activity or presence in history, all our earlier concrete concerns about maintaining the integral vitality of Judaism resurface. For the God of creation, covenants, Sinai, and redemption is altogether different, i.e., qualitatively, metaphysically, and morally other, than a "conductor" or "filament."

Given the dispassionate, disinterested, amoral nature of Cohen's deity, it is not surprising that the conclusion drawn from this descriptive recasting of God's role in "community and nexus" is, vis-à-vis the Shoah, finally, trivial (in the technical sense).

> Given these assumptions, it would follow that the *tremendum* does not alter the relation of God to himself, nor the relation in which God exists to the historical, nor the reality of creation to the process of eternal beginning within God, but it does mean that man not God renders the filament of the divine incandescent or burns it out. There is, in the dialectic of man and God amid history, the indispensable recognition that man can obscure, eclipse, burn out the divine filament, grounding its natural movement of transcendence by a sufficient and oppository chthonic subscension. It is this which is meant by an *abyss* of the historical, the demonic, the *tremendum.*[78]

That the Holocaust makes no difference to God's relation to Himself we can grant *in principle* for the purposes of this analysis. And, logically and structurally, i.e., ontologically, we can allow for the purposes of argument Cohen's conclusion that "the *tremendum* does not alter the relation in which God exists to the historical." But, if we grant both these premises, it is necessary to conclude, contra Cohen, that the *tremendum* is not, and *in principle* could not be, a theological problem. It is, on its own premises, irrelevant to God's existence, irrelevant to God's relation to history, and, on these criteria, irrelevant to God's relation to humankind whatever humankind's relation to God.

The *tremendum* is seen by Cohen to be crucially relevant to humanity's recognition of a creator, but this is anthropology, for it perceives the *tremendum* only as a human event with no consequences for God other than our indifference to Him. And our indifference does not appear to matter in any transcendental sense, for God apparently does not make any response to it. This is the logic of the free will position driven to its "nth" degree—to a degree that makes God all but irrelevant. This remarkable implication flows, ironically, from Cohen's consummate attempt to redefine and reconstruct the theological landscape in order to *protect the viability of some* (not the traditional) *God-idea* in the face of the *tremendum,* an end it accomplishes through the total disconnection of God and the *tremendum.*

The last thinker whose work needs mention in this context is Irving (Yitz) Greenberg. Greenberg has argued that as a result of the Holocaust the covenant between God and Israel is voluntary.

The Shoah marks a new era in which the Sinaitic covenant was shattered. Thus, if there is to be any covenantal relationship at all today it must assume new and unprecedented forms.[79] In this context Greenberg insists that the covenant always implied further human development. The natural outcome of the covenant is full human responsibility. "In retrospect," he argues, paraphrasing A. Roy Eckardt,

> It is now clear that the divine assignment to the Jews was untenable. In the Covenant, Jews were called to witness to the world for God and for a final perfection. After the Holocaust, it is obvious that this role opened the Jews to a total murderous fury from which there was no escape. Yet the divine could not or would not save them from this fate.
>
> Therefore, morally speaking, God must repent of the covenant, i.e., do Teshuvah for having given his chosen people a task that was unbearably cruel and dangerous without having provided for their protection. Morally speaking, then, God can have no claims on the Jews by dint of the Covenant.[80]

What this means is that the covenant can no longer be commanded and subject to a serious external enforcement. It cannot be commanded because morally speaking—covenantally speaking—one cannot *order* another to step forward to die. One can give an order like this to an enemy, but in a moral relationship, I cannot demand giving up one's life. I can ask for it or plead for it—but I cannot order it. To put it again in Wiesel's words, "When God gave us a mission, that was all right. But God failed to tell us that it was a suicide mission."[81] Moreover, after the horrors of the *Endlösung*, nothing God could threaten for breach of the covenant would be frightening, hence the covenant cannot be enforced by the threat of punishment any longer.[82]

Out of this complex of considerations, Greenberg pronounces the fateful judgment: *The Covenant is now voluntary!* After Auschwitz Jews have, quite miraculously, chosen to continue to live Jewish lives and collectively to build a Jewish state, the ultimate symbol of Jewish continuity, but these acts are, now, the result of the free choice of the Jewish people. "I submit that the covenant was broken but the Jewish people, released from its obligations, chose voluntarily to take it on again and renew it. God was in no position to command anymore but the Jewish people was so in love with the dream of redemption that it volunteered to carry on with its mission."[83] The consequence of this voluntary action transforms the existing covenantal order. First Israel was a junior partner, then an equal partner, and now, after Auschwitz, it becomes "the senior partner in action. In effect, God was saying to humans: you stop the Holocaust. You bring the redemption. You act to insure: never again. I will be with you totally in whatever you do, wherever you go, whatever happens but you must do it."[84]

In turn, Israel's voluntary acceptance of the covenant and continued will to survive suggest three corollaries. First, they point, if obliquely, to the continued existence of the God of Israel. By creating the state of Israel, by having Jewish children, Israel shows that "covenantal hope is not in vain."[85] Secondly, and very importantly, in an age of autonomy rather than coercion, living Jewishly under the covenant can no longer be interpreted monolithically, i.e., only in strict halakic fashion. A genuine Jewish pluralism,[86] a Judaism of differing options and interpretations, is the only legitimate foundation in the age of Auschwitz. Orthodox observance no less than Reform, Conservative, or "secular" practices are freely adopted—none can claim either automatic authority or exclusive priority in the contemporary Jewish world.[87] Thirdly, and repeating a theme sounded several times in earlier essays, Greenberg offers that

> the urgency of closing any gap between the covenantal methods and goals is greater in light of the overwhelming countertestimony of evil in this

generation. The credibility of the Covenant is so troubled and so hanging in the balance that any internal element that disrupts or contravenes its affirmations must be eliminated. So savage was the attack on the image of God that any models or behavior patterns within the tradition that demean the image of God of people must be cleansed and corrected at once.[88]

A note of caution in pushing this dramatic statement of a "voluntary covenant" too far is, however, now required because of Greenberg's, further, mediating remarks on this provocative thesis. He writes, "We are at the opening of a major new transformation of the covenant in which Jewish loyalty and commitment manifests itself by Jews taking action and responsibility for the achievement of its goals. This is not a radical break with the past. In retrospect, this move is intrinsic in the very concept of covenant."[89] And Greenberg goes on,

> The Rabbis [of the Talmud] put forth Purim, with its hidden, human agency and flawed redemption, as the new redemptive model to which the Jews gave assent in upholding the covenant. *Today we can say that the covenant validated at Purim is also coercive, for then the genocide was foiled, and it is less binding in a world that saw Hitler's murder of six millions Jews.*

In responding to the many genuinely interesting philosophical and theological positions Greenberg has advanced, one feels, to begin, a certain unease that one has not quite captured his meaning completely. The source of this disquiet lies not only in the limits of one's own understanding but also in Greenberg's imprecise use of essential terms and ideas. Such elemental terms as "revelation," "messianic," "messianism," "history," "redemption," "real," "secular," and "religious" are all used in a multiplicity of ways, aimed at a spectrum of differently informed listeners, and all are employed (perhaps in part intentionally) without any precise definitions being offered. Then again, his work suffers from a certain lack of logical rigor. This is evident both in the construction of particular arguments as well as in certain underlying architectonic features of Greenberg's thought as a whole. The most notable of these lapses, which is present so consistently that it should be seen as a structural flaw, is located in his hermeneutical overemployment of the notions "dialectic" and "dialectical" and in his unsatisfactory usage of the interrelated notion of "paradox." Merely holding, or claiming to believe, two contradictory propositions simultaneously is not a fruitful theological procedure.

Greenberg offers two seminal criteria of verification for theological discourse in our time. The first criterion is strikingly powerful in its directness and simplicity. It states, "No statement, theological or otherwise,
should be made that would not be credible in the presence of burning
children."[90] The second criterion, more philosophically sculpted and no
doubt shaped in response to the positivist verificationist challenge, reads
as follows:

> Faith is not pure abstraction, unaffected or unshaken by contradictory
> events; is subject to "refutation." Yet it is not simply empirical either. A
> purely empirical faith would be subject to immediate refutation, but in fact
> the people of Israel may continue to testify in exile and after defeat. It may
> see or hope beyond the present moment to the redemption which will
> inevitably follow. Thereby, it continues to testify despite the contradiction
> in the present moment. In fact, when the redemption comes, it will be all
> the greater proof of the assertions of faith and of the reliability of God's
> promises because it will overcome the present hopeless reality. On the other
> hand, if redemption never came or if Israel lost hope while waiting for
> redemption, then the status quo would win and Jewish testimony would
> come to an end. Thus, faith is neither a simple product of history nor insu-
> lated from history. It is a testimony anchored in history, in constant tension
> with it, subject to revision and understanding as well as to fluctuation in
> credibility due to the unfolding events.[91]

While modern Jewish philosophers have tended to ignore the all-impor-
tant challenge raised by requests for verification, here Greenberg, astutely
as well as courageously, meets it head on. The question to be put to him,
however, is whether his two formulations are adequate as principles of
verification.

Begin with the first formulation. It does not set out a straightforward
empirical criterion. Empirical evidence will neither simply confirm it nor,
as it is phrased in the negative, simply disconfirm it. There is no empirical
statement with which it is incompatible. That is, it is not, finally, a statement of an empirical sort. But this need not matter *decisively,* for it is not
put as an empirical criterion; rather, its appeal is to the broader category
of "credibility," and many things are credible that are not empirical. In this
way, the task before us transforms itself into showing that "credible" is not
used trivially, but this is a far more ambiguous and uncertain task than
at first appears to be the case. Consider, for example, the remarks of the

German Protestant pastor Dean Grueber that had such a profound impact on Richard Rubenstein.[92] The dean honestly held that Jewish children died for the crime of deicide committed by their first-century ancestors. Such "good" Christian theology was obviously "credible" to the dean in the face of the Holocaust. Likewise, Satmar Hasidim and other right-wing Orthodox Jews who continue to account for the Holocaust through recourse to the doctrine of "for our sins we are punished" (*mipnei chata'eynu*), remembering, for example, the terrible fate of the children of Jerusalem of old recounted in Lamentations, which is credited to "our sins," also believe that their propositions are "credible." It thus becomes evident that *credible* is not a self-explanatory category of judgment. What is credible to Dean Grueber and the Satmar Rebbe is *incredible* to Greenberg, and the dispute between them is not resolved by appeal to the criterion Greenberg has established, as it would be were it a viable criterion. It turns out that what is "credible" depends on one's prior theological commitments, the very issue at stake. Accordingly, the argument becomes circular.

Consider now the second, more formal, criterion. It is attested to be falsifiable, "subject to refutation," yet it is not, at the same time, a "simply empirical" proposition. The two conditions of "refutation" established are (a) "Redemption never comes"; or (b) "if Israel lost hope while waiting for redemption, then the status quo would win." The first criterion appears, at least in what has been called a "weak" sense, to be empirically verifiable—i.e., it states a specific empirical condition under which it would, in principle, be disconfirmed. However, the established thesis is inadequate as a criterion because it turns on the temporal notion "never comes." Logically, we could not make any use of this norm until world history ended, in redemption or otherwise. At any time prior to the end of history an appeal could be made to "wait a minute more," hence putting off the empirical disconfirmation indefinitely. It certainly is not, contra Greenberg, a "testimony anchored in history" in any strong sense, as immediate and available historical evidence, e.g., the obscene reality of the death camps, is deflected by appeal to the end that never is.

The second condition offered is of more interest. But it, too, is not sufficient for two reasons. First, the continued and continuing status of Israel's faith qua subjective affirmation is not a logical or ontological warrant for any proposition regarding "God's mighty acts in history," Greenberg's claim to the contrary notwithstanding. What is disconfirmed "if Israel loses hope" is, of course, Israel's faith—i.e., the strength of its commitment—but the ontological content of the commitment is unaffected.

Propositions such as "there is a God," or "God redeems," or "History reveals a loving providence" are neither confirmed by Israel's faith nor disconfirmed by Israel's apostasy.

Given the weak verification procedures proposed by Greenberg, his advocacy of faith in God after the Shoah would seem compatible with any empirical set of conditions. That is, there seems no empirical state of affairs that is actually incompatible with theism, especially Greenberg's particular expression of theism.

This review of several major theological positions formulated as responses to the Holocaust reveals both the creativity and limits of Jewish thought after the Shoah. In particular, analyzing each of these positions individually and then comparing and contrasting them in their totality makes it evident that no (single or multiple) way has been found to provide meaningful criteria of confirmation and disconfirmation in our theological discourse. And, thus, no real advance has been made relative to the absolutely fundamental questions of theodicy.

Accordingly, we need to begin to think about the essential theological issues all over again *from the beginning* if we are to advance the argument concerning Jewish belief after Auschwitz in a satisfactory way.

NOTES

1. It should be mentioned at the start of this paper, in the clearest possible terms, that my criticism of Rubenstein is intended to be *strictly* philosophical and *not* ad hominem. *I* wish to dissociate myself *totally* from those critics who, rather than discuss Rubenstein's ideas, have abused the man. No instances of such abuse will be singled out for citation here, but those familiar with the literature will recognize this as an all-too-prevalent, and odious, element in the critical response to Rubenstein's position. Let me add in connection with the present essay that Professor Rubenstein has taken the criticism offered by me over the years in a most generous spirit and has become a valued friend.

2. *After Auschwitz* (Indianapolis, IN, 1966). This is Rubenstein's earliest and most important collection of material dealing with the Holocaust and its implications. This paper will primarily deal with Rubenstein's views as presented in this work, which I take to be his most significant statement on the theological implications of this theme.

3. *After Auschwitz*, 49.

4. *After Auschwitz*, 47.

5. Those who would deal with the Holocaust need to master not only Holocaust materials but also the whole of Jewish history. This point has been well made by E. Berkovits in his *Faith after the Holocaust* (New York, 1973). To obtain some idea of what is involved in such a mastery of Jewish history, readers are referred to Salo Baron's magisterial *Social and Religious History of the Jews,* 18 vols. (New York, 1952–1983), and especially to his extraordinary notes.

6. On Rubenstein's appreciation of the state of Israel see, for example, his essay on "The Rebirth of Israel in Jewish Theology" in *After Auschwitz.*

7. See A. Flew's essay in *New Essays in Philosophical Theology* (London, 1964). For a useful introduction to the enormous literature generated by this issue see R. Heimbeck's *Theology and Meaning* (London, 1969), especially his bibliography and notes.

8. On the "verification principle" see the sources given in R. Heimbeck, *Theology and Meaning.*

9. Readers must not confuse "verification" and "meaning"—the essential error made by A. J. Ayer. Nor should they confuse "meaning" and "falsification," which is a common distortion of Karl Popper's extremely interesting and widely influential views. See Popper's own discussion of this matter in his *Conjectures and Refutations* (London, 1963).

10. Franklin Sherman, "Speaking of God after Auschwitz," *Worldview* (Sept. 1974), 27.

11. On this classical rabbinic doctrine see, for example, Saadiah Gaon, *Emunot ve Deot,* 5:3.

12. See M. Buber, *I and Thou* (New York, 1958). For a critique of this position see my essay "Martin Buber's Epistemology," in idem, *Post-Holocaust Dialogues* (New York, 1983), 1–51. That the Buberian account is not without its serious philosophical and theological difficulties, which may undermine it, is not unknown to Fackenheim. See in this connection his essay "Buber's Doctrine of Revelation," in *The Philosophy of Martin Buber,* P. Schilpp and M. Friedman (eds.) (La Salle, IL, 1967).

13. See E. Fackenheim, *Quest for Past and Future* (Bloomington, IN, 1968), 10.

14. See E. Fackenheim, *God's Presence in History* (New York, 1970), 8 ff.

15. See E. Fackenheim, ibid., 16 ff.

16. Thus the traditional rabbinic dictum that every Jew at the Passover Seder should participate in the event with the sense that *he* or *she* was personally redeemed from Egypt, i.e., it is not just a commemoration of a past, concluded, event.

17. Fackenheim, *God's Presence in History,* 11.

18. *God's Presence in History,* 84, repeated from Fackenheim's earlier essay, "Jewish Faith and the Holocaust," *Commentary,* vol. 46, no. 2 (Aug. 1968), 30–36.

19. Ibid., 84. Here Fackenheim spells out the implication of these "commandments" in some detail. See 85–92.

20. See here Fackenheim's essay, read at the conference held at St. John the Divine in New York City and printed in Eva Fleischner (ed.), *Auschwitz: Beginning of a New Era* (New York, 1977), 205–17. See also his more recent work, which increasingly emphasizes the significance of the state of Israel. These newer essays are collected in *The Jewish Return into History* (New York, 1980).

21. See my essay "Martin Buber's Epistemology: A Critical Appraisal," *International Philosophical Quarterly*, vol. 21, no. 2 (June 1981), 133–58. Fackenheim's appreciation of Buber's position is to be found in his *God's Presence in History*, in his contribution to *The Philosophy of Martin Buber*, and in his collected essays, *Quest for Past and Future* (Bloomington, IN, 1968).

22. See his outstanding study of Hegel, *The Religious Dimensions of Hegel's Thought* (Bloomington, IN, 1967), and again his important essay "Hegel's Understanding of Judaism," in *Encounters between Judaism and Modern Philosophy* (New York, 1973). See also the Hegelian influence in several essays in *The Jewish Return into History*.

23. Buber would not agree. He saw his treatment of Judaism as emphasizing the historical in comparison, for example, with the system of his friend Franz Rosenzweig, or again, of the older Hermann Cohen. However, despite his genuine attempt to make history matter, to do it justice, his dialogical mode of thought essentially eliminated this possibility from satisfactorily actualizing itself in his work. I have briefly noted the reasons for this in the essay on Buber's epistemology cited in note 21 above.

24. On Buber's role in the life of German Jewry under the Nazis, see H. Kohn's biography *Martin Buber: Sein Werk und Seine Zeit, 1880–1930; Nachwort 1930–1960*, Robert Weltsch (ed.) (new edition, Koln, 1961). See also the article by Ernst Simon in the *Leo Baeck Yearbook*, vol. 1 (1956) entitled "Jewish Adult Education in Nazi Germany as Spiritual Resistance," 68–104; and E. Wolf, "Martin Buber and German Jewry," *Judaism*, vol. 1 (1952), 346–52.

25. On Buber's handling of the problem of evil see M. Friedman, *The Life of Dialogue* (Chicago, 1976); G. Schaeder, *The Hebrew Humanism of Martin Buber* (Detroit, 1973). For criticism see N. Glatzer, *Baeck-Buber Rosenzweig Reading the Book of Job* (Leo Baeck Memorial Lecture, No. 10) (New York, 1966); Paul Edwards, *Buber and Buberism* (Lawrence, KS, 1970); William Kaufmann, *Contemporary Jewish Philosophers* (New York, 1976). It should be noted that Edwards and Kaufmann's critiques are too simplistic in some important respects and hence must be read with care.

26. M. Buber, *Eclipse of God* (New York, 1957).

27. For a more detailed analysis of Buber's views, see my papers referred to above, as well as my paper "Martin Buber's Theory of Revelation," read at the Sixth World Congress of Jewish Studies (Jerusalem, 1976).

28. On this sensitive issue see Arthur A. Cohen's "Revelation and Law: Reflections on Martin Buber's Views on Halakah," *Judaism*, vol. 1 (July 1952), 250–56;

and Marvin Fox, "Some Problems in Buber's Moral Philosophy," in *The Philosophy of Martin Buber,* op. cit., 151 ff. See also Eliezer Berkovits, *Major Themes in Modern Philosophies of Judaism* (New York, 1974), 68–137.

29. See the article "Richard Rubenstein, the God of History, and the Logic of Judaism," in my *Post-Holocaust Dialogues: Critical Studies in Modern Jewish Thought* (New York, 1983), 174–204, for more on this issue as it applies to his position.

30. E. Fackenheim, *Encounters,* 7–30.

31. "University Discussion," in A. Flew and A. MacIntyre (eds.), *New Essays in Philosophical Theology* (London, 1966) and A. J. Ayer, *Language, Truth, and Logic* (London, 1936); several subsequent revised editions.

32. E. Fackenheim, *Encounters,* 20.

33. Ibid., 21.

34. It is now recognized that the verification/falsification challenge must usually be carried on in the language of *in principle,* i.e., future possibilities rather than actual disconfirming instances. Of course this weakens the challenge first laid down by Ayer as subsequent editions of *Language, Truth, and Logic* clearly demonstrate. But this diminution of the challenge was the only way to retain its intelligibility. Whether it is intelligible even in this weaker form is an open question.

35. Ibid., 21.

36. Ibid., 21–22.

37. *Return,* 52.

38. *Faith,* 106.

39. Ibid., 107.

40. J. L. Mackie, "Evil and Omnipotence," originally published in *Mind,* vol. 44, no. 254 (1955). Reprinted in L. Urban and D. Walton (eds.), *The Power of God* (New York, 1978), 17–31. This quote is from 27. A similar position has also been advanced by A. Flew, "Divine Omnipotence and Human Freedom," in *New Essays in Philosophical Theology* (New York, 1955), ch. 8. A counterargument has been provided by, among others, Ninian Smart, "Omnipotence, Evil, and Supermen," *Philosophy* vol. 36, no. 137 (1961). Smart's position has in turn been criticized by H. J. McCloskey, *God and Evil* (The Hague, 1974), 103–5.

41. A. Plantinga, *God, Freedom, and Evil* (New York, 1974), 54–55. I have revised the numbering of the various propositions in this argument, Plantinga's numbering being different because part of a larger thesis, e.g., my number (2) is his (3), my (3) his (35), my (4) his (36).

42. I have technical philosophical reservations regarding Plantinga's argument. Given our present concern, however, we need not take them up here. For the sorts of issues that are relevant to a discussion of Plantinga's views see J. E. Tomberlin and F. McGuiness, "God, Evil, and the Free Will Defense," in *Religious Studies,* vol. 13 (1977), 455–75, which is critical of Plantinga's position. This paper has, in turn, been replied to by Del Ratzsch, "Tomberlin and McGuiness on Plantinga's Free

Will Defense," *International Journal for the Philosophy of Religion*, vol. 12, no. 4 (1981), 75–95; and by Robert Burch, "The Defense of Plenitude against the Problem of Evil," *International Journal for the Philosophy of Religion*, vol. 12, no. 1 (1981), 29–38. And idem, "Plantinga and Leibniz's Lapse," *Analysis*, vol. 39, no. 1 (Jan. 1979), 24–29. This should be taken as only a sample of the extensive secondary literature generated by Plantinga's important, if not fully convincing, work.

43. Ibid., 55 ff.

44. On this issue of miracles and its relevance see the argument below.

45. J. Hick, *Evil and the God of Love* (London, 1966), 255–56. A similar argument is advanced by Gordon Kaufman in his *God the Problem* (Cambridge, MA, 1972), 171–200. Berkovits is explicitly sensitive to the disanalogy involved in the Job metaphor per se (see *Faith*, 67–70), though he uses the same argument in a more general way.

46. *Faith*, 109. Berkovits's preference for the term "miracle" is both correct and misleading. That is, we can grant the term and the correctness of its usage, but this does not solve anything. The issue merely becomes why God did not perform a miracle.

47. Ibid., 105.

48. In his most recent book, *With God in Hell* (New York, 1978) Berkovits elaborates on this weakness at some length. In addition to the appeal to a "hereafter" he refers to three other Jewish "responses" to buttress the free will argument. They are the *Akedah*, the "Exile of the Shechinah," and the "Suffering Servant" motif. I shall not discuss Berkovits's treatment of these themes as they do not seem to me to advance appreciably the logic of the argument. Readers are referred to *With God in Hell*, 124 ff., for Berkovits's presentation.

49. *Faith*, 136. This, of course, is a standard proposal often made in the past by theists. See, e.g., Kant's moral theism as developed in a number of his works, and C. A. Campbell's *On Selfhood and Godhood* (London, 1959), among many other instances of this defense.

50. The possible counterargument some might advance, that heaven is good because it is earned by good deeds, would not be relevant in the case I present. This is because the causal mechanism whereby one gets to heaven does not account for, and is a different matter from, heaven's intrinsic goodness. Heaven is good per se not because this is where righteous souls ascend to. Rather, righteous souls ascend to heaven because it is good.

51. This position has also been adopted by Yitzchak Greenberg through, in all likelihood, Berkovits's influence.

52. *Faith*, 109.

53. *Faith*, 107.

54. *Faith*, 124.

55. See ibid., 109 ff., for Berkovits's views on Israel in history.

56. *With God in Hell*, 83.

57. Having said this I should also say that I disagree with Berkovits's further remarks on the interaction of Jewish vs. non-Jewish history in *Faith*, 111–12.

58. *Faith*, 111–12.

59. Ibid., 134. On the meaning of the rebirth of the state of Israel see also ibid., 144–69; and *Crisis and Faith* (New York, 1976), 159 ff.

60. Ibid., 136 ff.

61. The positivists' erroneous conflation of meaning and verification must be recognized and avoided. Again, Karl Popper's views on "disconfirmation" and the nature of scientific propositions must not be misapplied, as Popper himself acknowledges, to metaphysical propositions.

62. Ibid., 96 ff.

63. Ibid., 97.

64. Ibid., 97.

65. Cf. here my comments on Yitzchak Greenberg's redefinition of God and his notion of a "voluntary covenant" in my essay "'Voluntary Covenant': Irving Greenberg on Faith after the Holocaust," in Steven T. Katz, *Historicism, the Holocaust, and Zionism: Critical Studies in Modern Jewish Thought and History* (New York, 1992), 225–50.

66. Ibid., 97.

67. It is worth comparing Cohen's present description and understanding of the divine as dipolar with his comments made in conversation with Mordecai Kaplan over the idea of God in Kaplan's reconstructionism and printed in the volume *If Not Now, When?* (New York, 1973). There Cohen offered,

> I think it also implies a rather fundamental distinction within the tradition between God as creator and God as revealer. One of the things that I particularly love in Rosenzweig's discussion of the reality of God in his *The Star of Redemption* is the recognition that the distinction between God the creator and God the revealer is rather too sharp in traditional theology. The assumption that the creating God is not also a revealing God and that the revealing God is not also a creating God at one and the same time is mistaken. The God who brought the people of Israel out of the land of Egypt to be their God was not only revealing himself to the people and calling the people to himself, convoking the people as the object of the act, but at the same time was exhibiting an undisclosed aspect of himself. The notion in classical theology (which I dislike as much as you do) that God *is being* alone, *ens entissimus*, and that history is somehow oppositive to the divine nature; that God concedes to history, condescends himself to it, seems to me meaningless and defeating.
>
> God needs history. God needs his creatures. God as creator requires as much the thing that he creates as he does the capacity to create.
>
> The creation of the universe and the giving of the Torah are part of the same continuum of self-expression. God's nature demands self-expression as profoundly as his creatures demand it.

Cohen's presentation here seems more satisfying and closer to the reality of Jewish views of God than his statement in his new work. It is instructive to follow the whole of Cohen's debate with Kaplan. Also of interest is a comparison of his present views as to the nature of God with those voiced in his earlier *The Natural and the Supernatural Jew* (New York, 1962).

68. *The Tremendum: A Theological Reinterpretation of the Holocaust* (New York, 1981), 90. The emphasis of "assumed" is supplied by me.

69. Ibid., 94.

70. Ibid., 96.

71. Compare in particular Eliezer Berkovits, *Faith after the Holocaust* (New York, 1973) and *With God in Hell* (New York, 1978). See also my critical discussion of Berkovits's views in *Post-Holocaust Dialogues* (New York, 1983), 268–86.

72. For more on the issue of the relation of God and history see below.

73. Cohen, *The Tremendum*, 97.

74. Ibid., 97–98.

75. Here, that is, we raise issues as to meaning and related, but separate, questions as to verification, i.e., not conflating the two but asking about both.

76. Ibid., 97 ff.

77. See my paper on the "Logic and Language of Mystery," in S. Sykes and J. Clayton (eds.), *Christ, Faith, and History* (Cambridge, England, 1972), 239–62, for a fuller criticism of this common theological gambit.

78. Cohen, *The Tremendum*, 98.

79. The five articles by Greenberg I will be concerned with in this section are (1) "Cloud of Smoke, Pillar of Fire: Judaism, Christianity, and Modernity after the Holocaust," in E. Fleischner (ed.), *Auschwitz: Beginning of a New Era?* (New York, 1977), 1–55 (hereafter cited as "Cloud"); (2) "Judaism and History: Historical Events and Religious Change," in Jerry V. Dillen (ed.), *Ancient Roots and Modern Meanings* (New York, 1978), 43–63 (hereafter cited as JH); (3) "New Revelations and New Patterns in the Relationship of Judaism and Christianity," *Journal of Ecumenical Studies* (Spring 1979), 249–67; (4) "The Transformation of the Covenant" (not yet published); and (5) "The Third Great Cycle in Jewish History," printed and circulated by the National Jewish Resource Center (New York, 1981), 44 pages (hereafter TGC).

80. TGC, 23. Here it is to be noted, as already indicated, that in this paragraph Greenberg is paraphrasing a remark by A. Roy Eckardt and there may be some differences between Eckardt's position and Greenberg's over the final understanding of this seminal issue.

81. Ibid., 23.

82. Ibid., 23–24.

83. Ibid., 25.

84. Ibid., 27. Because of the significance of this doctrine and its apparent radicalness, it is important that we understand Greenberg's position correctly. In

further correspondence with this author he has given the following explication that I quote in full:

It is true that I go on to describe "the shattering of the Covenant" and "the Assumption of the Covenant." However, in the light of this whole essay the human taking charge, i.e., full responsibility for the covenant is God's calling to them. "If the message of the destruction of the Temple was that the Jews were called to greater partnership and responsibility in the covenant, then the Holocaust is an even more drastic call for total Jewish responsibility for the covenant" (TGC, 36). The more I reflected upon this insight, I grew more and more convinced that this third stage was an inevitable and necessary stage of the covenant. The covenant always intended that humans ultimately must become fully responsible. In retrospect, the voluntary stage is implicit in the covenantal model from the very beginning. Once God self-limits out of respect for human dignity, once human free will is accepted, the ultimate logic is a voluntary covenant. (Personal correspondence from Dr. Greenberg to the author, January 3, 1989)

85. TGC, 30.

86. See ibid., 33. For further adumbration of Greenberg's position on pluralism and its many implications, cf. also his more recent essay "Toward a Principled Pluralism," *Perspectives* (National Jewish Center for Learning and Leadership, New York, March 1986).

87. These ideas are more fully described in TGC, 37 ff. For Greenberg this means that it is God's will that humans take full responsibility for the outcome of the covenant. Such a grant of autonomy entails that even if the actual policy decisions reached and acted upon are erroneous, the error is, in some real sense, a legitimate error within the broader confines of the covenant rather than a wholly illegitimate form of religious behavior.

88. Ibid., 37–38. See also 16 ff.

89. TGC, 18.

90. "Cloud," 23.

91. JH, 47.

92. On the details of this encounter see R. Rubenstein's article in *After Auschwitz* (Indianapolis, IN, 1966), 47–58.

Chapter 3

Philosophical and Midrashic Thinking on the Fateful Events of Jewish History

Joseph A. Turner

In the following discussion, I would like to make a statement with regard to the interpretation of fateful events in Jewish history in the overall context of Jewish thought. More precisely, I would like to make a statement concerning the relative strengths and weaknesses of two types of Jewish thinking with regard to what I view as the two fundamental responsibilities placed upon those dealing in Jewish thought in the present. The forms of Jewish thinking that I am referring to are the traditionally oriented midrash, on the one hand, and the more systematic thought of Jewish philosophy, on the other.[1] My premise is that one of the responsibilities incumbent upon Jewish thought in the post-Holocaust world is to examine, and in many cases to reexamine, the character of particular historical events with regard to their cultural, religious, and philosophical significance. Another responsibility is to examine, and reexamine, the fundamental presuppositions of traditional thought in light of these events. My primary thesis is that while in the past the method of Jewish thinking, either midrashic or philosophical, did not radically influence the normative value of the conclusions reached in the examination of fateful events, this could no longer be the case in the Jewish thought of the post-Holocaust world.[2]

In the course of the paper it will become evident that I identify with the position that maintains that the Holocaust should be considered unique when compared with other fateful events of Jewish history. I shall further make the claim that because of the horrible uniqueness of the Holocaust, we must now consider the characteristic distinctions between philosophical and midrashic thinking in ways that did not seem to be necessary in the past. I believe that this reconsideration is necessary in order to acknowledge the uniqueness of the challenges arising before tradition in the wake of the Holocaust, as well as to respond to them appropriately.

As a first step toward demonstrating my point, let me state, in general terms, the overall character of some of the challenges arising before traditional thought from within the fateful events of the past. A proper formulation of these challenges may be stated in the terms of classical theodicy: if indeed God is wholly good, and is at the same time both providential and all-powerful, how is it that there is evil in the world? Eli Schweid states the problem in a somewhat existentially oriented fashion. "The questioning [of faith]," he says, "is not rooted solely in the independent challenge of a shocking event that testifies to the growing disparity between expectations already held by the man of faith and a given reality, but also in the relation between the degree of pain and injustice inherent to the event and [other contrasting] faith strengthening experiences."[3] I would like to point out that while the challenge we are speaking of may, in fact, be defined specifically as a challenge of faith in God, it is also a challenge to the preconceived truth of tradition.

It would certainly be foolish to say that the reality of evil is the only phenomenon that challenges faith in God or tradition. It is, nonetheless, that phenomenon that warrants a comparison between the type of challenge arising from the Holocaust and that arising from previous fateful events in Jewish history. Whichever formulation of the problem one may prefer, it is obvious that many of the fateful events of Jewish history call into question previously held notions from which Jewish thought has traditionally drawn the meaning of Jewish existence. The destruction of the First and Second Temples, exile, Jewish martyrdom at the time of the Crusades, inquisitions and expulsions, and, above all, the Holocaust, challenge the traditional belief in Providence and the overall goodness of the world. And yet, as has been emphasized again and again, there is a difference between the type of challenge arising from most of these events and that arising from within the world of the Holocaust. The difference between most of these events and that of the Holocaust corresponds to the distinction, made by many post-Holocaust thinkers, between relative and radical evil.[4] Shalom Rosenberg describes this distinction in the following manner:

> The principle thesis of this type of thought . . . is that [in the Holocaust we are speaking of] an essentially different type of evil. The persecution of men

for political reasons is wrong, and of course, we must fight against it. Mass murder is an unforgiving crime against humanity, but the Holocaust is still something different. The intent and activity that went into the murder of a [single] Jewish child, the reality in which the deed was done, as well as the end for which it was done, are absolutely different from all other actual and intended acts of murder in history.[5]

At this point, I believe we would do well in following Emil Fackenheim's analysis of the Holocaust as a world similar to the one we all live in, except that whereas we presume the end for which our world exists to be the principle of good, the end for which the world of the Holocaust was created was evil for evil's sake.[6] If one accepts (as I do) Prof. Schweid's reaction to Fackenheim's position to the effect that the Holocaust was not a world unto itself but part of our world,[7] then we have good reason to reconsider the justifications given to the seemingly evil events of the past.[8]

When I say that methods of Jewish thinking in the post-Holocaust world must influence the outcome of deliberations with regard to the challenge arising from historical events in ways that were not considered in the past, I am referring specifically to the above distinction between relative and radical evil. By and large, both midrashic and philosophical forms of thought were able to respond to the challenges arising from past events by viewing the evil manifest in present reality as relative to a more all-inclusive good. This is true of Maimonides' philosophical view of evil as an "absence of being" necessitated by divine activity so as to allow for the completion of creation[9] as it is of midrashic statements to the effect that the sorrows of exile are necessary as a prelude to an all-encompassing future redemption. Such justifications may have been possible, in the past, insofar as the events being considered could be seen as limited in scope. Disastrous as they were to the Jews whose lives they immediately affected, they could still be seen, in principle, as a necessary, if tragic, episode in God's overall plan for Jewish and world history. It is virtually impossible, on the other hand, to conceive of an all-encompassing good that could in anyway justify the dimensions of evil exhibited in the Holocaust. It is because of this point that I believe a careful consideration of the identifying characteristics of philosophical and midrashic thinking is crucial for present-day Jewish thought concerning the Holocaust.

In order to support the points I have made in these introductory remarks, the next two sections will be devoted to a consideration of the manner in which the problem of evil and suffering has been dealt with in the past, both in midrashic as well as in systematic philosophical thinking.

The Status of History and Tradition in Midrashic Thinking

With regard to midrashic thinking, we will first note that as a form of rabbinical thought, the problem of evil and suffering was generally considered in midrashic thinking in light of the earlier biblical position concerning the connection between suffering and reward and punishment.[10] The early biblical statement to the effect that "the sins of the fathers shall be visited upon the children," Ezekiel's later position that it is only the "soul that sins who shall die," and of course the blessings and admonitions of Deuteronomy all provide the basis for the theological presumption on the part of the rabbis that divine activity is ultimately just insofar as it is rooted in divine lawfulness.

Already the prophet Jeremiah asked why it is that that the ways of the wicked seem to be crowned with success while the righteous are relegated to suffering and dismay.[11] Jeremiah's protest, however, would be meaningless had it not been for the fact that he too expected the divine response to human activity to be in some proportional relation to that activity. The rabbis, in turn, defined the nature of divine retribution as "a measure for a measure" (מידה כנגד מידה).

The following Mishnah is one example of the manner in which midrashic thought deals with the question of divine retribution:

Seven kinds of calamities come to the world for seven chief transgressions:

Some [of the people] bring tithe while some do not—hunger from *batzoret* [mild drought] results—some will be hungry while others will not.

They [all] undertake not to bring tithe—hunger from *batzoret* as well as *mehumot* [violent upheaval] results.

[They undertake] not to bring *halah* [the priests share of the dough], hunger from *k'liyah* [extreme drought] results.

Pestilence ensues from [transgressions requiring] the death penalty not given to the [jurisdiction of the] courts, and from [transgressions regarding prohibited] fruits of the seventh year.

[Destruction by the] sword ensues from *inui hadin* [administering the law in a cruel manner], from *ivut hadin* [fallacious implementation of the law], and from teaching the law *shelo k'halakha* [improperly].

[Destruction by] wild animals ensues from [taking] unnecessary oaths and blasphemy.

Exile [from the land] results from idolatry, forbidden relations, murder and from *shmitat ha'aretz* [not letting the land rest during the Sabbatical year].[12]

This Mishnah portrays the punishments recalled in the curses of Deuteronomy as just retribution for specific transgressions of norms and values central to biblical as well as rabbinical law. It should be noted, however, that for the rabbis the correspondence between the transgressions and the calamities listed in this Mishnah is of existential, and not only legal, significance. Many, if not all of the calamities listed in this Mishnah had in fact occurred at the time of exile and destruction of the First Temple. The fact that the calamities are seen as punishments designed to correspond with specific transgressions of a religious and social nature offers both an explanation as well as a justification for the tragedy that God brought to bear on the people of Israel in the distant past.

According to the biblical principle of divine retribution, the tragedy may be seen as a punishment for social and religious transgressions that in and of themselves disqualified the legitimacy of a Jewish homeland in the eyes of the rabbis, as well as in the eyes of the Bible. When transgressions such as indicated with regard to the bringing of tithes are committed by the people as a whole, then it is the people as a whole that is to be punished. The reason for this may very well be that which was expressed less than a hundred years ago by Franz Rosenzweig: the land belongs to God, and only secondarily to humanity. "And so, even when it has a home, this people . . . is not allowed full position . . . it is only 'a stranger and a sojourner.' God tells it: 'The land is mine.'"[13] The land belongs to humanity only because of its ties to God. Therefore, it is only by his will that the people have a share in the land. Adherence to the divine word is therefore a condition for remaining in the land. The ritual bringing of tithes and making the land rest in the Sabbatical year reflect this status. Failure to observe laws tied to the land expresses indifference to divine sovereignty, and therefore brings destruction in its wake. On moral matters, it may even be the sin of the few that bring destruction upon the land and the people. The sins of idolatry, murder, and adultery destroy the core of the people's national-religious existence, and as such they too legitimize national destruction. This is certainly the case when it comes to transgressions committed by the religious, moral, and political leadership of the people. These sins, when done by public officials, also bring about the corruption of society, and therefore ultimate destruction.

For the purpose of comparison with a later rabbinical source, I would like to point out that save for one, all the transgressions mentioned above seem to reflect a historical reality already known to the Bible. The law they transgress may well have been the law of the land in the First and Second Temple periods. The passage that lays blame for "destruction by the sword" on crimes of the court, on the other hand, seems to reflect a period when the rabbinical leadership already saw itself as bearing responsibility for the fate of the people, perhaps in the absence of temple worship. In any event, this passage is found to be of significance when compared with a later midrash that also emphasizes the notion that *inui hadin* brings destruction by the sword.

We shall see in the following midrash that the matter of *inui hadin* is once again raised with regard to a great tragedy brought to bear on the people. In this later midrash, the rabbis still view *inui hadin* as a just cause for destruction. This time, however, the principle of divine retribution is wracked with irony. The result is that the notion of divine retribution is now used to explain and justify God's involvement in history in a way that is not entirely consistent with previous belief.

> When Rabbi Yishmael and Rabbi Shimon were about to be put to death, Rabbi Shimon turned to Rabbi Yishmael and said: my heart grieves for I do not know the deed for which I am to be executed. Rabbi Yishmael replied to Rabbi Shimon: Did it not ever occur that a man stood before you in judgement, or came to you with an inquiry and you detained him until you finished drinking from your cup, or until you finished putting on your shoes or your garment? [The Bible says] *Anoh Ta'aneh*[14]—One suffering is large, the other is small. With this he replied: *Nekhamtani Rabi* [My teacher, you have consoled me].[15]

The period reflected in the midrash on Rabbi Yishmael and Rabbi Shimon's martyrdom is one of great difficulty for the Jewish people. It reflects a situation in which traditional Jewish faith is challenged by a present historical event of extreme severity. Not only has faith in God's promise to care for his people been once again tested by the destruction of the Second Temple and the loss of Jewish autonomy, but now the most pious Torah scholars are being put to death for what appears to be no good reason. Rather than affirm God's relation to history as set out in the Bible, history, at first glance, contradicts it. The sages, we should note, are not being tortured and executed because they disobeyed God's word, but just the opposite: because they are fulfilling their responsibility to both God and their people in their role as national religious leaders.

The challenge to Jewish faith is clear: Does God consent to what is being done? Were we right in believing that God is just, that he cares for his people, and that all that happens in the world that he created is, in fact, a sign of his ultimate goodness?

The crimes noted for which the punishment is brought indeed suggest a degree of *inui din*. The midrash, however, admits to this being problematic in the present situation. Insofar as the crimes recalled are rather trivial examples of the crime, they certainly do not, in the final analysis, appear to fit the severity of the punishment. As a result the midrash does not focus so much on the transgression of *inui hadin* in and of itself, as it does on Rabbi Simon's "not-knowing." As is the case with much Jewish theology over the ages, Rabbi Shimon is convinced that God manages history in a just manner. His standing before torture and execution in this specific historical situation, however, challenges that belief in the deepest of ways. God has "hidden his face," and despite the assurance that it is Rabbi Shimon's own transgression that justifies his fate, he still does not know how that is so.

From an educational point of view, the midrash is powerful indeed: judges should always be aware that even by showing the slightest disrespect for those that come before them, they may eventually bring upon the people ultimate destruction. From the point of view of theodicy, though, it is pure irony. *Inui hadin* is not invoked in this midrash in order to substantiate the claim that divine retribution presumes "a measure for a measure," but just the opposite. It is as if the midrash is saying, "even if we do not know why it is that such a seemingly small sin warrants so cruel punishment, let us rest assured that the punishment follows, in some way, from that sin." With this, we are meant to say along with Rabbi Shimon, "*nekhamtani rabi*—my teacher you have consoled me."

We find that what could have been a most devastating challenge to the truth of tradition is neutralized by a rather moderate revision of that truth. The author of this particular midrash confronts the challenge to the traditional Jewish faith position by carefully choosing which aspect of this faith must be forfeited in order to save the others. It is not at all certain that the author of this midrash saw himself as providing an adequate solution to the questions raised above. And yet, the question posed regarding the reason for Rabbi Shimon's martyrdom already indicates a sincere desire for an answer that would justify God's actions, or at least his silence, even if the answer is not totally satisfactory.

"ענה תענה—One suffering is large, the other is small." In the attempt to preserve the notion of a just and providential God this specific midrash was willing to sacrifice the principle of "a measure for a measure." It is as if the midrash is saying, "we may continue to believe in a just God who rewards the righteous and brings suffering as a result of transgression even when we no longer understand in what manner the punishment fits the crime." The bottom line is that Rabbi Shimon sinned, and even if in our eyes the severity of his punishment in no way fits the severity of his crime, we may rest assured that there is a principle of divine justice at work here.

The midrash responds to a specific historical event and then interprets its meaning in light of a previously held truth. In so doing, it sometimes finds it necessary to reevaluate the specifics of that truth. The primary goal of midrashic thinking, however, is not the reconsideration of traditional presuppositions as such, but rather the reinstatement of the previously held truth in light of the challenge. The challenge itself is not a value, but merely a fact that needs to be acknowledged and resolved. Traditional presuppositions will therefore only be reevaluated to the extent necessary for its overall reinstatement, that is, to the extent necessary for the challenge to be met.

In response to the challenge, midrashic thinking expands the parameters of traditional thought so as to absorb the event that gave rise to the challenge and give it religious significance. Midrashic thinking makes the event a part of tradition as it succeeds in ascribing to it religious and cultural meaning.

How does midrash accomplish this task? It is clearly not through the use of philosophical criticism, but once again, through the particular literary expression chosen so as to enable a reinstatement of the preconceived truths of tradition in the given circumstances.

Because of the limited scope of this paper, I will not enter a discussion as to the variety of strategies used in other midrashim in order to reinstate the truths of tradition in light of historical challenge. It is sufficient to note that the character of midrashic thinking allows for such a reinstatement of traditional truth insofar as it is both historically situated as well as historically malleable. Midrashic thinking is a type of thinking that situates itself in history, and then allows itself to reinterpret its own truths in light of the specifics of historical occurrence. It thereby gives meaning to that occurrence, and makes its memory a vital aspect of present experience.

Truth as an Abstract and Universal Value in Systematic Philosophy

Like midrash, systematic Jewish philosophy also takes upon itself the role of interpreting the changing historical reality in light of a higher truth, and at the same time reevaluates that truth in the light of changing historical realities. But as we shall presently see, until recently philosophy's connection with history was long term. The problems with which it busied itself are the long-standing problems of human existence. True, when Maimonides is influenced by the categories of Greek philosophy so as to interpret the creation of humanity in the image of God in terms of intellectual perception[16] he is, in fact, engaging in midrashic activity. The same goes for Rabbi Nachman Krochmal, in the modern period, when he identifies the Lord of Hosts with the Absolute Spirit of historical development.[17] It is also true with respect to Hermann Cohen's identification of Kant's categorical imperative with the divine command to love one's neighbor and of the Day of Atonement as a day of moral and psychological catharsis necessary for adherence to that command.[18]

Systematic Jewish philosophy shares with its midrashic counterpart an orientation toward Jewish sources as a basis upon which tradition expands its own parameters. Nonetheless, as will immediately become apparent, Jewish philosophy, at least in the past, differs from midrashic thinking in that it is not able to reflect upon specific historical situations but only on history, and even Jewish history, in general. It therefore could not as readily integrate the uniqueness of the challenge to the preconceived truths of tradition posed by specific historical circumstances.

There is no doubt that Maimonides, Krochmal, and Cohen believed that the solutions to the problem of evil, of Providence and the goodness of the world inherent in their works, were immediately relevant to the challenges to traditional belief arising from within history. And yet, even when these themes become central to the philosophical thought of these thinkers, they become central not with regard to specific historical events but with regard to the general nature of God, humanity, and history. This is because the guiding truths of systematic Jewish philosophy, even when they are identified with the truths of tradition, do not rest upon the authority of tradition but are rather seen as universal truths resting on the authority of a universally oriented philosophical discourse.[19]

I follow Fackenheim[20] in maintaining that for this reason philosophy, in and of itself, is unequipped to recognize the uniqueness of the challenge to traditional faith arising from within the Holocaust. Because of its generalizing or universalizing character, systematic philosophical discourse has consistently been better equipped to criticize and transform the inner content of traditional thought in light of historical challenge. But it is less equipped than midrashic thinking when it comes to ascertaining the specifics of the challenge as they are manifest in particular historical occurrences.

This can clearly be demonstrated, for example, in the case of Maimonides. The interpretive quality of Maimonides' thought is clearly seen in the manner in which he applies the general orientation of the biblical story of creation, along with his own unique interpretation of the story of Job, to the principles of Aristotelian philosophy with regard to the problem of divine retribution.

Maimonides' position concerning the problem of evil is based upon the Aristotelian understanding of the relation between matter and form in the physical world.[21] What seems to be evil, for him, is in fact a result of the relationship maintained between substance and form in the context of creation. Evil is an "absence" of existence. It is a characteristic of substance, when it is not yet fully formed according to its potential as determined by infinite divine wisdom. Divine activity is from the start existence that contains within itself the potential for renewed existence. Evil results from the incomplete state of divine activity as presently manifest in creation. God is certainly not responsible for evil, insofar as evil is not, in the last resort, a part of his creation, but is rather an "absence" of created existence, a "not yet having been created."

Does this conception of evil allow for the traditional notion of Providence, including the principle of divine retribution? It certainly allows for a general theory of Providence in which the evil manifest in illness and disease, and even natural and social calamities such as earthquakes and war, are identified with the incompleteness of creation at any given moment. But what about Providence and the individual? What about the principle of reward and punishment with regard to individual responsibility?

Whereas the function of traditional midrashic thinking was initially to broaden the truth of tradition in light of historical occurrence, Maimonides uses midrashic interpretation in order to broaden the content of philosophical truth. Genesis I and II place humanity at the center of creation, making its destiny dependent on personal adherence to the divine command. How does this square with the notion of creation based on the Aristotelian position concerning the relation between form and matter as a basis for existence in general? Maimonides' answer is given by way of an expanded interpretation of the answer given to Job's search for an understanding as to the reason for his own suffering. This, for Maimonides, is the point of the story:

> The revelation that reached Job (chap. xxxviii, xli) and explained to him the error of his whole belief, constantly describes natural objects . . . the description of all these things serves to impress on our minds that we are unable to comprehend how these transient creatures came into existence, or to imagine how their natural properties commenced to exist, and these are not like things which we are to produce. Much less can we compare the manner in which God rules and manages His creatures with the manner in which we rule and manage certain beings. . . . This lesson is the principal object of the whole book of Job; it lays down the principal of faith, and recommends us to derive a proof from nature, that we should not fall into the error of imagining His knowledge . . . intention, providence, and rule similar to ours.[22]

In his discussion, Maimonides claims that Job's status as a prophet is linked to the truth he acquired as a result of his suffering. Job was convinced of his own righteousness. Much of the book shows Job's struggle not to relinquish his faith in the face of what must have looked to him as a pretty good proof against that faith. According to Maimonides, however, the challenge only seems formidable because of humanity's initial state of ignorance. The very assumption that Job's suffering may be unjust follows from the expectation that God's management of the world be similar to our own. The beginning of wisdom, more specifically prophetic wisdom, is therefore to know that this is not so.

Suffering, for Maimonides, contains deep educational import. The simple knowledge that God's "management" of the world is different from our own already constitutes, for Maimonides, an advance toward the sort of intellectual perfection that ultimately brings reward and lessens one's suffering in the world. "When we know this we shall find everything that may befall us easy to bear; mishap," he says, "will create no doubts in our hearts concerning God."[23]

In the midrashic framework now constructed, Maimonides returns to the Aristotelian conception of form and substance and uses it as a basis for the reinstitution of the belief in providence with regard to the individual. In true Aristotelian fashion, Maimonides views the intellect as the form of human existence. But at any given moment the individual person is, as is society in general, in a state of material imperfection. Humanity's world is imperfect on two counts. Firstly, the objects comprising it are material objects and are therefore in and of themselves imperfect. Secondly, human beings, being themselves objects in that world, are imperfect so long as they have not carried themselves to a higher level of being through intellectual perfection. This, for Maimonides, is the basis for human management. Providence, on the other hand, consists in the totality of creation as seen through God's eyes. Divine consolation is therefore derived from the knowledge that God's ways are not our ways.

It is through suffering that the prophet learns the difference between human and divine management. Suffering is, in fact, a function of that difference. Insofar as suffering results from the abyss separating the imperfect state of the material world and its intellectual perfection, it is through suffering that humans learns the limits of their existence. Consolation is a result of a divine wisdom attained through suffering insofar as a proper understanding of that suffering quiets the sense of injustice previously attached to it. A proper attitude toward suffering is the way to advance toward such a state of perfection as determined in the infinity of God's wisdom.

In this way suffering itself is seen as necessary for the ultimate completion of creation. An increased knowledge of a truth that is at once philosophical and prophetic, beginning with the awareness that divine management is different from human management, lessens the sense of suffering to the extent that it dispels the feeling that one has been hurt for no reason. At the same time, it serves as a basis for the claim that suffering is, as already presumed, necessary for the redemption of humankind.

What may we learn from Maimonides' discussion of evil, suffering, and providence? Once again, it is not the details of the philosophical position that concern us here but rather the manner in which the truth of tradition faces the challenges posed to it by an outside source. Should we say that Maimonides' discussion of Providence with regard to the problem of evil and suffering reflects the specifics of a particular historical event? Apparently not. It rather deals with concepts denoted by the word "Providence," such as God, humanity, sin, and wisdom in a general sense.

The same may be said, to take one more example, with regard to the place of suffering in Herman Cohen's modern philosophy of religion. Cohen, too, attributes metaphysical significance to human suffering. For him suffering could never be meaningless, nor could it be considered an imperfection in divine activity, insofar as for him, too, suffering is necessary for the improvement and ultimate perfection of humankind. As Maimonides did before him, Cohen saw Job as a prophet whose life story constitutes his prophecy. For both Maimonides and Cohen, Job is a prophetic witness to divine truth. Through recourse to that truth, Cohen, like Maimonides, seeks to expand the truths of philosophy.

For Cohen, too, the book of Job teaches that suffering is a prerequisite on the road to fulfillment of humanity's destiny. Whereas Maimonides believed that suffering is dialectically connected with the causality of creation, Cohen believed that it teaches human beings something of their nature, as beings whose spirit can exist only in a correlative relationship with divine transcendence.

In his classic work, *The Religion of Reason from within the Sources of Judaism*,[24] Cohen goes to great length to show that the significance of suffering, and therefore of humanity's fate, in monotheistic religion, is free from any and all dependence on natural and historical causality.[25] Suffering is seen, here, as a direct expression of humanity's relation with the transcendent. It represents, for Cohen, an area of existence that is unique to religion. Because of his contention that the structure of existence is rooted in a correlative relationship between the human and the divine, Cohen necessarily interprets Kant's categorical imperative as the obligating word of the divine creator. Throughout his philosophical career he emphasized the universality of truth as a fundamental principle of human ethics. In his later period, however, he also came to recognize the limiting effect of philosophy's universalistic orientation. Once again, philosophy knows only the general or the universal. Philosophical ethics therefore knows only the idea of humanity in general. It establishes the idea of humanity as the proper goal for all human activity, and yet remains oblivious to the finite flesh-and-blood individual required in order to make the idea of humanity a historical reality. Religion is therefore required to make the categorical imperative personally meaningful and motivating.

The religious sensibility, identifying God as He for whom humanity yearns and who commands human beings to love their neighbors, accomplishes this task. But it may only do so because of the human response to suffering. For Cohen, humanity's destiny is dependent upon repentance. Suffering lay at the heart of repentance. Just one generation after the destruction of the Second Temple, Rabbi Akiva was heard to ask, "Before whom are you purified, and who is it that will purify you?" and to answer, "Your father who is in heaven."[26] Cohen interpreted Rabbi Akiva to mean that repentance is indeed only possible because of humanity's correlative relationship with God, but nonetheless it is an act of purely human and not divine responsibility.[27]

Repentance is the process through which the individual creates himself or herself as a moral subject. Suffering is necessary for the ultimate fulfillment of the divine command for humanity because, Cohen maintains, humanity will not in truth exist until individuals are motivated to recognize the other as a "self like me."[28] The ability to see the other as a "self," however, requires a previous sense of the correlative relationship in which the individual already sees himself or herself as standing before God. Suffering is a necessary result of this relationship because its correlative character stems precisely from the fact that the God before whom humanity stands represents all that humanity has not yet become in history. The "I" becomes conscious of himself or herself and acquires responsibility for his or her existence, as such, only in the experience of standing before God. The recognition of the other's suffering, particularly when it stems from poverty or from social indifference, is what wakes us up to the fact of our neighbor's humanity, and hence of our responsibility toward our neighbor.[29]

The employment of midrashic thinking in a systematic philosophical context is, then, similar for Cohen and Maimonides. For Cohen, the Bible teaches the correlative nature of the relationship obtaining between God and humanity in history. From a psychological point of view, this knowledge is necessary in order to undertake the fulfillment of the divine command with respect to one's neighbor. Knowledge of the correlative relationship with God, along with the experience of suffering, serves as the psychological basis in which people judge their activity in terms of sin and guilt, reward and punishment. Through his understanding of the metaphysical and psychological significance of suffering, Cohen developed a unique religious philosophy that is faithful at once to the traditional Jewish belief in divine providence as well as to the principle of human autonomy so central to Kant.

With regard to this, Maimonides and Cohen are fairly representative of Jewish philosophers through the ages. Their interpretation of religious truth is historically oriented to the extent that they reflect a conflict between traditional belief and the present philosophical climate. And yet, as I mentioned above, their thought is not historically situated nor is it historically malleable in the sense that midrashic thinking is.

The manner of confrontation manifest in systematic philosophical discourse does not reflect the immediacy of crisis in a specific historical occurrence. Rather, the employment of midrashic thinking in philosophical discourse enables the absorption of systematic and universal philosophical terms into the fabric of tradition, while using the methodology connected to those terms as the basis of mediation between the two styles of discourse. It indeed is not, to use Ahad Ha'am's imagery, merely a matter of retaining the "barrel" after the "wine" has been removed.[30] Rather, Cohen, like Maimonides before him, is an example of a philosopher who used midrashic thinking to reinterpret the truths of philosophy on the basis of the religious presuppositions of tradition, only to return and interpret the meaning of traditional presuppositions in the universal language of contemporary philosophy.

The systematic Jewish philosophy of the past retained traditional terminology as well as the principle structure of relations among God, humanity, and world that are implied by that terminology. One cannot deny, however, that the meaning of traditional language and its structural implications was also reinterpreted in the context of philosophical conceptions that are, for the most part, foreign to all biblical and most rabbinical texts. There is no doubt that the critical approach characteristic of systematic philosophy, as well as the depth of probing enabled by it, contributed much through the ages with regard to the absorption of philosophical thinking into the tradition. Systematic philosophical thinking has always been able to deepen and broaden the Jewish conception of God, humanity, sin, history, and Providence. Yet, once again, it is not with the idiosyncratic character of the challenge, as it arises from an individual event, but rather with the abstract universal import of that challenge when considered in the totality of existence that philosophy is concerned.

This is certainly one of the reasons why systematic Jewish philosophy has never affected the personal orientation of the Jewish masses in the way that midrash has. Nonetheless, because of its sometimes radically critical approach and its commitment to the universal criteria of truth, I believe that a systematically philosophical component must be present in contemporary Jewish thought in order for the significance of the Holocaust to be properly considered by the community at large. In fact, as may be gathered from the discussion above, I believe that we require some sort of synthesis of midrashic and philosophical speculation in the present situation.

Midrashic and Philosophical Thinking in the Jewish Thought of the Post-Holocaust Era

It is very difficult to state how the various components of Jewish thought ought to be integrated so as to facilitate, in the present, a proper investigation into the significance of the Holocaust for Jewish tradition. Much post-Holocaust Jewish thought is still in search of this type of integration. Nonetheless, it is possible to make a statement as to what some of these components must look like if we analyze properly the challenge to tradition as it stands in the wake of the Holocaust.

In order to fulfill its responsibilities with regard to the problems facing Jewish existence in the present, it is necessary that contemporary Jewish thought demonstrate how the various unique and tragic meanings of the Holocaust may become integrated into Jewish tradition. The question is, can this be done without prematurely denying the depths of the challenge to those truths arising from within the world of the Holocaust?

As in previous events of Jewish history, and again in the Holocaust, the challenge first arises from a confrontation between traditional notions of Providence and the tragedy of history. As opposed to the past, however, the Holocaust does not require a revision of only this or that aspect of traditional thinking, but it rather threatens to refute all that traditional thinking is based upon. It is, therefore, here that I believe that a critical philosophical element is necessary in order for Jewish thought to ponder the problems of Jewish existence following the Holocaust.

Philosophically speaking, the challenge may be thus formulated: Are the dimensions of evil manifest in the Holocaust such that evil can no longer be considered secondary to the previously presumed overall divine and benevolent structure of existence? Through this question, philosophical thinking exposes an aspect of the problem that is, at this point, still beyond the grasp of the more personal midrashic thinking. Because the reinstatement of traditional truth is the prime function of midrashic thinking, a critical philosophical element is required before we can specify the depth of the challenge arising from within history, particularly when the challenge threatens to overrun the most fundamental presuppositions of that tradition. Midrashic thinking is indeed more historically influenced than philosophical thinking, but it is also more conservative when it comes to the possible need of revising presumed notions of truth.

The primary function of philosophical criticism, in this context, is to clearly formulate the particular aspects of the challenge to traditional thinking on the matter of divine justice and Providence that are unique to the Holocaust. Here Jewish thought must be willing to go beyond what either philosophical or midrashic thinking has done in the past. However, philosophy too is not self-sufficient.

Because of the universal character of its discourse, it will not suffice in the attempt to integrate the challenge arising from within the event of the Holocaust into the language of Jewish tradition. For that, philosophy requires midrash. Apparently, it is only the deeply intuitive midrashic comparison with the beliefs of the past that gives rise to the type of biting literary expression that would make the Holocaust's unique deviation from the presumed course of Providence a fact within tradition.

Emil Fackenheim has already commented on the ability of midrashic thinking to expose the confrontation between religious expectation reminiscent of the past with the possibility of its utter and complete repudiation in the Holocaust, by reference to a story by Eli Wiesel.[31]

The story tells of a madman who walks into a *shtiebel* in one of the towns of Nazi-occupied Europe and says, "Shhh, Jews! Don't pray so loud! God will hear you. Then he will know that there are still some Jews left in Europe." The midrashic quality of the story is apparent. The story reflects the traditional predisposition toward faith in God at the precise moment that it is challenged to the point of utter absurdity by the situation of the Holocaust.

Wiesel's story raises the problem of past belief and its possible reinstatement in the present. But, rather than reinstate the past presumption of God's benevolence, it projects the notion of Providence into the world of the Holocaust as an absurdity. In this manner, Wiesel's story acts as an interpretation that traditional thinking gives to the impossibility of its own presuppositions in the present situation.

The story of Wiesel's righteous madman arouses in Fackenheim's mind an allusion to another madman, who was created by Friedrich Nietzsche, almost a hundred years before the Nazi domination of Europe, in order to proclaim the death of God. With regard to the two of them Fackenheim points out something essential for the consideration of Jewish thought in the present: "An abyss yawns between the prophecy of a dead God and a prayer to a living God, but spoken softly; lest it be heard. . . . Nietzsche's madman comes too late to have gods for company and too soon to bear the new solitude, his present madness is therefore, of the spirit alone. . . . Wiesel's 'madman,'" on the other hand, "has all along held fast to a God who is Lord of actual history."[32]

Though the determination of truth implicit in Wiesel's story is, if at all possible, a matter for philosophical and theological discourse, it is already convincingly displayed, here, in midrashic language. As Fackenheim remarks with regard to hermeneutic thinking,[33] in general Eli Wiesel's story still presumes that the present exists in a relation of continuity with the past, in which the past interprets itself to the present. But it is precisely in its attempt to interpret the past to the present that the story focuses on the unique character of the challenge to tradition arising from within the present reality, as one that may ultimately preclude the said relation of continuity with the past.

In the past, it was expected that God hear the prayers of his people. Despite their suffering, they were constantly reassured that they were his chosen. In Wiesel's story, the people still expect God to hear their prayers. With the advent of radical or absolute evil in the Holocaust, however, that expectation, along with all the truths of tradition supporting it, becomes an absurdity. On one level the dialogue with the truths of the past is broken, but on the other it is maintained. The dialogue between past and present that is traditional thinking can now be maintained only so long as the expectation of the possibility of its continuation survives in the face of its own absurdity.

The implications of the crisis here described are certainly far reaching. The threat facing the possibility of a continued relationship with our past in matters concerning the overall structure of reality seems to have a paralyzing effect upon the ability of Jewish tradition to educate with regard to its most fundamental beliefs, i.e., with regard to the notions of good and evil, reward and punishment. One possible result may be that continued consideration of the Holocaust will ultimately bring about a change in the Jewish understanding of these notions, as well as in the way in which Jewish people perceive of themselves and their past, even while the religious presuppositions of the past remain in a state of crisis. In any event, in order for there to be at least the possibility of a continuous relation with the past, it is necessary, once again, to synthesize midrashic and philosophical thinking.

Midrashic thinking must go beyond its own parameters and critically address the depths of evil arising from within the world of the Holocaust, in order to stand before the challenge at hand. At the same time, systematic philosophical and theological discourse as to the nature and import of that evil requires midrashic expression in order for the newly learned facts of existence to become a part of the body of tradition, whatever form it may take in the future.

NOTES

1. When I refer to philosophical thinking, in this context, it should be noted that my interest is not with philosophy in the abstract, but rather with Jewish philosophical thinking as practiced by specific Jewish thinkers through the ages. Similarly, when I mention the term "midrash," I am not referring to an abstract concept of midrashic thinking but rather to the concrete use of midrashic thinking as manifest in traditional sources. In this sense, philosophy and midrash need not be seen as forms of thinking that are diametrically opposed to each other in every respect. Quite the contrary: many traditional midrashim in fact contain deep philosophical content. As will be pointed out in the course of the paper, much Jewish philosophy may be similarly described as engaging in midrashic activity. Nonetheless, it is essential that we take note of certain identifying characteristics that apply to each individually. Philosophy generally situates itself in a world of universal discourse. It often subscribes to some form of universal truth that subsequently obligates or demands a critical approach to the character of existence that precedes traditional authority. Midrashic thinking, on the other hand, rests upon the authority of tradition even as it reflects upon specific historical events in order to ascertain and resolve the challenges arising from within these events with regard to the truths of tradition.

2. This position follows from an understanding as to the nature of the challenge to tradition arising from within historical events in the different periods, particularly with regard to the problem of evil. Generally speaking, the challenge to traditional thinking arising from the events of the past was such that differing methods of thought could still lead to similar conclusions. So it is that we find in both Jewish philosophical as well as in midrashic thinking a tendency to justify the appearance of relative evil in light of a more all-encompassing or absolute good. It is, however, precisely the reconsideration of this position, in light of the Holocaust, that I feel requires us to distinguish between elements characteristic of

midrashic and philosophical thinking in ways that were not deemed necessary in the past. This point will, of course, be developed further in the course of the paper.

3. Eliezer Schweid. *To Declare That God Is Upright* (Bat Yam, 1994), 22 [Hebrew]. The translation is mine.

4. See especially Emil Fackenheim. *To Mend the World* (New York, 1982), 9–14, 130–36.

5. Shalom Rosenberg. *Good and Evil in Jewish Thought* (Tel Aviv, 1995), 83–84 [Hebrew]. This translation is my own.

6. See Emil Fackenheim. *To Mend the World* (New York, 1982), 187–88.

7. Eliezer Schweid. *Wrestling until Daybreak* (Tel Aviv, 1990)]Hebrew].

8. If indeed it turns out that the character of evil exhibited in the Holocaust can no longer be explained by the theodicy of the past, then the challenge arising from this event not only requires a response that is different from past responses. It also requires that the philosophical and theological presuppositions underlying those responses be reconsidered. That is to say, the challenge to tradition arising from within the world of the Holocaust calls into question all previous understanding as to the nature of existence, including the relations obtaining among God, humanity, and the world. The point is that the challenge to traditional belief arising from within the Holocaust is not only relevant with respect to the Holocaust as a specific event. Beyond the question, "Where was God at Auschwitz?" the dimensions of evil made manifest in the Holocaust force a radical change in our understanding of the proportion between good and evil exhibited in world history.

9. Moses Maimonides. *Guide for the Perplexed.* Part 3. Section 10.

10. For a more comprehensive explication of this topic see E. E. Urbach. *The Sages: Their Concepts and Beliefs* (Jerusalem, 1975), 436–48.

11. Jeremiah 12.

12. Mishnah *Avot.,* Chap. 5, 8.

13. Franz Rosenzweig. *The Star of Redemption.* Trans. by William Hallo (New York, 1970), 300.

14. The midrash refers to the double form of the verb "cause to suffer" in verse 22 of parshat Mishpatim, chapter 22: "And if you shall cause him [the orphan] to suffer (ענה תענה), and he will beseech me, I will surely hear his call."

15. Mekhilta Mishpatim, Chap. 18.

16. Maimonides. Part 1. Section 1.

17. R. Nahman Krochmal. *The Guide for the Perplexed of Our Time* (Berlin, 1924), Gate 7.

18. Hermann Cohen. *The Religion of Reason from the Sources of Judaism.* Chapters 11 & 12 ("Atonement" and "The Day of Atonement").

19. It should, of course, be pointed out that the status of universal truth is not the same for each of the thinkers mentioned above. Whereas Maimonides uses

midrashic interpretation to equate the truths of philosophy and religious tradition, Krochmal and Cohen seem to use it as a means of expanding the one in order to include the other. For Krochmal such an interpretation involves an expansion of the truth of tradition so as to include the higher truth of contemporary science. Cohen, on the other hand, seems to use midrashic interpretation in order to expand current philosophical notions of truth so as to include a more traditionally acceptable understanding of divine transcendence in a manner that goes beyond what is normally considered to be the bounds of philosophical reason. It would be fair to say that the three of them perceived of themselves first and foremost as philosophers committed to the authority of a universal truth as the basis for a critical understanding of reality in general. The differences between them, on the other hand, stem from their consideration of the extent to which the various dimensions of that truth are attainable through and beyond the use of reason.

20. Compare with Fackenheim's discussion of Spinoza, Hegel, Heidegger, and Rosenzweig in *To Mend the World.*

21. For a more thorough discussion of this topic emphasizing the central themes that we will presently consider, see *To Declare That God Is Upright,* 275–329.

22. *Guide for the Perplexed,* 303.

23. Op. cit., 190.

24. Hermann Cohen. *The Religion of Reason out of the Sources of Reason.* Trans. S. Kaplan (New York, 1972).

25. Op. cit., 227.

26. Yoma, chap. 8, Mishnah 9.

27. *Religion of Reason,* 199–204.

28. Op. cit., 113–43.

29. Op. cit., 128.

30. "Between the Holy and the Secular," in *The Collected Writings of Ahad Ha'am* (Tel Aviv, 1947), 74.

31. Emil Fackenheim. *God's Presence in History,* 67.

32. Op. cit., 68.

33. *To Mend the World,* 256–60.

Chapter 4

The Holocaust
Lessons, Explanation, Meaning

Shalom Rosenberg

Just as standing upon sacred ground requires us to remove our shoes, and those entering the Holy of Holies remove any golden garments, so do I feel myself obligated, when writing about the Holocaust, to, so to speak, remove my academic robe—and declare that I am not speaking in the name of any academic discipline, but purely in terms of my own most intimate feelings, in the sense of "things that come from the heart."[1]

The focus of the present study is theological. But in order to present my arguments fully, I shall first need to situate my views vis-à-vis the broader Jewish discussion of the Holocaust. In my opinion, an understanding of this subject requires that we confront ideological and cultural categories and frameworks. I shall divide this preliminary discussion into three foci, which I will refer to by the brief and simple rubrics of "lessons," "explanation," and "meaning."

Zakhor: *Remember*

I do not think that it would be incorrect to say that the initial religious Jewish reaction to history is to remember. I am not referring to an academic or sterile remembrance but to a free, existential remembrance that penetrates to the innermost part of the human being. Memory sanctifies the historical dimension. Even though nature is not absent from it, the Bible teaches us the centrality of history. Nature and history are intermingled within the Jewish year. But this mingling connects two different concepts of time. Natural time is cyclical; historical time is linear and cannot be turned back. It does not repeat itself; hence, it is dominated by forgetfulness. The first commandments that Israel was given upon leaving Egypt are thus related to the need to preserve this singular historical experience. The Paschal sacrifice and the festival of unleavened bread, and in their wake the family Seder as known to us, are an attempt to preserve the historical heritage. "To remember the exodus from Egypt" is thus the first mitzvah. This is the archetypal memory that influences all other remembering.

But the cause of forgetting is rooted not only in the nonrepeatable nature of time and the uniqueness of historical events but also in the transience of human existence. One generation goes and another generation comes. Beneath the external facade of stability, the nation and the society change their essence after only a few years. Individual memory cannot be the guarantor for the possibility of collective memory. Collective memory is not a natural phenomenon but a cultural and educational imperative.

"When your son shall ask you tomorrow" provides the surety of collective memory. But the opposite thesis—namely, that the Torah speaks of four different types of sons—indicates that memory depends upon the existential identity of the inquirer and of the one remembering. Even prior to memory there must be a certain identification that determines whether what we are remembering is in fact our own memory. In the archetypal memory, we must ask whether we are in fact the successors of that same generation that went out of Egypt. The answer is found in the call in the Haggadah: "In each generation a man person must see himself as if he went out of Egypt, as is said, 'And you shall tell your son on that day, saying, Because of this the Lord did for me when I went out of Egypt.'" The Haggadah emphasizes that even after many generations the father must say "for me." Memory is thus inextricably connected with the issue of identity that transcends history. I remember in the first person—both my own memories and those of my people. Before I remember I must know myself and my identity, what is mine and what is not.

One of the central elegies recited on the Ninth of Av is built upon the contrast between "when I went out of Egypt" and "when I went out of Jerusalem." "Remember what Amalek did to you" intermingles with "remember the exodus from Egypt." The memory of the Holocaust is another archetypal memory: "In each generation a person must see himself as if he is part of the saven remnant, in the sense of, 'You shall tell your son on that day, saying: "the Lord did this for me when I went out of Auschwitz." For, "If I had been there then, I would not have been redeemed.""" Here too, as we shall see, the question of identity is a crucial issue.[2]

Memory is based upon identity, but it also creates identity. This brings us to the second component of memory. Not the "for me," but the "what." What do we need to remember? And how? We do not remember an inchoate event. Before remembering it, we need to give it a structure.

I will not go into the philosophical question of the method of "constructing" events. Nor shall I relate to the school of the classical historians, trained on and guided by scientific objectivity, nor that of the new historians, who think, like Nietzsche, that "no facts exist, but only interpretations."[3] Yet for us there is no meaningful difference.[4] Even if we agree that a purely historical realm does exist, we must state that this "construction" of the historical event is in our case problematical. This brings us to the issue of the "lessons" and their pitfalls.

Lessons and Dangers

From the outset, I must say that I "derive" a Zionist "lesson" from the Holocaust, but I am prepared to forego it. In retrospect, I refuse in the deepest and most existential way to "derive" lessons from the Holocaust altogether. I shall attempt to explain my reasoning and arguments.

Let us begin with the initial point to which I alluded above. The lesson derived from the Holocaust is often, though not always, a function of the worldview of the person deriving the lesson. However, there is no doubt that the Holocaust left behind it an imperative that is the collective lesson of the Jewish people, which is the legitimacy and need for Jewish politics. First of all, worldwide Jewish politics—the establishment of the Jewish state—that led to the construction of a political entity that not only returned the Jewish people to the stage of political activity but also gave it the prerogatives of power insofar as possible. But more than that: the Holocaust gave legitimacy to the Jewish politics of Jewish communities in the Diaspora, wherever possible—and this notwithstanding the danger of dual loyalty.[5]

This returns us to another claim made at times, in my opinion unjustifiably. According to this argument, we have committed a sin—sin in a certain sense, but sin nevertheless—in repressing the awareness of the Holocaust during the first years following the war. The harsh initial shock was followed by a period of repression during which any significant confrontation with the traumatic experience of the Holocaust was absent. This description is both incomplete and factually incorrect. The Shoah experience in all its seriousness broke out within the life of the Jewish people. The rendering of accounts with those that served as Kapos in the death camps and the Kastner trial—that dealt with issues arising out of the murder of Hungarian Jewry—are only a few examples. But there is undoubtedly a deeper reason. The initial period after the Holocaust was guided by the awareness that we needed to devote ourselves to creating a practical answer to the Holocaust—to resolving the fundamental problem that enabled the Holocaust to take place as it did—by the establishment of the state of Israel. Precisely the thought that we were able to return to "normality" was the strongest Jewish reaction following the Holocaust. Just as the Jews in the Holocaust discovered a new significance to resisting the enemy, so did the Jewish people instinctively understand that there was meaning to the struggle for life—that biological existence bears ideological significance. Now, decades later, we can again ask about the meaning of the trauma, since we also enjoy the perspective of the state. The return to the search for meaning thus derives from both reasons.

So we stand and ponder our relationship to the Holocaust. Seemingly, matters are quite clear. The differences that separate and divide all of us, including thinkers and scholars, into different camps, are erased in moments of grace, in light of the memory of the Holocaust. The Holocaust is the symbol and the event that unites all of us. All of us were candidates for Auschwitz. But we are witnesses to a terrible phenomenon: that at times the lessons of the Holocaust not only fail to unite us but even divide us among ourselves—that they are harnessed to horses that gallop in different and at times opposing directions. The respect due to the Holocaust, to the saving remnant and the memory of the martyrs, obligates us, in my opinion, to refrain from any use of this symbol in arguments and disputes having a political component and practical contemporary implications. Let us leave the lesson of the Holocaust on the individual level, as something of profound existential meaning, but refrain from drawing political conclusions, be it in the negative or the positive sense.

What is meant by refraining from this positive step? I again emphasize that deep within my heart of hearts, I would prefer without hesitation to derive from it the Zionist lesson, primarily because Zionism spoke in a vague way of the danger of such a catastrophe from its very inception.[6] But despite all this it seems to me that, even within this Zionist context, the use of the symbol of the Holocaust demands that we engage in deeper thought. We often begin our Zionist information with the Holocaust. The visit of a foreign personality to Israel begins with a visit to Yad Vashem, or a Zionist educational film may begin with modern anti-Semitism and the horrors of the Holocaust. In my opinion, such a connection between the Holocaust and Zionism entails a certain degree of distortion of the contents, as well as a tactical error.

I call it a distortion and an error, for if the Holocaust provided a strong impetus to the struggle to establish the state, our Zionism does not begin with the Holocaust: it did not set out to solve the European Jewish problem by creating a problem in the Middle East, as is frequently emphasized by the Arab propagandists. Zionism is not sustained by the Holocaust. Moreover, even the connection between Zionism and anti-Semitism is in my eyes problematic. Zionism is none other than our generations-old struggle to return to our homeland. In light of all this, it seems to me that we are closer in our approach to the classic harbingers of Zionism than we are to the Zionism that was born in the wake of modern anti-Semitism. This was the stance of those people who felt that, just as Rome was liberated, so does Jerusalem need to be liberated. Sadly, one might also say the opposite: that we as Zionists live in the land of Israel and will continue to live here, notwithstanding the fact that, in the words of the late Yeshayahu Leibowitz, the land of Israel is evidently the most dangerous place for Jews to live.[7] Our state is not a giant refugee camp, but the birthplace of a people struggling for its national liberation who are "fed up" with living under foreign rule.

Thus far we have been regarding the "positive" side in the remembrance of the Holocaust. However, one may easily demonstrate that at times the consciousness of the Holocaust can be specifically negative. This may be exemplified by two illustrations. During the Lebanon War the identification between the Holocaust and our own destiny worked against us. Without going into a discussion of the problem per se, I may exemplify my words through two contrasting incidents that embody the problematics of which I am speaking. It seems to me that underlying the attitude towards the Maronites in Lebanon there was a conscious or unconscious sense of identification: a sense that we, as the victims who during a time of destruction did not enjoy any help from an apathetic world may not stand aside when others find themselves in a similar situation. On the other hand, there seems no doubt that the reaction to that war of many of the nations of the world was guided by the desire to prove that, when they have the power, the children of the victims are no better than the hangmen. Sabra and Shatilla were understood as a kind of purification of the acts done at Auschwitz. The true atonement was attained through the acts of the former victim, who played the part of the hangman. By way of analogy, one might say that the traumas of the children of those saved troubles our collective "I." We are guilty for having survived. We need to be different from everyone else, purer in our politics, without any marks or stains, for if not, what right do we have to complain about the Holocaust?

But the distortion does not only derive from the outside, from the world of the nations. A striking example of this may be found, for example, in Yehoshua Sobol's play "Ghetto."[8] Nazism was not only an external circumstance but also an inner one. Kittel, the Nazi commander, tells Weisskopf, the organizer of the Jewish labor brigades in the ghetto, in the name of Nazism,

> You have made yourself productive. I only created for you the proper conditions, allowing an unknown side of your Jewish nature to be revealed. . . . The painful, but so fruitful, combination between the German soul and the Jewish soul will yet do great things. (p. 41)

Another hero, the Nazi Dr. Poll, tells us that to "the Zionist Jews in Israel . . . aggressiveness . . . is not alien to them... Is this the death impulse, that we have finally succeeded in infusing from our own souls into the Jewish soul?" (p. 93). And so too the Bundist, Kruk, director of the ghetto library, tells Gens, the head of the ghetto, "the true Jewish patriot and nationalist,"

> *Kruk*: It's a shame that Dr. Paul isn't here. They succeeded more than they
>   imagined to themselves.
> *Gens*: What? what are you talking about?
> *Kruk*: Nationalism inspires nationalism.
> *Gens*: What are you trying to suggest? That I'm influenced by the Germans?!
> *Kruk*: Understand it as you wish. (p. 84)

The message conveyed by these things, in my opinion, is that a terrible process occurred in the Zionist state, whereby the victims internalized the aggression of their executioners. Such a use of the Holocaust is not new. It may have originated with Arnold Toynbee, who drew a parallel between, in his view, what the Nazis did to the Jews of Europe and what the Israelis did to the Palestinian Arabs.

Toynbee is of course aware of the quantitative difference, but this does not prevent him from drawing the parallel: While every increase in numbers brings about an increase in human suffering, it is impossible to be more than 100 percent evil. Whether I kill one man or one million, I am a murderer.

This is the decisive question. There is a clear distinction between murder and genocide, just as there is, in my opinion, a difference between genocide and the Holocaust. In any event, these remarks of Toynbee illustrate the significance of a new definition of a crime beyond the far "weaker" or more "moderate" crime of murder. It is obvious that any legal or conceptual difficulty arising from such an attempt is not a rebuttal, but rather a sign of intellectual poverty of the one who is taken aback by this difficulty. This is not only a matter of quantity creating quality, but that we find here a new, essential quality of evil and of crime revealed before our eyes.

The sophistication of such an accusation does not in any way detract from the injury and insult felt when we consider these things in our memory and in our consciousness. And to this insult is added as well a feeling of sacrilege. It is interesting to note Toynbee's response to this insult:

> I have been surprised at the vehemence of the reaction to it in the Jewish community. I have wondered myself why, if it [the comparison between the acts by the Nazis and those of the Israelis] is a preposterous suggestion, as you obviously felt it to be, you haven't said: "Here is a silly man, saying this silly thing. Why bother about it? If it is so silly we should leave it alone." But the reaction has not been like that. It was been, as we know, very vigorous. . . . I would say that, inadvertently, in this comparison I have drawn, I have given the Jewish people a piece of what psychologists call "shock treatment."[9]

Toynbee evidently forgot that, following acts of such a "crazy" coloration, we are more sensitive to dangerous "stupidities" and unable to ignore them. True, "shock therapy" once more presents us with the terrible dilemma in which we find ourselves. Because we have been victims of a satanic politics, we are now unable to conduct realistic politics. If it is at all permitted for us to return to history, we must live a humane or even utopian politics; anything less than that is a crime that is forbidden for us —and only for us—to perform. If we become like all the nations, we will be Nazis. It is not redundant to emphasize that, of course, international ethics obligates us as well. But the voice of this obligation is not the voice of neurotic ethics that comes from the Holocaust, but a sane voice coming from elsewhere. For us, believers and sons and daughters of believers, it is the voice of the Holy One, and blessed be He who speaks to us by means of His prophets and through our own conscience. We hear other voices from the Holocaust. The other nations, who have not been judged for their actions nor for their failures, should not be our judges and should not deal with this trauma of ours!

In light of all these things, and many others of a similar ilk, the demand, perhaps quixotic, to refrain from use of the memory of the Holocaust becomes self-evident, in any event within the context of our internal political disputes. We can learn the Zionist humanistic lessons from other pages in our long history. For the Zionist lesson it suffices to remember the Kishinev pogrom, while for the humane (not humanistic!) lessons we may make use of any of the myriad examples from the history of harsh persecution that we have suffered over the course of many generations. Examination of any page in the history of totalitarianism and fascism will suffice for us to repudiate them.[10]

Nor would I wish to connect the struggle against racism with the Holocaust. I do not think that the Holocaust is identical to racism; moreover, it does not begin with racism, but long before that. It begins with the rape that takes place before our eyes in the streets, it begins with human beings turning their fellow human beings into instruments. The Holocaust was unique in that it synthesized all the varieties of evil together and in that each one of them may be exemplified from within it. But despite that, it entailed something new. It was more than garden-variety evil. The very substitution of the specific noun "Holocaust," or "Shoah," by the general noun "genocide" is an unforgivable sin.

But despite my instinctive tendencies, I am almost forced to cease using the Holocaust as a weapon, that which we use almost daily to shoot at one another. I refer to the ongoing struggles between the two principle "lessons" derived from the Holocaust: the Zionist and the humanistic.[11] These are perhaps ideological battles, but the stances of the thinkers are also reflected in the street. Against the background of social tensions we occasionally hear such unfortunate expressions as "the job that was not finished." In certain neighborhoods one can hear cries of "Nazi" used against the police. Advocates of certain policies are called "Judeo-Nazis" by their sharp-tongued opponents. It does not help to invoke talk about a common enemy nor descriptions of the dangers of destruction that confronted Oriental Jews. Such words simply need to be uprooted from our lexicon, for the sake of the spiritual and social hygiene of our environment.

I learned from my teacher, Prof. Shoshani, of blessed memory, that the difference between objects used to perform a mitzvah and objects that are sacred (*tashmishei-mitzvah* and *tashmishei-kedushah*) lies in the following: one must continue to treat sacred objects with reverence after one has used them. That is, they are not merely instrumental. By contrast, after one has used a *lulav* and *etrog,* even if one has recited a blessing upon it, one may do with it as one wishes. By contrast, sacred objects must be hidden away, because they are in a certain sense an end in themselves. Unfortunately, it is clear that the politics that surrounds us on all sides will not agree to a "moratorium," to a "sabbatical year" on the instrumentalization of the memory of the Holocaust. From a religious viewpoint, I wish to say that the memory of the Holocaust is also "holy" in my eyes! The testimonies and experiences of the survivors, their cries and their testaments, are holy. But the studies of the experts, the theories of the thinkers, and the lessons learned by politicians are the most profane of the profane, if not less than that.

Explanation and Its Lack

Let us leave the political message and turn to the question of its religious meaning. Here too, it seems to me, a kind of moratorium on theories is called for. The various religious positions have been surveyed and analyzed any number of times, and I do not wish to add here to what has already been written. I will only say that at this stage we confront a mystery that has no theological explanation. Of course, this stance sounds apologetic by its very nature but, in my opinion, it is not so. This is so because of the thesis in which I believe and that I shall present without making any attempt to confirm it—a thesis that, notwithstanding the problematics involved, seems to me to be correct: namely, that there is no explanation for the Holocaust—neither a religious explanation nor a scientific explanation.

The Holocaust was an historical event, and like any historical event it requires explanation. Why did it take place, and how was it at all possible? In order to explain the above thesis, I wish to argue that we are mistaken when we offer the same explanation for anti-Semitism and for the Holocaust, as they are two entirely different phenomena. One is of course based upon the other, one is the sequel of the other, but they are not identical. For our purposes, there is a fundamental difference between them. I am able to "understand" and possibly even to agree with the psychological, sociological, economic, and even historical explanations of anti-Semitism, but I am unable to understand the Holocaust. We find ourselves confronting a unique and strange phenomenon, which has neither parallel nor explanation. Regarding this issue, we do not even have "retroactive hindsight."[12]

This is a question that thinkers and scholars—whose greatness is beyond doubt—have attempted to answer. They may have succeeded in explaining its background and the operation of its mechanism, but they have not given an explanation of the Holocaust itself, of the absurdity of the why and wherefore. The central lesson that emerges after reading their works is that many—if not the vast majority, or even all of them—have not derived any new "lesson" from the Holocaust, but continue to use accepted theories and categories in order to understand it.

Because of this claim, I expose myself to harsh accusations of mystification and even mythologization of the Holocaust. I shall discuss these concepts further on but, if you wish, I accept the accusation. This is precisely my claim. And I shall formulate things even more sharply: The claim that we are dealing with an embodiment, an incarnation of the devil in the person of Hitler, may his name be obliterated, seems more rational, and in a certain sense truer, than any other explanations that have been offered.

True, various solutions have been offered to resolve the enigma of explaining the Shoah. The most extreme explanation, in my opinion, is the argument that we are dealing here with a collective insanity. The use of this sort of language indicates that this presents a particularly severe problem for the psychologists, and the transition from personal pathology to collective pathology is to my mind extremely problematic. But the real problem lies elsewhere. The father of modern psychology succeeded in finding the key to understanding this "insanity" and in explaining phenomena that seemingly have no meaning whatsoever. He found reason in insanity, thereby creating a science. But the use of insanity in our context is no more than verbal manipulation. True, the term "insanity" is used in everyday language to designate phenomena that have no rational explanation. But here the talk of collective insanity serves the opposite purpose: to obscure, rather than to explain. The same holds true of other terms and concepts taken from the realm of psychology that are likewise unsatisfactory if we do not assimilate the unique nature of the Holocaust, one that was expressed in a tragic way by the term "a different planet."

Is there in fact a historical explanation for the Holocaust? Are psychologists and sociologists able to explain the facts? My answer is negative, and I will give several examples. One striking example is to be found in the approach of Bruno Bettelheim, which we may attempt to understand by way of comparison with another similar approach: the sociological position of Hannah Arendt.[13] The central thesis of both these thinkers may be understood as an attempt to explain the Holocaust as an episode in the struggles of authoritarian regimes to control the world. But this is not all. Bettelheim attempted to explain the camps, where he was "privileged" to live for a certain period. His position may be summarized by saying that he viewed the camps as an attempt on the part of the Nazis to find the means by which it would be possible to change and to influence the masses. Bettelheim saw himself as a laboratory animal in an experiment, in which there was tested in miniature a system that was thereafter to have been applied to the general public, a system based upon total supervision of human beings. Bettelheim thought, as did his teacher Freud, that he had found the logic within the absurd.

He lived in the camp and tried to render an account of his experiences, which belonged essentially to the initial period of Nazi rule. According to his description, an attempt was made in the camp to return the prisoner to the situation of a child, for whom others decide what is permitted and what is forbidden, regarding even the smallest details of life. The purpose of the experiment was to bring him to a state of total loss of his free will as a human being. This was a laboratory intended to accomplish the ultimate goal of Nazism—the transformation of humankind as a whole into a great automaton, who acts, without protest, according to the will of the Führer.

The most important aspect of Bettelheim's interpretation is the assumption that the persecution of the Jews may be seen as one chapter in a global struggle in which they were merely guinea pigs. This idea is particularly striking in Hannah Arendt. She sought to describe the mechanism of totalitarianism and of authoritarianism. Totalitarianism is built upon three circles, in which responsibility is confined to a very small group of people who belong to the innermost circle. In the second circle were those people who happened to be SS members, of whom Eichmann was a prime example. Beyond them were the German people as a whole, with their masses. The paradox in this explanation is that not only the dead martyrs were victims of authoritarianism but also the hangmen themselves, whom the system caused to lose their individuality and make them into part of a mere bureaucratic system. Arendt's application of this principle to the Eichmann trial and the basic comparison she draws between the murders and the victims was deeply hurtful, in a way that was almost unforgivable. But Arendt's statements were not intended as a personal reaction to the trial, nor as a historical polemic concerning what happened, but as the application of an ideology that explains the phenomenon and why it took place. The key to her explanation lies in the fact that this was not a uniquely Jewish phenomenon, but that the Jews were merely a small and marginal factor within a far more fundamental experiment.

These explanations are not correct, in my opinion, because there is no continuity between xenophobia and anti-Semitism, and the Holocaust. Moreover, that which may have been true concerning the initial expressions of Nazism experienced by Bettelheim does not necessarily hold with regard to its later manifestations. There is no single "great" ideology that encompasses within it the possibility of explaining what happened in the Holocaust. It is an empirical fact that there is no narrative to the Holocaust.

Moreover, in the cases noted above, and in many others, the explanation offered is no more than a kind of misleading and "theft" of the Holocaust. This is the same "theft" that, in a less sophisticated manner, finds expression in monuments to the memory of the victims in which their Jewishness is not mentioned; it is the same "theft" as is committed by those who proclaim Edith Stein to be a Christian saint, notwithstanding the fact that she died because of her being "Jewish"; it is the same "theft" that is performed by others on the ideological level.[14]

I now wish to return to the concept that I mentioned above. In the abovementioned discussion, Prof. Yehudah Bauer refers to a semantic question: "'Mystify' is defined by the dictionary as 'to envelope in excessive secrecy; to obscure or obfuscate.'"[15] One can agree with this lexicographical comment, but there is a decisive difference between "to envelope in excessive secrecy" and "to obscure." When we seek an explanation we find ourselves confronting an alternative. One may attack the approach of those thinkers who emphasize the unique and demonic nature of the Holocaust as "mystification," but the alternative is, in my eyes, banalization—banalization, not of the crime, but of the explanation: the marshalling of the explanation of the Holocaust to support every ideology in the world. What we have seen regarding the "lesson" of the Holocaust reappears in our discussion of its explanation. When we speak of uniqueness, we do not mean to deny other tragedies, nor to claim that this is the greatest human tragedy of all times. Indeed, there are more than a few examples of genocide. But no other genocide is the Holocaust. It is unique because of its nature, because of its absurdity, because of its belonging to a "different planet." The perception of the Holocaust as unique is not offered in the place of scientific historiography, nor does it refuse to learn the history of the tragic events. However, it does unconditionally refuse to accept pseudo-explanations that are recruited to ideologies or scientific approaches.

There is no doubt in my mind that, as in the case of the "lesson," a clear correspondence may be drawn between the explanation and the guiding ideology, and even between the explanation and the Jewish identity of the one offering the explanation. For example, Hannah Arendt's attempt to prove that the victims of the Holocaust were killed not because they were Jews but because they represented democracy and liberalism in the eyes of those who developed a regime of dictatorship and authoritarianism is rooted in Arendt's a priori political philosophy. This is an inauthentic reaction, in my opinion, of people who were confronted anew by their Jewishness only by the Holocaust, in a very tragic manner, without finding any meaning to what befell them. The historical Jewish identity, and even the most fundamental categories that related to anti-Semitism and that accompanied this identity, were alien to them. We find here a phenomenon that reappears repeatedly in different guises and reincarnations, the stealing of the Holocaust. As the result of a certain identity, ideology, or philosophy, such thinkers steal the Holocaust from their Jewish brethren, and even from themselves, by erasing the victims' own identity as Jews.[16]

Meaning

The quest for the explanation of the Holocaust exposed us to the cunning of philosophy. What I say here is not intended, heaven forbid, to cast aspersions upon the important work of scholars and researchers who have enriched our knowledge in this field. Historical science has doubtless succeeded in elevating itself to a high level of objectivity. But once we abandon the "empirical" realm and turn from knowledge of facts and processes to a deeper understanding and to questions of meaning and significance, we continue to read the same old philosophy as of yesteryear. Indeed, when we seek the moral and explanation in the third generation after the Holocaust, there appears a figure characterized not only by distortion but also by ugliness: the person who utilizes the Holocaust in order to learn a lesson and who consciously or unconsciously attempts to harness it to his or her own petty or "lofty" interests.

But perhaps, as we said above, a third level to our discussion also exists. The work of the Jewish psychologist Victor Frankel likewise draws upon the experience of the Holocaust, and especially upon his own years in Auschwitz. He learned there, in his words, that people are capable of living even with total lack but that if one takes away from them one fundamental thing—meaning—then they are lost and are condemned to death. But this is not included among those things that sociologists and psychologists have researched so assiduously. The Holocaust also reveals to us the person seeking meaning, who in his or her own private realm confronts these questions, which at times "cannot be uttered by the mouth."[17] The quest for meaning repeatedly confronts us with the religious question.

The Holocaust in all its horrors confronts us with a world in which God's face is hidden. The last commandment in the Torah is to teach the children of Israel "the Song." A day will come, we are told there, when "I will hide My face from them, and they will be devoured; and many evils and troubles will befall them, so that they will say on that day, 'Have not these evils found us because God is not among us?'" (Deuteronomy 31:17). The Song referred to there is the Song of Moses (Deuteronomy 32; known in Hebrew as *Ha'azinu*), which attempts to teach us to hold fast onto faith even in light of a reality in which "our enemies shall provoke us" and to say that "the Lord has not wrought all this" (32:27). I will not enter into an analysis of this chapter but shall merely note that it points out the consciousness of the religious problematic of history. Despite the way things seem at first glance, Jewish thought, certainly postprophetic thought, did not speak of the history of our people in categories of reward and punishment. It saw the tragedy of history subject to the hand of evil and attempted to teach that there is meaning even in the face of despair. As Rabbi J. B. Soloveitchik, of blessed memory, hinted in his essay, "The Voice of My Beloved Knocks," history is a marvelous wall carpet interwoven with pictures of rare beauty, but we look at the carpet from the wrong side.

These teachings imply, in my opinion, a warning to whoever presumes to understand the secrets of history and of providence. But this is true not only with regard to ourselves, as believing human beings, but also with regard to science. This is so because the Holocaust does not constitute a mystery from the religious, theological perspective alone. Scientists are also unable to explain what happened. Human understanding, to which everything is lucid and comprehensible, cannot cope with the Holocaust. We can understand evil that is done for some economic or political interest. We can "understand" the dastardly Polish peasant who betrayed a Jew because he wanted his boots. But it is impossible to understand what might be called absolute evil, the foregoing of one's own interest simply in order to do evil: evil as an end in itself. At times we hear the claim that Nazism was a collective insanity. This is precisely the confession of the litigant of the impossibility of answering the question. In this "other planet," absolute evil is satanic evil!

And despite all this, the call for meaning cries out to us from hell. And precisely in the wake of this, there is something that speaks to us even from within this terrible Holocaust. One of the conflicts that arises from time to time in relation to the site of Auschwitz relates to determining the nature of the place. Here one must ask a very simple question, to which we have already alluded above. Why did the Communists insist on not mentioning that those murdered at Auschwitz were Jews? Why, to this very day, do monasteries strive to establish a foothold in Auschwitz? These questions were a riddle for me, until one day I understood that perhaps the people who insist upon this themselves do not understand their own demands and their own acts.

Were we able to return to Mount Sinai and to see the *Shekhinah* (Divine Presence) descend and declare, "You are My beloved," we would be able to say that we are the chosen people. Our souls were at Mount Sinai, but we ourselves did not merit this. However, our generation saw something else. We saw Satan descend upon earth and declare of us, the Jewish people, "You are my enemies." And the enemies of Satan are the chosen people.

This is an absurd but true jump, and it is understood by every honest and intelligent person. I have often heard directed towards me the covert or overt expression, "Too bad that the Nazis didn't finish the job." There are anti-Semites in the world, but there are also decent and ethical non-Jews, and they understand that one who was not a candidate to go to Auschwitz does not constitute a spiritual option for humanity. So one needs to invent Christian martyrs that the Nazis murdered, and their presence in the valley of destruction.

What can I tell my son, my daughter, or my students? I am not able to free you from the fears or from the nightmares that afflict me as well from time to time. I can only say that I am proud of two things. One is that we are the children of those who were murdered and not, heaven forbid, the children of the murderers, or even the children of those who looked on apathetically, or the collaborators. But more than that, Satan appeared and pointed to us as his enemies—not because of our political affiliation, or because we were a threat to him but only because we are Jews, even infants or elderly people who could not possibly do any harm. This is the unique significance of the Holocaust that many people try to deny. Indeed, Satan properly identified his enemies. This is the voice that we hear over and beyond the tragedy and the pain: "They are loathed as absolute evil by absolute evil. In this manner they are indeed the chosen people."[18]

There is no doubt in my eyes that my remarks about Satan will sound bizarre and even outlandish to rationalistic ears who will rightly demand an explanation. I do not wish to explain them. I wish the reader to relate to them at this stage, not as philosophical claims, but as *aggadah.* I also ask of my reader to consider another possibility, namely, that throughout the darkness of the Holocaust, it may be that the world can be explained only by means of *aggadah,* and not by philosophical systems.

The Holocaust and Philosophy

But perhaps, nevertheless, the meaning that I wish to find is no more than mystification? After all, other groups were also persecuted. But we must also take note of the difference. If we were indeed perceived as a biological danger, like the gypsies, why did they persecute Judaism? Why did they desecrate Torah scrolls and all sancta of Israel? If, indeed, the war was waged against an inhuman subspecies, how are we to understand acts of cruelty against parchment scrolls? The war was conducted against a people whose very existence was a symbol and a source of ideas that were diametrically opposed to those of Nazism. Otherwise, we cannot at all comprehend the struggle against Judaism, the ban on Jewish prayer, the war against the symbols of Judaism, against its holy books, against Jewish faces adorned with beard and *payot.* There was something here that goes beyond an economic, historical, or even biological struggle.

To understand the essence of the Holocaust means, first of all, to discover our own Jewish identity "by way of negation," namely, to discover that this was a war against Judaism. Nazism killed us because we were

Jews. The second stage is to discover the second war, that which was declared against Judaism. The Holocaust was not only a biological or political battle: it was a religious and philosophical war.

A profound attempt to deal with this confrontation may be found, in my opinion, in the sermons for *Parshat Zakhor* and Purim of the saintly Rabbi Kalman Kalonymus Shapira.[19] Elaborating an earlier Hasidic idea, the Rebbe of Piaseczno relates to the conflict with philosophy. *Amalek* is "that which chanced upon you on the way"—that is, which presented a path, a way of thought, that was an alternative opposed to faith. To this classic motif, another dimension is added. The alternative presented to us is that of human autonomy, namely, "the wisdoms and intellectual structures that they invented . . . from their hearts." The conflict with such autonomy finds tragic expression in the festival of Purim:

> It states in the holy *Tikkunei Zohar* that Purim is compared to Yom Kippur. This may also allude to the fact that, just as on Yom Kippur a person does not perform the fasting and repentance of that day only if he wants to do them, but whether he wants to or not, he fulfills them because such is the edict of the Holy One blessed be He, so too is it the case regarding the rejoicing on Purim: not only if the person is himself in a state of joy, or in any event in a state where he is able to make himself feel joyful, must he rejoice, but even if he is in a state of lowliness and broken-heartedness, when his mind and his entire body are downtrodden, it is nevertheless the law that he must bring some spark of joy into his heart.

These religious notions relate to what the Rabbi of Piaseczno said on *Shabbat Zakhor* concerning the confrontation of the Jews with philosophy —doubtless alluding to German philosophy, even if he did not know it in its full breadth and depth. He describes Judaism as "the commandments and laws of God, whether or not a person may also understand them with his intellect. . . . One who learns it and fulfills it becomes attached to it with all his body and vitality, spirit and soul, until he also sees their goodness a little bit." The same confrontation is expressed in the confrontation between Nazism and Judaism:

> They can preach beautifully, but within themselves be filled with filth and corruption. And when they need to or simply wish to do so, just as they had previously invented wisdoms and intellectual constructions to preach about the beauty of good character, now do they invent wisdoms and intellectual

constructions to preach about theft, robbery, murder, and other corrupt things, that these are good things.

The rabbi concludes his words by saying that, just as on Yom Kippur "the day itself atones, even if a person had not completed his repentance," so too does the day of Purim have an effect upon the Jew, "even if a Jewish person was not in a state of joy as he should have been." This is an extraordinary case, the service of God in a liminal situation. The greatest test is the possibility of redeeming joy from one's enslavement.

The rabbi of Piaseczno saw Nazism as the final chapter in a philosophic tradition, whose central expression—we may complete his words thus by way of conjecture—was found in the teaching of Emmanuel Kant. This leads us to a much broader question that is not without theological importance. What is the place of the Nazi "philosophy"? Or, to give a more specific example, do Nazism and the Holocaust, which was its sequel, constitute an offspring of Christian anti-Semitism, or do they perhaps have a different pedigree?

I do not wish to fix any rules here concerning this matter. An alternative answer to that of the rabbi of Piaseczno may be found in various attempts—for example, in the studies of the late Jacob Talmon. According to this approach, we may take a further step by understanding Nazism as a high point in the development of a certain direction in European thought. The intellectual pedigree of Nazism begins with various modern approaches, the most outstanding of which is a social Darwinism that turned into violent and unrestrained racism.

But this explanation is only partial. I have no doubt that Nazism is to be seen as a revival of paganism in its renewed struggle against Judaism and its influence upon the Western world. But the most striking example, albeit one based upon a number of different motifs, is to be found in the work of Richard Wagner.[20] Teutonic mythology must be the option that will bring the world to redemption from the forces that have subjugated it.[21]

One of those who anticipated this tragedy in a general way was Rabbi A. I. Kook, who saw the beginning of a rebellion against "the Judeo-Christian oppression." On the one hand, Rav Kook blamed Christianity for truncating and distorting healthy Judaism; on the other hand, he discerned a profound gap between the collective psychology of certain peoples and the principles of ethics that were imposed upon them by Christianity from the outside, and to a certain extent even by the power of the sword. These peoples were not yet prepared to accept the reign of ethics. The counterrevolution is yet to break out. A poetic expression of these ideas was given by Uri Zvi Greenberg in his poem "Rehovot Hanahar":

> And from the day that pagans of the generation of Abram
> Until the generation of the Crusade
> Received from us knowledge of the One God. . . .
> We know not any refuge from the fury of the nations
> Their blood cries out for their primeval idol
> And they return to the ancient paths
> Covered with hyssop
> Bringing with them our blood, as a new gift offering to him.[22]

I have no doubt that Sigmund Freud, at the end of his life, also understood things in this manner. The Jewish people has been portrayed by many people, and justly so, as a kind of collective "superego," and the Holocaust as none other than an act of patricide. It seems likely that Freud's last and highly problematic book, *Moses and Monotheism,* is none other than a desperate, and possibly also vain, attempt to break the connection between the image of the father and Judaism. This was accomplished by means of a theory that claims that Moses, who was really responsible for the covenantal tablets of ethics, was not a Jew, and that the Jews killed him. The sin of the Jews was thus that they attempted to deny this universal sin. The Gentiles took the consequences of that sin upon themselves and atoned for it by the Christian myth of the death of the son—which does not exist in Judaism.

I do not wish to enter into an analysis of the historical basis of Freud's arguments. However, the book must be catalogued, not only among the works of science fiction but also among the documents of Jewish reaction to the Holocaust. This brings me to Freud's remarks in another work when, in the wake of the First World War, he discovered that the world is dominated not only by the libido (sexual urge) but that alongside it there also exists another force of tremendous potency—Thanatos, the death urge. Freud thought then in terms of the urge to suicide that is transformed into the murder of others. But the Second World War has taught us, to my mind, the opposite model. What was revealed then was that the impulse to murder may be transformed into that for suicide. This was the discovery of the satanic Other Side.[23]

The "Satan" thus revealed is the embodiment of evil for its own sake, and not for any political, economic, geographical, or social benefit—not murder for the sake of desire, but the desire to murder for its own sake, as an end in itself. It is clear that this was done by human beings of flesh and blood. I do not know what is meant by "responsibility" or "justice" in a context in which all legal and ethical categories are destroyed, but I know that the final testament and command of those killed was to wage relentless war against the murderers and to bring them to justice. Recognition of the absurd, satanic quality of Nazism does not exempt the German people from responsibility for the Nazi regime. The Holocaust is not isolated from its historical context; it flourished against a particular human, social, and ideological background that bears the blame, but it cannot be explained by this background alone.[24]

But not only the Nazi "philosophy" but all philosophies stand on trial. Could they have opposed Nazism? This is the question that is being asked today, in the third generation after the Holocaust. The example of Heidegger is the most striking example. And indeed, as the Rabbi of Piaseczno thought, *Amalek* is more than just a political concept. In the words of Yoss'l Rakover, in a conversation with his Creator:

> God hid his face from our world and thereby brought people closer to their wild urges. I therefore think that, unfortunately, it is quite natural, at a time when urges are dominant in the world, that all those within whom there lives the Godly, pure [instinct], should be its first victims. . . .
>
> And if you are not my God—then whose God are You? The God of the murderers?
>
> If all those who exterminate me, murder me, are so dark, so evil—What am I, if not the one who carries within himself something of Your light, of Your goodness?[25]

History as Theater

One of the foci of the lifework of Yeshayahu Leibowitz was the attempt to separate Judaism from history. History is not relevant from a religious viewpoint—neither the tragedy of the Holocaust nor the heroism of the establishment of the state of Israel.

At first glance, Leibowitz's position seems opposed to the classical Judaic assumption according to which history expresses and realizes a divine plan. There is a certain truth to this basic assumption, but it also involves no little reservation. In any event, the divine plan does not need to be that portrayed by a certain part of classical Jewish theology, that which relies upon the principles of reward and punishment.

As we shall see below, among the approaches that negate this approach is that of the Maharal of Prague. In his book *Netzah Yisrael,* the Maharal teaches us that while it is indeed true that punishment was the cause of the Destruction, there was also a cause for that cause, a second-level cause, which is not at all related to sin. Maharal's approach is very radical, and we shall relate to it further on. Here I wish to briefly discuss the approach of the Ramhal, R. Moshe Hayyim Luzzatto. And this because it seems to me that the things that we have observed thus far are in a certain way close to his approach. In his mature thought, which found expression in *Da'at Tevunot* and in *QL''H [138] Pithei Hokhmah,* he sees the Kabbalah, in its Lurianic formulation, as a system that requires deciphering. The answer to this is found in history: the question of the sufferings of the righteous, of the unjustified suffering of the Jewish people. Luzzatto explains the entire complex system of Lurianic teaching on this basis.

Rav Yehudah Amital, for whom the Holocaust made it impossible to accept the innocent and optimistic position of Rabbenu Saadya Gaon, according to whom the rational mitzvoth of religion are based upon the principle of gratitude, once said to me, "The intellect requires us to duplicate every good act"[26]—that is, to repay Him good for good, whether by doing good deeds in return or by giving thanks. From this tragic comment one may infer, in my opinion, two things. The questioning of the intellective or rational mitzvoth expresses the fact that rationalism is lost. On the other hand, one of the central motifs in theology, the meaning of the creation, the idea that the world was created for humanity's benefit, is also impossible.

Here, in my opinion, is to be found the central focal point in Ramhal's mature thought. The first approach, the Maimonidean, reached its full philosophical development in the generation of Ramhal in the thought of Leibniz. This world is the best of all possible worlds. Offhand, this approach is close to the classical rabbinic assumption according to which God builds worlds and destroys them. Those that were destroyed were destroyed, it would seem, because they were insufficiently perfect. But my teacher, Prof. Shoshani, of blessed memory, taught us that Ramhal in fact taught the exact opposite. The good worlds were rejected. The world that

God chose to create was an incomplete world, not only in the absolute sense—i.e., as compared to the perfection of the Holy One blessed be He —but even relatively, in comparison to the perfection that could have been our lot. Herein lies the significance of the idea of *tzimtzum,* the act of divine contraction.

This approach of the Ramhal indeed finds expression in the emendation that he makes to his earlier views. He now thinks that, in addition to the idea of gratitude, the idea of unity lies at the focus of the creation. God's unity must find expression in the negation of opposites. Illusions— metaphysical, religious, and moral—need to be created that seemingly negate the principle of unity.

According to Ramhal the playwright, history is thus in fact a kind of play in a cosmic theater, a theater of the absurd, in which an illusion is created in the eyes of the viewers, but the play must end with the fact that evil itself announces its own negation.

These things are developed further in Hasidic mysticism. The theater is not real. The most extreme expression of this view finds expression in the metaphor of the dream. One of the harshest things ever said about the Holocaust was the testimony of Katzetnick, who heard his neighbor groaning during a nightmare. He did not want to awaken him, because he was certain that reality was harsher than any nightmare he could be having. According to Hasidic belief, reality itself is considered to be on the order of a dream, and redemption means that we are able to awaken from it. The words of the psalmist, "we were as dreamers," do not refer to the redemption, but rather to the exile. The exile is a nightmare, and the only answer to the question posed by the Holocaust is that at some time we shall awaken and feel that it had been no more than a nightmare.

Ramhal did not give reality a mystical interpretation of this sort. But he thought that history would create the possible horrors when they are needed to contradict themselves. Satan himself must announce its nullification.

History as Riddle

I have discussed Ramhal's approach, which touches upon history, albeit only in a fragmentary manner. Among the numerous questions connected with the discussion thus far, there remains open the question, to which I wish to relate here, that lies at the focus of the attitude to history. In my opinion, there is a basic debate within Jewish thought, whose two fundamental options are represented by the Maharal of Prague and Rav Kook.

In my opinion, the approach of the Maharal of Prague teaches us the doctrine of estrangement. The Jewish people needs to be in this world, despite the fact that it belongs to another world. In absolute contrast to Arnold Toynbee, who thought that the Jewish people are a fossilized people from the past, the Maharal views them as a representative of the future thrust into this world. But this incompatibility carries in its wake alienation and suffering. This is the meaning of exile. Of course, the redemption will ultimately take place, but it will be the result of catastrophic and apocalyptic change. The Maharal thinks that there is a kind of ontological necessity in the existence of the Jewish people in the world. It is a divine mission, but one involving suffering and pain.

As against that, Rav Kook thought that history has significance, and it is that which will bring us to the redemption, to the world that is entirely good. Rather than the revolutionary and destructive change of which Maharal spoke, Rav Kook believes that there is a continuity to the process of redemption. R. Judah Halevi had restored the historical outlook to Jewish life in exile.[27] Rav Kook continues this approach and brings it to its ultimate conclusions. Zionism is the return to history. On the face of it, this return means that we are again taking our destiny into our own hands. But this is only one stage: the return to history is guided by a more positive conception, of the possibility of history and of its power.

The works of all the philosophers constitute an attempt to read the secrets of history. The rebirth of the state of Israel supported the interpretation of Rav Kook. Indeed, on the face of it the Holocaust erased history from Jewish theology. The rise of the state of Israel restored it. This restoration was seen as significant, not only for Jewry and Judaism but also for other religions. Christianity, with all its factions, is the most striking example. It is this connection that gave the Holocaust an apocalyptic character. This is the first time that apocalypse has validity and significance.[28]

But despite this, the history of the state of Israel shows that it, which was expected to bring normality to Jewish existence, lives a life of alienation, this time not on an individual but on a collective level. We have seen in our brief political history the shadows of the Holocaust, during the days of waiting prior to the Six-Day War and during the opening days of the Yom Kippur War. But there too we felt that a political solution could not resolve the deeper existential questions, questions that are a function of "Jewish destiny." The meaning of that history has not yet been determined, and without doubt constitutes the greatest riddle of our lives.

In Face of the Absurd

Thinking about the Holocaust means confronting the absurd. Do we have the strength to gamble on meaning after the absurd? I would like to conclude my remarks by quoting something said by Prof. A. J. Heschel in one of his conversations, as they were recorded by Robert Alter: "A father cannot educate his son as a Jew after the Holocaust, except with the recognition that he is bringing his child into an eternal covenant with God."[29]

These are cruel words, expressing the dilemma of the Jew in certain situations, but its very presentation teaches us a great deal. First of all, it teaches us that there can be destiny even without a covenant of destiny. They teach us that, beyond the covenant of destiny of the Holocaust, we need to gaze upon the horizon of the covenant of purpose. The religious perspective on the Holocaust, the question that is asked in the theological discussion of the Shoah, is the question of the existence of such a perspective. But perhaps it is specifically so. Perhaps even the destiny itself has meaning. A religious response to the Holocaust means faith in meaning beyond the absurd. The absurd means opening a frightening door to our own Jewish essence.

NOTES

1. On the historian's approach, see the important interview with Prof. Yehudah Bauer, "A Historian's Viewpoint" [Hebrew], *Shoresh* 2 (Nissan 1983), and also Yehuda Bauer and Nathan Rotenstreich (eds.), *The Holocaust as Historical Experience* (New York, 1981).

2. In this fact is rooted, of course, the critical difference between Jewish memory and that of the nations. The nations of the world can identify with the memory of the martyrs; in a deep sense, we are those that identify with them.

3. *The Will to Power*, sect. §481.

4. It is interesting to analyze the ideological zigzags used by the new historians in their discussions of the Holocaust. Application to the Holocaust of the method they use with regard to Zionism would entail approval of historical revisionism

and legitimization of Holocaust denial. As we shall see below, in this respect too the Holocaust is a turning point that casts doubt upon philosophies and upon methodologies.

5. There are those who point towards the attitude of the Jewish people towards the Jews of the Soviet Union as one of the results of the new consciousness that was born after the Holocaust. But this argument is in my opinion not valid. The process to which I refer is illustrated well by the organizations of American Jewry, albeit there one finds a fortuitous coinciding of interests. For example, the struggle on behalf of Soviet Jewry advanced the interests of the Jewish people, but since the processes against which they struggled occurred on the soil of the main political and ideological adversary of the United States, it was popular not only as a Jewish cause but also as suitable to the American identity of those engaged in the struggle. We can easily imagine a different scenario in which, God forbid, the meaning of the struggle would be put to a more serious test. The same holds true regarding the attitude toward the state of Israel.

6. The comments of the late Prof. Jacob Katz as to the impossibility of anticipating the Holocaust are irrelevant in this context. Jabotinsky's remarks about Bartholemew Night were more than prophetic, and were sufficient to awaken us to a Zionist lesson. The same is true of the words of other Zionist leaders. See Jacob Katz, "Was the Holocaust Predictable?" in Bauer & Rotenstreich, *The Holocaust* (op. cit., n. 1), 23–41.

7. Leibowitz's struggle to separate Zionism from the Holocaust, even though it was in my opinion a justified struggle, prevented him from properly seeing the rebirth of anti-Semitism literally before his eyes.

8. The page numbers are based upon the Or-Am edition, 1984.

9. Quoted in Yaacov Herzog, *A People That Dwells Alone* (London, 1975), 26–27.

10. The humanistic moral underlay the soul-searching of Buber conducted in 1939, in the Hebrew essay "Them and Us," one year after the riots in Germany: see his *Teudah ve-Yi'ud* (Jerusalem, 1961), vol. II, 296 ff. Buber called upon people not to "serve the god of Hitler after calling him by a Hebrew name" (ibid., 300) and promised in the name of a hidden providence that "he who performs the act of Hitler—will be obliterated together with him." It is interesting that Buber offers an economic explanation for what happened to our people in Europe: "The problematic of the relationship of Jews to the economy of the dominant peoples . . . whose participation therein usually begins not on the ground level but on the second storey" (ibid., 298). According to him, the responsibility does not fall upon the German people but on "the German state," that is, the organization that the German people establishes for itself or agrees to, or "on those forces that it places over itself or that it suffers, and not on the German people itself" (ibid., 296). Again, that which may have been true regarding the stage before the war is not correct regarding the Holocaust itself. The tragedy of this moral from what occurred in Europe is that the desire to build a nonexilic society in Israel led us,

without a doubt, to turn our mind away from the fact that the primary goal, cognitively, was saving Jews, in the simple literal sense.

11. I will not attempt to analyze these arguments here but wish to emphasize one side of the problem: that there is a fundamental difference between the two lessons learned. The Zionist lesson is descriptive, while the humanitarian lesson is normative. The Zionist lesson is derived from reality itself, while the ethical lesson is concerned with norms—it engenders values. Failure to understand this difference stands out in a grotesque way, when one reads the attempts made at times to prove that, because Nazi Germany was undemocratic and unethical, it failed to win the war. Before our eyes there has been woven a new theory of neo-providence that assures that the just, the ethical, and the democratic will be victorious in the final analysis: "In the final analysis the free world defeated the Nazi monster not only by power, but also by spirit." This stance is either naive or absurd. We were not freed because we were in the right, as may be seen by the vain struggle of Spartacus and the slaves who were not freed. From the Exodus we learn of the Passover, but the proper attitude to the stranger and the alien is learned, not from the Exodus, but from the memory of our enslavement. The values of the good and the ethical are not instrumental, and obligate us even if they are not successful from a utilitarian viewpoint. The confusion, rooted in cruel reality and that teaches us, quite rightly, that we are surrounded by wolves, requires that we also allow room for faith, in which the norm will be rooted.

12. I shall allow myself to state, with all due reservation and reverence, that ultimately not even fascism or Nazism are to be identified with everything that pertains to the Holocaust. See on this Saul Friedlander's article, "On the Possibility of the Holocaust: An Approach to a Historical Synthesis," in Bauer & Rotenstreich, *The Holocaust* (op. cit., n. 1), 1–21.

13. We shall ignore the problematics of her approach to the Eichmann trial in her book on the subject (*Eichmann in Jerusalem: The Banality of Evil* [New York, 1961]) and the political implications of this stance, and concern ourselves here only with its philosophical implications. See on this Gershom Scholem, "Letter to Hannah Arendt" [Hebrew], in *Devarim bego* (Tel Aviv, 1976), 91–95. Deserving of quotation in this context are Scholem's remarks concerning "the love of Jews, no trace of which I find in you, dear Hannah" (92). Her stance derives from her own sense of identity, which included an intense hatred of Zionism. This hatred found expression in her words about Eichmann, who "became a Zionist." However, it may be that there is another, "suppressed" side to her personality, which finds expression in the testimony of her biographer (Elisabeth Young-Bruehl, *For Love of the World* [New Haven, 1982]) concerning her reactions to the Six-Day War and the Yom Kippur War.

14. The church faced, in my opinion, two valid options: to canonize a "gentile" who was killed for his assisting of Jews; or to transform into a saint an "honorary" Christian, a Jew who died as a Jew. But when they canonized a Jewess who had

converted, who died because of her Jewishness, they stole her after her murder. The death of Edith Stein was a central point in the play by Rolf Hochhut, "The Deputy." His criticism, in this case, did not receive a suitable response.

15. *Hashoah: hebetim histori'im* (Tel Aviv, 1982), 71.

16. In Emil Fackenheim's thought, the Holocaust serves as a turning point that returns the individual to his or her lost Jewish essence. In the earlier approach, Fackenheim emphasizes that beyond the 613 commandments there is a 614th commandment embodied in the Holocaust—that which prohibits us from giving Hitler any posthumous victories: i.e., the disappearance of the Jewish people. Such disappearance is a dangerous option that confronts us, even if it will be a "death of the kiss" through assimilation or insufficient birthrate. In his later writings, Fackenheim notes the philosophical significance of the Holocaust: the idea of the 614th commandment teaches us that the Shoah, which seemingly erased all meaning, in a radical way gave new meaning to the biological existence of the Jewish people per se. In the Warsaw ghetto, Zionist leader Rabbi Yitzhak Nissenbaum coined the term "sanctity of life": "Previously our enemies demanded our soul, and the Jew sacrificed his body to sanctify the holy Name; now the enemy demands the Jewish body, and the Jew is required to protect it, to defend it." See G. Eck, *Ha-to'im bedarkei hamavet; havai vehagut beyemei hakilayon* (Jerusalem, 1960), 73.

17. For a survey of personal balance sheets of this type among Holocaust survivors, see the excellent work by Reeve Robert Brenner, *The Faith and Doubt of Holocaust Survivors* (New York, 1980). And cf. Yehoshua Eibeschutz, *Bi-kedushah uve-gevurah* (Tel Aviv, 1976); Mordecai Eliav (ed.), *Ani ma'amin: Eduyot al hayyeihem ve-emunatam shel anshei emunah beyemei hashoah* (Jerusalem, 1969); Rabbi E. Oshri, *She'elot u-teshuvut Mima'amakim*, 3 vols. (New York, 1949–69); and the collection (no ed.), *Emunah ba-Shoah; Iyyun be-mashma'ut ha-Yehudit datit shel ha-Shoah* (Jerusalem, 1980). The reader may find analysis and comprehensive bibliography on this topic in the M.A. thesis of Moshe Werdiger, "The Holocaust as Theological Turning Point" [Hebrew], Ramat Gan: Bar Ilan U., 1996.

18. In the wonderful words of Theodor Adorno and Max Horkheimer, who prophesied unknowingly. Quoted in *Yesodot ha-Antishemiut u-gevulot ha-ne'orut*, a collection from the Frankfort school (Tel Aviv, 1993), 279.

19. *Eish Kodesh* (Jerusalem, 1960), 29 ff.

20. In my opinion, this brings us closer to the truth in another respect as well. Various attempts have been made, particularly in Germany, to interpret what occurred in the Nazi era as a chapter in the struggle between two Germanys: that of Lessing and Goethe, which draws upon a deep and complex culture, against that of Hitler and Goebbels, which utilizes Teutonic myth. I do not know if it is correct to see things thus, but it seems clear to me that the Holocaust gave expression to a struggle between ideologies and philosophies and was not merely a struggle for political rule or economic dominance. As we have seen, one must say

here, quite simply, that there was a struggle against Judaism—but one that was not only biological.

21. From this perspective, the thought of Richard Rubenstein and his struggle to return Judaism to pagan pantheism constitutes, to use E. Fackenheim's words uttered in another context, a posthumous victory for German paganism.

22. U. Z. Greenberg, *Arba'ah Shirei Binah: Sefer ha-Idalyot veha-koah* (Jerusalem, 1972), 32.

23. Arthur Cohen, the late American Jewish thinker, wished to see the Holocaust as an expression of the *tremendum* (attribute of judgment), in my view incorrectly. This is a central category in Rudolph Otto's philosophy of religion. Using traditional Jewish language, one might formulate things thus: In the Holocaust we did not encounter the Sefirah of *Gevurah* or *Middat ha-Din,* but the *Sitra Ahara* (the Other Side in kabbalistic terminology; the satanic reality). See Arthur A. Cohen, *The Tremendum: A Theological Reinterpretation of the Holocaust* (New York, 1981).

24. I cannot concur with the criticism of Yermiyahu Yovel, "The Holocaust as a Component in Our Self-Image" [Hebrew], *Ha-Aretz,* 8 April 1975. The Holocaust was not "an uniquivocal human event." The task of history is not measured through the creation of subjective consciousness. This is a legitimate and necessary task, but it is also called upon to explain events. In this task—that of explanation—history has failed.

25. This text, written after the war by Zvi Kolitz, was published a number of times. See *Ani ma'amin,* ed. Eliav (op. cit., n. 17), 302 ff.

26. *Emunot ve-De'ot:* III.1.

27. It seems to me that this is the root of the lack of interest in history in the world of the sages. When history does not express divine providence, it is no longer significant: "that which was, was." These words have a double meaning. On the one hand, it expresses the impossibility of changing the past (*B.T. Nazir* 23a), "And what could he do? That which was, was." As Rashi comments at *B.T. Yoma* 37a: "'That which was, was'—it is already past, and it is impossible to go back." Similarly R. Obadiah Bertinoro (*M. Berakhot* 9.3) says, "One who prays concerning that which has already happened, engages in vain prayer, for that which was, was." But this concept also means that there is a past from which one cannot learn, and therefore its description is of no significance (*B.T. Yoma* 8b): "How did he dress them? How did he dress then? That which was, was. Rather, How will he dress them in the future." Thus the rabbinical sages spoke of a prophecy that is needed for future generations, and a prophecy that was made for its time alone.

28. I will allow myself to make use of the beautiful idiom of David Novak, in the opposite direction. Indeed, the apocalypse claims that "Post hoc ergo propter hoc."

29. Robert Alter, "Deformations of the Holocaust," *Commentary* (February 1981), 48–54.

Chapter 5

Between Holocaust and Redemption
Silence, Cognition, and Eclipse

Gershon Greenberg

My subject is the history of Jewish thought that existed during and through the years of the Holocaust in ultra-Orthodox circles. I will not be dealing with a central concept of Jewish thought, such as exile or chosenness, systematically, and will be covering material only from 1938 to 1947. In particular, I will focus on the issue of messianism within ultra-Orthodoxy, especially as it was concerned with the area between the historical Holocaust of the present and the metahistorical redemption of the future. My hypothesis is that this area "between" differed according to the spatial and temporal relationship of the particular religious thinker to the catastrophe. In terms of concentric circles, one could describe this difference as follows: at the center, within the catastrophe, there was silence; around it there was knowledge; after the catastrophe there was an eclipse.

Some thinkers invoked silence about the passage from Holocaust to redemption, others provided exegesis, and still others were blocked by the catastrophe from detecting any passage whatsoever. Each group can be described more specifically:

1. From within the war zone, there was certainty that redemption would occur, but a withdrawal into silence when it came to describing how the calamity would lead to it—whether historically (i.e., empirically and bound by time and space) and metahistorically (i.e., beyond time and space, of mythic proportions) or historically alone. In place of probing the passage, i.e., exploring in depth the content of the path from present (historical) Holocaust to future redemption, the thinkers called for pious action—which filled the silence while prayer bridged present history with future, metahistorical redemption.

2. In Palestine and America, wartime religious thinkers did probe the passage, bringing it to the level of cognition. Whether due to an experience of revelation that enabled an apprehension of the universe sub specie aeternitatis; or because of God's compassionate presence; or because of the ability of a particular *Tsadik* (charismatic Hasidic leader) to perceive the common point to existential and ontological experience, the passage to redemption was detectable—metahistorically, historically, and individually. Other wartime thinkers in Palestine and America believed they understood the passage from historical catastrophe to metahistorical redemption, either in terms of *Da'at Torah* (Torah knowledge) or in terms of restoring the land of Israel.

3. Religious thinkers whose writing began after the war recoiled from the attempt to describe the passage, or even to be consciously silent about it, because the darkness of the catastrophe eclipsed the light of future redemption.

The Core of Silence

Shlomo Zalman Ehrenreich of Simleul-Silvaniei, Transylvania

Ehrenreich led and consoled his congregation through siege, through ghettoization (May 1944), and finally into Auschwitz (June 1944), where he was killed. His sermons (the last one, prepared for Shabbat Hagadol, 1 April 1944, was never delivered) drew from the sources of rabbinic and Hasidic traditions. Speaking in historical terms, he was certain—and he declared this after his encounter with mutilated victims from Oradea passing through his little city—that God was using the nations to force Jews to retreat from their assimilation and (both secular and religious) Zionism (citing Ephraim MiSuldikov, *Degel Mahaneh Ephraim*). He predicted that once the assault was over, God would destroy the attackers—thereby eliciting recognition (i.e., sanctification) of His name in the world, a nation's smallest amount of goodness (e.g., Pharaoh's honoring Joseph) qualifying it to be sanctified by its destruction (citing Levi Yitshak of Berdichev, *Kedushat Levi*). He also was certain that the nations could act out their pathological hatred of Israel only when God allowed them to. God was doing so now. His fury over modern assimilation and Zionism was of such intensity that once He transferred His indignation to them, the nations were at liberty to hurt the Jews indiscriminately (*Metsudat David* to Isaiah 10:5).

But Ehrenreich could go no further. While deliberating the notion that the pious were included among the Oradea victims because "together with the thorn [the sinners] the cabbage [the pious] is smitten" [*B.T. Baba Kama* 92ᵃ], he broke off to declare,

> One need not reflect about whether or not this is the judgment of the Holy One Blessed be He. When the Blessed Name will help us and will redeem us, then we will understand all this. In the meantime, it is forbidden to open one's mouth, to talk rebelliously, or to question. One has only to do *Teshuvah* as our forefathers did in Egypt. It is absolutely certain that God will rescue us, and that the rescue is near. [In the meantime] it is necessary to attribute [the suffering] to the magnitude of our guilt. And the [internal] trespasses and sins should be hurting us more than the [external] troubles.

Even if he was inclined to ask why God did not seem to stand by His people, Ehrenreich would never criticize God. He would be as Job and "ascribe righteousness to my maker" (Job 36:3). And he dismissed outright those who challenged God, questioning why He was letting the *Yereim* suffer, or asking where God was as the catastrophe went on. The very language of their questions, Ehrenreich said, was unbearable to him. He did not seek to explain his arbitrary line between the knowable and the unknowable, or how explanation could cut itself off without explanation. He only pointed out that silence in the face of tragedy was in the tradition of an exemplar such as Aaron, who remained silent upon the inexplicable death of his two sons (Leviticus 10:3).

His explanations blanketed in silence, Ehrenreich set his sights upon future redemption, which would reveal the wisdom about the unanswered questions. But having surrendered comprehension of the present, he did not attempt to probe the passage from the historical present into the future. Because he had been silenced about the present, there was no epistemological threshold to the future—and he projected his silence about current suffering into silence about how it might be alleviated in the future. All he could say was that the future would necessarily be other than the present. For example, he contrasted the progressive salvation within history, which involved a human messenger such as Moses, with the complete redemption in the future, which came from God alone. He discouraged feelings of expectation—explaining that they would likely lead to despair; had the Jews of the temple era contemplated that it would be at least another 1,870 years before redemption, he pointed out, they would have either killed themselves or died of sorrow. He would not speak of redemption's coming within or outside the land of Israel. Nor would he speak in metahistorical terms, about the birth pains of the Messiah or about a metaphysical light following darkness.

In his mind, the inability to comprehend God's role in the present catastrophe implied that future comprehension would be mutually exclusive with what he could say now. The path from history to redemption was filled with silence. At the same time, it was silence alone that could relate to the transcendental wisdom that redemption could and would offer— about the present as well as about the passage from present to future.

The epistemological and verbal silence, however, was not Ehrenreich's final response in confronting the disaster. The Jew had to fill his life, between now and the future, with piety—the piety of Torah, *Teshuvah,* prayer, and *Mesirat nefesh.* Each had a synthetic power to link present history with future, metahistorical redemption—and to draw redemption and present earthly existence closer to one another. Specifically, by cleansing Israel, Torah study allowed the Jew to participate in, and possibly advance, the onset of redemption. *Teshuvah* could remove the evil decrees and make way for the messianic reality. Prayer could restore God's *Kavod* and *Malkhut.* In turn, Torah, *Teshuvah,* and prayer were at their most intense when they coalesced into *Mesirat nefesh.* The life of piety, of course, still unfolded within the realm of silence.[1]

Shlomo Zalman Unsdorfer of Bratislava

Unsdorfer, a student of the Da'at Sofer, shared the leadership of wartime Bratislav Orthodoxy with the Heshev Sofer. He carried on after the latter left for the land of Israel in summer 1943, through ghettoization in 1944. In the fall of that year he was taken from nearby Mariathal to Sered and then to his death in Auschwitz.

Like Ehrenreich, Unsdorfer sought to explain the growing catastrophe in terms of rabbinic tradition. He explained that Esau's contemporary attack came about because Israel allowed Jacob's legacy of *Da'at Torah* to be weakened and then projected the failure to the outside by assimilating, thus inciting the eruption of Esau's latent, pathological hatred. The eruption was under the auspices of God—who sought to punish the errant Jewish nation.

Also as with Ehrenreich, there were questions that Unsdorfer would not confront or attempt to answer. Some were implicit in his explanations:

Was the relationship between the specific assaults (e.g., yellow badge, expulsion from housing, deportation) and the religious decline causal, coincidental, correlative, or associative? How did Esau's direct assault relate to God's indirect assault through him? How could the wishes of the good God be carried out by an evil instrument?

Others, he openly confronted: If God recompensed people with kindness according to their deeds and placed evil upon the wicked according to their wickedness ("*Yigdal Elohim hai*"), why were the pious being persecuted (January 1942)?[2] He suggested different possible answers. Once the fire of God's fury broke out, it could not be controlled and so the pious were consumed as well (Exodus 22:6). Or, once the righteous had guaranteed the observance of Torah upon its acceptance, when Torah was imperiled they became victims (*Or Hahayim* to Exodus 22:6). Or, he suggested, there had to be some small element of sin present. The suffering was then an act of divine *Hesed,* for it produced return by the pious. He used the metaphor of birth pains. They were necessary if there was to be a child— and the mother prayed only to endure them, not for them not to happen at all. He cited the Hatam Sofer's concept of miracle-amidst-catastrophe (*Nes leporaniut*), where such a miracle was tied to opportunity for the pious to restore themselves ("Thou hast given a miracle to them that fear Thee, to elevate themselves because of the truth," Psalms 60:6). The Hatam Sofer observed how, after Napoleon's assault upon Pressburg in summer 1809 (an assault so unnatural that even the soldiers were shocked), there was practically no damage (bodily or structurally) to the Jews. If God was going to rescue the Jews, why did He allow for the assault (which, as unnatural, had to come from Him) to begin with? The catastrophe and miracle, the Hatam Sofer said, followed as the letter *vav* followed the letter *hay.* In His *Hesed,* God introduced the catastrophe. The miracle of rescue coincided with the return—such that retroactively the troubles would be seen to have been for the good.[3] But these possible answers did not satisfy Unsdorfer.

In the end, Unsdorfer was led to draw a blanket of silence over his inquiries. He averred that there was a categorical difference between the knowledge of God and the knowledge of humanity—God's knowledge being able to go deeper than the measure of time. He was offended by those who tried to remove the difference:

> Who do you think you are, anyway, to imagine yourself so high and mighty as to want to understand the ways of the Blessed Name? You are but mortal

human beings, who wither as the grass, whose days are as the passing shadows. And you want to understand the ways of God? The God who lives, exists, was and will be? Who do you think you are?[4]

Unsdorfer invoked the paradigmatic silence of the patriarchs. Abraham could not find a place to bury Sarah, after God promised him land. He finally paid for the plot—but did not probe God's intentions. After God told Isaac that He would be a blessing to him in the land, Isaac's servants could not find water. When they did, they were forced to dispute over it. But Isaac raised no questions. Jacob had to pay to use land for his tent, after God had promised him land, but he too raised no questions (B.T. *Sanhedrin* 111a).[5]

Unsdorfer believed in redemption but, unable to explain the present suffering, he had no basis for finding the way into the future. Like Ehrenreich, stymied over the suffering of the righteous, he could not begin to explain how the tragedy around him could pass into divine redemption. Citing the Hatam Sofer and *Yalkut Shimoni*—"Then I will take My hand away and you will see My back; but My face must not be seen" (Exodus 33:23)—he averred that a person could understand an action only after it took place, not before. Before the divine light of redemption emerged from the darkness, it was impossible to see the light; the eternal light could not be understood from within temporal darkness. First the light had to overwhelm the darkness.[6]

Unlike Ehrenreich, however, Unsdorfer did not surrender the possibility of apprehending the passage on a metahistorical level. Drawing from the Hatam Sofer, he invoked a structural, metahistorical connection between catastrophe and redemption. The Hatam Sofer spoke of the presence of the *Shekhinah* amidst *Tumah,* providing a means to rescue Israel.[7] He affirmed that decline led to ascent. In commenting on Genesis 43:19— "So they went up to Joseph's house steward and spoke to him at the entrance of the house. If you please my Lord, they said, we came down once before to procure food"—the Hatam Sofer said (citing Rashi) that when the troubles were worst (the taking of Benjamin), there was an upturn (Judah's confronting Joseph). Freedom followed slavery, and light followed darkness. The Tenth of Tevet (when Nebuchadnezzar laid siege to Jerusalem) was more severe a fast day than the Ninth of Av (when the Temple was destroyed)—and could not be postponed for the Sabbath (B.T. *Rosh Hashanah* 18b)—because destruction implied revival. That was the message of Rabbi Akiva, who was merry when he saw the utter destruction of the holy of holies (B.T. *Makkot* 24b). For the Hatam Sofer, indeed, not only would Israel be rescued in the end, but the assailants would be punished.[8] Unsdorfer connected the fact that the Hatam Sofer escaped injury during the 1809 siege to the birth pains of the Messiah.[9]

This metahistorical dialectic, Unsdorfer believed, was in turn reflected in history. In fall 1941 he wrote that as Joseph was once thrown into a pit and enslaved, so Jews were now being thrown into ghettos and enslaved. Israel would nevertheless survive, while the enemies would be lost in oblivion (*Midrash Tanhuma: Vayigash* 10. Warsaw). The Hatam Sofer said about the passage "nor does wickedness deliver those who practice it" (Ecclesiastes 8:9) that those who hurt Israel would eventually be punished. Those who were now hunting Jews and abandoning everything else to do so, Unsdorfer wrote, were precipitating their own fall. In June 1943 he assured that even after the last year's expulsions, the oppressed would stand upright (B.T. *Shabbat* 104a). And he believed that this was the generation of *Ikveta dimeshiha* (the beginnings of redemption), implying that God would bring comfort to, and avenge, His nation (Isaiah 51:3).[10]

Thus, Unsdorfer was certain that redemption would come, and he also could discern the transition metahistorically. But the path from history to redemption was cleft with silence. A partition separated what was known about God's relationship with Israel in the past from the messianic future. The silence, the partition, would be removed and God's "face" seen only when redemption itself would take place. Unsdorfer invoked the way of the patriarchs as paradigmatic for pious conduct in the meantime—the way of suffering in silence. When Abraham was thrown into the fiery furnace by Nimrod in Ur Kasdim, he still sanctified God's name (B.T. *Sanhedrin* 111a; *Midrash Bereishit Rabbah* 38:13; Rashi to Exodus 3:22). Isaac was silent for the entire three-day journey to Mount Moriah. He walked with his father in joy, the Hatam Sofer observed, even after Abraham had been cast down by the command to sacrifice him. In these tragic days, Unsdorfer wrote, thousands of Jews in Poland and Germany sacrificed themselves in silence and sanctification of God's name. Now, "We too can say what Hannah said to her seven sons: 'My sons, go and tell Abraham your father, you bound one [child for] sacrifice but I bound seven [children for] sacrifices' [B.T. *Gittin* 57b]." For him, the silence should be broken only by prayer. The messianic birth pains were inevitable; but an unclean child, he said, could be cleansed gently or harshly—and prayer eased the pain.[11]

In sum, within the war zone itself, these two religious thinkers were silent about the passage to redemption—Ehrenreich on the levels of history and metahistory, Unsdorfer on the level of history. They surrendered to the dilemma of God's role in the Holocaust, notably regarding the suffering of the pious. This did not mean that they lost faith. Rather, they proceeded to posit redemption beyond a wall of silence—lest their faith be endangered, perhaps, by any further inquiry. Cognition was irreconcilable with faith, while silence fostered faith. Silence provided a space for the life of piety (but not a self-conscious piety that would provide a path of cognition) and was a way to emulate the patriarchs and Aaron. It also allowed for the affirmation of messianically revealed wisdom—by the fact that it was mutually exclusive with present, historical knowledge.

From a Distance: Cognition

Mendel Piekaz observes that while Kalonymous Kalman Shapira described the *Hevlei mashiah* (birth pangs of the messiah) and spoke much of quick salvation in the Warsaw ghetto, his was not an actual messianic mindset. But Yosef Yitshak Schneersohn, far from the catastrophe, in Brooklyn, issued warnings from his ivory tower about the nearness of redemption and reckoned when the end would take place.[12] The data I have found suggests that those outside the war zone were indeed more explicit and forceful about their messianic expectations—but I found no basis to impute to these thinkers any psychological or emotional separation from, or superiority to, those caught in the misery in Nazi-dominated Europe.

Metahistorical Frameworks

Religious thinkers during the war in Jerusalem and Brooklyn discerned the passage to redemption, and did so on both metahistorical and historical levels. They also discerned the role of the historical individual—within Israel's collectively historical path and within the metahistorical drama. In the first instance (Harlap), this discernment was made possible by his access to the revealed wisdom of Kabbalah and by his transforming the entire universe (metahistorical, historical, individual) into an inclusive apocalyptic drama. In the second (Sarna) it was made possible by the existential apprehension of divine presence in the suffering of Israel. In the third (Schneersohn), it was possible because the *Tsadik* (the charismatic leader), Rav Schneersohn, had access to the esoteric knowledge of Joseph's "*Pakod yifkod*" (promise of redemption in Genesis 50:24).

Ya'akov Moshe Harlap, Rav Kook's successor as head of Yeshivat Merkaz Harav in Jerusalem, did speak of silence, but only as a prelude to comprehension rather than as a barrier to it. Silence enabled him to be receptive to revealed wisdom. The children of Israel were silent as they were about to enter the Red Sea, where the *Shekhinah* enveloped them (Exodus 14:14). The world was silent when God spoke at Sinai (*Midrash Shemot Rabbah* 29:9). Once he was silent and unclouded by the words of worldly experience, Harlap could understand the higher knowledge—a primary means to which, he said, were the works of the Gaon of Vilna. Once accessed, the higher knowledge integrated what was known from time with what was known from eternity. Collective and individual historical experience was sublimated into transcendental wisdom.

This higher knowledge provided ground for knowing the passage to redemption. For Harlap, the Holocaust was the era of *Mashiah ben Yosef*. He explained that the time for redemption had come, but since the people of Israel could never have withstood its intense and all-encompassing light, it entered the world through the dark and sorrowful vessel of history. The light coalesced with the people of Israel as a collective entity, whose holiness (*Kedushah*) was surrounded with unholiness (*Tumah*). The tension between the darkness and light, between the constructive universe (*kulo zakai*) and the destructive universe (*kulo hayav*) (B.T. *Sanhedrin* 98a), was becoming unbearable (the Holocaust), and soon there would be an explosion—leaving the universe to the light of redemption, the era of *Mashiah ben David* (See Ha'gra, *Biur* to *Tikunim Mizohar Hadash* 27a). Harlap averred that the nations were rooted in the realm of *Tumah* (impurity) and resided there—while Israel was rooted above in *Kedushah* (holiness) and branched downward toward *Tumah*. At an earlier time, the nations could have shed their *Tumah* and sanctified themselves by drawing, through the channel of Israel, from the sacred reality that surrounded God and Torah. They failed to do so. Now they would, as *Tumah*, be destroyed upon the imminent manifestation of Torah and sacred being of the *Mashiah ben David* era. At this time, they were trying desperately to prevent redemption itself in a perverse and mistaken assault upon Israel, the vessel of redemption. Harlap continued to say that with the advent of *Mashiah ben David*, history itself, which had become immersed into *Tumah* and transformed into antibeing (*Sitra ahra*), would be shorn away.

While for Ehrenreich and Unsdorfer, history preceded the metahistory of redemption, Harlap sublimated history into the apocalyptic metahistory of redemption—and then cast history into oblivion.

The role of the individual Jew of history was also sublimated into the higher drama. According to Harlap, the most pious Jews would be separated from *Tumah,* survive the catharsis of history, and be redeemed. Through mitzvot, especially the mitzvah of martyrdom, the pious Jew could hold onto the light of the present era of *Mashiah ben Yosef* as it exploded into the light of *Mashiah ben David.* The martyrdom of Jews in Europe broke the bounds of the finite, enabling them to escape the polluted realm of history and ascend into eternity. As the universe passed from *Mashiah ben Yosef* to *Mashiah ben David,* the Jewish martyr moved out of history and into the redeemed realm. Harlap did not recoil from the final implications of the drama. Theoretically, for him, passage into redemption could involve the martyrdom of all Israel: even if, God forbid, the soul of the entire nation should be taken, the love for God would not be exhausted. The legacy of Israel's *Mesirat nefesh* (sacrificial suffering of the soul) could apply to the entire nation. In this era of *Ikveta dimeshiha* (beginning of the messianic era), it was possible for all Israel to die, without the love for God being exhausted (see B.T. *Berakhot* 54a).[13]

Yehezkel Sarna, head of Keneset Yisrael-Slobodka Yeshivah, also of Jerusalem, offered a less otherworldly approach to redemption. He described a metahistorical triad of Holocaust (*Hurban*), *Teshuvah* (repentance and return to God), and redemption (*Geulah*), and the individual's participation in the higher process through a life filled with *Teshuvah.* While Harlap's knowledge came from revealed wisdom, Sarna's knowledge was instilled by the consoling presence of God. In 1944, he stated that the tragedy was unprecedented—while the destruction of Jeremiah's time was also severe, he could at least embrace the bones of the dead (*Midrash Eykhah Rabbah.* Proem 34)—and therefore incomprehensible. But God was present. He was present in Babylon during the days of Ezekiel (*Zohar: Shemot*: 6–12) and has been present in every catastrophe since. By His presence, God first made it possible for humans to cry, and then for them to perceive the transcendental meaning to the catastrophe—enabling them then to construct an immanent meaning.

While Harlap's higher drama involved the transition from light and darkness to light alone, the transcendental meaning perceived by Sarna involved a single, ontological point that unfolded for humanity as a triad of *Hurban, Teshuvah,* and *Geulah.* Sarna brought the triad into a

worldly context and explained that *Hurban* brought *Teshuvah* and *Teshuvah* brought *Geulah*—that *Geulah* evoked the *Hurban* of *Ikveta dimeshiha,*
and *Ikveta dimeshiha* evoked *Teshuvah.* The threefold relationship was
also retraceable to two—*Din* (identifiable with the present *Hurban*) and
Rahamim (divine grace) (identifiable with *Geulah*). How this twofold relationship applied to particular historical circumstances was indicated by
Sarna's *Musar* colleague Ephraim Sokolover of Ra'anana. He told of a critically ill child, whose hands and legs had to be amputated. But not even
that was enough. There had to be further operations, until it was as if only
the soul remained. Would it have been better to let the child die? When it
came to morally debased non-Jews, the world would be better off if they
did die. When it came to Israel, not so—for its suffering (*Din*) came from
God, and was bound up with His love and *Rahamim* for the nation.[14]
Sarna also referred to the triadic dimension to Israel's history, pointing
out that when the First Temple was destroyed (*Hurban*), potential *Geulah*
was implanted by God, along with *Teshuvah*—and it would be actualized
in the coming generations. The triad was crystallized in the present. At this
point, Sarna said, the faith of *Geulah* and the faith of *Teshuvah* were one.
God promised *Geulah* and He promised *Teshuvah,* and *Teshuvah* contained the secret of *Aharit hayamim* (the end of days). Should the *Aharit
hayamim* be delayed, the *Rahamim* of heaven would be intensified. This
was the generation of the *Hevlei mashiah,* the ultimate *Aharit hayamim,*
during which *Teshuvah* would be fulfilled.

While Harlap's explanation of the individual's passage into redemption
centered on martyrdom, Sarna explained it in terms of *Teshuvah.* The
metaphysical *Teshuvah* (accessible to human consciousness) made existential *Teshuvah* possible, and now a life of *Teshuvah* could integrate the individual into the higher triad, with its redeemed dimension. Because the
individual was too broken and depressed by the tragedy, he could not initiate the return (Psalms 90:3). God, therefore, initiated it for him. God
opened a threshold in the heart of the individual, the size of a needle's eye
(*Shir Hashirim Rabbah* 5:3), Sarna stated, enabling the individual to draw
from the higher sources of *Teshuvah.* The tiny opening would ultimately
expand into a threshold appropriate to a great hall, and *Teshuvah* would
lead the *Hurban* of the individual to *Geulah.* While Harlap thought in
terms of a revealed wisdom, according to which all existence was lifted up
into an apocalyptic drama, Sarna began with God's compassionate presence in the historical context and ended with God's enabling the individual to do the *Teshuvah,* which would include him within the *Geulah.*[15]

Yosef Yitshak Schneersohn, the Lubavitcher Rav of Brooklyn, gained his insights from secret apprehensions. He accessed the esoteric knowledge from Joseph's *"Pakod yifkod"*: "I die and God will surely remember you and bring you out of the land [of Egypt]" (Genesis 50:22). The statement hid the principle that death meant life—on the larger scale, the principle of transition from exile and catastrophe (death) to land of Israel and redemption (life). This esoteric knowledge was made available to Schneersohn's Hasidim, and it enabled them to survive in the invisible Goshen ("Only in the Land of Goshen, where the children of Israel were, was there no hail," Exodus 9:26) where, living a life of *Teshuvah,* they could wait out the storm and share in redemption. His Hasidim formed a secret society, the *Mahaneh Yisrael*; they told no one about their membership, and they communicated with each other via upside-down Yiddish acronyms in their periodical, *Hakeriyah Vehakedushah.*

There were three levels of passage into redemption—ontic, metahistorical-historical, and individual. On the highest level, like Sarna, Schneersohn accepted the existence of a higher triad—*Galut, Teshuvah,* and *Geulah.* Then, metahistory and history coalesced into a combined path of suffering and redemption. Schneersohn explained that Israel's exile came about in consequence of sin, and that it was intended by God to serve as an incentive to *Teshuvah.* When Israel failed to return, the suffering of exile intensified. Finally Israel faced the choice between utter destruction and *Teshuvah.* For Schneersohn, Nazism was ultimately traceable to a divine plan to bring the people back to God: "When thou art in distress and all things are come upon thee . . . if thou turn to the Lord thy God" (Deuteronomy 4:30), God would deliver Israel from exile. The sufferings were the *Hevlei mashiah,* intended to "tear open [Jewish] hearts and to instill the deepest feelings of *Teshuvah.*" According to the editors of *Hakeriyah Vehakedushah* who communicated Schneersohn's thought, he believed that God had placed Israel into a gigantic concentration camp, abandoned by the whole world, and the only means of escape was *Teshuvah.* At the same time, *Geulah,* drawn from the metahistorical dimension to Israel's history, was inevitable. Indeed, in May 1941 Schneersohn offered that it would come at war's end; in September 1942, he offered that exile would end in the next twelve months. And he spoke of restoring the geography of the land of Israel, which was to be free of Arabs, in terms of Torah and *Teshuvah*—lest it be destroyed irrespective of the physical reconstruction (Rashi to B.T. *Yoma* 86b). The fact that *Geulah* was inevitable meant that, at least to some extent, the required *Teshuvah* would take place as well. Schneersohn was confident in the *Teshuvah* of some Jews. Those who remained outside Goshen, however, would be killed— along with the Haman peoples, who bore no Noahide imprint.

As to the individual Jew, like Sarna, Schneersohn expected *Teshuvah* to be initiated by God, whose spirit was indeed calling out from above: "Turn, my backsliding children" (Jeremiah 3:14, 24). To get out of the prison of exile, his *Hakeriyah Vehakedushah* editor wrote, the prisoner had to deal with the highest (divine) judge. Through *Teshuvah,* the individual blended himself or herself into the ontological sequence. He or she also contributed to the culmination of the historical-metahistorical path in redemption. *Teshuvah* was the *axis mundi* of Schneersohn's cosmos. It bridged the existential, the ontological, and the historical.

In sum, according to Harlap's revealed wisdom, the universe was caught up in an apocalyptic drama. *Mashiah ben Yosef* (the Holocaust era) was yielding to *Mashiah ben David* (redemption). Through liberation from *Tumah* and the world of history polluted by it, i.e., through martyrdom, the individual shared in Mashiah ben David's realm. With each Jewish soul rooted in the collective sanctity of Israel, death to the profaneness of the body meant life for the soul in the sacred. According to Sarna's enlightenment, occasioned by divine presence, divine intervention enabled the individual to do *Teshuvah* and thereby participate in the higher triadic process. Schneersohn shared Sarna's perception of the higher transition but was more concerned with Israel's road through history and metahistory. He also shared his view that individual passage into redemption turned upon *Teshuvah.* Schneersohn shared Harlap's anticipation of the termination of the profane upon the redemption of the world—but he included Jews along with Gentiles in this end. And while Harlap envisioned the end to history as a whole, Schneersohn held onto the temporal and spatial boundaries to Israel's combined historical and metahistorical existence.[16]

From History into Metahistorical Redemption

Mizrahi and *Agudat Yisrael* thinkers in Palestine and America thought in the terms of Ehrenreich and Unsdorfer, whereby Israel's history would culminate in metahistorical redemption. But they removed the silence and delineated a direct path from history into redemption. They also set aside the comprehensive, inclusive metahistorical stage upon which history played a role, according to Harlap, Sarna, and Schneersohn—Harlap sublimating individual and history into a metahistorical, apocalyptic drama; Sarna delineating a metahistorical dynamic in which the historical individual sought inclusion; and Schneersohn describing a path to redemption that blended the historical and metahistorical. *Mizrahi* and *Agudat Yisrael* thinkers believed that the path to redemption led from out of history; they did not think that history was blocked by the unknowable or blanketed in silence. The path they delineated was, respectively, that of the land of Israel and *Da'at Torah* (knowledge of Torah); respectively, they filled the silence with land and *Da'at Torah*.

The *Mizrahi* perspective was rooted in the thought of Yitshak Nissenbaum in Warsaw in the 1930s. Nissenbaum correlated the contemporary forms of Amalek-Haman with the messianic advent, and the troubles of his time with what he believed to be the imminent Jewish state. Specifically, the more intense the persecution, the more intense the process of restoration. The sharpening of the *Hevlei mashiah* in 1939, he said (i.e., the burning of holy structures, the impending slaughter of Jews in Germany, and the potential expulsion of millions of Jews in Europe), demanded a proportional commitment to the land—with its implications for redemption. To state this differently, against the background of the renewed presence of Amalek and its implications for the Messiah, Nissenbaum called for land building. The Jew was to build the land in history, and thereby move the world from Amalek to messiah.

The *Mizrahi* leader in Jerusalem, Shlomo Zalman Shraggai, brought Nissenbaum's perspective into the war years. He presumed a permanent enmity between Esau and Jacob, and believed that it would have remained dormant had Israel not acted provocatively. God, he explained, exiled Israel because of Torahlessness, as a way to teach the people that it was impossible to live without Torah-in-the-land. Instead the people went further away from Torah and land, adopting false messianic redemptions and assimilating. Israel's landless status was dangerous, especially coupled with assimilation and the ever present enmity. Finally, Germany was provoked to attack. Shraggai conceded that Hitler was evil enough—and it was not as though Israel's *Teshuvah* could have prevented or stopped him. But Hitler needed a catalyst—and Israel provided it. Ironically, by this time religious nationalism and Zionism were underway. But by now there was an added factor: Israel's enemies feared the redemptive ramifications of Israel's return in terms of their own well-being. Still, Shraggai sought the return of Israel to the land, there to live the life of Torah. In turn, this would bring redemption.

The return, however, did not take place as Shraggai wished, and now the war made it impossible. At the end of the war, he abandoned his historically based scheme and invoked an apocalyptic drama. Whether because Israel failed in history to restore the land, or because the nations now made it impossible, or because the bloodshed was of *Hevlei mashiah* proportions, Shraggai allowed the historical restoration to become swept up in a higher drama of *Hurban* and *Geulah*. God, not humanity, now led the way to redemption. Specifically, as the UN General Assembly provided grounding for the Jewish state, Shraggai spoke of God's breaking into history, calling the *Hevlei mashiah* to a halt, and having the light of the Messiah break forth.

However, Shraggai's perspective remained essentially historical—irrespective of the apocalyptic element. Thus, for example, he was furious over the mass desecration at Kibbutz Daliyah in May 1947. The violation, he observed, was taking place in the world in which six million Jews had been burned to death with *Ani ma'amim* on their lips. A year earlier he had written,

> Our revival [as a people] is not solely a matter of changing the location of one million or many millions of Jews from Europe to the Land of Israel. Nor is such a revival some sort of [equal] exchange for the destruction, or an atonement for destruction. That is, not unless it mends the very sin which brought about the destruction in the first place. Namely the sin of Torahlessness which brought about the exile ["On account of our sins we were exiled from our Land," *Musaf*, Rosh Hashanah]. And the revival will not be lasting unless Israel is revived internally, as a nation defined in its own terms, according to Torah.

Shraggai understood how redemption would come about—through the historical restoration of the land in Torah. In the end, God had to intervene into history and raise it into an apocalyptic framework to enable this to take place—Israel having failed to do so in time. But once this occurred, redemption would remain elusive until the historical restoration of the land in Torah was complete.[17]

A parallel approach was taking place among *Agudat Yisrael* thinkers. While Nissenbaum was identifying the onset of the Messiah with the historical restoration of the land, Elhanan Wasserman in Baranowicz identified it with the historical restoration of *Da'at Torah*. He believed that the emergence of Nazism was an outer expression of the demise of

Torah within Israel, a mirror of the intrusion of Amalek within Israel itself. The historical failure reverberated above—where the *Shekhinah* itself mourned—and set off the *Hevlei mashiah*, and in turn the redemption. Wasserman despaired over the possibility that *Da'at Torah* could be restored (especially with the secularist Jewish *Medinah* underway) so as to revoke the *Hevlei mashiah*—or perhaps accelerate them and bring redemption about immediately. The assault, a product of the external Amalek of Nazism (under divine auspices) below and the release of *Hevlei mashiah* from above, would have to run its course. But it would do so in time for Israel, however exhausted, to be restored and to restore *Da'at Torah*—so as to align Israel with the messianic realm's *Da'at Torah* content. The essentially historical path into redemption, interrupted because of Israel's failure, would continue after the catastrophe—and until redemption. Indeed, given the intensity of redemption's presence following the calamity, the return of Torah to Israel's history would be unavoidable.

Agudat Yisrael leader Yitshak Meir Levin of Jerusalem looked for an explanation for the Holocaust, which he said could not be explained naturally, in the divine wisdom transmitted by the rabbinic tradition. He concluded that it was attributable to Israel's violation of the ontic division between Israel and the nations. As long as the distance was preserved, the hatred of the cruel and evil nations for the people who received revelation at Sinai remained contained. When the assimilationists breached the separation, which coincided with the loss of *Da'at Torah*, Israel was attacked. As with Wasserman, the coincident Torah-loss and Nazi assault on the plane of history reverberated above, and Levin's "*Akeidah* of six million" became the *Hevlei mashiah.* Levin was certain that the consolation of redemption would follow catastrophe ("*Ha'azinu*," Deuteronomy 32); that the terrible assault of Hitler's evil upon good (albeit Torah-wanting) Israel would be succeeded by the *Aharit hayamim.* But this would happen only in tandem with the restoration of *Da'at Torah.* In July 1947 he pleaded for Jews in Palestine to remove the Gentile dust that stuck to them from the exile; like Shraggai he condemned the desecration at Kibbutz Daliyah —where the dancing and torches evoked images of Hitler's pagan celebrations.

As with Shraggai, Israel's historical path was interrupted for Levin by apocalyptic events. The extremity of Israel's assimilation evoked divine action in history, releasing the hatred to stop Israel's Torahlessness, lest Israel lose itself entirely: "Hitler's animosity was sent upon us in all its horror, for the sake of our existence as a chosen nation." This in turn elicited the *Hevlei leida* of redemption. But now, with history about to pass through the threshold of redemption (a passage enabled by the era of *Hester panim*), *Da'at Torah* had to be restored immediately. Given the imminence of redemption, presumably it would be.[18]

Shraggai and Levin, albeit interrupted by the apocalyptic episode, never removed their eyes from Israel's history. For Shraggai, history was land-of-Israel based; for Levin it was based on *Da'at Torah*. The advent of redemption was contiguous with that history. The fact that they could understand the passage, while Ehrenreich and Unsdorfer withdrew into silence, that they were self-conscious and cognitive while those within the catastrophe prayed, sacrificed, and studied but not self-consciously or cognitively, may be understood in context: for the latter, Israel's life in history according to Torah (neither was a religious nationalist, and Ehrenreich opposed Zionists and Mizrahi) was being horribly disrupted, and while they insisted on Torah piety, it would have been difficult indeed to conceive of Torah-life in the ghettos of Simleul-Silvaniei and Bratislava as leading to redemption. From their distances (although Shraggai also visited the D.P. camps in June 1948) and their presence in vibrant Jewish communities in Jerusalem, it was possible for Shraggai and Levin to think differently.

After the Catastrophe: Hiddenness of Redemption

Religious thinkers within the war area were brought to silence about the onset of redemption and the paths (whether metahistorical and/or historical) to it. Those in Jerusalem and Brooklyn during the war were able to enunciate the content of the passage, claiming to have cognition about it (whether by divine revelation, God's consoling presence, "Gnostic"-like knowledge of Joseph's insight at death, or rabbinic traditions brought forward by Nissenbaum and Wasserman). Two religious thinkers who began to explicate their positions after the war concluded not only that cognition about the onset was impossible but that even silence as a means of bridging history to redemption was impossible. Future redemption could not be accessed, cognitively or silently. This was because the enormous historical catastrophe eclipsed redemption. Redemption existed, but could not be detected.

In 1947, like Ehrenreich and Unsdorfer, the rabbi of the Hasidei Sokolover-Kotsk congregations in Tel Aviv, Hayim Yisrael Tsimerman, spoke of the impossibility of understanding why God allowed the Holocaust to happen. Of course, God knew why—but God's knowledge was not available to humanity. His was infinite and humanity's was finite (Ramban, *Hilkhot Yesodei Hatorah* 2; 4:2); humanity had no way to evaluate His mercy and righteousness. When his congregants prevailed upon him to explain such matters as God's intention regarding the suffering of the pious, Tsimerman insisted that not only the answer but the question itself belonged to God. Quandaries about why God acted as He did should be allowed to recede, for humanity's ability to know was disconnected from God's judgments. Instead of painful questions, the Jew should immerse himself or herself, and find consolation, in the rabbinic and Hasidic traditions, and the reality of God's presence within those traditions.

What, then, did the tradition offer? According to Ezekiel, redemption would come with the revitalization of the land of Israel (Ezekiel 36:8). Before the war, the land did in fact have cities, villages, forests, fields, and vineyards—demonstrating that redemption had begun. The Holocaust further evidenced its presence. According to Maharsha's explanation of B.T. *Sanhedrin* 98a, after the process of redemption began, Israel was to be judged to be worthy (*kulo zakai*) or unworthy (*kulo hayav*). Inevitably, the latter would be the case (Ha'gra, *Biur Litekunei Hazohar* 126a). In turn, *Teshuvah* would be necessary, and *Teshuvah* would take place de facto by the suffering of Israel. The suffering would continue until the divinely chosen "appropriate moment," whether or not the people chose to assume the responsibility for *Teshuvah* by themselves. The Jew was to accept the suffering. Abraham's life was paradigmatic: he suppressed his natural objection to the command to sacrifice his son (Yonatan ben Uzziel to Genesis 17:1), and even the natural reaction, a heart attack, and in an act of *Mesirat nefesh* he followed God's command. The Jew should think of Bahya Ibn Pakuda's declaration, "My God, Thou hast made me suffer, left me naked, set me in the darkness of the night, and Thou hast shown me Thy might. If Thou merit to burn me in the fire, it would only increase my love for Thee" ("Sha'ar Ahavat Hashem I" in *Hovot Halevavot*).

For Tsimerman, redemption could be understood up to the point of the Holocaust—both of history and of metahistory. But he had nothing to say about how redemption would emerge from it. It existed for him, but he could see it only in the past. The present suffering eclipsed its future.[19]

In 1946 in Shanghai, Simha Elberg also stressed the inability to understand or explain the calamity. Not even a total life of suffering could be compared to a single hour in Treblinka. Murder had been present in the world since Cain, but the mass murder by Hitler, which polluted all of creation, was outside of nature, unprecedented. Human language had no words for the *Hurban*—indeed, to apply any would be "the greatest profanation of the tragedy." Elberg could not even begin to express himself, he said, with tears—for all his tears were exhausted (Ezekiel 24:15)—let alone in words.

But Elberg was nevertheless able to ask a question—the very question raised from Moses through Job: Why do the righteous suffer and the evil ones prosper? And how could God let six million Jews be killed, after He promised not to allow Israel's existence to end (Jeremiah 5:18)? Once he could express the question, Elberg was able to begin to frame an answer. It was that sacrifice and suffering were at Israel's innermost being—making questions about why Jews suffered almost irrelevant. Jewish history from Abraham's *Akeidah* (the binding of Isaac) through 1946 was in fact a process in which the substance of Treblinka was being realized. Isaac, for Elberg, never descended from the altar, and *Akeidat Treblinka* was the national conclusion to the individual *Akeidat Yitshak*. His answer was also about holiness. Both *Akeidat Yitshak* and *Akeidat Treblinka* sanctified Israel's history and existence. This was why, he averred, the Jews of Poland and Lithuania—the holiest of Jews—bore the brunt of the assault. The meaning of "through those near to Me I shall make Myself holy" (Leviticus 10:3) was "through the death of those close to Me, I will become sanctified."

The ultimately holy sacrifice of Treblinka coincided with the very destruction of world history. As with Harlap, the history of the world belonged to the *Sitra ahra* (the "left side," i.e., the power of evil), and now it had been cast into oblivion. But while for Harlap the disappearance of history came with the light of redemption, Elberg envisioned no *Mashiah ben David,* only the *Tehom* (deep) and the *Tohu va'vohu* (chaos) that had been there before creation. The world was destroyed, and the historical destruction eclipsed any vision whatsoever of redemption. For Tsimerman, redemption was refracted into the past, a process underway up to the point of the Holocaust. For Elberg, a new creation of the world would have to take place, this time around the Torah and the Torah nation, before any redemptive light could even be imagined. There were some allusions to redemption in the 1946 tractate: the "overflowing fury" of Ezekiel (Ezekiel 20:33–34) having taken place, "the hour of divine revelation for all mankind should come soon. And that is indeed our essential mission, to redeem the world with our blood." The fact that one individual could personify total evil, that such a satanic reality came to bear, implied that everything positive could be embodied in a single individual who would rebuild the world from destruction. "And perhaps that person is standing behind our backs with the message of redemption in his mouth." But these allusions were fleeting, and overwhelmed by the sense of the destruction of the world and a pervasive attention to *Akeidah*. For Elberg, the *Akeidah* became an absolute reality—which overshadowed redemption.[20]

Summary and Conclusion

Ultra-Orthodox Jews persisted in their expectation of messianic redemption through the catastrophe. They did so framed by the lines of history and the dialectics of metahistory. Within the center of the catastrophe, there was a blanket of silence when it came to how redemption would happen—an extension of the silence about why the Holocaust itself happened (especially about why the righteous were suffering); they projected the theological paralysis about the present ahead towards the future.

Around the center, geographically but not, I would stress, psychologically, there was cognition about the passage—how it would take place ontically, metahistorically, historically, and individually. The thinkers here were not paralyzed by the issue of the suffering of the pious, and their knowledge about the present flowed into the future. The cognition ranged from inclusively apocalyptic (Harlap) to mystical-existential (Sarna) to a blend of the historical and metahistorical (Schneersohn) to those who held onto the category of history through the apocalyptic moment (Shraggai and Levin).

After the war, future messianic redemption could not be faced. Tsimerman was able to speak of redemption's prelude in the period up to the Holocaust, but not about redemption after the Holocaust. Elberg was blinded by *Akeidat Treblinka*. The confidence in redemption, whether in silence at the geographical center or in words at the periphery, was no longer present. Redemption, albeit not denied, was now eclipsed by history.

To conclude: the long-lasting messianic urge within exilic Judaism endured through the catastrophe. Those thinkers who were simultaneously subject and object, namely, those whose reflections about the catastrophe emerged from and turned back to their own suffering, could perceive redemption only in silence—their apprehension did not reach cognition.

Those for whom the catastrophe was an object separated by space did achieve this cognition, while those for whom it was an object separated by space and time were surrounded by the darkness of tragedy and could not reach redemption either by silence or by wisdom-in-words. Perhaps these three concentric circles complemented each other in such a way as to preserve thoughts of redemption for the future. Taken together, they kept redemptive hope intact—there to be drawn upon in later years.

NOTES

1. Ehrenreich, *Derashot Lehem Shelomo* (Brooklyn, 1976); *Tiyul Bepardes* 1 (Simleul Silvaniei, 1938/39); *Tiyul Bepardes* 2 (Szilagy Somlyo: 1941/42); *Igeret Hatiyul Hashalem* (Jerusalem, 1961/62); *Even Shelomo al Hatorah* (Jerusalem, 1963).

2. Unsdorfer, "Avayehi . . . 5702" in *Siftei Shelomo*, 84–89.

3. Hatam Sofer, *Sefer Zikaron*, 17–18; Unsdorfer, *Siftei Shelomo*, "Shabbat Hazon 5703 [7 August 1943]," 137–39. See *Midrash Tehillim* 20:4.

4. Unsdorfer, "Shofetim 5703" in *Siftei Shelomo*, 144–46.

5. Unsdorfer, "Va'eira . . . 5702"; and "Va'eira . . . 5703" in *Siftei Shelomo*, 93–96, 308–10. See B.T. *Sanhedrin* 100b and Hatam Sofer, "Va'yeira" in *Hatam Sofer al Hatorah* (Jerusalem, 1957/58), 1: 72–73.

6. Hatam Sofer, "Ki Tissa" in *Torat Moshe Hashalem* (Jerusalem: 1990/91), 2: 303a; "Ki Tissa," *Hatam Sofer al Hatorah* (Jerusalem: 1957/58), 2: 146b; Unsdorfer, "Ki Tissa . . . 5702 [6 March 1942]," in *Siftei Shelomo*, 117–18.

7. Hatam Sofer, "Derush Lezayin Adar" in *Derashot* (New York, 1960/61), 1: 128; Unsdorfer, "Tetsaveh: Beyom 13 Adar Rishon 5702," in *Siftei Shelomo*, 113–15.

8. Hatam Sofer to Genesis 43:19–20 as cited in Unsdorfer, "Vayigash . . . 5702" in *Siftei Shelomo*, 78–81. I was unable to find the citation. See Hatam Sofer, "Mikets" in *Torat Moshe Hashalem* 1, 168–79 and "Parashat Miketz" in *Hatam Sofer al Hatorah* 1, 204–15.

9. Hatam Sofer, *Sefer Hazikaron* (Brooklyn: 1974/75), 17–18 and Unsdorfer, "Shabbat Hazon 5703" in *Siftei Shelomo* (Brooklyn, 1972), 137–39.

10. Hatam Sofer to Ecclesiastes 8:9 as cited in Unsdorfer, "Velo yakhol Yosef," *Siftei Shelomo*, 81–82. I was unable to find the citation. See Hatam Sofer, "Lehag Hasukkot" in *Derashot* 1: 72–111. Unsdorfer, "Vayeshev . . . 5702 [13 October 1941]"; "Terumah . . . 5703 [13 February 1943]"; "Beha'alotekha 5703 [19 June 1943]"; "Veze she'amar [*Pirkei Avot* 3:1]" in *Siftei Shelomo*, 64–66, 111–13, 316, 236–38.

11. Hatam Sofer, "Vayeira" in *Hatam Sofer al Hatorah*, 271–72. Unsdorfer, "Shenat 5700 [*Pirkei Avot* V:4]" and "Vayeira . . . 5702," in *Siftei Shelomo*, 271–72, 40–44. Unsdorfer, "R. Shimon omer" [*Pirkei Avot* 2:17] in *Siftei Shelomo*, 232–34. See *Midrash Tehillim* 20:4.

12. Piekaz, *Hasidut Polin* (Jerusalem, 1990), 379.

13. Harlap, *Mei Marom 4: Haggadah shel Pessah* (Jerusalem, 1954/55); *Mei Marom 6: Mi'einei Hayeshuah* (Jerusalem, 1981/82).

14. Sokolover, *Penei Ephraim* (Tel Aviv, 1965/66). See also Eliahu Botschko, *Der Born Israel* (Montreux, 1944), 1: 19–20; Menahem Mendel Schneersohn, *Emunah Umadah* (Brooklyn, 1977): 115–24; and Samuel Usque, *Consolations for the Tribulations of Israel,* transl. Martin Cohen (Philadelphia, 1977), 229.

15. Sarna, *Liteshuvah Velitekuma* (Jerusalem, 1945).

16. Greenberg, "Redemption after Holocaust according to Mahane Yisrael-Lubavitch, 1940–45," *Modern Judaism,* vol. 12 (1992), 61–84; "Assimilation as *Hurban* according to Wartime American Orthodoxy: Habad Hasidism" in *Jewish Assimilation, Acculturation, and Accommodation* (Lanham, MD, 1992); "The Sect of Catastrophe: Mahane Yisrael-Lubavitch, 1940–45," in *Jewish Sects, Religious Movements, and Political Parties* (Omaha, NE, 1992); "Mahane Yisrael-Lubavitch, 1940–1945: Actively Responding to the *Hurban*" in *Bearing Witness to the Holocaust, 1939–1989,* ed. Alan Berger (Lewiston, ME, 1991).

17. Nissenbaum, "Shenei Alafim Yemot Hamashiah" in *Ha'yahadut Haleumit* (Warsaw, 1920), 41–58; "Doro shel Mashiah" in *Ketavim Nivharim* (Jerusalem, 1947/48), 319–22; "Gormei Hageulah," "Yad Hahashgahah Haelyonah," and "Al Saf Tekufah Hadashah," in *Masoret Veheirut* (Warsaw, 1939), 87–97, 117–25, 174–89. Shraggai, *Tehumim* (Jerusalem, 1951/52); *Zemanim* (Jerusalem, 1969); *Tahalikhei Hatemurah Vehageulah* (Jerusalem, 1958/59); "Fun a Medina Untervegs," *Di Yidishe Shtime,* vol. 1, no. 18 (4 April 1947), 2, 6; "In fustn Roym," *Di Yidishe Shtime,* vol. 2, no. 2/whole no. 37 (28 September 1947), 2, 8; "In di Eybikayts-Momentn," *Di Yidishe Shtime,* vol. 2, no. 18/whole no. 53 (20 February 1948), 3, 8; "Oro shel Mashiah: Im Tekumata shel Medinat Yisrael," *Di Yidishe Shtime,* vol. 2, no. 33/whole no. 68 (18 June 1948), 1.

18. On Wasserman see Greenberg, "Elhanan Wasserman's Response to the Growing Catastrophe in Europe: The Role of Ha'gra and Hofets Hayim upon His Thought," *Journal of Jewish Thought and Philosophy,* vol. 8, no. 1 (2000), 1–34. Levin, "35 Shanah Le'agudat Yisrael," *Haderekh,* no. 116 (5 June 1947); "Heshbono shel Olameinu," *Haderekh,* no. 5 (15 October 1942), "Hem Kidshu Et Hashem Be'-motam-Nikadesh anu Et Hashem Behayeinu," *Haderekh,* no. 37 (27 May 1943).

19. Tsimerman, *Sefer Tamim Pa'alo: She'elot Uteshuvot Bidvar Hahashmadah Haiyumah shel Shishah Milyon Hayehudim, Hashem Yinkom Damam* (Jerusalem, 1947).

20. Elberg, *Akeidas Treblinka* (Shanghai, 1946). Elberg's commitment to this position is evidenced by the fact that *Akeidas Treblinka* was translated into Hebrew and republished thirty-eight years later in the land of Israel. Elberg, "Akeidat Treblinka," *Hamodiyah* (18 May 1984).

Chapter 6

Ultra-Orthodox Jewish Thought about the Holocaust since World War II
The Radicalized Aspect

Gershon Greenberg

An element of theological absolutism has emerged within ultra-Orthodox Jewish thought since World War II. The anti-Zionism of the wartime period has been radicalized to the point of alleging an association between secular Zionism and Nazism. Religious Zionism has moved from the wartime theme of Israel's change of mind about ascending to the land of Israel, because of the catastrophic acts by the nations (under divine aegis), towards the concept of God's direct physical intervention to implement the ascent. Elements of conceptual assimilation and the cooption of ultra-Orthodoxy into the assimilation process have been added to the wartime allegation that cultural assimilation caused the catastrophe. While during the war Amalek (as Hitler) was seen as a divine instrument used for positive purposes in history, after the war Amalek represented the realm of darkness in a cosmic mortal struggle against the light as represented by the people of Israel. The suffering process deliberated upon during the war was transformed in postwar thinking into suffering as a fait accompli, as crystallized in the *Akedah* of Isaac both as the binding for sacrifice and the sacrifice itself. Finally, during the war messianic redemption was conceived of as a metahistorical process ("metahistory" referring to the drama of Israel's covenantal relationship with God, touching upon and manifest within empirical history), which involved knowledge of the explicit Torah and required human initiative in terms of Torah and land. After the war redemption became a matter of seeking the internal, secret knowledge of Torah (Kabbalah). There were also intimations of a shift towards a heteronomous apocalyptic drama.

Anti-Zionism

During the Holocaust era, blame for the catastrophe was laid at the feet of secular Zionists. The language used was a mixture of metahistorical, metaphysical, mythic, and empirical elements. For example, Elhanan Wasserman, head of the Baronovichi, Poland, yeshiva, condemned secular Zionism in his 1938–1939 writings as a blatant example of the "we will be as the nations" mentality spelled out by Ezekiel, where God reacted by pouring out fury (Ezekiel 20:32–33). Secular Zionists, he complained, thought that all it took to be a Jew was to "pay a Shekel [for the land of Israel] and sing *Hatikvah*." This evoked the nations' measure-for-measure punishment, under divine aegis.

The Mizrahi leader Mosheh Avigdor Amiel, chief rabbi of Tel Aviv, paired Herzlian Zionism with the *Haskalah* legacy of Moses Mendelssohn as a line of development that diminished Torah (meaning Hebrew scripture and ongoing rabbinic tradition) and neutralized the separate collective identity of Israel, evoking divine punishment. Jakob Rosenheim in New York, the world president of the Agudat Yisrael rabbinical organization, spoke in terms of political identity and attributed the developing catastrophe to a world plagued by quests for national sovereignty. For secular nationalists to seek national sovereignty in the land of Israel, according to Rosenheim, was to court disaster. Indeed, a sovereign Jewish commonwealth, with Torah-reality marginalized, was in danger of generating a third *Hurban*.

The anti-Zionism of Shlomoh Zalman Ehrenreich of Simleul-Silvaniei, Transylvania, consisted of categorical opposition to active restoration of the land and to any mass *aliyah*. Invoking the three oaths of *B.T. Ketubot* 111ᵃ, which inveighed against Jews' revolting against the ruler and also inveighed against mass settlement, Ehrenreich attacked those who participated in the Betar movement and in the uprisings in Palestine against the British. Ehrenreich was committed to awaiting God's intervention: "The [secular] Zionist sect wants to conquer and build the Land by its own power, without Torah and without our righteous messiah. [But] we have none to rely upon except our Father in Heaven, who acts without the help of those of flesh and blood." Indeed, even to give money to Mizrahi religious nationalists or to the *halakah*-based Agudat Yisrael organization for restoration of the land, Ehrenreich declared, amounted to assisting Haman to destroy Judaism. The violation of the three oaths would incite God's judgment, and the "flesh would become like prey, like the gazelles and hinds in the field" (*Ketubot* 111ᵃ).[1]

In the years following the war, ultra-Orthodox thinking about the Holocaust removed secular Zionism out of Judaism completely and posited it as belonging to an anti-Israel realm of being that was already inhabited by Amalek and Nazi Germany. Yoel Taytlboym, the Satmarer Rav (Satu Mare, Romania), was a survivor of Bergen Belsen who escaped Europe in July 1944 and settled in America in 1947 after a brief period in the land of Israel. As Ehrenreich alleged during the war, Taytlboym wrote in *And It Pleased Moses* (1959) and *Treatise on Redemption and Change* (1981) that secular Zionism was responsible for violating the three oaths of *B.T. Ketubot* 111ᵃ. As stipulated there by the rabbinic sage Eleazar, the people of Israel were sworn not to rebel against the nations that ruled them in exile, and they were not to hasten the end of history (i.e., the moment set by God for redemption) by ascending to the land of Israel en masse. The nations, conditional upon these two oaths, were sworn not to overly oppress the people of Israel. If the people of Israel abided by their oaths, Rabbi Eleazar explained, matters would go well for them. If not, God would let Israel's flesh be hunted down by the nations of idolaters as gazelles and hinds were hunted as prey in the fields. Having in fact violated the oaths not to rebel (presumably by the activism in Europe and aggressive activity in the land of Israel) and not to hasten the end of history, secular Zionists released the animosity that had been building up towards the people since Esau. The result was an explosion of persecution and oppression. Taytlboym condemned Zionism categorically as a manifestation of profanity (*Tumah*), for it displaced divine providence with human initiative and sought to transform the land of Israel into a place like all others. He made a series of specific, unproven accusations: Zionist leaders advised government officials to expel Jews because they were dangerous; they incited the German government by supporting England in the war; they plotted to have gates of refuge closed during the war so as to force Jews to go to the land or else be killed; and they excluded non-Zionists from the escape train of Rudolf Kasztner, leaving them to die in Germany. In their totality, according to Taytlboym, the violations on the part of secular Zionists were worse than all the violations of the current generation in toto.[2]

There was opposition to Taytlboym's view. Mordekhai Atiyah was a kabbalist from Mexico City who had settled in the land of Israel by 1948. In 1963–1964 he cited Shemuel Yaffe Ashkenazi's sixteenth-century *Midrash Rabbah* commentary, which held that Rabbi Eleazar's teacher Rav Yohanan (along with Resh Lakish), contrary to Taytlboym's interpretation, took the position that it was a trespass not to ascend en masse. Both sages in fact held in contempt those Babylonian Jews who did not themselves ascend or who failed to encourage others to ascend: had there been an en masse ascent, God Himself would have supported it. It would, indeed, have evoked the coming of the Messiah. For Rav Yohanan, entering into the earthly Jerusalem led to entry into the Jerusalem of redemption. For his own part, Rabbi Eleazar averred that if the people did not ascend en masse they would become as prey in the fields. Atiyah also cited positions from the seventeenth and eighteenth centuries: for Efrayim Landshits, it was evil for the ancient Israelites to want to stay in the land of Egypt and resist going to the land of Canaan. Mosheh Hagiz characterized anyone claiming that premessianic settlement would profane the land and judging those who advanced settlement worthy of being obliterated as being "rotten to the core." To try to cite *Ketubot* 111ª in opposition to settlement, Hagiz wrote, was like "whistling in the wind."

For Atiyah, there was also the matter of higher, kabbalistic unity. He pointed out that in *Gate of Intentions* Hayim Vital (1542–1620) wrote that the covenant of God would be fulfilled by unifying the letters of His name, two of which (letters *hay* and *hay*) stood for the land of Israel (*ha'arets*). That is, the land's restoration was indispensable to the name's unity. In the eighteenth century Shalom Buzaglo wrote in *Sanctuary of the King* that the unity of God's name was impossible during exile. Ascent to the land, however, evoked unification of the higher realms above as well as of the nation of Israel below, both aspects of the redemption. Buzaglo wrote of the devastating consequences of not ascending to the land. The "I" cited in the three oaths of *Ketubot* 111ª ("If you abide by the oath it will be well and good for you. If not, I will permit your flesh to be hunted by idolators as the hinds of the fields") referred to the divine *Shekhinah* (presence). In exile, the *Shekhinah* remained imprisoned. This meant there could be no unity above. Below, the disunity of the people generated disaster. God called out for the people of Israel to return to the land. But they failed to respond, and so God did not respond to them when they called out to Him in distress. The nations that prevented the return of the people of Israel, thereby precluding the higher and lower unity, would also be punished, leading to greater havoc. It was as if they placed a sheet between the lion and the lioness when they wanted one another. They would suffer terrible consequences: "Woe to the nation found there when God redeems His children."[3]

But Taytlboym's views endured. Among those who subscribed to them,

Benyamin Mendelssohn accused secular Zionists of being Kapos during the war. Avraham Yeshayah Roth accused them of sabotaging Mikhael Dov Weissmandel's rescue efforts in Slovakia and the efforts by Agudat Yisrael to send aid packages to Europe. In an attack upon Mapam Kenesset member Hayka Grossman, Elazar Halevi Shulsinger accused secular Zionists of attempting genocide of the 2,000-year-old Jewish religious culture. The Naturei Karta movement (begun in 1935) took the matter to its extreme and identified Zionists with Israel's paradigmatic enemy, Amalek and the Nazis.[4]

During the war the secular Zionists were attacked by ultra-Orthodox thinkers as being responsible for the developing disaster. By reducing Torah Judaism and becoming as the nations, blurring the metaphysical division between Israel and the nations, pursuing national sovereignty, and violating the oaths listed in *Ketubot* 111^a, they were responsible for the troubles. The direct cause of the attacks could be covenantal (Wasserman), cosmic (Amiel), political (Rosenheim), or legalistic (Ehrenreich). After the war, the catastrophe was taken as evidence of secular Zionist wrongdoing. The disaster having actually taken place, the wrongdoing amounted to participating in the crime against the Jewish people. This made the secular Zionist the enemy of Israel, ultimately no different than Amalek. The fact of ultimate disaster corresponded with the unmitigated evil of those responsible.

Religious Nationalism

During the war, religious Zionist ultra-Orthodox thinkers interpreted the disaster as an action of the nations under divine aegis, which mandated the conclusion that the moment had come for return to the land of Israel. In 1943 in Budapest, Yissakhar Taykhtahl observed that the tragedy was the worst to befall the people of Israel since the time of Haman, and the first where nations allowed no refuge to which Jews might escape. Meanwhile, as the catastrophe unfolded, the process of restoration had begun in the land. The latter, for Taykhtahl, evidenced the revealed end that heralded redemption (*Kets hameguleh*; see B.T. *Sanhedrin* 98b): "But ye, O mountains of Israel, ye shall shoot forth your branches, and yield your fruit to My people Israel, for they are at hand to come" (Ezekiel 36:8). Taykhtahl interpreted the synchronism of the threat to Israel's life in Europe (with no way out) and the beginnings of restoration of the land as the expression of a divine imperative to recognize and implement the end of exile and the beginning of land-centered redemption. The absolute closing off of the Diaspora and the simultaneous opening of the land of Israel for restoration and redemption required a complete change in religious orientation, and Taykhtahl renounced his earlier anti-Zionism, rooted in absolute reliance upon divine miraculous intervention for en masse ascent to take place. Mizrahi leader Shlomoh Zalman Shraggai of Jerusalem explained that God had decreed exile as a means of educating the people of Israel not to assimilate (as they had in the ancient land of Israel). Instead, the people assimilated even more, up to the point where the concept of redemption itself came to mean the French Revolution. There was long-standing antagonism between Israel and the nations. When combined with the Jews' condition of landlessness, a furious reaction (under divine aegis) to assimilation was inevitable. The conclusion to be drawn was unambiguous: the people of Israel had no place in exile and had to have their own land.[5]

For Taykhtahl, God, the trapped people of Israel, and the attacking nations constituted a triangular, metahistorical relation with land-centered redemption at its center. For Shragai, the triangle was constituted by God, the people of Israel (landless and assimilating), and the alien nations. For both, God overlooked the interactions between Israel and the nations at the bottom of the triangle. The actions of the nations, for Taykhtahl persecution and imprisonment and for Shragai the outburst of antagonism, mandated a change of mind, namely, the awareness that the moment for restoration of the people in the land of Israel had arrived.

After the war, God was thought of as moving into the position of participant from below, intervening in history at the bottom of the triangular structure through the nations. While mediated by the nations as before, the distance of aegis between God and the nations was removed and the distance of cognitive decision between the destruction and move to the land was eclipsed. Drawing from a principle set down by the medieval biblical commentator Abraham Ibn Ezra in 1947, Hayim Yisrael Tsimerman, leader of the Sokolover Hasidim in Tel Aviv, asserted that God destroyed the generation of the Holocaust in order to remove any obstacle to the next generation's building the land of Israel. He explained that the restoration process towards the end of the nineteenth century and during the earlier twentieth century belonged to the *Kets hamegulah* (redemptive end-time). But the people failed to recognize it. While pious Jews during the Crusades made terrible sacrifices to get to the land, during the years of the *Kets hameguleh,* when there was relative calm, Jews—including the pious—remained outside. Tsimerman believed that "on account of this trespass alone, namely of not ascending to the Land of Israel, the people of Israel suffered the calamitous annihilation of one third of their number." He drew from the medieval commentator Abraham Ibn Ezra's commentary about the desert generation. The children of Israel internalized their slavery in Egypt to the point that they lacked any courage to take the land (Abraham Ibn Ezra *ad* Exodus 14:13: "And Moses said unto the people, 'Fear ye not, stand still, and see the salvation of the Lord'"). God therefore let the males of the older generation die out in the desert to allow for a new generation, unobstructed by slavishly minded elders, to move upon the land. In the Holocaust, Tsimerman continued, God let the generation that failed to recognize the *Kets hameguleh* die out, so a new generation with a fresh outlook could arise.[6]

The following year, Mordekhai Atiyah added details. He cited the commentary of Hayim Ibn Attar (1696–1743) that God "sold" the land of Israel to the nations because Israel sinned. God planned to return it to them when piety and desire to return so merited. Instead, the nation became so enslaved psychologically that liberation could hardly be grasped, let alone be acted upon. Then, following Tsimerman, Atiyah cited Abraham Ibn Ezra *ad* Exodus 14:13. The six hundred thousand escapees from Egypt were so afraid, because of their slavish psyche, that when the Amalekites confronted them they had to turn to Moses to pray for divine intervention. God therefore let the generation die away to make room for a young, courageous generation. Atiyah pointed out how the interwar generation had squandered the opportunity offered by the Balfour generation, because of meekness and lack of confidence in being able to go and build the land. God let it die, through Hitler, so a new generation like that which entered ancient Canaan could be free to act.[7]

The motif of Abraham Ibn Ezra was also echoed in New York in 1957 by Aharon Petshenik, son of the Rav of Dombrovitsa Nahum Petshenik (d. 1942) and nephew of the Rav of Belz Isaakhar Dov Rokeah. He added the medieval Jewish philosopher Yehudah Halevi's point that tragedy purified Israel and enabled the divine presence to renew itself.[8]

A second version of direct divine intervention emerged from the Tsevi Yehudah Kook school of thought. Kook, who succeeded Ya'akov Mosheh Harlap, the successor to Avraham Yitshak Kook (Tsevi Yehudah's father) as head (*Resh Mesivta*) of Merkaz Harav Kook yeshiva in Jerusalem, identified the interwar period as the *Kets hameguleh.* It was the era that heralded redemption, when the "dry bones" of Israel were to be resurrected—a symbol of which was the 1917 Balfour Declaration. Diaspora Jews, however, did not choose to participate in the metahistorical turn of the *Kets hameguleh* with their own historical return. Instead they remained stuck in the "tar" of exile. God therefore acted to extract them from the tar. In a metaphor invoked during the war itself by Eliyahu Botschko of Montreux and Efrayim Sokolover of Ra'anana, and traceable to Yehudah Halevi's *Kuzari*, Kook spoke of a divine act of surgery, a "hidden, internal procedure to purify the Jewish people," to remove the *Tumah* portions of the body of Israel and to enable penitent return (*Teshuvah*) and thereby land-of-Israel-centered redemption. The empirical enactment took the form of Hitler's mad conduct. Citing the French edition of Hermann Rauschning's *Gespräche mit Hitler*, Kook explained that Hitler's world was divided into a Germany chosen by God and a nation of Israel chosen by Satan. Echoing the apocalyptic description of Zadok Rabinowitz's (1823–1900) *Holy Ones of Israel*, he said that the *Kets hameguleh*, with its aspects of return, land-centered redemption, and subsequent universal sanctification, made Hitler frantic and he set out to sabotage the process towards redemption by desecrating the name of God through the destruction of God's people.[9]

In 1998–1999 Uri Sharki, a follower of Tsevi Yehudah Kook, compared Israel's exile to sickness, redemption to health, and the premessianic sufferings (*Hevlei mashiah*) to convalescence. During the convalescent stage, which was the interwar period, the people of Israel failed to align themselves with the metahistorical process by turning towards the land. The failure spelled danger. The medieval philosopher Yehudah Halevi asserted that sluggishness with regard to return to the land diminished the holiness of the people and even the holiness of God. For Halevi "divinity only rests upon a person in accordance with a person's receptivity to it, be it great or small"—and the sluggishness compromised this receptivity. According to Ya'akov Emden (1697–1770), citing "and the land of your enemies shall eat you up" (Leviticus 26:38), it was dangerous for the people of Israel to stay away, and Jews who were mindful of God must rush to the land. Israel's desert forefathers exhibited contempt for the land, and by doing so they generated tears that would continue for generations to come as the nations of the world rose up against them. Emden attributed the fact that "in every generation they rise up against us to destroy us" ("Vehi She'amdah," in *Haggadah shel Pessah*) to that original resistance. During the era of the *Hevlei mashiah*, Sharki explained, the need to return intensified—the Gaon of Vilna, for example, convinced that the *Kets hameguleh* was in place, urged his students to go to the land to participate in and accelerate the onset of redemption. Likewise, the dangers of not returning sharpened. Because the Jews of the interwar period failed to rush to return, according to Sharki, God acted to remove His presence from the people of Israel and let the nations devour them. In the chaos that ensued as God removed Himself, no distinctions were made between the good Jew and the bad (Rashi *ad* Genesis 6:13). Sharki also brought forward the kabbalistic interpretation of Mosheh Hayim Luzzatto (1707–1747): when the Temple was destroyed, the higher gates through which the world's blessings flowed were shut while the lower gates remained open so that enough blessings for Israel to survive the Diaspora could flow out. With the *Kets hameguleh,* the windows below closed in anticipation of the opening above. The transition was filled with tribulation and tension. God went into hiding—and only great trust in God enabled the people of Israel to endure (see Deuteronomy 4:30; Psalms 10:1, 31:25).[10]

In the wartime period, God oversaw a horizontal (anti-) relationship between the nations and Israel, which led to the unavoidable conclusion that the time for restoration-as-redemption had come. After the war, God entered into the horizontal relationship. He had the slavishly minded generation die off so the next generation would be free to take action, and He cut off the *Tumah* of exile so the people would no longer be stuck in its tar. The proximity of redemption and the intensity of the dynamics of apocalypse, all scripted by God, involved destruction of the people on one side and their liberation and salvation on the other. The postwar thinkers reduced the mediation between God and historical reality and conceived of Him as an actor in the drama rather than its director. And they reduced the cognitive mediation between persecution and *aliyah* by making the Holocaust the direct impetus for *aliyah.* The catastrophe having actually taken place, ultra-Orthodox thought responded to the urgency and condensed the triangle among God, the attackers, and Israel into a single point in which God's physical assault in the form of the Holocaust implied the move to the land.

Assimilation

During the war, the tragedy was often blamed on attempts by non-Orthodox Jews to assimilate into the social and intellectual culture of the Gentiles. The theme was enunciated at the onset of the war by Avraham

Yitshak Bloch of Telsiai (Lithuania) and Elhanan Wasserman. It was carried into the tragedy by Shlomoh Zalman Unsdorfer (Bratislava), Shlomoh Zalman Ehrenreich, Yitshak Meir Levin (Jerusalem), and Eliyahu Henkin (New York). According to the essential dynamic involved, by moving into the cultures of the Gentiles the people of Israel undermined their own sanctity and upset the metaphysical balance between Israel on the one side of the universe and the nations of the world on the other. Chaos and destruction followed. Invoking the principle formulated in Ezekiel 20:32–33 that becoming as the nations precipitated the outpouring of divine force against Israel, the interpreters enunciated how specific acts of assimilation evoked corresponding measure-for-measure retaliatory acts by the nations. They were equally convinced that a recession of assimilation would restore the balance with Israel's sacred status intact. Indeed, it would bring about redemption. The tear in Israel's relationship to God caused by assimilation could not be repaired historically or metahistorically, for the relationship was only partly historical or metahistorical. The repair had to address the realms of finite and infinite together. Only redemption could do so. Inevitably, given the metaphysical structure, it would.[11]

After the war, a conceptual element was added to the dynamic, framed in terms of a Gnosticlike division between wisdom (that of Torah) and the denial and perversion of wisdom (all non-Torah knowledge). In 1953 in Monsey, New York, Holocaust survivor Avraham Weinfeld described how his entire family had been slaughtered in a single day, sending his mind into religious chaos. He was unable to understand why God did such things to His own people. By an act of providence, he believed, he chanced upon Yosef ben Hayim Jabez's *Light of Life,* written in response to the Spanish Inquisition. Jabez argued that the slaughter, starvation, and expulsion were divine punishment, resulting from His wrath over the people's exposure to wisdom other than Torah (see II Kings 22:13 and Jeremiah 9:13). God was just, and He delighted when His people were engaged in Torah. He punished them when they were not. Jabez found it particularly reprehensible that the very same Spanish Jews who filled the yeshivas went on to study the "external wisdom" of philosophy after they graduated. This crime was even worse than that of philosophers when they claimed that God did not see humanity. To substantiate his conviction that the division between internal and external knowledge was categorical and absolute, Weinfeld traced its ongoing affirmation over the centuries. For example, Yair Hayim Bacharach (1638–1702) inveighed against scientific research.

Eleazar Loew (1758–1837) warned against the contention that the way of the temporal world demanded acquaintance with literature other than Torah and alleged that embracing external wisdom was a heretical act with mortal consequences (see Proverbs 5:21–22). Commenting on Jabez's work, the rabbi of Munkacz Tsevi Elimelekh Shapiro of Dynow, Poland (1785–1841), categorically denounced the *Haskalah* (the Jewish Enlightenment) and its alien concepts. The Hofets Hayim (Yisrael Meir Hakohen of Radin) considered it an abomination to even have external literature in the home (see Deuteronomy 7:28). To actually read it meant to abandon any potential place in the world to come (B.T. *Sanhedrin* 90a). Barukh Dov Laybovitch (1866–1939), *Resh Mesivta* of Keneset Beit Yitshak yeshiva (Kovno-Slobodka) considered the act of sending Jewish children to a *Gymnasium* or university as heresy. For Laybovitch, all outside wisdom, without qualification, was forbidden (he cited the sixteenth-century legalist Mosheh Isserles). It pushed souls out of Israel and was not to be studied even if it meant saving life during a crisis. For Weinfeld, in sum, the very idea of non-Torah literature, any compromise to the transcendental idea of pure Torah wisdom, above and beyond any cultural assimilation, spelled disastrous empirical consequences—and indeed brought terrible troubles to Israel, from the Spanish expulsion to the Holocaust.[12]

The division of the universe between sacred Israel and profane nations that stood during the Holocaust was sharpened in its aftermath by Tsimerman's inclusion of pious Jews in the violation. According to the rabbinic sages, he explained in *All His Ways Are Righteous* (*Tamim Pa'alo*), if it was at all possible to keep a member of one's household or community from sinning, the pious Jew had at least to try. The citizens of Ezekiel's Jerusalem, for example, were culpable because they had the power to protect against trespasses but failed to do so (B.T. *Shabbat* 54b–55a). Or King Zedekiah committed a sin because he had the power to protest when his contemporaries turned to evil but did not (B.T. *Sanhedrin* 103a). Tsimerman cited Orthodox Jews in Germany for not trying to stop family members from intermarrying, and Orthodox Jews in Warsaw for not attempting to stop publication of Jewish newspapers on the Sabbath. That is, the dualism between the sacred realm of Judaism and the Gentile world was deepened to include the factor of collective responsibility.[13]

During the war, the mythic and metahistorical language of the ultra-Orthodox gave expression to the belief that world order depended upon Israel's existence remaining blended into the sacred reality of Torah. The order was violated and chaos ensued. But the metaphysical condition meant that repair would take place. On the anthropological level, this meant assimilation followed by persecution, and finally Israel's return to the Torah-domain. After the war, the dualism was sharpened, adding an ideational dimension to the cultural Torah-compromise and including the pious who failed to stop the assimilators in the non-Torah realm. Once the catastrophic consequences of being as the nations unfolded, the dynamic was absolutized. It was extended into the realm of the transcending idea and left no neutral ground at all in the encounter between the mutually exclusive realms of Torah and non-Torah.

Amalek and Evil

According to Hebrew scripture and its traditional interpreters, Amalek's attack against Israel at Refidim (Exodus 17:8, 14; Numbers 24:20; Deuteronomy 25:17–19), an attack without rationale or provocation, went beyond the people of Israel and assaulted God Himself. The people of Israel were never to forget what happened, while God would remain in a state of war with Amalek forever (see, for example, *Pesikta Rabbati* 12:9–12; 13:1; *Midrash Shemot Rabbah* 51:5; *Midrash Eykhah Rabbah* 5:6). During the war years Amalek was perceived as present in the form of Hitler. Amalek-Hitler functioned as God's weapon to force the people of Israel back to their authentic selves, centered in Torah and Torah-of-the-land-of-Israel. Having no space among the nations, the people of Israel were de facto located in their own sacred space. While Amalek had no idea of this—nor could he—he served a positive purpose in God's metahistorical scheme.

Mosheh Avigdor Amiel offered a metahistorical explanation, which included historical factors, whereby the people of Israel failed to maintain the dividing line between themselves and the Gentile nations that kept the cold war begun at Sinai in check (see *Ein Ya'akov ad Shabbat* 89^b)—specifically, by compromising Torah with Mendelssohnian *Haskalah* and Herzlian Zionism. God responded furiously through Amalek-as-Hitler (see Ezekiel 20:32–33): "For over a hundred years our German brethren did everything possible to push Israel into the other side. What did this produce? Hitler."

Shlomoh Zalman Ehrenreich went a step further to explain how it was possible for the absolutely good God to employ the unconditionally evil Amalek. First, he pointed out, the use of Amalek did not blur the line between good and evil, so as to compromise either. Citing Levi Yitshak of

Berdichev's (1740–1809) *Kedushat Levi* (*Sanctification of Levi*) he explained that functioning as divine instrument was coincidental, in the sense that Amalek would have made Israel suffer anyway. Had Amalek's attack been solely a matter of divine instrumentalization, Amalek would have given Israel the opportunity to perform *Teshuvah* to avert the suffering. Second, the absolutely good God could use the evil Amalek because the use was not essential and enduring, but temporary. God would eventually destroy Amalek. Further, Levi Yitshak explained, Amalek's destruction would evoke recognition of God's name in the world, aligning his temporary evil function with the metaphysical goodness of God's universe—aligned to such an extent, indeed, that Amalek's destruction would fall into the category of sanctifying God's name (*Al kiddush Hashem*). Ehrenreich added that for Levi Yitshak this could happen because there was always some positive element, no matter how small, in the respective Amalek manifestation that served *Al kiddush Hashem*—for example, Pharaoh's recognition of Joseph. Ehrenreich did not attempt to locate any such element when it came to Hitler.[14]

After the war the positive instrumentality of Amalek disappeared. In its place, he sunk into a realm of dark being that confronted a realm of light in apocalyptic (Zoroastrianlike) combat. With the advent of redemption, light would fill the universe and the Amalek of darkness would be destroyed. In 1947 the religious Zionist Bentsiyon Firer, *Resh Mesivta* of the She'erit Yisrael yeshiva in Ulm outside of Munich, identified the Holocaust with the culmination of the collective history of the people of Israel. That collective history was essentially one of submitting the soul in life-risking self-sacrificial acts (*Mesirut nefesh*), which were required to maintain Torah in the face of Amalek. At this juncture in metahistory (with its historical dimension), Firer argued, there was nothing more important for the people of Israel to do than to hate Amalek absolutely and to blot out his memory. Amalek's destruction was inevitable, Firer assured—whereupon redemption would reveal itself. In 1946 in Shanghai, Simhah Elberg, a student of Warsaw's Hasidic Rebbe Natan Spigelglas who escaped Warsaw in 1939, wrote in *The Sacrificial Binding of Treblinka* (*Akaydas Yitshak*) that the Nazi Amalek, who built gas chambers for Jews while claiming to do so in God's name, would be obliterated when the chemicals that seeped through the Jewish corpses in the ground would explode.[15]

The metaphysical-level opposition between Israel and Amalek persisted in ultra-Orthodox thought and resurfaced in the 1990s. Yeshayah Shtaynberger, *Resh Mesivta* of Hakotel yeshiva in Jerusalem, explained that

Amalek met the criterion set down by Maimonides (*Commentary to the Mishnah. Perush Lamishnayot* and *Mishneh Torah-Hayad Hahazakah*) and Rashi (*ad* Esther 3:2) for idolatry: his conviction that no being stood higher than he. Amalek had to dominate everything around him (see *Midrash Bamidbar Rabbah* 13:3), Shtaynberger wrote, and launched a genocidal assault when anything stood in his way. Amalek-as-Hitler worshipped himself as a deity and construed a metaphysical superiority for Germany by invoking Teutonic myth. He was unconditionally evil, and as a (self-conceptualized) deity, certainly never acted (even self-deceptively) as an instrument of God. He set out to obliterate the Jews in particular, because he imagined they had an extraordinary ability to survive and that he could never dominate them. The obsession was so all-consuming that even self-destruction (notably the diversion of military resources) did not stand in Hitler-Amalek's way (see Rashi *ad* Deuteronomy 26:18).[16]

A similarly absolutistic picture was drawn by Yoel Shvarts of the Devar Yerushalayim yeshiva in Jerusalem. Hitler was the Amalek of the present, as evident from their identical characteristics: the original Amalek cast the phalli of Israelites up towards heaven and shouted to God, "Here is what You delight in [so take it]" (*Midrash Bereshit Rabbah* 13:3) and Hitler destroyed all signs of Jewish identity. Amalek was out to destroy the people of God and through and with them, the God of Israel (see *Midrash Shemot Rabbah* 51:5), and so was Hitler. Both were bastards (Rashi *ad* Genesis 36:12) and liars (B.T. *Megillah* 13b). Both attacked when the faith of the people was weak (B.T. *Sanhedrin* 106a). Finally, they both sensed that redemption was imminent, Amalek vis-à-vis the promised land and Hitler vis-à-vis a cosmic redemption—which, Shvarts pointed out, the Hofets Hayim (1838–1933) predicted would take place after World War I. The implications of Israel's redemption for Hitler's obliteration drove him to insane action (Shvarts cited Rabinowitch's *Holy Ones of Israel*).[17] Layb Minzberg, *Resh Mesivta* of the Hamatmidim yeshiva in Jerusalem, echoed Shtaynberger's point, saying that ever since Esau struggled with Jacob in their mother's womb, Esau-become-Amalek was out to overcome Israel— even at the cost of his self-destruction with the advent of redemption.[18]

Other thinkers rooted the absolute division in the moment of creation or in the era of redemption. In the 1980s Shalom Noah Brazovsky (the Admor of Slonim, Byelorussia), *Resh Mesivta* of the Beit Avraham yeshiva in Jerusalem, wrote that God implanted holiness-sanctity (*Kedushah*) and unholiness-profanity (*Tumah*) in the universe when He created it. Israel was the inevitable outcome for *Kedushah. Tumah* inevitably gave birth to

Hitler, the paradigmatic representative of the realm of evil being (*Sitra ahra*). "This terrible [Holocaust] was set down in the calendar of events from the very beginning." Citing Shabbetai Hapstein of Kozienice (early eighteenth century), Brazovsky explained that everything was planned in advance, beginning with the six days of creation and Adam's sin, and running through Israel's exile and suffering. Human choice was free, but its correspondence with outer reality belonged to advance divine planning. When it came to the (planned-in-advance) bad choices by Israel and angry divine responses, the anger was sometimes delayed. This was the case with the anger manifest in Nazi destruction—although Brazovsky did not cite the specific bad choice of Israel that originally set it off. For Brazovsky, Amalek's instrumental role in expressing divine anger in response to Israel's bad choices was rooted in the metaphysical dualism that belonged to creation.[19] Hayim Druckman, dean of the Etsiyon yeshiva in Jerusalem, brought this structure forward in 1990. God's creation, he explained, included the opposing forces of darkness (chaos, lies, and *Tumah*) and light (order, truth, and Messiah). They emerged in stages over the course of history. Darkness surfaced at Mount Sinai (see B.T. *Shabbat* 89a), presumably with Amalek, and in Babylon, Persia, Greece, and Rome (anticipated at creation by *Tohu, Bohu, Hoshekh,* and *Tehom,* as described in Genesis 1:2; see *Midrash Bereshit Rabbah* 2:5), and ultimately with Hitler. The light surfaced with the *Akedah* (binding for sacrifice of Isaac by Abraham), the Sinai revelation, acts of *Mesirut nefesh* in Jewish history, and acts of holiness within the catastrophe—for example, the outcry of Mosheh Friedman, the Boyaner Rav, who was killed at Auschwitz, that Germany would be destroyed before he recited the *Shema* ("Hear O Israel, the Lord our God, the Lord is One"). The end of history, the messianic redemption, would bring the original light to fullness and remove darkness from the universe.[20] As with Brazovsky, Hitler-Amalek belonged to a metaphysical reality set in place at creation—to the realm of *Tumah* opposed to *Kedushah*.

Others turned their eyes to the absolute dualism of the apocalyptic process. In the years following the war, Ya'akov Mosheh Harlap, *Resh Mesivta* (head) of the Merkaz Harav Kook yeshiva in Jerusalem, drew from the work of Eliyahu ben Shlomoh, Gaon of Vilna (eighteenth century) to understand the Holocaust. According to the Gaon of Vilna, the Messiah son of Joseph entered the world through vessels of darkness, lest his sudden blaze of light overwhelm the people of Israel. For Harlap, the apocalyptic drama was underway and the darkness was the Holocaust. A battle was taking place between unworthiness-guilt, (*kulo hayav*), which was a dark external phenomenon, and worthiness-innocence (*kulo zakai*), which was internal light—that is, between Amalek's heirs and the collective soul of Israel. Until this point, the nations of the world had the option of sharing in the realm of holiness, equivalent to existence itself, that Israel channeled into history. But instead they chose *Tumah*, for themselves, and also as something to impose upon the people of Israel. Following the motif of *The Holy Ones of Israel*, Harlap explained that with redemption getting close, and with it the sanctification of the universal that spelled death for the *Tumah* nations, the nations launched an all-out, insane attack upon Israel to stop the process. In doing so, they shut themselves off from any source for continuing their own existence.[21]

This eschatological dualism remained within the ultra-Orthodox universe of thought and expressed itself again in the 1990s. Hayim David Bakon, a Bobover Hasid in New York, detailed how, with the Holocaust, the universe moved through a preredemptive battle between satanic *Tumah* (in the form of *Kelipot*, shards of the vessels that shattered from vibrations of cosmic light at creation) and *Kedushah*. Within the battle, sparks of divine light penetrated into the darkness as individual acts of holiness (see Leviticus 26:44).[22] Moshe Blaykher, *Resh Mesivta* (head) of Shevi Hevron yeshiva in Hebron, spoke of Hitler's bringing the ongoing metaphysical antagonism between the realms of divine eternity-morality (as crystallized by the Jewish people) and of the hatred thereof (by the Gentile nations) to a climax. Hitler found it impossible to be on the same planet as Israel, and sensing the imminence of redemption and the potentially permanent, primary status of Israel, he attacked them without control.[23]

While the Holocaust unfolded, ultra-Orthodox thinkers held to the God of metahistory and the attackers remained under His control. Once the Holocaust became a fait accompli and was processed by their consciousnesses, Amalek assumed independent metaphysical being. Instead of confronting the reality of the Holocaust vis-à-vis divine control in metahistory, they moved Amalek into a metaphysical realm beyond metahistory and of the apocalypse. No longer under God, emptied of any possible bit of sanctification, Amalek would not be absolutely destroyed.

Suffering and Sacrifice

During the war, suffering was understood as a process, either metahistorical (with historical ramifications) or existential, or both combined.

The Rav of Lubavitch, Yosef Yitshak Schneersohn, then of Brooklyn, expounded upon the metahistorical theme that Israel's exile was intended by God to bring *Teshuvah* (penitent return) but that sin increased instead and God responded with incremental punishment. The sin, however, did not stop, and God finally enclosed the people of Israel between two existential choices—*Teshuvah* or death (which would be the Holocaust). Those who chose *Teshuvah* and joined the eschatological community known as *Mahaneh Yisrael*, would share in redemption—and there had to be some who did so choose because redemption was inevitable and *Teshuvah* bearers were an indispensable condition of it. All other Jews (along with the entire Gentile world, less those who adhered to the seven Noahide laws) were doomed. In Jerusalem, the *Musar* (moralistic) movement leader Yehezkel Sarna spoke of a metahistorical interrelationship of metaphysical proportions among suffering-into-annihilation (*Hurban*), *Teshuvah,* and redemption (*Geulah*). Composing a triad, each implied the other: the telos of *Hurban* was *Teshuvah* while *Teshuvah*'s telos was *Geulah.* Each individual had to find his/her existential position in the triad, in terms of performing *Teshuvah.* In the Warsaw ghetto, the process of suffering assumed an existential form, one without metahistorical context. The Piaseczner Rebbe Kalonymous Kalman Shapira concentrated on individual suffering, and held that if the believer could transcend finite limits and touch the infinite suffering of God, suffering could be diminished in the here and now and absorbed into the infinite suffering of God.[24]

After the war the suffering process was crystallized into suffering as a fait accompli and became identified with the *Akedah* (the binding of Isaac) on Mount Moriah combined with actual sacrificial death (see *Midrash Vayikra Rabbah* 36:5 and *Mekhilta Bo: Parashah* 7). In the immediate aftermath, Bentsiyon Firer in Ulm identified the Holocaust totality as an *Akedah.* He blended the two into a metahistorical entity, a collective sacrifice that ended the thread of *Mesirut nefesh* that ran through Israel's existence over the centuries. The *Akedah* was simultaneously the birth pangs of the Messiah (*Hevlei mashiah*) and the "colossal outflow of blood" that came with birth. In 1946 in Shanghai, Simhah Elberg transformed the *Akedah* from a metahistorical entity into a metaphysical one. He held that the mass death of Treblinka (paradigm for the death camps) was a massive *Akedah* that stood at the final end to the line of *Akedah* after *Akedah* in Jewish history, beginning with Mount Moriah. The essence of binding-into-sacrifice trailed Israel's movement through time. A poet as well as a religious thinker, Elberg wrote that Mount Moriah moved with the people of Israel from land to land until it ended up in the death camp. There, in Treblinka, the *Shema* broke forth from the flames of death, ascended, and split the heavens open. This *Akedah* was the ultimate and purest one, necessarily carried out by Israel's holiest Jews, those of Poland and Lithuania. It sanctified all of Israel's existence—leaving the rest of the universe, its history irretrievably polluted, to plunge into oblivion. With history destroyed, it remained for God to create an entirely new universe through Torah.[25]

Yehoshua Grinvald coalesced the events of Sinai and Auschwitz into a single metahistorical reality. Grinvald, a disciple of the Rav of Belz Aharon Rokeah, survived Auschwitz, Mauthausen, and Ebensee. When he reached Paris in 1945, he said he felt he belonged to the legacy of Abraham and Isaac, having experienced the *Akedah* of Mount Moriah in the camps. The slaughter there was a precious sacrifice. Its smoke was sweet to God (see Genesis 8:21 and B.T. *Yoma* 19b), as was the aromatic smoke that wafted from the fiery furnace into which Abraham was cast by Nimrod (*Midrash Bereshit Rabbah* 38:13) as well as from the furnace into which Hananiah, Mikhael, and Azariah were thrown (*Midrash Bereshit Rabbah* 34:9). In a rabbinical responsum written a year and a half later in Brooklyn, citing Hayim Yitshak (the Or Zarua), Mosheh Schreiber, and the Hatam Sofer, Grinvald made the point that all those who were sacrificed were holy, for they were killed because they were Jewish. In 1948 in *Weeping Eye* he condensed the moments of *Akedah* in Israel's history into the Sinai event and blended Auschwitz and Sinai into one another. At Sinai, flashes of fire sent forth the holy words of God. At Auschwitz, the *Shema* burst forth from the flames of the ovens. But this time, he added, redemption appeared on the horizon. These *Akedah* sufferings atoned for the trespasses of those who were sacrificed and constituted the *Hevlei mashiah* of the onset of redemption (*Ikvetah dimeshihah*).[26]

Ya'akov Mosheh Harlap spoke of the individual *Akedah,* in the context of the Gaon of Vilna's apocalyptic drama. The murder of each Jew shattered the body, while the soul ascended to God in love (see B.T. *Berakhot* 54a). Each was a point of light that entered into the inner light of the Messiah son of Joseph, and passed into the universal light of the Messiah son of David. The soul of each murdered Jew broke out of empirical historical reality, filled with the evil, other side to being (*Sitra ahra*), and passed into the transcending reality of redemption. For Harlap, each individual was also an actualization of the *Akedah,* participating in the redemption while enhancing it. He cited the rabbinic sages' view that Israel would be redeemed by the merit of Isaac (B.T. *Shabbat* 89b).[27]

Two decades later, the theologian Eliezer Berkovits, then in Chicago, spoke of the *Akedah* in terms of *Emunah* (trusting faith). God's "face" and His covenant were hidden during the Holocaust. This created an opportunity for *Emunah* of the level of Abraham's at the *Akedah*: "In this situation I do not understand You. Your behavior violates our covenant. Still, I trust You because it is You, because it is You and we, because it is us." The acts of pious observance and *Mesirut nefesh* during the Holocaust implemented Abraham's *Emunah* (faith). They were mitzvot, enactments of divine commandments, that remained suspended in metahistory, enduring after the death of the one who bore them, as history-as-Holocaust plunged into the depths of oblivion. When the Jewish state was created, history rose from oblivion to touch the mitzvah retained in metahistory.[28]

Other thinkers embedded the *Akedah* in a dialectical relationship between ashes of death and sanctified life. In the 1980s Shalom Noah Brazovsky channeled the *Akedah* and its impact into holiness instilled within history. All the Jews who were killed—whether willingly and lovingly or simply because they were Jews—were joined in death in the most sublime expression of sanctification of God's name (he cited Avraham ben Shmuel of Slonim, d. 1933). Brazovsky identified the deaths of the Holocaust as a collective *Akedah*. The sanctification of God's name that it brought about uplifted creation itself. Their *Kedushah* (holiness) displaced the *Tumah* (impurity) of the universe; it mended the cosmos (*Tikkun*) and prepared the world for redemption. The catastrophe, that is, constituted the onset of the Messiah (*Ikveta dimeshihah*). Further, the *Akedah* was responsible for the present postwar revival of Torah study and mitzvah observance: "Every spiritual event contains something of eternity which is not lost. How much more so with such a great *Akedah*. Each holy one [who was killed] left holiness in the world after him."[29]

Eliyahu Karlebakh of Newark, New Jersey, the son of Naftali Karlebakh and brother of Shlomo Karlebakh, like Hayim Bakon a Bobover Hasid, drew the same thread of *Akedah* through Jewish history as did Yehoshua Grinvald. The *Akedah* and the sanctification of God's name into death (*Kiddush Hashem*) ran from Abraham, who was cast into the fire by Nimrod (*Midrash Bereshit Rabbah* 38:13), sanctified, and transformed into a spiritual essence; through Isaac, whose ashes were spread across the altar (see *Midrash Vayikra Rabbah* 36:5 and *Mekhilta Bo: Parashah 7*); through the Ba'al Shem Tov, whose life of *Mesirut nefesh* ended with a holy fire from heaven that sent holy sparks across the universe; through sanctification of self and sanctification of God's name at Auschwitz. The reality of the holiness of the ashes was borne out, Karlebakh added, by the fact that Auschwitz, Maidanek, and Treblinka were near, respectively, the homes of the Hasidic dynasties of Kotsk in Kock, Alexander in Aleksandrow-Lodzki, and Tsants in Nowy Sacz. To Karlebakh, the ashes of Isaac blended with the ashes of the death camp into a single metaphysical essence, and this essence constituted the *Hevlei mashiah*. As did Harlap, he observed that the rabbinic sages anticipated that the world would be redeemed by the merit of Isaac (B.T. *Shabbat* 89b).[30] Elazar Menahem Man Shakh, Resh Mesivta (head) of the Panevezys yeshiva in Benei Berak, described how Jews who were entering the gas chambers to be killed suddenly remembered that it was the holiday of *Simhat Torah*. Metahistorical reality dominated empirical existence for them, and in accordance with the holiday they were obligated to rejoice. So they broke out and sang, and they danced with God who was present. In this way their deaths were transformed into acts of *Mesirut nefesh* in sanctifying God's name, and their lives coalesced with life in the world to come. Shakh concluded, "Is this to be called death? This is life!"[31]

During the war, suffering belonged to a process. As such it could conceivably be affected and conceivably diminished. Ultra-Orthodox thinkers conceived of doing so through *Teshuvah*, which functioned above and below simultaneously, or through self-transcendence into God's infinitude. After the war, the suffering now complete, ultra-Orthodox consciousness processed it into the objective reality of the *Akedah*. As an *Akedah*, it became the outflow of blood of the birth process of redemption (Firer) or fulfillment of Israel's metaphysical *Akedah*-essence as a victim of persecution (Elberg). For Grinvald, the *Akedah* of the Holocaust belonged to the holy fires of Israel's history, from the furnaces of biblical times to the flames of Mount Sinai. Harlap spoke of the individual *Akedah* where the soul entered the stream of the Messiah's light. Brazovsky and Karlebakh blended the ashes of *Akedah* with holiness. By conceiving the reality of mass death as the *Akedah*, these thinkers were able to immerse it in sanctity, blend it into the sacred metahistory of Israel, and attribute to it a redemptive dimension.

Messianic Redemption

Messianic thinking during the war included the element of human effort. There were two overall types. In one, historical activity was the path to messianic redemption, and messianic redemption entered into time. Beginning with Yitshak Nissenbaum's 1939 writings in Warsaw, Mizrahi thinkers held that the restoration of the land of Israel in terms of Torah would enable redemption to unfold, and that redemption would be contiguous with the restoration. According to the Agudat Yisrael view, which followed upon the 1939–1940 writings of Hayim Ozer Grodzensky, the head of the Va'ad Hayeshivot in Vilnius, the Torah (according to its esoteric meaning) had to be revived in study and practice on a universal basis. Once this took place redemption would come about, a redemption contiguous with Torah-life in history. In the other type, there were parallel movements underway in empirical historical activity below and in metaphysical dynamics above (both intertwining with metahistory). As catastrophe became transformed into redemption above, the people of Israel reverberated from, and contributed to, the higher drama by pious activity below. For Yosef Yitshak Schneersohn of Habad and Yehezkel Sarna of Musar, Holocaust, redemption, and *Teshuvah* interrelated in a tripartite dialectic above. Each Jew was impelled by the metahistorical process to participate in the process from below, primarily through internal and external acts of *Teshuvah*.[32]

After the war, Holocaust-inspired messianism assumed new emphases. The first was that of internal Torah (Kabbalah). In Jerusalem, Yehudah Ashlag maintained that neglect of the authentic, internal Torah precipitated the Holocaust. Restoration of internal knowledge would mean both recession of catastrophe and the advent of redemption—which included the sublimation of historical (empirical) reality into the messianic realm. He himself started to contribute to the process by publishing the *Sulam*, making the *Zohar* accessible in Hebrew translation with explanation, already in 1943.[33] In 1963–1964 Mordekhai Atiyah brought attention to the fact that the (mythical) author of the *Zohar*, Shimon bar Yohai (second century), attacked teachers who divided kabbalistic wisdom from the written and oral Torah and insisted that Torah's meaning was exoteric and not esoteric. These teachers stopped the flow of divine wisdom into the world. This left the world "dry," i.e., impoverished, abandoned to slaughter, plunder, and murder—in sum, to the chaos that reigned before creation. It would have been better, he added, had such teachers never even existed. It was because of the dry universe that the Messiah abandoned the world, and with no intention of returning (see "Tikkun 30" and "Tikkun 40" in *Tikkunei Hazohar*). Atiyah also cited the eighteenth-century kabbalist Shalom Buzaglo, who asserted that pious scholars had to study Kabbalah and deserved punishment if they did not. One hour of Kabbalah study was worth an entire month of exoteric study (Buzaglo, *Kise Melekh ad* "Tikkun 30" in *Tikkunei Hazohar*). Atiyah was convinced that Israel's suffering would be replaced by messianic redemption if, and only if, the people gathered in the land of Israel and studied Kabbalah. God Himself, as Hayim Vital pointed out, would support the endeavor.[34] In 2001 Meir Yannai of Jerusalem wrote that the absence of the study of Kabbalah before World War II had left the universe a mass of *Kelippot,* pieces of broken vessels that once were whole and held the primordial light (*Shevirat hakelim*). God's presence as light (*Shekhinah*) was replaced by darkness and harsh judgment (*Din*), and the unity of God, Israel, and Torah (*Zohar: Aharei mot* 73ᵃ) was broken. There was no longer any distinction between good and evil. This was the catastrophe of the Holocaust.[35]

Some thinkers centered their explanation of the Holocaust and redemption on knowing one particular idea of Kabbalah as a key to the Holocaust—the doctrine of transmigration of souls. In 1947 Hayim Yisrael Tsimerman, citing Hayim Vital, explained that the Holocaust was a process of purifying sinners of earlier generations. Those who sinned in Noah's generation were purified immediately by their physical obliteration. Those who stoned the prophet Zechariah (II Chronicles 24:20) were not. They were reincarnated to be purified during the destruction of the Second Temple. Tsimerman, observing the dramatic Jewish population growth over the last century, concluded that a massive reincarnation of sinners of earlier generations was underway, brought back to be purified by the Holocaust. Elazar Menahem Shakh brought this interpretation forward in 1990.[36]

A second element was that of a messianic advent empty of human effort. Yehoshua Grinvald held that redemption was appearing of itself on the horizon, simultaneously with the flames and the *Shema* ("Hear O Israel" prayer) at Auschwitz, which were joined to the flames and holy words of Sinai. Menahem Mendel Schneersohn, the Rav of Lubavitch, was also led to the extrahuman dynamic. In 1941, representatives of Habad's *Mahaneh Yisrael* had declared that the people of Israel were standing before redemption, but because the required *Teshuvah* had not taken place, they faced a choice of *Teshuvah* or the extreme punishment of death, and in 1972 Menahem Mendel Schneersohn wrote that God had in fact proceeded with the punishment. Acting as a surgeon, God removed the diseased part of the body so the rest could recover and the soul could enter redemption. When he was challenged by the Socialist-Zionist Hayka

Grossman (Mapam member of the Kenesset), he wrote her that "with regard to the metaphor (*Dugmah*) that I chose, I never heard anyone claim that when surgery was performed on a sick person it was a punishment. To the contrary, it was for the patient's good"—adding that the scalpel (Hitler) was a tool of the surgeon (God) and no more (see Jeremiah 25:9). But then Schneersohn switched and acknowledged that no *Tikkun* could ever justify the suffering of the Holocaust. In the end, the tragedy had to be seen in terms of a higher dialectic between death and life, between catastrophe and redemption, which unfolded independently of human action. He wrote as follows:

> As to the "task" of Hitler, may his name be erased: What I said [in 1972] was nothing new. It was drawn from the light of Torah. Of the *Hurban* of the First Temple, with its murder, cruelty and exile, Jeremiah said, "Behold, I will send and take all the families of the north, saith the Lord, and Nebuchadnezzar, the king of Babylon, My servant, and will bring them against this land, and against the inhabitants thereof" [Jeremiah 25:9]. Regarding Assyria, Isaiah said, "O Assyria, the rod of Mine anger, and the staff in their hand is Mine indignation" [Isaiah 10:5]. Still, there is a difference between the situation then and that of our own generation. Then it was a matter of punishment after several warnings. Now it is a matter of surgery and *Tikkun*. The *Tikkun*, I emphasize, is intended to mend the patient. True, the suffering is out of proportion to the *Tikkun*. But there is life and there is its opposite. As stated in Rambam's *Thirteen Articles,* it is a principle of our faith to believe unequivocally that the dead will be resurrected [in the redemption].

The transhistorical motif to suffering and redemption also appeared in his 1991 statements that the painful suffering could not be justified even by the sins of Satan, and that it desecrated the victims to think that it could. Instead, drawing from Maimonides and Hayim Yitshak (the Or Zarua), he wrote that insofar as the victims were murdered because they were Jews, they died in sanctification of God's name and *Kaddish* was to be recited for them whether or not they were observant.[37] In the 1990s Hayim Druckman (Jerusalem) and Mosheh Blaykher (Hebron) identified the Holocaust as the ultimate, metaphysical confrontation between *Tumah* (focused in Hitler) and *Kedushah* (concentrated in Israel), which would terminate in redemption—as reflected by holy acts within the catastrophe. The dynamic took place in and of itself.[38]

The messianism of the wartime period included the element of human and historical participation. For some this was a matter of building the land of Israel in Torah, for others, the life of Torah on a universal basis. Others paired that activity with parallel processes taking place supernaturally. After the war, the disaster having taken place, messianism was shifted into ahistorical realms. For some, it was shifted into the internal wisdom of the Kabbalah. Secret knowledge, disconnected from empirical time and space, became the source, basis, and means to the messianic reality. Or human effort was separated out of redemption.

Concluding Note

While ultra-Orthodox thinkers after the war continued to use the metahistorical, mythical, metaphysical, and empirical language of their wartime predecessors, there were distinctive characteristics: radicalized dualism, lessening of human power, and apocalypticism. They may be seen as responses to the fact that the Holocaust was now an objective reality. It became circumscribed as an event of the past and positioned as an object of consciousness. Postwar thinkers moved secular Zionism into the realm of Israel's antagonists, because once the disaster became known in its extremity, the guild of those responsible (the secular Zionists) grew proportionally extreme. Religious nationalists faced the fact that the Holocaust took place and return and restoration had begun. They removed the temporal and spatial differences among overseeing God, the nations that acted at His direction, and the response by the people of Israel and spoke of the realities of the Holocaust (specifically God's "surgical" act and His letting the weak generation die) and of the land and state of Israel affecting one another immediately and directly. After the war the factors of a Gnosticlike division of wisdom and guilt of the pious were added to the attack upon assimilation. The reality of the Holocaust left a radical division between the sacred and the profane, leaving no neutral ground—not even in the realm of ideas or in terms of piety. With the Holocaust before them, the concept of Amalek being of service to God's metahistory became impossible. To accommodate the reality, i.e., Amalek's evil, ultra-Orthodox thinkers changed the subject away from metahistory and to the apocalypse—where Amalek became uncontrolled evil—and was doomed for destruction upon the advent of redemption. When it came to the matter of suffering, once the reality was clear, the wartime idea that pious behavior could have an effect became impossible. The suffering took place, and there was nothing left to prevent. So it was transformed in religious thought into the actual sacrifice of Isaac, with its implications for redemption. Finally, wartime conceptions of humanly generated messianic redemption were transformed to the extent that internal knowledge (Kabbalah) and elements of transhistorical redemption entered in. When redemption did not follow the Holocaust, the aspect of human effort in history was to some extent marginalized and attention drawn to ahistorical contexts.

NOTES

1. See Gershon Greenberg, "Elhanan Wasserman's Response to the Growing Catastrophe in Europe," *Journal of Jewish Thought and Philosophy,* vol. 10 (2000), 171–204; "Sovereignty as Catastrophe: Jakob Rosenheim's *Hurban Weltanschauung,*" *Holocaust and Genocide Studies,* vol. 8, no. 2 (July 1994), 202–24; "The Religious Response of Shlomoh Zalman Ehrenreich (Simleul-Silvaniei, Transylvania) to the Holocaust, 1940–1943," *Studia Judaica,* vol. 9 (2000), 65–93; "Mosheh Avigdor Amiel's Religious Response to the Holocaust," *Eleventh World Congress of Judaic Studies* (Jerusalem, 1994), 93–100.

2. Yoel Taytlboym, "Hakdamah" and "Ma'amar Shalosh Shevuot," in *Vayoel Mosheh* (Brooklyn, 2000), 5–18 and sections 81–82, 88, 110–11, 139; and *Kuntres al Hageulah Ve'al Hatemurah* (Brooklyn, 1981), 12, 17–18, 79, 85. See Shlomoh Hayim Aviner, "Berurim Be'inyan Shelo Ya'alu Kehomah," *Noam,* vol. 20 (1977/78), 208–31. On Taytlboym see Yitshak Kroyz, "Shnayim Shelo Yelkhu Yahad-Mishnato Haradekalit Shel R. Yoel Taytlboym-Ha'admor Misatmar," *Hatsiyonut,* no. 22 (2000), 37–60; Aviezer Ravitsky, "Facing the End: Radical Anti-Zionism," in *Messianic Zionism and Jewish Religious Radicalism* (Chicago, 1996), 40–78; Amos Funkenstein, "Theological Interpretations of the Holocaust: A Balance," in *Unanswered Questions: Nazi Germany and the Genocide of the Jews,* ed. Francois Furet (New York, 1989), 275–303; and Allan Nadler, "Piety and Politics: The Case of the Satmar Rebbe," *Judaism,* vol. 31, no. 2 (Spring 1982), 135–52.

3. Shemuel Yaffe Ashkenazi, "Beur Lemidrash Shir Hashirim 8:11–13," in *Yefeh Kol Limegilat Shir Hashirim* (Jerusalem, 1989 edition), 187a. Mosheh Hagiz, *Sefat Emet* (Vilna, 1775/76 edition), 10a, 44a; Hayim Vital, *Sha'ar Hakavanot* 53 col. 4 as cited by Atiyah in *Sod Hashevuah.* Hayim Vital, *Olat Tamid* (Jerusalem, 1996/97 edition), 4 col. 2. Efrayim Luntshits, "Leviticus 18:13," in *Keli Yakar: Beur Al Hatorah* (Jerusalem, 1987/88 edition). Shalom Buzaglo, "Emor," in *Mikdash Melekh* (Benei Berak, 1973 edition), 93b. Mordekhai Atiyah, *Sod Hashevuah* (Jerusalem, 1963/64).

4. Benyamin Mendelssohn in *Diglenu* as cited by Dina Porat, "Amalek's Ac-

complices," *Journal of Contemporary History,* vol. 27, no. 4 (1992), 695–735. Avraham Yeshayah Roth, *Sha'arei Aharon* (Benei Berak, 1981/82), Elazar Halevi Shulzinger, "Mikhtav Gilui," in *Al Mishkenot Haro'im* (Benei Berak, 1987/88), 155–60. See also Mosheh Shonfeld, *The Holocaust Victims Accuse,* vol. 1 (New York, 1977); Mikhael Dov Weissmandel, *Min Hametsar* (New York, 1960); and Yehezkel Salmon, "Teshuvot Hatsiyonut Lashoah," in *Shoah Mishamayim* (Erets Yisrael: 1998). See further Menahem Friedman, "Medinat Yisrael Kedilemah Datit," *Alpayim,* vol. 3 (1990), 24–68 and "The Haredim and the Holocaust," *Jerusalem Quarterly,* vol. 53 (Winter 1991), 86–114.

5. See Pessah Schindler, "Tikkun as a Response to Tragedy: 'Em Habanim Semeha' of Rabbi Yissakhar Shlomoh Taykhtahl—Budapest 1943," *Holocaust and Genocide Studies,* vol. 4, no. 4 (1989), 413–33. Shlomoh Zalman Shragai, *Tehumim* (Jerusalem, 1951) and *Tahalikhei Hatemurah Vehageulah* (Jerusalem, 1958/59).

6. Hayim Yisrael Tsimerman, *Tamim Pa'alo* (Tel Aviv, 1947). See Gershon Greenberg, "Tamim Pa'alo: Tsimerman's Absolutistic Explanation of the Holocaust," in *In God's Name: Religion and Genocide in the Twentieth Century,* ed. Omer Bartov and Phyllis Mack (Oxford, 2001), 316–41.

7. Hayim Ibn Attar, "Leviticus 25:25," in *Or Hahayim* (Jerusalem, 1988/89 edition), 111. Mordekhai Atiyah, *Mahashavot Shalom* (Jerusalem, 1948), 19–20.

8. Yehudah Halevi, *Kuzari* 2:44. Aharon Petshenik, "Onesh, Segulah Veyi'ud," *Or Hamizrah,* vol. 3, nos. 3–4 (August–September 1957), 61–66.

9. Eliahu Botschko, *Der Born Israels,* vol. 1 (Montreux, 1944), 19–20. Efrayim Sokolover, *Penei Efrayim* (Tel Aviv, 1965/66), 114–19. Yehudah Halevi, *Kuzari* 2:44. Zadok Rabinowitz, *Yisrael Kedoshim* (Benei Berak, 1966/67 edition), 48. Hermann Rauschning, *Hitler M'a Dit* (Paris, 1945), 269. Tsevi Yehudah Kook, "Hashoah," in *Sihot Harav Tsevi Yehudah Asarah Betevet Hashoah* (Jerusalem, 198[?]) and *Linetivot Yisrael* (Jerusalem, 1966/67): 35–37, 47, 53, 60, 64, 74–75. See Dov Shvarts, "Seder Lenisim Veseder Ligeulah: Motivim Meshihi'im Bemishnat Harav Tsevi Yehudah Kook," in *Etgar Umashber Behug Harav Kook* (Tel Aviv, 2001), 15–138.

10. Yehudah Halevi, *Kuzari* 2:24. Ya'akov Emden, "Hakdamah: Sulam Beit El," in *Siddur Beit Ya'akov* (Lemberg, 1904 edition), 13. Eliyahu ben Shlomoh, Gaon of Vilna, according to Hillel Mishklov in *Kol Hator* as cited by Menahem Kasher, *Hatekufah Hegeulah,* vol. 1 (Jerusalem, 1968), 535. Mosheh Hayim Luzzatto, *Ma'amar Hageulah* (Jerusalem, 1997/98 edition), 108–11. Uri Sharki, *Shoah Veshe'elah: Le'asarah Betevet Yom Hakadish Hakelali* (Jerusalem, 1998/99).

11. See Gershon Greenberg, "Shlomoh Zalman Unsdorfer, Disciple of the Hatam Sofer: With God through the Holocaust," *Yad Vashem Studies,* vol. 31 (2003), 61–94; "Ontic Division and Religious Survival: Wartime Palestinian Orthodoxy and the Holocaust (*Hurban*)," *Modern Judaism,* vol. 14, no. 1 (1994), 21–61; "Wartime American Mizrahi and Agudat Yisrael Religious Responses to the Holocaust," *Mikhael,* vol. 15 (1999), 102–38; and "Holocaust and Musar for the Telsiai Yeshivah: Avraham Yitshak Bloch and Eliyahu Meir Bloch," in *The Vanished*

World of Lithuanian Jews, ed. Stefan Schreiner, Darius Staliunas, and Alvydas Nikzentaitis (New York, 2004), 211–67.

12. Yosef bar Hayim Jabez, *Or Hahayim* (Lublin, 1911/12 edition), 4a–4b, 40a. Yair Hayim Bacharach, "Siman 219," in *She'elot Uteshuvot Havat Yair,* vol. 2 (Ramat Gan, 1996/97 edition), 623. Eleazar Loew, *Shev Shema'atata: Derush Sha'arei Yirah. Derush Revi'i* as cited in Akiva Joseph Schlesinger, *Lev Ha'ivri,* vol. 2 (Jerusalem, 1989/90), 29–30. Yisrael Meir Hakohen, *Beit Yisrael* (New York, 1934 edition), 39–40. Tsevi Elimelekh Shapira of Dynow, "Mayan Ganim," in *Or Hahayim* (Lemberg, 1874 edition), 2. Barukh Dov Laybowitch, "Siman 27," in *Birkat Shemuel,* vol. 1 (New York, 1946/47). Moshe Isserles, "Siman 246," in *Darkhei Mosheh: Mitur Yoreh Deah* (Sulzbach, 1692 edition), 85. Avraham Weinfeld, "Ma'amar Be'inyan Hovat Hahitbolelut Bemashma'ut Hurban Yahadut Eiropah," in Yosef Ben Hayim Jabez, *Or Hahayim* (Monsey, NY, 1953).

13. Hayim Yisrael Tsimerman, *Tamim Pa'alo* (Tel Aviv, 1947).

14. See Gershon Greenberg, "The Amalek of the Holocaust," in *Nuremberg Revisited: Bioethical and Ethical Issues,* ed. Jacques Rozenberg (New York, 2003), 120–48; and "Amalek in the Era of the Holocaust: Orthodox Jewish Thought," in *Eliezer Schweid Festschrift,* ed. Aviezer Ravitsky and Yehoyada Amir (Jerusalem, 2004) [Hebrew].

15. See Greenberg, "The Amalek of the Holocaust."

16. Maimonides, "Hayesod Hahamishi," in "Hakdamah Leperek Helek Sanhedrin," in *Mishnah Im Perush Harambam* (Jerusalem, 1969/70 edition) and "Hilkhot Avodat Kokhavim Umazalot Vehukot Ha'akum," in *Mishneh Torah* (New York, 1975 edition), ch. 1, Halakah 1 and Halakah 2. Yeshayah Shtaynberger, "Hashoah Vetarbut Meholelehah: Hatakdim Ha'ameleki Lenatsizm Hagermani," *Shanah Beshanah* (1992/93), 393–404.

17. Yoel Shvarts, *Zakhor* (Jerusalem, 1992/93).

18. Layb Minzberg, "Milhamah Lashem Be'amalek," *Torati Bekirvam,* vol. 8 (February–March 2002), 12–20.

19. Yisrael ben Shabbetai Hakohen Hapstein of Kozienice, "Gam Zeh Shayakh Lo: Be'er Revi'i," in *Yehudah Layb Betsalel Be'er Hagolah* (Jerusalem, 1970/71 edition), 154 and "Parashat Beshallah," in *Nezer Yisrael* (Yoseffof, 1870 edition), 3a. Shalom Noah Brazovsky, *Kuntres Hahareigah Alekhah* (Jerusalem, 1987/88) and *Ma'amar Galut Vegeulah,* in *Netivot Shalom,* vol. 2 (Jerusalem, 1982), 305–10.

20. Hayim Druckman, "Hashoah: Bitui Si Lenetsah Yisrael," *Iturei Kohanim* 58 (December 1989–January 1990), 11–15. On Friedman see Esther Mark, "Arba Teudot Mi'auschwitz-Birkenau," *Galed,* vol. 1 (1973), 309–32.

21. Eliyahu ben Shlomoh, "Beur," in *Tikunei Hazohar: Im Tikunim Mizohar Hadash* (Vilna, 1867 edition), 27[a] and *Beur Lesifra Ditseniuta* (Vilna, 1820/21 edition), ch. 5. Hillel Mishklov, "Tikkun Het Hameraglim," in *Kol Hator: Pirkei Geulah Me'et Hagaon Hamekubal R. Hillel Mishklov . . . Bo Hazon Nifla Shel Rabo Ha'gra* in Menaḥem M. Kasher, *Hatekufah Hagedolah,* vol. 1 (Jerusalem, 1968),

534 ff. Ya'akov Mosheh Harlap, *Mei Marom: Mima'ayenei Hayeshuah,* vol. 6 (Jerusalem, 1981/82) and "Le'et Dodim," *Sinai,* vol. 11, nos. 4–5 (December 1947–January 1948), 126–38.

22. Hayim David Bakon, *Shtraln in der Finsternish* (Brooklyn, 1990).

23. Mosheh Blaykher, "Hashoah," in *Megillot Litekumah* (Hebron, 1996), 8–13.

24. See Gershon Greenberg, "A Musar Response to the Holocaust: Yehezkel Sarna's *Liteshuva Velitekumah* of 4 December 1944," *Journal of Jewish Thought and Philosophy,* vol. 7, no. 1 (December 1997), 101–37; "Redemption after Holocaust according to Mahaneh Yisrael-Lubavitch, 1940–1945," *Modern Judaism,* vol. 12, no. 1 (February 1992), 61–84; and Nehemiah Polen, *The Holy Fire: The Teachings of Rabbi Kalonymus Kalman Shapira, the Rebbe of the Warsaw Ghetto* (Northvale, NJ, 1994).

25. Simhah Elberg, *Akeydas Treblinka* (Shanghai, 1946) and "Hagaon Harav Natan Spigelglas," in *Sefer Einei Ha'edah* (Brooklyn, 1996), 355–435.

26. Hayim Yitshak Or Zarua, "Mispar 14," in *She'elot Uteshuvot Maharah Or Zarua* (Jerusalem, 1974/75 edition), 7. Mosheh Schreiber, "Siman 333," in *She'elot Uteshuvot: Helek Yoreh Deah,* vol. 2 (Jerusalem, 1999/2000 edition), 486. See "a person to whom God has awarded the merit of rising to the great level of being killed in sanctification of God's name had a place in the world to come, even if the person's sins were like those of Jeroboam ben Nebat and his colleagues." Maimonides, "Hamin Hashlishi," in *Igeret Hashemad* in *Igrot Harambam,* vol. 1 (Jerusalem, 1987 edition), 51. See also Yekutiel Yehudah Taytlboym, *Yitav Panim,* vol. 1 (Brooklyn, 1962/63 edition), 108[a]. Dov Rapaport, "Hakdamah," in Yehoshua Grinvald, *Kuntres Ein Dimah* (Brooklyn, 1990), 1–29. Yehoshua Grinvald, "Ein Dimah" and "Al Devar Ha'efer," in *She'elot Uteshuvot Hesed Yehoshua* (New York, 1948), 5–20, 9a–9b.

27. Ya'akov Mosheh Harlap, *Mei Marom: Mima'ayenei Hayeshua,* vol. 6 (Jerusalem: 1981/82); "Le'et Dodim," *Sinai,* vol. 11, nos. 4–5 (December 1947–January 1948), 126–38; "Ayom hu matsavam shel Yisrael [undated]" (Letter 249); "Nahamu nahamu ami [October 1946]" (Letter 138); and Barukh Duvdevani's letter from St. Caesarea to Harlap of 12 September 1946, in Beit Zevul Archives, Jerusalem. See also Gershon Greenberg, "The Holocaust Apocalypse of Ya'akov Mosheh Harlap," *Jewish Studies,* vol. 41 (2002), 5–14.

28. Eliezer Berkovits, *Faith after the Holocaust* (New York, 1973) and *With God in Hell* (New York, 1979).

29. Avraham ben Shemuel of Slonim, "Behar," in *Beit Avraham* (Jerusalem, 1968/69), 143–44. Shalom Noah Brazovsky, "Besha'ar Hasefer," in *Beit Avraham* (Jerusalem, 1968/69), i–vii; "Ma'amar Galut Vegeulah," in *Netivot Shalom,* vol. 2 (Jerusalem, 1982) 305–10 and *Kuntres Hahareigah Alekhah* (Jerusalem, 1987/88).

30. Eliyahu Hayim Karlebakh, *Kuntres Hevlei Mashiah* (Hillside, NY, 198[?]).

31. Elazar Menahem Man Shakh, "Hayim Shel Mesirut Nefesh-Rikud Im Hakadosh Barukh Hu Beta'ei Hagazim," in *Bezot Ani Boteah* (Benei Berak, 1997/98), 34–38.

32. See Gershon Greenberg, "A Musar Response to the Holocaust: Yehezkel Sarna's *Liteshuvah Velitekumah* of 4 December 1944," and "Redemption after Holocaust according to Mahaneh Yisrael-Lubavitch, 1940–1945," *Modern Judaism,* vol. 12, no. 1 (1992), 61–84.

33. Yehudah Ashlag, *Sefer Hazohar: Al Hamishah Humshei Torah Mehatana Rabi Shimon ben Yohai. Im Perush Derekh Emet Ve'im Habeurim . . . Hasulam,* 10 vols. (Jerusalem, 1964); "Hakdamah Lesefer Hazohar," in *Sefer Hahakdamot Lehokhmat Ha'emet* (Jerusalem, 2000), nos. 65–70. See Eliezer Schweid, "Hahitgalut Hago'elet: Hatsdakat Elohim Bemishnato Hakabalit Shel Harav Yehudah Ashlag," in *Bein Hurban Liyeshuah* (Tel Aviv, 1994), 193–215.

34. Shalom Buzaglo, "*Kise Melekh ad* Tikkun 30," in *Tikkunei Hazohar* (Warsaw, 1883 edition), 107ᵃ. Hayim Vital, *Ets Hayim* (Jerusalem, 1995 edition), 15 col. 1. Mordekhai Atiyah, *Sod Hashevuah* (Jerusalem, 1963/64), 30–33.

35. I was unable to verify several sources cited by Yannai. Meir Yannai, *Tamtsit Hashoah* (Moshav Ben Shemen, 2001).

36. Hayim Vital, "Sha'ar Shishi," in *Sha'ar Hakavanot,* vol. 1 (Erets Yisrael, 1961/62). Hayim Yisrael Tsimerman, *Tamim Pa'alo* (Tel Aviv, 1947). Elazar Menahem Man Shakh in *Yated Ne'eman* (26 December 1990), 4–6 as cited by Shmuel Koll, *Kuntres Shoat Yahadut Eiropah Uporaniyut Yisrael Bizemanenu* (Jerusalem, 1996). Additional references to this motif may be found in Hayim David Bakon, *Shtraln in der Finsternish* (Brooklyn, 1990), 26–27 and Ovadiah Yosef in *Ma'ariv,* internet edition (August 2000).

37. Hayim Yitshak Or Zarua, "Mispar 14," in *She'elot Uteshuvot Maharah Or Zarua*; Maimonides, "Hamin Hashlishi," in *Igeret Hashemat.* Menahem Mendel Schneersohn, "Hashoah," in *Emunah Umada* (Kfar Habad, 1972). Hayka Grossman, "Harabi Milubavitch Vehashoah," *Al Hamishmar* (18 August 1980). Schneersohn, Letter to Grossman (28 September 1980), provided by Grossman to the author. Schneersohn, "Devar Malkhut," *Kfar Habad,* nos. 457–59 (December 1990–January 1991), 1–7 as cited in Mosheh Verdiger, *Hashoah Kinekudat Mifneh Teologit* (Ramat Gan, 1997/98). See Gershon Greenberg, "Redemption after Holocaust according to Mahaneh Yisrael Lubavitch, 1940–1945."

38. The activist messianism of the *Gush Emunim* movement as a response to the Holocaust should be seen as a complement and counterweight to these heteronomous elements. See Dov Schwartz, *Etgar Umashber Behug Harav Kook* (Tel Aviv, 2001) and Aviezer Ravitzky, *Hakets Hameguleh Umedinat Hayehudim* (Tel Aviv, 1993). Hayim Druckman, *supra.* Mosheh Blaykher, *supra.*

Chapter 7

Theological Reflections on the Holocaust
Between Unity and Controversy

Michael Rosenak

Ethnic and Theological Perspectives

The Holocaust is, first and foremost, a feature and segment of history, that of the European Jews and that of the Christian nations of Europe and their largely post-Christian societies. But the educational, social, and existential concern with the subject is not primarily located in the discipline of history.

On the firm basis of historical studies, two fundamental ways of presenting the Holocaust to consciousness, our own and that of the coming generation, are available to us. One is the ethnic-national way that views the Holocaust as the moment of horrible truth about what Herzl euphemistically called "the Jewish problem," namely, the problem of the Gentiles. The other is a religious-theological way that wonders what is presently the truth of the God-Israel or, if you will, the God-humankind relationship, and what can be said of it after the apparent silence and indifference of God at Auschwitz.

Both approaches, the ethnic-national one and the theological one, may have humanistic or nonhumanistic orientations. The ethnic-national approach may just as easily draw ethnocentric and distrustful conclusions from the historical facts as universalistic and hopeful ones. Likewise, theological approaches may be oriented toward returning the divine image to the faces of all people and peoples or it may dwell on the destruction of Amalek, which, alas, can be taken to refer to a great many people and even to many nations.

What distinguishes the educational thrust of the ethnic-national approach is that it seems to galvanize united consciousness and united efforts. It evokes, as Rabbi Soloveitchik would formulate it, the covenant of fate,[1] that which binds Jews together regardless of their beliefs and practices, simply by virtue of their being in the world as "others" vis-à-vis everyone else. School curricula and Jewish Studies programs at universities informed by this view implicitly bear the slogan, "We are all in this together," a slogan in which "we," once again, may be understood as limited to "the Jews" and as wide as "humankind." Moreover, the ethnic-national approach is intent on solving what appear to be real problems and on thinking about them rationally, in terms of real experience, passed through the prism of modernly informed intelligence and creativity. It seems hard to argue with that!

In contradistinction, the theological approach sounds suspect: it appears to be divisive, inviting scholastic controversy, inciting endless polemic. It raises the issue of Rabbi Soloveitchik's "covenant of destiny," dealing, sometimes tendentiously, with the substance of Jewish uniqueness and what constitutes authentic commitment and true significance. And while R. Soloveitchik believed that only Orthodox Jews are true and conscious members of that covenant,[2] this judgment is obviously part of the very polemic that theological discourse so readily evokes. Indeed, there are numerous theological approaches, each a platform for decision making and action, that restate the differences among Jews, that delineate conceptions of destiny and perhaps accentuate them.

What then can speak in favor of taking theology seriously in the context of Holocaust consciousness and education? Don't we deserve the scant yet significant comfort of unity, at least here? The advocates of the national-ethnic approach will, of course, deny that their preference is therapeutic. They may sincerely state that the questions of belief and ultimate significance are simply not where the action is—that it is more important to understand the status of the Jew in prewar European society, to fathom the socioeconomic crises of Europe between the wars, and to understand the Christian and post-Christian habits of the heart vis-à-vis the Jews than to ask covenantal questions to which most Jews appear indifferent. Only those who understand the past, they tell us, are not condemned to repeat it.

If we are yet intent here on taking these issues seriously in an age that is largely secular and skeptical in any case, it is because we consider Judaism and its bearers, the Jews, to be in a state of severe crisis—normative, halakic, and spiritual—in the wake of the Holocaust. For those who do view Judaism as a religious demand and a religious presence in the world and for those who may come to see Judaism that way, to neglect theological questions is to despair of that demand and to turn one's back on that presence.

Five Theological Orientations

There are at least five fundamental theological approaches that clamor for our attention and allegiance. One of them ostensibly denies the necessity for theological rethinking by denying the premise of such rethinking, namely, that God was "really" silent or absent during the Holocaust. The other four take cognizance of divine silence. We may categorize them as follows:

(1) The first, the most traditional approach, maintains that nothing is wrong at all. While much is awry with the contemporary world and with Jews who have fallen under its pernicious sway, the classic teachings of Torah concerning divine retribution for transgression are, if anything, vindicated by the horrendous events. On the central theme of this position we find several variations: for some thinkers and rabbinic leaders, the rebellion of Israel is reflected in the pernicious enterprise of Zionism; for others, it is a denial of the significance of Israel that constitutes rebellion. Some view the events as birth pangs of the Messiah and others view them as, purely and simply, God's punishment for the transgressions of secularism, accompanied by the salvation of chosen righteous ones.[3]

(2) The second approach we may characterize as stating, "Something seems to be wrong"—*seems* rather than *is* because, according to this way of thinking, it is inherent in our tradition that unprecedented situations create a sense of crisis and it has happened before. And whenever it happens, a restatement of Judaism's fundamentally halakic theological principles is mandated. When the response demanded by the situation is understood, the crisis may be overcome and God's presence may again be clearly perceived, from within the pristine tradition of Torah.

The positions within this approach are generally presented as traditional doctrine. Thus, for example, Eliezer Berkovits[4] addresses God's silence as an essential and perennial prerequisite of human freedom to choose, a freedom that would be neutralized and nullified by constant human intervention, even though Jewish faith has been kept alive by the memory of Jewish-divine encounter and the anticipation of it. Guided by his halakic perspective, Berkovits finds a hero in R. Akiva who, while being flayed to death by the Romans, recited the Shema, not for innovative dramatic effect but rather for the explicit halakic reason that it was "the time for saying the Shema." Much like the Holocaust victim who could "brush off" his oppressors by musing or exclaiming, "Let them go to hell," so R. Akiva was too engaged with the mitzvah of reciting the Shema at its proper time to, as it were, pay attention to his torturers and killers. They were extrinsic elements in a situation that gave him the privilege of loving God with all his soul in the manner in which he himself had interpreted the verse, "Even when he takes your soul." Berkovits's approach is reminiscent of Soloveitchik's: Speculation as to the meaning of events is futile and diverts religious energies from the actual service of God.[5] The position of Yeshayahu Leibowitz, that the locus of Jewish faith is in the halakah and not in history, also seems close to Soloveitchik's.[6] In each case, the halakic reformulation suggests that while the problem of Judaism is indeed acute, it has been fundamentally misunderstood. What is required to restore a proper perspective is a reiteration of the halakic response of commitment, even unto absurdity.

(3) A third approach candidly states, "Something is wrong"; there is a flaw in the present Jewish-divine relationship and we are indeed distant from the biblical ideal of covenantal encounter and intimacy. For the covenant promises that the commanding God is also the God of our salvation. In the Holocaust world, this, our saving God, was silent.

Consequently, all attempts to fathom the meaning of the Holocaust, for example, by interpreting the catastrophe as divine retribution for sin, are ludicrous and even blasphemous. They are ludicrous because there never was or can be enough sinfulness to justify such punishment and they are blasphemous because they portray God as undeserving of either loving reverence or devoted service. And yet, we are commanded to respond to the events. In Fackenheim's celebrated phrase, though there was no saving Presence at Auschwitz, there was a "commanding Presence" that uttered the "six hundred and fourteenth commandment," obliging Jews to survive. Jews are not to give Hitler "posthumous victories" by abandoning Judaism, its people, and its God.

In this orientation we also find Orthodox positions such as Norman Lamm's.[7] The unavailability of divine meaning he categorizes as divine eclipse, *hester Panim,* "which denotes God's self removal from the context of Israel's company into His transcendence and remoteness. *Hester Panim* began with the destruction of the Second Temple; since then, there is no clear 'sense' or 'meaning' in Jewish history. Yet, such distance is not intrinsic but historical: it has a beginning and it shall certainly end. The anticipated *nesiat Panim* is (perhaps!) evidenced by the dramatic events marking the rebirth of Israel in its land. In any case, the religious response to *hester panim* is prescribed. Even when 'it may seem impossible to feel His presence . . . feel we must, as we bend all our energies and innermost devotions to His service.'"

(4) A fourth position insists, "There is something radically wrong." God's silence during the Holocaust does in fact threaten the entire structure of Jewish faith. Before there can be the authentic and sincere cultural reaffirmations that contemporary Jewry vitally needs, there must be radical rethinking of faith questions and positions. Only then can religious renewal perhaps become feasible.

We must bear in mind that all "answers" (like in (1) above) and all "responses" (like in 2–3 above) are part of what Fackenheim has called "the midrashic framework."[8] Other thinkers insist that, while theological thinking must be placed in a historical framework, it must yet be rooted in the biblical conception of covenant as a moral and reciprocal relationship.

Eliezer Schweid has extensively spelled out this view.[9] Schweid notes that the pain and despair of personal suffering occasioned by the organic nature of human life may yet lead the suffering person to find God as not only the cause of his or her pain and helplessness but as also "being with him or her" in the very midst of suffering. The historical situation is more problematic. For the historical covenant between the human (and the Jewish) and the divine is based on trust. In times of crisis, its human members look back reflectively at historical antecedents and attempt to incorporate the present crisis into the tapestry of tradition. In doing so, they cannot avoid asking what is demanded of both of them and of the divine partner to the covenant. When there seems to be great incongruence between the divine promise of *tzedakah* (i.e., what Israel has the moral right to expect as a partner to the covenant) and the facts on the ground, of solitude and abandonment, there must be rethinking. When there is an excess of human *tzedek* (moral commitment) over the divine *tzedakah*, the *tzedakah* (that God demands as His moral right from Israel) becomes implausible. Then the consciousness of historical tradition that seeks to mend each breach by recalling past love, trust, and reciprocity cannot be carried on.

The greater the seeming injustice of God, the greater the challenge to the moral balance of faith. This may mean that, after the Holocaust, the traditional faith in providence and in the historical covenant is no longer automatic and may no longer be tenable, though the faith in the God who is with the individual in his or her "natural" suffering may remain unaffected or even strengthened.

(5) Finally, there is the position that states, "The entire theological enterprise of Judaism is wrong." In this approach, the previous responses and questions are thoroughly radicalized in a nontheistic theology. As Richard Rubenstein insists,[10] the mythic world picture of classic Judaism is false; God is not only silent but "dead." In the real and meaningless world, there is neither a divine moral commander nor a divine redeeming presence. Yet, paradoxically, the significance of Torah remains, for it is a system of community patterns and rituals that allow us to "huddle together" in a hostile cosmos. The function of leaders, whose task it is to structure this cultural collective existence, remains vital. Israel still needs its priests. But the message of prophets, who spoke for a redeeming and demanding God, is now, and fully, revealed as illusionary. In our world of continuous upheaval and growing chaos, the illusion is dangerous and potentially fatal.

Fate and Destiny

How shall we view the various theological positions that are available to community leaders, planners and educators?

First, they should help make it clear to us that "the lessons" of the Holocaust are by no means self-understood or simply derivative from a grasp of the (historical) facts. Through the prism of diverse religious and theological viewpoints, as well as ethnic-national ones, we may arrive at widely disparate goals in dealing with the Holocaust. For example, against the backdrop of the Holocaust, some may teach or otherwise foster a sensitivity to social and moral wrongs; others may make "self-reliance" their motto. For some leaders, whether museum curators, foundation leaders, teachers, or rabbis, the motif may be that heroism in abject circumstances is the height of human achievement and experience. For yet others, the "meaning" of the Holocaust may be pride in the transformation of the Jews, from pitiful victims to proud self-defenders.

Secondly, diverse theological positions, while indeed creating contro-

versy and possibly even enmity among Jews, can also foster, if not understanding, at least empathy among them. For that to become feasible, I suggest, three valuative decisions must be made:

(1) It must be admitted, specifically by Orthodox Jews, that what unites all
Jews is not only a covenant of fate that leaves most outside the realm of
Jewish significance but also the search of diverse Jewish communities for
their own understandings of our common destiny. We are suggesting that
R. Soloveitchik's notion, that only Orthodox Jews are party to "Jewish destiny" while "the others" are merely partners in fate, be reexamined and
revised by traditional communities. These communities were meant to be
the beneficiaries of that position but, in fact, they stand to be isolated by it
and rendered incapable of hearing what other Jews are saying.

(2) The various theological positions must be seen as responses to a common question: namely, how to maintain the spiritual entity that is the
House of Israel and how to carry on its spiritual life, even in widely diverse
forms. This decision does not carry the requirement that there be agreement about the answers but only that thinkers have the right to posit
them.

(3) At the same time, standards for what will count as Jewish discourse on
faith may be and should be put in place, and they will make argument
possible while hopefully minimizing acrimony. These standards, I suggest,
relate to the *truthfulness,* the *coherence,* and the *plausibility* of the theological positions presented.

By "truthfulness," I refer not to the propositional truth of the theological position but to the trust that those who hear it may place in the spiritual integrity of those presenting it. This trust is somehow related to the
ability and willingness of those who confront the particular theological
position to "find" it, even vaguely, in their own religious experience and
behavior. The theology that is truthful "rings a bell"; it is illuminating and
worth thinking about and thinking through, and tools for doing so are
readily found in our tradition.

The "coherence" of a theology refers to the requirement that diverse
features or propositions within it not contradict one another. Though
there may well be paradoxes among them, given the depth of the objects
of theological discourse (e.g., God, the human soul, the text as a pointer to
ultimacy), the various aspects of the proposed theology yet support one

another and "come together" in some way that fosters the integration, the wholeness, of religious personality.

As for "plausibility," it refers here to the feasibility of explaining the proposed point of view, even if only partially, to an outsider. Such a person will be able to "get the drift of" the position without necessarily accepting it or agreeing with it.

Which of the positions can meet these standards, for whom, and under which circumstances is a subject for further and varied investigation. Clearly, what will be truthful in a community committed to halakic observance and eager for enlightenment in *ta'amai hamitzvot* (rationales for the commandments) is less likely to "strike a bell" for American Reform Jews whose "truthfulness" will have to touch base with many aspects of experience that traditionalists will consider "incoherent" with the Jewish faith tradition. Likewise, those who are fully integrated into a liberal non-Jewish society will consider plausibility more of a prime condition for coherence than those who ideologically favor self-segregation.

Theology and Silence

If we posit that one is to take various theological positions as deserving of (at least) initially respectful treatment, as testifying to sincere struggle and search, and if we attempt to enter into dialogue with them, we are brought up short by Yitzhak Greenberg's often-cited assertion that any theological statement made about the Holocaust should be one that can be made in the presence of burning children. This statement is compelling, but it may require reformulation. Should *any* statement be made in the presence of burning children? Is the religious consciousness of the *haredi* person witnessing such death and bearing such sorrow identical with that of the secularized yet (also) committed Jew?

The reformulation we are suggesting points to the fact that all the positions, even those in the first, ultraconservative category, proceed from the experience of God's silence, a silence that some attribute to His justice while others, at the opposite extreme, attribute to His (supposed) nonexistence. For educators, certainly, a theological approach that will not be simply divisive suggests proceeding from the fact of that silence and from the question, what are we to do with that silence and what should be learned from it for our collective life in the twenty-first century? Our reformulation, then, is, which theological statements help us to decide what to do and what to say about Jewish faith, as educators and leaders who know about silence but who believe that silence "speaks" within a framework, not of chaos but of the struggle for a meaningful existence? And when is theological speech inappropriate? When should it leave the field to decision and to action?

A theologian who has well articulated the potential religious significance of divine silence is the Israeli-French scholar and teacher Andre Neher.[11] In his homily on chapter 20 of Ezekiel, which tells of "certain of the elders of Israel" who, during the Babylonian exile, "came to inquire of the Lord," he notes that God instructs the prophet to dismiss their request. "Are you come to inquire of Me? As I live, saith the Lord God, I will not be inquired of by you."

The elders, as Neher imagines them, are not necessarily unhappy at God's refusal to speak. Rather, following Rashi on verse 1,[12] Neher sees them leaving the presence of the prophet like school children let out of school, released into freedom. If God is finished with them, if the covenant has been annulled, so be it!

Then, strangely, God embarks upon a long tirade in which He recounts Israel's transgressions in tedious detail. And when the divine Preacher returns to His original declaration in 20:31, namely, that He refuses to be "inquired of," He, as it were, suddenly takes notice of the absence of His assumed listeners. Neher sees the prophet as now ordered to run into the street to bring them back, to "take them by the scruff of the neck and forcefully regain their attention." They are forced to listen to God's new word, no matter how incongruous it is with His previous outburst. "So you think yourselves free? . . . As I live, saith the Lord God, surely with a mighty hand and with an outstretched arm, and with fury poured out, will I be king over you" (20:33).

And Neher explains, "It is as though the Doctor, in refusing to receive the patient, had prescribed for him the correct remedy . . . as though the Master, in withdrawing Himself in silence, had imported the true word to His disciple." And then he asks the bitter and pressing question that is the question of us all: How can silence instruct? What prevents the elders from simply responding to that strange and seemingly heartless Doctor that they are finished with Him?

Shall we see at least part of the answer in the very ludicrousness of the situation, of people turning to the source of their identity and asking that Source whether they may relinquish it? Isn't such a question likely to evoke laughter and rebuke? Can't we expect that Source to turn scornfully to the "petitioners" and to say, "If you wish to lose your identity, why come to Me? Your turning to Me is itself an affirmation of your identity! As long as you know who you are, 'I shall be King over you.'"

But such terms of reference are, for Neher, possibly too overtly theoretical-educational and perhaps even reductionistic. He himself suggests a further interpretation as to the identity of these "certain elders of Israel." A midrash in *Song of Songs Rabbah* (7:13) teaches that the men who came to "inquire of the Lord" were none other than Hananiah, Mishael, and Azarya, the companions of Daniel called into exile by the Babylonian king, Nebuchadnezzar, to learn the Chaldean tongue and wisdom, and to stand in waiting upon him. The king had warned them that they would be cast into a fiery furnace if they refused to worship his idols (Daniel 3:15), to which threat they responded, in the opinion of the midrash, in seemingly untroubled certainty, that their God would deliver them. Now, suddenly seized by anxiety, they come before the prophet to seek reassurance; they want to know for a certainty that God will indeed save them. But, surprisingly, shockingly, God spurns their request. "No, I will not be inquired of them," meaning, "No, I will not save them."[13]

The prophet weeps and cajoles, but to no avail. God remains silent, and when the three men ask Ezekiel what God has replied, the answer is, "That He won't deliver you." And this new word of silence creates a new insight and commitment, a new response, a new situation. "Very well, then," they respond, "whether He delivers us or not, we are ready for martyrdom." The midrash anchors this dialogue in Daniel 3:18 where the three "cast at Nebuchadnezzar the eternal challenge of the martyrs, 'hen-lo,' 'despite all.'" "If that God Who is ours and Whom we serve will not deliver us, despite all of this (*hen-lo*) be it known unto thee, O king, that we will not serve thy gods nor worship the golden image that thou hast set up." Neher comments,

> *Hen-lo*, a contradictory formula, is nothing else but the juxtaposition of "yes" and "no." But whereas elsewhere this juxtaposition would be a sign of indecision, of equivocation, of balancing "yes" and "no" leading to neutral passivity, here it is the supreme symbol of voluntary action, of deliberate and irreversible choice. Whether "yes," He is close, or "no," He is silent and remote, we shall serve Him.

Several features of Neher's conception may engage our attention. First, God's silence, the divine refusal "to be inquired of," appears as a form of speech; the human listener, who hears only silence, is galvanized into a response that creates a new religious situation. Martyrdom, for Neher, becomes an existential possibility when the human being is totally alone, when it can be assumed that God will not save. Secondly, at the moment of silence, one may anticipate God's speech—which may well come, as it does in Ezekiel 20 as Neher interprets it, when no one wishes to listen. Third, we note that Neher dwells on "inquirers" who certainly have prior experience of God's speech. These, after all, are the very young men who would not eat at the king's nonkosher food table (Daniel 1). They know God, they have experience of Him at least through His Torah. Moreover, if they had no trust, why defy the earthly king? And why go to the prophet to hear the (anticipated) reassuring word?

Yet God's inscrutability is a fact. Even the prophet is appalled by His silences. And even if it be said that his silence is also speech, that it creates the space for human activity, it is still shocking. The reasons that God gives for his silence may make theological and existential sense but they are not consoling. One may say that the seeming silence is inscrutable yet deserved and unerring justice. One may posit, with Berkovits, that human freedom demands divine withdrawal, or with Lamm, that eclipse, however painful, is radically demanding, a demand that emanates from what Fackenheim calls "the commanding Presence." One may suggest that God speaks to those who "listen" to his commandments and that these righteous ones "locate" the isolation that requires martyrdom in the spiritual space shaped by the prohibitions not to eat the nonkosher food of even the most exalted earthly king and not to bow down to his idols. Does it also make possible a radical rethinking, or even the radical denial of humans "to be inquired of" by what they conceive to be an uncaring and distant God?

The theology that relates divine silence to human responsibility can make theological sense only if God can be somehow and somewhere experienced. For the persons and the communities who find that God is distant and who are "addressed" by that silence, there is the memory of when He was near. This may refer to no more than the moment of (halakic) revelation in a distant past, retained as vital memory within communities of faithful observance. Most likely, it also refers to the moments of love bestowed, beauty shared, confidence engendered at moments when "all's right with the world." Good parents, it seems safe to say, present the world to their children as a place in which God is plentifully to be found: in blessings they teach them to recite for everything they may enjoy or even for what they can risk enduring, in a sense of safety created by love and order, and in the internal language and discipline of a meaningful life. They teach about God through what can be learned and mastered, by fostering their ability to accomplish, by initiating them into a prevailing sense of right that "fits in" with an ordered, rich, and hopefully beautiful world.

But even without holocausts, everyone experiences God's absence. Job is everyone. There are moments in the life of every child in which the terror of thunder is not mitigated by the blessing to be recited, when the world seems ugly and menacing and too painful to be borne. And just as parents and teachers must bring the child into the world where God's presence seems obvious, so they must prepare children for the silences, so that they can do what all theologies of silence require—so that, at times when God is distant, they may stubbornly do what was learned in moments of closeness: enact an identity that is loyal and reliable, whether God or others are there to approve and reassure or not—or rather, especially when they are not. For character, as has been truly said, is what a person does *and is* when no one is looking.[14]

A pithy interchange arising from the experience of God's silence is that recorded in the Talmud between Rabbi Akiva and Pappus ben Yehudah. Pappus asks the rabbi why, despite the edict of the Roman authorities prohibiting Torah study, he continues to teach and study. Is he not afraid of what the authorities will do to him? Akiva responds with a parable of fish who are advised by the fox to escape the fishermen's nets by jumping onto dry land. To this "suggestion" the fish reply, "do they really call you the cleverest of animals? You are not clever but foolish. If we are afraid in the element in which we live, how much more so in the element in which we would die" (B.T. *Berachot* 61a). Like the friends of Daniel who were seemingly abandoned by God, R. Akiva argues, when God is distant all that remains is to be oneself, to stay with oneself, in the "element" in which one lives. *Hen-lo*, whether He will ultimately save or not. In a sense this is also the response of Abraham to Satan, who accosts him on the way to the binding of Isaac. Despite the silence that envelops him in the three-day trek to Mount Moriah, Abraham "stays with himself." And though Satan callously tempts him by intimating how implausible the entire venture is, Abraham remains truthful, and he stays with his faith in the ultimate coherence of it all. In the words of Elizabeth Shanks, "Abraham replies [to Satan] that he does not seek evidence of God in the world around him. All he can know is the rhythm and meter of his own holy trek. 'In my innocence, I will walk forward.'"[15]

We are here today to recall the silence of those terrible years, and to ask, can we, still experiencing much eclipse, yet act in religious truthfulness, simply because of who we are, as the people of Israel? Can we, despite so much disorder and fear in our collective and personal experience, bring the divine Presence into our lives and those of our children, testifying to a religious truth and to lives of significance, yet paving the way for courage and even heroism when they are needed? Can we transform the commonwealth bestowed upon us in an hour of divine challenge, and compassion, into a place worthy of the divine Presence?

Theological reflections on the Holocaust in the twenty-first century, I suggest, will bring our attention to the educational questions: What shall we do to make children encounter God in the world? How shall we prepare them for the times of silence when they must decide, on the basis of who they are, whether to be His witnesses? How shall what we *do* inform what we *say* about such lofty matters so that we bear no false witness?

NOTES

1. On this and on the "covenant of destiny" noted below, see J. B. Soloveitchik, *Kol Dodi Dofek* in Soloveitchik, *Ish Ha-emunah* (Jerusalem, 5731) (second printing), (Hebrew), especially 43–47.

2. Rabbi Joseph B. Soloveitchik, "Wait Here with the Donkey," *Five Addresses* (Jerusalem, 5743), 43–47.

3. For the "sin of Zionism," see Menachem Friedman, "The Haredim and the Holocaust," *Jerusalem Quarterly*, no. 53 (Winter 1990). A major exponent in the religious world of the approach that it was sinful not to recognize the dawn of redemption in Eretz Yisrael is R. Issachar Shlomo Teichthal, *Em Habanim Simehah* (Jerusalem, 5743). For an extensive discussion, see Eliezer Schweid, *Ben Hurban L'Yeshuah* (From Ruin to Salvation) (Tel Aviv, 5754–1994), (Hebrew), chapter 5. The "ironical" comment on National Socialists is that of R. Elhanan Bunim Wasserman himself, like Teichthal a victim of the Holocaust. See his *Kovetz Maamarim* (Tel Aviv, 5746), (Hebrew), 119. On the alleged relationship between the Holocaust and the state of Israel as part of an alleged messianic process, see Uriel Tal, "The Land and the State of Israel in Israel's Religious Life," in *Proceedings of the Rabbinical Assembly* 1976 (New York, 1977). For a popular and already classic exposition of the "birth pangs of the Messiah" conception applied to our times see Menahem M. Kasher, *Israel Passover Hagaddah* (New York, 1983) (seventh edition).

4. Eliezer Berkovits, *Faith after the Holocaust* (New York, 1973). On his discussion of R. Akiva, 80–85.

5. Soloveitchik, *Kol Dodi Dofek,* 65–71.

6. Yeshayahu Leibowitz, *Yahadut, Am Yehudi U'Medinat Yisrael (Judaism, the Jewish People and the State of Israel)* (Jerusalem and Tel Aviv, 5735–1975), (Hebrew). See particularly "Hinukh L'Mitzvot" ("Education for the Commandments"), 57–67; "Hamoreshet Hayehudut-Notzrit Hamishutefet" ("The Common Judeo-Christian Heritage"), 327–33.

7. Norman Lamm, "The Face of God: Thoughts on the Holocaust," in *Theological and Halakhic Reflections on the Holocaust,* edited by Bernhard H. Rosenberg and Fred Heuman (Hoboken, NJ, 5752–1992), 119–36. Citation from 133.

8. Emil L. Fackenheim, *God's Presence in History* (New York, 1970), 20–21.

9. See particularly Eliezer Schweid, *Lehagid ki Yashar Hashem (To Declare That God Is Upright: Theodicy in Jewish Thought)* (Bat Yam, 5754–1994), chapter 1, and extensive additional writings.

10. Richard L. Rubenstein, *After Auschwitz: Radical Theology and Contemporary Judaism* (Indianapolis, 1966). See also Rubenstein, "Jewish Theology and the Current World Situation," *Conservative Judaism,* vol. 28, no. 4 (Summer 1974) for a statement of his pessimism.

11. Andre Neher, *The Exile of the World: From the Silence of the Bible to the Silence of Auschwitz,* translated from the French by David Maisel (Philadelphia, 5741–1981), 199–207.

12. "They came to inquire of the Lord out of their own interest. If He refuses to listen to us, well, He will no longer have any claim upon us. A slave sold by his master, a wife driven out by her husband, are they not free of their responsibilities to one another?"

13. In the biblical narrative, God does, of course, save them: they are unharmed by the fires of the furnace.

14. For religious Jews, I venture to state, Jewish identity is not only a function of historical belonging but of having been "inquired of" by God. To deny that appears to make theology incoherent with the totality of Jewish experience, even if it appears plausible to many in the secular world of contemporary Western civilization.

15. Elizabeth Shanks, "Dialogues on the Theme of Martyrdom," *Post-Modern Jewish Philosophy Network Journal,* vol. 5, no. 1 (March 1996), unpaginated.

Chapter 8

Building amidst Devastation

*Halakic Historical Observations on
Marriage during the Holocaust*

Ester Farbstein

The conventional combination of words in the phrase "halakah in the Holocaust" is an ostensible oxymoron. "Halakah" denotes continuity, permanence, an ordering of personal and public life in view of Torah laws, an adherence to a path paved since time immemorial. The origin of the word "halakah" is the Hebrew root *heh-lamed-khaf*—a "walking" on a path already laid out.

"Holocaust"—the literal meaning of this term, like its historical meaning is discontinuity, dissociation, a descent into a deep pit. The Holocaust was a collapse of worlds, both the personal and the public, and a shattering of all systems: those of ethics and thought, those of existence and society.

Therefore, the combination "halakah in the Holocaust" makes one ask if both ends of an oxymoron can possibly be discussed in one breath. How did these two concepts, continuity and discontinuity, become linked? The distance of years and the progression of research allow us to understand that life amidst contrasts such as these is one of the traits of the Jewish response during the Holocaust. Jews strove prodigiously to make sure that the outer circle of their lives—the one imposed on them, one of unparalleled enslavement, humiliation, and suffering—would not consume the inner circle—the one they preserved, their staff of support, the remnant of free choice, the struggle to maintain their identities as human beings and Jews. Thus, amidst a collapsing world, links of continuity—of morals, halakah, faith, and ideals—were preserved. The confrontation of halakah with the Holocaust was one of the most impressive links of continuity amidst discontinuity.

In the past few years, research on this topic has developed in several ways. First, it has moved from a generalized approach to an individualized one (as has occurred with many themes in Holocaust research). This approach is based on the integrated use of historical and halakic research tools, because only by understanding the specific reality in each situation can one discern the methods, meaning, and dynamic of *pesiqa,* halakic decision making. I will give two examples of this. The first concerns how to define the general halakic situation in the Holocaust. At an international conference at Yad Vashem in April 1968 on the Jewish stand during the Holocaust, where the halakic response was "recognized" for the first time as part of the concept of resistance,[1] Professor Joseph Walk noted, also for the first time, the dilemma that rabbis faced in defining the halakic situation during the Holocaust. In the main, Walk distinguished between two halakic definitions that, in his opinion, reflected a difference in the way the overarching goals of Nazi anti-Semitism were perceived.[2]

> One cannot possibly consider *pesiqa* in detachment from the thinking of the Torah sages. Only in view of the attitude of leading rabbis toward the phenomena of Nazi Germany and the Holocaust can one understand and explain the substantive differences in halakhic arbiters' responses to questions that the circumstances of the time forced them to answer.

Therefore, in his opinion, some rabbis defined the era as a time of *shemad,* an all-out onslaught against the Jews. In such an era, the observance of every religious precept should be upheld so stringently that the individual should accept death rather than commit any transgression. This is indicated in the Talmud (B.T. *Sanhedrin* 74b): "When a decree of *shemad* is in effect, one should die rather than transgress even in matters of sandal straps."[3] Others considered the Holocaust era a state of *piquah nefesh,* in which saving Jewish lives is the paramount value. In such a case, one may breach all commandments (except for idol worship, incest, and murder) because of the principle of *va-hay bahem*—commandments are to be "lived in," not died for. From this perspective, every ruling would be biased toward lenience.

The very fact of drawing this distinction was an important step, but today one may say that even this distinction is generalized in various respects. First, are there only two possible definitions? Second, was the halakic situation constant or fluid? Are halakic rulings in the Lodz ghetto in 1940 comparable to those in 1941, let alone in 1942? In other words, changes in circumstances and differences in historical reality in different locations, or in one location, had halakic ramifications because the halakic debate flows from given situations. For example, even the rulings of one rabbi reflected a revision in halakic definitions during the period.[4] This dynamic exists even with respect to a concept as basic as *qidush ha-hayim,* "sanctification of life."

Another example of the issue at hand concerns one of the most difficult questions: What attitude did rabbis take toward the selection of Jews by the Judenrat for deportation? Here, too, a transition has occurred—from a generalized perception arguing that the halakic view was inconsistent,[5] since the situation was unprecedented, to an individualized view that reached a different conclusion in the aftermath of case-by-case examination.[6]

An additional sweeping example is the belief that the traditional leadership, chiefly the community rabbis (as distinct from Hasidic rebbes), seemingly vanished. Those who expected to find evidence in Holocaust research about the houses of rabbis being magnets for discussion of dilemmas and reinforcement of religious faith during the Holocaust ignored the special kinds of persecution that rabbis faced. These persecutions transformed them into underground rabbis for those who sought them out and made their official leadership into a voluntary vocation. Their activity changed drastically, depending on circumstances in different locations and their own personalities. However, most rabbis—thousands in number—accompanied their communities at the various stops on their path of afflictions and many of them discharged their duties under all circumstances, up to the edge of the grave.

Another factor in the individualized direction in research on this topic is access to new sources: manuscripts kept in archives that have been deciphered, personal documents turned over in the course of expanded testimony-collecting projects, and even new documents from Poland—since much material on Jewish history is still circulating on Polish soil, and some of it is trickling into our possession. These sources allow us to develop discerning and analytical approaches in various directions, such as tracing the halakic rulings of one rabbi at various junctures of his life during the Holocaust. This type of research permits us to deal not only with the outer product, the halakic ruling, but also with the process of judgment and the development of the halakic approach. It also enables us to observe the rabbis' personal experiences at the time. Another direction of individualized research is related to the shift to specific topics in halakic rulings, a broad thematic cross-sectioning of sorts. An example of this is the question I presented earlier concerning selection; another example is the topic that I will attempt to present today.

Thus, one may say that the fertilization of Holocaust research and the enrichment of halakic research on the Holocaust have become paired because they express two facets of one reality. Only knowledge of the historical process, an understanding of the reality of consciousness in each location, and the steady expansion of documentation are facilitating genuine debate and making halakah in the Holocaust an inseparable part of historical research.

The topic through which I shall present this approach concerns marriage dilemmas during the Holocaust. The Jeremiah who would lament the destruction of the Jewish family during the Holocaust—a solid structure that was razed stone by stone—has not yet stepped forward. Nevertheless, new cornerstones were laid amidst these events: weddings were conducted and "families" of sorts were established. Beyond the broad significance of this phenomenon, it has a specific connection with halakah. The stationing of a *huppa* (wedding canopy) and performance of *qidushin* (consecration of marriage) are among the main functions of rabbis, along with the dissolution of marriages in bills of divorce. Halakah also includes marital rules that require the spouses to consult rabbis routinely.

Who wished to get married during that period? Who were the rabbis who dealt in such matters? Were old and new questions asked, to whom, and how? Were the halakic rulings based on precedent? Did these matters have implications for the post-Holocaust era? We will explore these issues on the basis of several sources that reflect a broad spectrum in terms of locations (Warsaw, Lodz, the Netherlands, Kovno) and conditions (before ghettoization, ghetto, labor camp, D.P. camp).

The first sources we discuss are from the Warsaw ghetto in 1940. The document at issue originates in the writings of a community rabbi in Poland, Rabbi Joshua M. Ahronson, rabbi of the town of Sanniki, who produced most of his writings while interned in the Konin labor camp. His writings are one of the sources from which we may understand the thinking and experiences of the halakah arbiter under those circumstances.[7] On one of the pages, written shortly after the liberation in a D.P. camp in 1946, the rabbi reconstructed several halakic dilemmas with which he had dealt during the Holocaust. The page presents a list of facts and rulings in a simple and succinct form, evidently as chapter headings of sorts, to prompt the author's memory or for reexamination. The rabbi gave these writings the modest title *Nisyones*—ordeals. The list includes the following paragraph:[8] "In the presence of important rabbis in Warsaw in 5700 [1940], I expressed my humble opinion that weddings should not be performed."[9] The very fact that decisions were being presented to an assembly of rabbis under the circumstances of 1940 is significant.[10] The question is why the rabbis of Warsaw debated the matter comprehensively. One of the answers may be found in a document by Rabbi S. Huberband, a member of Ringelblum's *Oneg Shabbat* group—a document that has not yet been discussed in a broad context. Huberband wrote the following:[11]

> A migration and a race to the East began. Most of the migrants were young people, and weddings for young couples who were about to migrate became a mass phenomenon. . . . For the purpose of registration, the couples brought notes from the official rabbis who performed their weddings. Since travel by rail was impossible at that time, the trips to the other side of the frontier were made by car. It sometimes happened that, as they sat in the car, a couple decided to get married, and then the car stopped for a few minutes, the couple went to the rabbi, they set up a wedding canopy—and resumed their trip. . . . Generally speaking, wartime marriages were commonplace. Many marriages that were originally postponed because of objections from parents were culminated during the war. Another reason for the proliferation of marriages was the state of war, in which men lost their wives and vice versa. An especially large number of weddings took place at the time of ghettoization. Grooms and brides wed and rented one apartment instead of two separate ones. Since the war began, these weddings have been perfunctory events only, without a trace of happiness. Wedding banquets are rare.

Notwithstanding the writer's reportorial tone, the drama of hasty weddings in the midst of mass flight comes through powerfully. The reader can imagine the wagons stopping along the way, passengers asking for the rabbi's address, getting married, and returning to the road. Afterwards, however, at the time of ghettoization, weddings also proliferated, perhaps to consummate old relationships while it was still possible, or perhaps in response to individuals' loneliness. Housing conditions also affected this behavior, it being easier to find one dwelling than two.

These two segments of documentation evidently complement each other: it was the phenomenon of mass weddings that prompted the rabbis of Warsaw to discuss the subject comprehensively.[12] Many details from this dramatic assembly are unknown to us, but Rabbi Ahronson expressed his attitude clearly in his writings: he spoke resolutely against performing weddings and cited several reasons for his view. First, "it will result in many *agunot*" (women not allowed to remarry because of uncertainty about their husbands' fate). Many men had been taken away for forced labor, and the rabbi, because of his position, had the foresight to wish to prevent a proliferation of *agunot*. This had been one of the grimmest results of World War I; it had become a preoccupation among rabbis who attempted to extricate women from this condition. The second rationale was also related to the rabbi's assessment of the realities: "Single women can also hide in labor camps and may hope to survive as long as they are not married and not pregnant." In other words, single and, in the main, childless women had better prospects of survival. The third rationale originated in concern about the moral situation and its implications for the future: "Since [morals] are widely abandoned at a time of siege and distress, it is best that the women be single and not married." The fourth reason had to do with the difficulty of observing the *halakhot* concerning marital relations: "The household would be established in a state of impurity because in Warsaw, the capital, there was no halakhically sound *mikve* [ritual pool] at the time since the Nazis had closed them all on pain of death." Huberband also described this serious problem—the closure of the ritual pools in Warsaw—in 1941:

> All the ritual pools were closed and sealed with the authorities' stamp. . . . A notice was imprinted on their gate: use of or immersion in a ritual pool shall carry a penalty such as that given for sabotage. Such a penalty means twelve years up to death. Jewish Warsaw was left without a *mikve,* and the problem of purifying the Jewish daughters became as immediate as in the days of the Romans.[13]

He recorded information about women who endangered themselves by traveling to nearby towns to immerse themselves in a river or in clandestine ritual pools. The problem worsened steadily in various locations in Poland, although not in all. In Lodz, for example, the Judenrat Committee of Rabbis operated the ritual pool and, until a certain stage, the Judenrat provided coals to heat the water.[14]

Rabbi Ahronson, a unique figure who tackled the most difficult questions with particular courage and frankness, also documented another halakic question related to family life: whether to encourage or discourage conception during the war.[15] The question also pertained to subsequent periods in the ghetto. Here again, he addressed himself to the moral, halakic, and historical aspects of the issue. In the background was a midrash that reenacted a conversation between Yokheved, wife of Amram, and her daughter Miriam at the time of Pharaoh's decrees.[16] Although the Israelites in Egypt accepted the decision to wed and procreate—"They all stood up and remarried their wives"—the rabbi deemed the very fact of the ancient discussion to be a basis for the possibility of prohibiting procreation in wartime, and a fortiori in a situation that he defined as direr than war:

> In my opinion, our woes—the woes of the Jews in this war—are wholly incomparable to what had been. . . . In particular, at such a woeful time as this is—since the Jews became a people, there has not been such an era of devastation and killing, especially of children and pregnant women, who were the first to be consigned to the terrible slaughter—[procreation] may be forbidden even to one who has not yet observed the commandment of "Be fruitful and multiply." All the more in our times, when they decreed the annihilation of every Jewish root, starting with children and pregnant women (*Nisyones*).

The rabbi attests that some of the Jews honored this ruling: "And so, in fact, the [God-] fearing and the haredim behaved, abstaining [from intercourse] at that time of woe."

These are the first halakic sources concerning weddings; they take up initial aspects of the matter. However, their contents belie their paucity: the terse writing alludes to a piercing debate over a very basic dilemma that took place across a wide spectrum of opinion and an assessment of the unique situation that the German occupation, from its inception, had created.

The question of conducting weddings in the ghetto surfaced in other locations as well. In the Kovno ghetto, for example, it was presented to Rabbi Shapira, the chief rabbi of this city, who was staying in the Slobodka ghetto along with his community:[17] "Should we refrain from performing weddings . . . or not?" In Kovno, the rabbi ruled in favor of continued weddings. However, study of the background of the questions and the rationales behind the rulings apprises us of the relationship between the ghetto reality and the nature and the dynamic of the ruling.

The circumstances in Kovno were totally different from the very beginning. Kovno was one of the first places where mass murders of Jews occurred. Thousands of Jews were slaughtered at the forts near Kovno; ten thousand Kovno Jews were murdered in the great *Aktion* in October 1941. When the question was asked, fewer than half of the Jews of Kovno remained alive. Although the Jews were assured at the time of ghettoization that the *Aktionen* had ended, rumors about a thinning of the ghetto population were rampant, and one of the rumors spoke of single women being in particular danger. Marriage seemed to offer the possibility of salvation. Fictitious marriage was perceived as a path of escape, and many asked the rabbi to help by performing "rescue weddings" to spare them from an *Aktion* against single women. The rabbi was seriously perturbed by this question. On the one hand, since the conditions of life in the ghetto made it difficult to observe the marital laws, he feared that halakic marriage would place a "stumbling block before the blind."[18] On the other hand, if halakic marriages were not arranged, these frightened women would resort to civil marriage, thus creating halakic obstacles no less daunting. Thus, pinned between the hammer and the anvil—a situation typical of various decisions at the time—the rabbi was asked to choose and, since the mortal danger in Kovno had become palpable, he chose in the affirmative. This was the nature of halakic inquiry in the ghetto: with fear slicing the air and a rabbi, elderly and ill, courageous and broken, seeking answers to questions concerning situations that the Jewish world had never encountered before.

Totally different questions were posed in the Lodz ghetto. In this ghetto, the central issues in the documentation on marriage questions were the characteristics of this, the most tightly sealed ghetto, and the personality of Chaim Rumkowski, the chairman of the Judenrat there. Since the earliest years in the ghetto, marriages were recorded systematically on the basis of civil registration and, with Rumkowski's approval, a religious ceremony. The religious ceremony was performed in the conventional way, by rabbis. On December 2, 1941, as committee of rabbis associated with the Judenrat received a number of rabbis from Germany, the requisite procedures were recorded: the initial registration would take place at the registration offices, and the rabbi would attach his consent to the documents. Then the Judenrat registration office would advertise twice, as public announcements, the names of those registering for marriage; if there was no objection, the registration office would authorize the rabbinical council to perform the wedding. The couple had to remit three to fifteen marks to the community chest, and the rabbis received a monthly salary.[19] On December 27, 1941, Rumkowski himself remarried in this fashion,[20] with Rabbi Yosele Feiner officiating.

Over the years, the authors of the *Lodz Ghetto Chronicle* recorded the number of persons marrying in the ghetto. For example, forty-two weddings were held on one day in May 1942 in the new hall of the Registration Department and the Rabbinate Department. Notably, even though this occurred during the counting of the Omer, when Jews do not marry, marriages were allowed for two days. Why was this two-day dispensation given, and why did so many couples exploit it? The answer in this case, as in the cases described above, is rooted in events in the ghetto. It was a time of deportations, and although the deportees' destination was not yet widely known, it was feared that unmarried people would be deported first; furthermore, some young people in the ghetto did not wish to be separated. Furthermore, getting married in Lodz resulted in benefits from the Judenrat: an apartment and a special food ration. Under the conditions of hunger and quarantine in the ghetto, this was a serious incentive.

The great change in the field of weddings, unparalleled anywhere else, was determined in October 1942. After the great *Sperre*, in which most of the ghetto rabbis, among other people, were deported, Rumkowski introduced a revolutionary change: he canceled the religious weddings and took over the functions of both rabbi and recorder. From then on, ghetto inhabitants had to wed in civil ceremonies, the rabbis were deprived of an authority that had been considered central in all generations, and Rumkowski attempted to endow the civil ceremony with a religious nature, just as he tried in various ways to pose as a man of tradition.[21] The authors of the *Lodz Ghetto Chronicle*, members of the ghetto archives staff, preoccupied themselves at length with the new characteristics of weddings in the ghetto. Thus they wrote in October 1942, when the new ceremonies began —a change that, they said, could not be imagined even in a dream,

> Yesterday, at the former Rabbinical Council building at 4 Koscleny Square, on the second floor of the second wing, seven couples got married using the new ritual. At 18:00, in the brightly lit hall, His Honor the President took his place at a table covered with a green cloth. Next to him stood a stool, on which a typewriter was positioned. One by one, the young couples and the witnesses whom they had brought were summoned from the room next door and were arrayed around the table in a semicircle. Strangers were barred from the outset; entrance was by appropriate invitation only.

The President delivered a speech to the assembly, in which he described briefly the situation that had come about when weddings following the rules of the faith were banned. He explained to them that the new wedding ceremony was tailored to the requirements of the time and the circumstances but, nevertheless, did not clash with the requirements of the halakha. Everything had been worked out in coordination with people of authoritative stature and definitely placed the participants in a binding state of matrimony. In the performance of a wedding and an engagement, the most important thing is the phrasing of the vow and the second blessing. These have been preserved; all the rest are just remnants of an ancient tradition that had to vanish under the circumstances of the times. . . .

In fact, these remarks and the new ceremony have no basis whatsoever in halakha and Jewish tradition. No oath is taken in a marriage ceremony, the cup of wine has no halakhic significance and is used only for the purpose of reciting a blessing, and only the tendering of the ring for the purpose of consecrating the marriage in front of witnesses is the gist of the wedding. Thus, in addition to usurping rabbinical powers, Rumkowski created a ludicrous ritual.

At the end of the aforementioned religious rites, His Honor the President recites the seven blessings, loudly but sadly. This sadness well reflects the state of mind of those in attendance, on whose faces one can perceive a certain insecurity and depression. Their faces give no indication that these people are experiencing so important a change in their lives. Afterwards, the couples and the witnesses report to B., the clerk of the Civil Registration Department, and sign the appropriate ledger. After the ceremony is over, His Honor the President parts from the assembly and advises the newlyweds to rush to the cooperative, in order to redeem that very day the coupon that they were given and honor this evening with an appropriate meal.

Thus, this seemingly modest wedding ceremony, held amidst a small group of select invitees, has recorded a new and interesting page in the history of local Jewish public life![22]

In the course of 1944, the number of marriages in the ghetto diminished, and the ceremonies were transferred to smaller locations. In the early summer of 1944, however, a new spate of weddings occurred, and in July of that year Rumkowski married nineteen couples en masse. The authors of the *Chronicle* explained the background for this: the great deportations were underway; the inhabitants had the impression that singles were being deported first and regarded marriage with protected persons and those who held jobs as a chance to save themselves. Thus, the dilemma that came up in Warsaw in 1940 and in Kovno in 1942—marriage as a vehicle of rescue—surfaced in Lodz in 1944.[23]

We have described the wedding system in Lodz at such length because it reflects both the historical and the halakic aspects. What were the implications of these marriages? How did observant Jews, who considered a halakically sound wedding a sine qua non, marry in this ghetto? Several sources allow us to answer this question in part. One of them is comprised of special documents that came into our possession only in recent years since, for understandable reasons, they had not been buried along with the voluminous ghetto archives: underground *ketubot* (marriage contracts). Many people, it turns out, did not settle for Rumkowski's ceremony and surreptitiously asked surviving rabbis to perform halakically correct ceremonies. Ready-made *ketubot* were not available, because such would constitute an expression of rebellion against Rumkowski's rule and lead to the penalties of deportation or withholding of food. Nevertheless, rabbis were not deterred from drawing up handwritten *ketubot,* from memory, in underground ceremonies. Fortunately, at least a few of these documents have survived, attesting to those nuptials that the Jewish historical memory naturally associates with those of the forced converts in Spain.

Only after the war were Rumkowski's ceremonies subjected to broad halakic debate. Such questions were referred to Rabbi Zvi Hirsh Meisels, former rabbi of the community of Waizen, Hungary, who was deported with his students to Auschwitz in 1944.[24] Rabbi Meisels gathered the halakic questions that had been asked there in a volume entitled *She'elot ve-teshuvot meqadeshey shem* (Responsa of the Martyrs). When he was appointed as the rabbi of the survivors in Bergen-Belsen, the main D.P. camp in the British zone, Jews asked him to endorse their wartime marriages. When couples from the Lodz ghetto approached him, he found it difficult to rule on the post-facto validity of these marriages and sought the opinion of one of the greatest halakic arbiters of that generation, Rabbi Yehezkel Abramsky. Meisels and Abramsky discussed these marriages in two detailed responsa and concluded that Rumkowski's weddings could be approved after the fact, provided that "the bride was unmarried and [the groom] consecrated her in front of two qualified witnesses and gave her the ring for the purpose of marriage." However, the second phase of the wedding, the wedding proper, must be completed. Therefore, Rabbi Meisels ordered the couples from Lodz to erect a canopy, have the seven blessings recited, and draw up a *ketuba,* as the halakah requires. And Rabbi

Meisels added, "I believe it would be a holy duty to issue a manifesto ordering anyone married by Rumkowski to refrain from living with his wife until the [halakic requirements of] canopy, seven blessings, and *ketuba* are fulfilled."[25]

As it turns out, however, the question of weddings was discussed in the Lodz ghetto from another perspective, a broad and surprising one. Documents that recently made their way to Israel were found to contain the minutes of several meetings of rabbis in the Lodz ghetto. The minutes bring to light a special debate that took place in 1941 on the so-called retroactive bill of divorce (also known as a "Davidic" bill of divorce or a bill of divorce from a husband about to be sent to war). The question was whether to require all married men in the ghetto to give their wives such a document. The source for this option is in the Talmud, *Ketubot* 9b: "Every man being sent to a Davidic war writes his wife a bill of divorce." The *Tosafot* explain: "If the husband does not return from the war, the bill shall apply from the date on which it was written."[26]

This approach had additional applications in various times, e.g., in a bill of divorce written by a mortally ill person (mainly to exempt his wife from a Levirate marriage) or community ordinances pertaining to persons embarking on lengthy voyages. The *Chronicle of the Lodz Ghetto* also alludes to this sort of bill of divorce, but the context in this case was the issue of the bill by candidates for deportation. An article dated January 13, 1942, reports,

> In regard to the deportation operation, the rabbinical board was empowered to conduct divorces using a simplified procedure, i.e., in circumvention of the panel for bills of divorce. This is in respect to people to whom the deportation requirement applies. A series of events of this type was submitted to the rabbinical board. Most of these cases pertained to spouses who were living apart and wished to divorce, where one of the sides has to leave the ghetto.[27]

This discussion reflects not only a ruling meant to solve regular problems in the ghetto but also a long-term debate that points to an awareness of the Nazi policy. Moreover, it attempted to create a tool that would avert the danger of the *aguna* situation after the war—a retroactive bill of divorce. Unfortunately, we do not know what the decision was and we lack additional sources from this ghetto. Therefore, we can only appreciate the ghetto rabbis' sense of responsibility for the future of the women and the families, in view of their realization, at relatively early stages, that a time of danger was at hand.

Concurrently, we have obtained sources on the same issue from other locations. Far from Lodz, in the Netherlands, the question came up at a very early stage, in July 1941, at a meeting of the board of chief rabbis, at the initiative of Rabbi Philip Frank.[28] When it became known that Dutch Jews who had been sent to Buchenwald were dying, Rabbi Frank suggested that husbands write their wives conditional bills of divorce. Opponents of this measure believed that it would foment panic, but eventually they adopted a retroactive bill of divorce prepared by Rabbi Aaron Issachar Davids, the chief rabbi of Rotterdam. A specimen of this document was sent by Chief Rabbi Sirlowy to Rabbi Levisson, who as rabbi of the vicinity had access to the camp.[29] These bills were used mainly in 1943. Professor Dan Michman found a list of twenty such cases; other documents in this matter remain in the possession of survivors from the Netherlands. One of them was handed to me during my participation in eliciting testimonies from *haredim* for Steven Spielberg's Survivors of the Shoah Visual History Foundation. It is a halakic document, a question-and-responsum, sent by Rabbi Frank from the Westerbork transit camp in the Netherlands to Rabbi A. S. Levisson, the witness's father, who was still in Amsterdam. Rabbi Levisson suggested to his colleague in Westerbork that a form be prepared for each person in the camp to fill out. The document is, in fact, a "Davidic bill of divorce" as applied in the Netherlands during the Holocaust. As the rabbi and the witnesses looked on, the prisoner signed his wife's retroactive bill of divorce in the following cautious and sensitive phrasing: "Herewith is your bill of divorce, and you shall not be divorced thereby except after five years, and then you shall be divorced thereby from me and permitted to any man."[30]

When the war ended and the gates of the camps were flung open, as the survivors began to fathom the magnitude of the disaster and attend to their physical rehabilitation, many weddings were conducted in the D.P. camps and new families began to form. The motives for this were clear: a remedy for the terrible loneliness, an expression of the existential need for a home, a reflection of personal and collective resurrection, and a way of ensuring continuity of the family and the Jewish people, as well as desire for revenge against the Germans. The spate of marriages led to a halakic rediscussion. The war had left a thick residue of unanswered questions in regard to marriages, foremost among them questions concerning *agunot*. The rabbis were under time pressure to decide quickly, examine information hastily, and provide an essential infrastructure for married life in accordance with halakah, by study of the halakic rules and construction of ritual pools. The D.P. camp rabbis acted with celerity in this matter. Rabbi Ahronson, mentioned above in the context of the discussion in Warsaw, was named rabbi of the D.P.s in the Austrian occupation zone. He acted personally and in conjunction with rabbinical committees to seek halakically sound ways to enable *agunot* to remarry. To accomplish this, he established relations with rabbis around the world. His archives contain some one hundred letters on this topic from various locations. A central figure in them was Rabbi Shlomo David Kahana of Warsaw-Jerusalem, who devoted all his time to this matter.[31] Rabbi Kahana recorded in his notebook the names of all couples married by his rabbinical association, along with an explanation of their personal status. Other questions concerned mixed marriages during the war, including some involving Jewish women who wished to convert German men in order to marry them. Other problems included Levirate-marriage situations and mixed couples from the war and afterward.[32]

The issue of sustaining marital relations under halakic requirements also resurfaced. With alacrity, twenty-six ritual pools were constructed in D.P. camps. A special booklet with a concise presentation of halakic marital laws was published and distributed in hundreds of copies. Some rabbis who officiated at weddings were survivors; others came from the free world and conducted many weddings while on morale-boosting visits. An example of the latter is Rabbi Hizkiyahu Yosef Miszkowski of Kriniki/Palestine. A prominent personality in the D.P. camps in this matter, as in other respects, was the Klausenberger Rebbe, Rabbi Yekusiel Halberstam. Although he was headquartered in Fernwald, in the American occupation zone, his influence reached many D.P. camps. He personally entertained brides and grooms, dancing in front of those whose parents were only harsh memories. He also established an organization named Hakhnasat Kalla to meet the couples' initial needs. His enterprises even included a free-loan collection of wedding dresses in the D.P. camp.

The deceptive, camouflaged, and sudden nature of the deportation process had left the fate of many deportees shrouded in uncertainty. For this reason, coupled with the survivors' loneliness and the celerity with which they wished to establish new households, halakic questions from *agunot* rose in intensity. Special rabbinical courts were established in D.P. camps and around the world. Rabbi S. Meisels presents some of these questions in his work *Kuntres ha-Agunot*.[33] Despite the world-spanning

inquiries, erroneous decisions occurred, such as the one involving a husband who returned from the Russian occupation zone after his wife had
been allowed to remarry. Thus, the mass murders during the Holocaust
also came to light during these months in the course of a halakic inquiry
that, to some extent, may have been the earliest research on the death
camps and the extermination of the Jews. I present as an example one
document that reflects this in the power and simplicity of its elocution.
The author was Rabbi Hayyim Yehuda Leib Auerbach, one of the leading
rabbis of Jerusalem, head of the kabbalists' yeshiva Sha'ar ha-Shamayim, a
noted rabbinical judge and the father of Rabbi Shlomo Zalman Auerbach,
the leading halakic arbiter in our generation. The elder Rabbi Auerbach
asks the Jewish Agency a simple question: "What is Sobibór?" A woman
survivor has turned to him in Jerusalem and asked his permission to
remarry since her husband had been sent there. The rabbi wishes to know
whether Sobibór was a ghetto or a camp, and how likely it would be for
a person to survive it.[34] Thus, even a query concerning the essence of
Sobibór is vested with a halakic aspect.

We have attempted to provide an overview that uses a single mirror to
reflect both the history of the time and the history of halakah. By means
of one theme, I wished to create a path toward a new approach to the
topic, rooted in an understanding of the need for an individualized attitude and avoidance of inclusive statements, an awareness of the essential
relationship between halakah and historical research, an understanding
of the continual dynamic of halakic decision making, access to the world
of rabbis who continued to carry the burden of their role, an attempt
to find trends of constancy and variance in their rulings, and an attempt
to respond to them. The standpoint adopted reflects the challenge of finding and deciphering still-new sources of research on halakah in the Holocaust and the need for sensitivity to this special manifestation of the agony
of that time, in which the distresses of the questioner and the respondent
intermingled to tell so grim a tale. The confrontations of halakah and faith
with the Holocaust are the narratives of thousands of people, a story still
untold.

The topic of this paper ostensibly deviates from the other papers at this
conference, since it deals with the Holocaust era itself and not with its
educational and religious implications. However, the discerning listener
will notice that the perception reflected in the essay, in terms of its contents, typifies the outlook of a large *haredi* public that, perhaps, does not
often illuminate its viewpoints with the tools of research but that lives

with the memory of the Holocaust in its own way and, thus, remembers and commemorates the Holocaust as a link in the chain of ordeals that the Jews have endured.

One of the great answers to the question of continuity is rooted in the very act of laying new cornerstones in the Jewish edifice amidst and immediately after the devastation—joyless ceremonies in which the two components of ordinary Jewish weddings, as expressed in Jeremiah 33:11—the sounds of delight and glee and the voices of newlyweds—did not intermingle, but were girders in personal and national resurrection.

NOTES

1. The lectures were published in *Ha-'amida ha-yehudit bi-yemey ha-sho'a* (Jerusalem, 1970). For the history and meanings of the term "resistance," see Dan Michman, "Jewish Resistance in the Holocaust and Its Significance," in Dan Michman, *The Holocaust and Holocaust Research* (Tel Aviv, 1998), 159–89 (Hebrew). Michman distinguishes between "resistance" and "armed resistance" by defining the latter as part of the former.

2. Joseph Walk, "The Religious Leadership during the Holocaust," *The Image of the Jewish Leadership in the Nazi-Controlled Countries* (Jerusalem, 1980), 325–35 (Hebrew). Additional basic works in research on the topic are I. J. Rosenbaum, *The Holocaust and Halakhah* (New York, 1976) and H. J. Zimmels, *The Echo of Nazi Holocaust in Rabbinic Literature* (London, 1975).

3. The expression "sandal strap" is meant as a symbol of a trivial, typical Gentile object that a Gentile forces a Jew to use in order to make the Jew resemble him.

4. Definitions of assorted relevant concepts—saving of life, duress, the persecuted Jew, fear of desecration of God's name, etc.—appear in Rabbi Ahronson's various rulings. See Esther Farbstein, "In the Company of the Writings of a Community Rabbi during the Holocaust," Part B, *Sinai*, vol. 18 (Spring 1996), 59–62 (Hebrew).

5. Yosef Nedava, "Problems of Halakha in the Ghettos," *Pages for Study of the Holocaust,* vol. 1 (Jerusalem, 1979), 44–55 (Hebrew).

6. Penina Feig, "Rabbinical Rulings concerning Selection during the Holocaust," *Shana b'Shana* (Jerusalem, 1991), 321–40 (Hebrew).

7. Rabbi Ahronson wrote extensively, and through a lengthy path most of his writings have reached us in recent years: diary, memoirs, book of rabbinical records from his tenure as chief rabbi of the D.P. camps in Austria, and philosophical writings that he produced from the end of the Holocaust until his death in 1993. Some of the writings are in the Ghetto Fighters' Archives and the Yad Vashem Archives; some are in the family's possession. They are gathered in his

book *'Aley merorot* (Benei Berak, 1996). See also Esther Farbstein, "Diaries and Memoirs as a Historical Source," *Yad Vashem Studies,* vol. 26 (1998), 87–128.

8. The original sheet was in my possession when I did historical editing for the book. For a photocopy, see *'Aley merorot,* 241.

9. "*Nisyones,*" *'Aley merorot,* ibid., 230. See also Farbstein, "In the Company of the Writings of a Community Rabbi," ibid., 153–54.

10. Was the rabbinical conference in Warsaw after the beginning of the Nazi occupation a nonrecurrent event? Several sources inform us about additional conferences or joint decisions in Warsaw. For example, Ahronson's memoirs describe a conference on welfare matters. The memory of these rabbinical assemblies remained with him throughout the period, and when as one of the few surviving community rabbis from Poland he was named chief rabbi of the survivors in Austria, he described this conference and considered himself virtually the only rabbi in attendance who survived. Documents in our possession speak of additional rabbinical conferences and their joint broadsheets.

11. Rabbi Shimon Huberband, "Qidush ha-shem" [Sanctification of God's Name], *Writings from the Ringelblum Archives in the Warsaw Ghetto* (Jerusalem, 1969), 92–93 (Hebrew).

12. Some, however, disagreed. For example, Leib Yod, a Ger hassid from Warsaw, testified that the Gerrer rebbe's brother, R. Moshe Betsalel Alter, authorized weddings in the ghetto and said the merit of this commandment served the Israelites well during the slavery in Egypt and was a great virtue in the faith. Moshe Prager, *Those Who Did Not Surrender* (Jerusalem, 1977, second printing), part A, p. 71.

13. Huberband, Rabbi Shimon, "Qidush ha-shem," ibid., 89.

14. Letter from the Committee of Rabbis to the manager of the coals warehouse at the Judenrat, signed by four rabbis, April 1941, *Qidush ha-shem* archives, file "Women."

15. *'Aley merorot,* ibid., 232–33.

16. According to B.T. *Sotah* 12a,

And a man from the House of Levi went . . . Where did he go? R. Yehuda said . . . "he went [following] his daughter's advice." It is learned: Amram was the greatest sage of his generation; when he saw that the wicked Pharaoh said, "Hurl every newborn boy into the Nile," he said: "we are laboring for naught." He stood up and divorced his wife. They all stood up and divorced their wives. His daughter said to him, "Father, your decree is more severe than Pharaoh's. For Pharaoh decreed concerning only the males, and you have decreed concerning both males and females. Pharaoh decreed in the present world only, and you— in the present world and for the world to come. The wicked Pharaoh's decree may come to pass and may not; you are righteous; your decree will surely come to pass. . . ." He stood up and remarried his wife. They all stood up and remarried their wives.

17. Ephraim Oshry, *Responsa mi-ma'amaqim,* 51 (1959–1980), 9 volumes (New York, 1979), vol. 1, part 4, 22–37.

18. *Lodz Ghetto Chronicle* (Jerusalem, 1990), part A, 268–69.

19. *Chronicle,* part A, paragraphs 26–28. The rabbi from Kovno made special and strenuous efforts in the interwar period to bolster observance of the marital laws, gave lectures, and wrote an important halakic pamphlet for women.

20. *Chronicle,* 314.

21. Only those who understand the consequences of abolishing the halakic framework of marriage can appreciate the grotesqueness of this representation, to which even historians fell prey.

22. *Lodz Ghetto Chronicle,* vol. B, 301–302 (Hebrew). The many ghetto documents that survived include copies of the *ketuba* that Rumkowski printed in the ghetto, bearing his prominent signature in the place that halakah reserves for the signatures of the witnesses. The texts were commemorated in numerous photographs in which Rumkowski appears with couples that he married. On November 23, 1942, the "president" augmented the benefits with a clothing coupon—it, too, in an ostensible connection with the tradition: "to reinstate the old practice of giving sermon gifts to the groom and bride" (part B, 361). By this time, weddings were no longer personal events; it became a norm in the ghetto—for reasons that evidently included efficiency—to conduct nuptials for many couples at once. In the course of 1943, the authors of the *Chronicle* recorded the collective weddings of eleven to twenty couples by "His Honor the President" (throughout part C of the *Chronicle*). In May 1942, the weddings were moved to Rumkowski's summer apartment in Marisyn because of his illness, and groups of twelve to thirteen couples, without the participation of their families, marched there on foot. The *Chronicle* explains, "With the brides' hairdos made untidy by the winds of Marisyn [and with] the President in festive attire, twenty-five couples reached the safe haven of matrimony under unique conditions." These weddings were so dependent on Rumkowski that doubts about whether or not they would take place were expressed in routine writing (e.g., June 1943). Most weddings were held on Sundays to avoid loss of work. As time passed, Rumkowski modified the wedding ceremony in additional ways, such as a mutual exchange of rings, "even though this is not a Jewish custom" (*Chronicle,* 267).

23. In the Netherlands, there was a wave of weddings in March–April 1942, shortly before Passover that year. This corresponded with the beginning of deportations to "labor camps," it being assumed that married men would not be sent to slave labor. On the eve of Passover, Rabbi Shuster in Amsterdam married sixty couples, using a ceremony worked out in advance by the rabbis, in three synagogues, in groups of five couples, each ceremony lasting about one hour. Another wave occurred in the summer of 1942. See Dan Michman, "The Rabbinical Leadership in the Netherlands during the Holocaust," in *Pages for the Study of the Holocaust,* vol. 7, 81–106. In Slovakia, Rabbi Frieder married many couples to save them

from deportation, in view of the deportations of girls and teenagers. There are additional examples. See Dan Michman, "The Daily Life of the Religious Jew under the Conditions of the Holocaust," in Dan Michman, *The Holocaust and Holocaust Research*, esp. 221–22 (Hebrew).

24. The halakic questions presented to him in Auschwitz have been published in his book, *Responsa meqadeshey ha-shem* (Chicago, 1955–1967), (Hebrew).

25. Rabbi Zvi Hirsh Meisels, *Responsa binyan Zvi* (New York, 1956), part B, 32, paragraph b (Hebrew).

26. The source for this is an exegetic reading of a verse in I Samuel 17:1.

27. *Lodz Ghetto Chronicle*, 57. See also Dan Michman, "Rabbinical Leadership," in *In Days of Holocaust and Reckoning*, Unit 10 (Tel Aviv, 1990), 156 (Hebrew).

28. Rabbi Levisson, rabbi of the vicinity of the Westerbork camp, had been active among the camp prisoners since the camp was established for refugees from Germany in 1939. He assured the existence of extensive religious activity, was nicknamed "Rabbi Simcha" (denoting "joy" or "joyous occasions"), and was held in great esteem. Dan Michman, "Rabbinical Leadership," 85.

29. Dan Michman, "Rabbinical Leadership," 92–93, 156. Rabbi Philip Frank, of Haarlem, was chief rabbi of northern Holland. An important public figure, he was executed in January 1943. Dan Michman, "Rabbinical Leadership," 84.

30. The document is in my possession.

31. Additional noted rabbis in Palestine/Israel dealt in these matters, e.g., the chief rabbi of Israel, Isaac Halevy Herzog, and Rabbi Shimon Katz of Petah Tiqva.

32. Rabbi J. M. Ahronson, *'Aley merorot*, 416.

33. Rabbi S. Meisels, *Kuntres Agunot* (Bergen-Belsen, 1947).

34. Rabbi Hayyim Yehuda Leib Auerbach, letter to members of the Jewish Agency rescue committee, December 6, 1944. Central Zionist Archives, 851/12 5613.

Chapter 9

Two Jewish Approaches to Evil in History

Warren Zev Harvey

In his classic book *Major Trends in Jewish Mysticism,* Gershom Scholem, who was not only a historian of the Kabbalah, but also, to use the expression of Moshe Idel, a "theoretician of the Kabbalah," contrasts the approaches of Kabbalah and Jewish philosophy. His contrast amounts to an appreciation of the Kabbalah and a critique of Jewish philosophy. One focus of his contrast is the problem of evil in history. The theoretician of the Kabbalah writes as follows:

> The fact of the existence of evil in the world is the main touchstone of [the] difference between the philosophic and the Kabbalistic outlook. On the whole, the philosophers of Judaism treat the existence of evil as something meaningless in itself. . . . To most Kabbalists . . . the existence of evil is . . . one of the most pressing problems, and one which keeps them continuously occupied with attempts to solve it. They have a strong sense of the reality of evil. . . . They do not, like the philosophers, seek to evade its existence with the aid of a convenient formula.[1]

Scholem often returned to this theme. In his celebrated article on "Kabbalah" in the *Encyclopaedia Judaica,* he formulated it as follows:

> The question of the origin and nature of evil was one of the principal motivating forces behind kabbalistic speculation. In the importance attached to it lies one of the basic differences between kabbalistic doctrine and Jewish philosophy, which gave little original thought to the problem of evil.[2]

In the alleged philosophic view that the existence of evil is "something meaningless in itself," Scholem saw a clear expression of the irrelevance of philosophy to the fundamental existential concerns of human beings. He writes, in the aforementioned discussion in *Major Trends*, about how Jewish philosophy lost touch with flesh-and-blood human beings:

> Kabbalism . . . did not turn its back on the primitive side of life, that all-important region where mortals are afraid of life and in fear of death, and derive scant wisdom from rational philosophy. Philosophy ignored these fears . . . and in turning its back upon the primitive side of man's existence, it paid a high price in losing touch with him altogether. For it is cold comfort to those who are plagued by genuine fear and sorrow to be told that their troubles are but the workings of the imagination.[3]

Scholem's accusation against Jewish philosophy is grave. By ignoring primitive human fears, the philosophers made themselves utterly irrelevant. Whereas the kabbalists had something important to say to suffering human beings, the philosophers did not; *for it is cold comfort to those who are plagued by genuine fear and sorrow to be told that their troubles are but the workings of the imagination.*

The main medieval target of Scholem's comments about Jewish philosophy is the greatest of all medieval Jewish philosophers, Moses Maimonides. In his *Guide of the Perplexed,* part 3, chapter 10, Maimonides had indeed written that evil is a "privation" or "nonexistence" (Arabic: *'adam*; Ibn Tibbon's Hebrew translation: *he'der*); and he had argued in *Guide,* part 1, chapter 2, that the notions of "good" and "evil" are not objects of the intellect, and a purely rational individual could not even conceive of them. Moreover, in *Guide,* 3, 12, he attributes the multitude's obsession with the problem of evil to their "imagination."

If Maimonides was Scholem's main medieval target, his main target among the modern Jewish philosophers was Hermann Cohen, whose approach to evil may have been influenced more by Maimonides than by Kant. He quotes Cohen as stating in his *Ethics of Pure Will* that "evil is non-existent," and "a power of evil exists only in myth."[4]

In responding to Cohen's statement of the alleged position of the Jewish philosophers, Scholem fastens onto his use of the word "myth." Myth does not have for Scholem the same negative connotations that it had for Cohen. He sees myth as being connected to "the primitive side of man's existence"—that is, as being connected to the most profound human emotions, to true human life. He then addresses himself to the conflict between philosophy and myth implicit in Cohen's statement: "One may doubt the philosophic truth of [Cohen's] statement [that a power of evil exists only in myth], but assuming its truth it is obvious that something can be said for 'myth' in its struggle with 'philosophy.'"[5] In other words, it may or may not be true that a power of evil exists in reality; but even if it does not, the mythic approach to evil has some advantages over the philosophic approach. The main advantage, of course, is that myth addresses itself to the fears that inhabit "the primitive side of man's existence," while philosophy is irrelevant to them. Having expressed his sympathy with myth in its struggle against philosophy, Scholem reminds us that the kabbalists are "true seal-bearers of the world of myth."[6]

I should like now to say some words about the two Jewish approaches to evil suggested in Scholem's comments: the *mythic* kabbalistic approach and the *rational* philosophic approach. To be sure, Scholem's distinction between "the kabbalists" and "the philosophers" is overly simplistic. Not all kabbalists fit his description of "kabbalists," and not all philosophers fit his description of "philosophers." Nonetheless, there is a heuristic advantage in this simplicity, and so I shall accept his distinction as is, without calling attention to counterexamples.

Let me begin by trying to clarify briefly what the philosophers mean by saying that evil is a privation or nonexistence. I wish to defend reason against myth, philosophy against Kabbalah, Maimonides against Scholem. In our urgent search, after the Holocaust, for an understanding of the problem of evil in history, I believe that we have a need to turn to Maimonides and our other Jewish philosophers, and it is at our peril that we turn to our kabbalistic mythmakers.

Evil as a Privation vs. Evil as a Power

Maimonides teaches that evil is not a power, but a privation. What about the Satan of our myths, who is admittedly mentioned in the Bible? Is not Satan the power of evil? To dispel such ideas, Maimonides cites a rabbinic dictum: "Satan, the evil inclination, and the angel of death are one and the same" (B.T. *Baba Batra* 16a). Satan is thus not an independent power but a literary personification of the psychological principle known as the "evil inclination" (Hebrew: *yeser ha-ra'*).[7] Maimonides further explains that "the imagination . . . is the evil inclination."[8] "Satan" would thus seem to be a mere metaphor for the imagination. It is not clear whether Maimonides means that Satan is the faculty of imagination, the act of imagination, or the imaginary object. He may mean that Satan is "privation" or "nonexistence," which is the object of the faculty of imagination (since what does not exist cannot be known by the intellect, but only imagined).[9] In any case, Satan is the cause of hallucinations, delusions, fantasies, irrational thought, and—yes—myth. The name "Satan," Maimonides reminds us, comes from the root *satoh,* meaning "to stray" or "to deviate."[10] Satan represents the psychological principle that leads us astray from the way of reason. Understood thus, Satan is not a product of myth, but myths are a product of Satan.

The identification of Satan with the privation of reason fits the following passage from *Guide,* 3, 11, in which Maimonides speaks about the causes of the evils that human beings wreak upon other human beings.

> The great evils that come about between the human individuals who inflict them upon one another because of purposes, desires, opinions, and beliefs, are all . . . consequent upon privation [or "nonexistence"]. For all of them derive from ignorance, I mean a privation of knowledge. . . . For through the cognition of truth, enmity and hatred are removed, and the inflicting of harm by people on one another is abolished.
>
> [Scripture] holds out this promise, saying, "And the wolf shall dwell with the lamb . . . ," and so on [Isaiah 11:6–8]. Then it gives the reason for this, saying that the cause of the abolition of these enmities, these discords, and these tyrannies will be the knowledge that human beings will then have concerning the true reality of the Deity. For it says: "They shall not hurt nor destroy in all My holy mountain, for the earth shall be full of the knowledge of the Lord, as the waters cover the sea" [ibid., v. 9].[11]

Maimonides explains that the great evils human beings inflict upon other human beings in history are a result of a privation or a nonexistence—the privation or nonexistence of knowledge. Wars, oppression, terror, and murder are a result of ignorance. Rational human beings know that peace and cooperation are necessary in order to fulfill their true physical and spiritual needs. Irrational human beings, motivated by their imaginary desires, by their delusions, that is, by the psychological principle personified in the Bible by Satan, do not know how to cooperate with other human beings but quarrel with them, hurt them, oppress them, and murder them. Maimonides defines the messianic era as that time when reason, the rule of God, will be victorious over delusion, the rule of Satan.

For Maimonides, the problem of evil in history is not fundamentally a metaphysical problem but a psychological and political one. It is a problem concerning human behavior.

If the evils human beings inflict upon each other in history are the result of the privation of knowledge, then there are measures we can take to prevent them. We can give our children a strong education in the sciences in order to develop their reason and to protect them against the delusions of the imagination. We can teach them ethics, and explain to them the importance of peace and cooperation. We can run our political communities in accordance with reason, not delusion, and we can take prudent and firm action against irrational individuals who would foment hate, strife, and violence.

Interpreting the verse "our fathers sinned and are no more" (Lamentations 5:7), which refers to the destruction of the First Temple by the Babylonians, Maimonides writes that our ancestors sinned in that they consulted astrologers instead of studying the art of war. Therefore, Maimonides continues, the prophets called them "fools and dolts" (Jeremiah 4:22). Their *sin* was that they were *fools and dolts,* who thought they could defeat the invading Babylonians by astrology instead of by the art of war. Their sin was their irrationality, and their punishment was the destruction of the Temple and the Babylonian captivity. The evil of the destruction and the captivity was caused by a privation, the privation of reason.[12]

The kabbalistic or mythic idea of evil in history is, as Scholem had rightly observed, much different from that of the philosophers. For the kabbalists, evil is not a privation but a real entity, and Satan is not a metaphor but a cosmic power. Satan is the power of evil. He is known also as "the Other Side" or "*Sitra Ahra,*" that is, "the Rival of the Divine." As God is present in the universe by means of His ten emanations or *sefirot,* so the Other Side is comprised of ten alternative *sefirot,* which are a sort of shadow government challenging the rule of the King of the Universe. Satan is so powerful that he poses a threat to God Himself.

For the kabbalists, in contrast to Maimonides, the problem of evil in history is not fundamentally a psychological or political one, but a metaphysical one.

Action vs. Comfort

Scholem had ridiculed the philosophic approach to evil, saying, "It is cold comfort to those who are plagued by genuine fear and sorrow to be told that their troubles are but the workings of the imagination." It is presumably more comforting to be told that the evils that plague us are the workings of the *Sitra Ahra*. There is perhaps comfort in the belief that we human beings are not primarily responsible for the evils that befall us. It is consoling to imagine that we could not have prevented them, for they were wrought by a power who can be defeated only by God. The kabbalists do say that we can assist God in his apocalyptic war against the *Sitra Ahra* by praying and doing pious deeds. However, in the end, the belief that the *Sitra Ahra* is the cause of the evils that afflict us leads to a severe diminution of human responsibility.

The Kabbalah, like astrology, may provide comfort in the face of evil, at least in the short run. However, this comfort is achieved at the price of ignorance of the true causes of our plight and of a consequent inability to ameliorate it. By turning the problem of evil in history into a metaphysical problem, the kabbalists drew attention away from its true psychological and political causes.

The Maimonidean philosophers, unlike the kabbalists and the astrologers, were not primarily concerned about providing comfort as a response to evil. They were more concerned about *preventing* evil. They were concerned about human *responsibility,* and the awareness of human responsibility often causes discomfort, not comfort. They insisted that the source of the evils that human beings inflict upon one other is not in some external Satan, but inside the human beings themselves. Since the source of evils is human, we humans can prevent them. *We are responsible.* One can prevent evils by acting in accordance with reason. One prevents defeat in war not by consulting horoscopes or writing amulets with the names of the proper *sefirot* on them, but by studying the art of war. Maimonides and his followers sought to understand the psychological and political causes of evil in history in order to determine what *actions* need to be taken in order to prevent its recurrence.

The Kabbalah and Maimonidean philosophy do represent two opposing approaches to the problem of evil in history. If the former tried to comfort the people with myth, the latter tried to improve their situation with reason.

The Holocaust

The kabbalistic approach, according to which the Holocaust was caused by the *Sitra Ahra*, implies that the prevention of future tyranny and genocide is not primarily in the hands of us human beings. Human beings were not responsible for the Holocaust and are not responsible for preventing a future Holocaust. As opposed to the kabbalistic approach, the Maimonidean one begins with the fact that the evils of the Holocaust were perpetrated by human beings against human beings, and could have been prevented by human beings. It seeks to understand the psychological and political causes of those evils—that is, to identify the privations of knowledge that made them possible. To understand how the Holocaust came about is to understand how a future Holocaust can be prevented.

It was a desire to restrain the mythical interpretation of the Holocaust that in recent years led the survivor-author K. Zetnik to question his own powerful and unforgettable description of "the planet Auschwitz," whose laws of nature differ from those on our planet. Auschwitz, he now stressed, was run by human beings, not Satan, and was located here on earth.[13]

That regular human beings are capable of great evil is the true horror that Maimonides, unlike the kabbalists, dared to face squarely.

Arendt vs. Scholem

In my comments until now, I have been responding to Gershom Scholem in the name of the Jewish philosophers. Let me now conclude by quoting a famous response to Scholem given to him in his lifetime by an important Jewish philosopher.

In the fascinating exchange of letters between Gershom Scholem and Hannah Arendt in 1963 concerning Arendt's *Eichmann in Jerusalem*, Scholem took exception to Arendt's thesis about "the banality of evil." He did not understand how Arendt, who in the past had written eloquently and eruditely about "radical evil," could now affirm the contrary thesis: evil was not radical but banal. She replied to him as follows:

> You are quite right: I changed my mind and do no longer speak of "radical evil." . . . It is indeed my opinion now that evil is never "radical," that it is only extreme, and that it possesses neither depth nor any demonic dimension. It can overgrow and lay waste the whole world precisely because it spreads like a fungus on the surface. It is "thought-defying" . . . because thought tries to reach some depth, to go to the roots, and the moment it concerns itself with evil, it is frustrated because there is nothing. That is its "banality." Only the good has depth and can be radical.[14]

With these words, Arendt was responding not only to Scholem's remarks in his letter to her, but in effect also to his pro-kabbalistic and anti-Maimonidean statements about the problem of evil in *Major Trends in Jewish Mysticism* and elsewhere. Evil, she asserted, has no demonic dimension: "There is nothing." Alluding to those rare individuals who during the Nazi regime bravely acted to save Jews, she concluded, "Only the good . . . can be radical."

NOTES

1. Gershom Scholem, *Major Trends in Jewish Mysticism* (New York, 1941), 35–36.

2. *Encyclopaedia Judaica* (Jerusalem, 1971), vol. 10, 583.

3. *Major Trends,* 35.

4. Ibid., 36. On 355, Scholem cites *Ethik des reinen Willens,* 2nd edition (Berlin 1907), 452.

5. *Major Trends,* 36.

6. Ibid.

7. Maimonides, *The Guide of the Perplexed,* trans. S. Pines (Chicago, 1963), part 3, chap. 22, 489.

8. Ibid., part 2, chap. 12, 280.

9. In identifying the imagination with the evil inclination, Maimonides does not use the term "*mutakhayyilah,*" which usually denotes the imaginative faculty, but "*khayy_l,*" which may refer to the phantasm or the imagining.

10. *Guide,* part 3, chap. 22, 489.

11. Ibid., part 3, chap. 11, 440–41.

12. Maimonides, *Letter on Astrology,* in R. Lerner and M. Mahdi (eds.), *Medieval Political Philosophy* (Glencoe, IL, 1963), 229.

13. See the testimony of Jehiel Dinur or De-Nur (K. Zetnik, Ka-Tzetnik) at the Eichmann trial in Jerusalem, session 68, 7 June 1961; and see his *Shivitti,* trans. E. N. De-Nur and L. Herman (New York, 1987), 106–9. K. Zetnik, who died in 2001, expressed reservations about his phrase "the planet Auschwitz" on various occasions during his last years.

14. Hannah Arendt, *The Jew as Pariah,* ed. R. H. Feldman (New York, 1978), 245, 250–51.

Chapter 10

A Call to Humility and Jewish Unity in the Aftermath of the Holocaust

Rabbi Shmuel Jakobovits

I am profoundly challenged, indeed humbled, by the task of presenting, in this collection of important essays, a distinctly *haredi* perspective on the terrible Nazi Shoah—and in particular on its ramifications for Jewish unity today.

The Shoah and the question mark hovering over Jewish unity today, for many with implications for their very survival as Jews, are both subjects fraught with agony and—in the absence of actual prophecy—with perhaps totally unfathomable perplexity. I am keenly aware that my thoughts and emotions on the two subjects are intensely personal and subjective, exceedingly finite and inadequate. I offer them here in the belief that our very participation in this discussion together is a powerful statement that underlying Jewish unity is alive and kicking, and in the fervent hope that my few words may strike a responsive note in some minds and thus contribute, even if only minutely, to a new consolidation of Jewish unity. For, to the best of my awareness, even sixty-five years after Nuremberg and fifty-five years after its fearful sequel had run its searing course, the threat to Jewish unity originally unleashed by the Emancipation remains the most basic and fateful issue facing us as a people today.

Allow me a reference to my sainted father, *hareini kaparat mishkavo*, who was a recent president of our host organization, the Memorial Foundation, for several years. He was fond of contrasting the two *mitzvot* of counting *sefirat ha'omer*, the yearly counting of forty-nine days, and *sefirat ha'yovelot*, the counting of fifty-year cycles. The counting of the *omer* is done by every individual, while the counting of the *yovelot* is done only by the *Beit Din Hagadol*. This is to teach you—my father would say—that the layperson is bound to look at the short term, whereas a spiritual leader must have a purview that spans fifty years at a time.

But, in our context, more than fifty years have already passed since the trauma of the Shoah ended, and still no one—not layperson and not spiritual leader—understands. Apparently, this is different.

My father would also often point out that *Yetziat Mitzrayim* (the exodus from Egypt) followed a veritable Shoah, wherein, according to a midrash incorporated by Rashi in his commentary on the verse *vahamushim alu B'nei Yisrael me'eretz Mitzrayim*, four-fifths (!) of the Jews had perished. Yet the survivors did not, morbidly, make the calamity their prime focus of self-awareness; rather, they looked to the future and sang, *az yashir Moshe uv'nei Yisrael et ha'shirah ha'zot leimor*—"*yashir*," in the future tense, "*leimor*," that future generations might continue to sing.

Perhaps it was because the calamity—that aspect—could not be understood. Not by *B'nei Yisrael*; not even by Moshe . . .

Coming back again to our own traumatic experience: what seems most noteworthy about our reactions to the Shoah is the almost total lack of reaction. To be sure, there have been remarkable bursts of new energies, whether in the realization of Zionism by Zionists or in the revitalization of Torah learning and *hassidut* by the *b'nei* Torah and the Hasidim. But there have been no sweeping changes of heart, no dawning of new direction, no new *shirah*. Even the silence seems sadly lacking in profundity.

Now, this may be partly due to the general spiritual superficiality that is growing inexorably on modern humanity. But (and no doubt in a reciprocal relationship of cause and effect with this factor), it is also a measure of the endless depth and of the numbing enormity of the Shoah; the Six-Day War, and even the Yom Kippur War, evinced vastly more significant responses. At least as religious Jews, we have been painfully aware that, in the Shoah, our community was spiritually decimated and thoroughly orphaned.

Another keenly insightful midrash (*Yalkut Shim'oni, Parashat Hukkat*) describes B'nei Yisrael on leaving *Mitzrayim* as unable to give appropriate expression, on their own, to their surely overwhelming, but perhaps numbed or incoherent, feelings. "Even as a child repeats his *parasha* verse by verse after his teacher, so did Moshe Rabbeinu have to say the *shirah* with B'nei Yisrael." Hence, *az yashir* Moshe *uv'nei* Yisrael—Yisrael with Moshe. Only after forty intensely educational years in the wilderness did the next generation "come of age," whereupon *B'nei Yisrael* said another *shirah* on their own, as it says (in *parashat Hukkat*), *az yashir Yisrael et ha'shirah ha'zot leimor*—Yisrael on their own.

But today we are not forty, but fifty-five, years after the deliverance as survivors of the Shoah, and we still have not found our voice. In our fragmented and friction-ridden condition, we are not even poised to begin to find it. For our tragedy was such that we were left, as it were, even without a Moshe Rabbeinu to show us the way—not a Hafetz Hayyim of Radin, not a Rav Meir Simcha of Dvinsk, and hardly even the conditions to produce giants of the spirit of their—or any—kind.

We hear talk of "a new Jewish theology," or "a Holocaust theology." My friends, don't buy it. If we are to be truthful with ourselves, we must recognize that it is neither new nor, historically speaking, essentially Jewish. And its connection with the Shoah is coincidental at best. In its essence, it was already around in the days of the Haskalah and early Reform, which, quite simply, compromised with the prevailing, agnostic European culture.

To my mind, as, I believe, to the mind of every normative, believing Jew, the Shoah can ultimately be only an affirmation of our eternal faith—which (having no papacy!) is unchanging in its essence from Sinai to posterity—as against the ephemeral, though deeply entrenched, humanism of the modern era.

For there is no way the experience of the Shoah can be believed to have any kind of positive meaning whatsoever in a world in which humanity is believed to reign supreme. Indeed, there is no way the appearance of a Hitler can be resolved with the elevation of autonomous humanity to the status of G–d. Theodor Herzl, in countering critics who feared a political Jewish agenda might prompt a backlash against the Jews by European governments, wrote in "The Jewish State" that once the nations had granted Jewish rights there could be no backtracking. Naively indeed did modern humanity put its trust in humanity! And once the wishful pipe dream was so shockingly shattered, the nonideological running amok of most of civilization into a hedonistic materialism was, evidently, inevitable.

Conversely, only the word of the true G–d, of G–d the Creator, can encompass—and indeed foretold—all. "*Mispatecha t'hom rabba*," G–d's judgments are unfathomable. But they are the judgments of a trustworthy G–d, Who is true to His word and will ultimately fulfill His ultimate promise too. The passages in the Torah and the Prophets foretelling the unspeakable sufferings of Israel at the hands of human enemies—but also foretelling our survival despite those sufferings and even because of them (see Rashi, Num. 29:12)—are explicit and hardly understood. One verse, in the book of Daniel, clearly seems to relate specifically to the Shoah:

"And it shall be a time of misfortune such as there never has been from when this people came into being and until that time; and at that time Your people will survive" (Daniel 12:1).

Now, to be sure, our faith and our allegiance to the G–d of Israel were sorely tested in the abyss of the Shoah. That is unassailable. Yet, in kind if not in degree, we have been through that test before, already in the days when there were prophets in Israel—and the ultimate outcome of their soul searching was enshrined for all future times in our daily prayers by the *Anshei Kenesset Ha'gedolah,* a body that included several prophets, at the beginning of the Second Temple period. I believe this piercing saying of our sages in the Talmud (B.T. *Yoma* 69b) says it all:

R' Yehoshua ben Levi said,

> Why were they called "*Anshei Kenesset Ha'gedolah*" (Men of the Great Assembly)? Because they restored the crown [of G–d's glory] to its original stature. Originally, Moshe came and said (Num. 10:17), "the great, the powerful and the awesome G–d." Then came the prophet Yirmyahu and [foretelling the destruction of the First Temple] said: "Behold, strangers are croaking in His Sanctuary! Where are the displays of His awesomeness?" So [in his prayer—Jeremiah 32:18] he omitted the word "awesome"! Then came Daniel and said [during the Babylonian exile]: "Behold, strangers are enslaving His children! Where are the displays of His power?" So [in his prayer—Daniel 9:4] he omitted the word "powerful"! Then came the *Anshei Kenesset Ha'gedolah* and said: "On the contrary! This is His greatest display of power—for He conquers His will, in that He displays extreme patience with the wicked [the oppressors]. And these are His displays of awesomeness: for were it not for the awe of the Holy One Blessed Be He, how could [this] one solitary nation survive amidst the nations of the world?!"

Asks the Talmud, "But how could the earlier teachers, i.e. Jeremiah and Daniel, act thus, and abolish that which Moshe Rabbeinu had introduced?" Answers R' Elazar, "They knew about the Holy One Blessed Be He that He is truthful [and despises falsehood]; therefore they did not speak falsely to Him."

Of course, I fully recognize that even today there are those among us who (in my eyes tragically) do not find it truthfully within themselves to respond to the Shoah—and indeed to the whole of the modern experience —with a reinforced Jewish faith, in its classical terms. Their predisposition is different. And yet, I thoroughly believe we are called upon to do all within our power to hold our basic unity intact. This is the message I have internalized from all the Torah sages of recent generations, without exception. Here I come, then, to the main thrust of my few words, and I hope I will make myself totally clear, while being necessarily concise.

I see two themes arising powerfully from the Shoah that impact importantly on the unity question.

Firstly, while we are all too hopelessly small to judgmentally apportion blame on anyone for the fury that struck us in the Shoah, I submit that we can confidently say this: the Shoah was facilitated by the profound disunity that beset us after the Great Emancipation.

The writings of the rabbinic sages abound with teachings dramatically emphasizing the power of unity among Jews to protect against misfortune, "even if they serve idols(!)" (e.g., *Bereshit Rabba* 38:6).

Secondly, the classically correct response to suffering, or *yissurim,* is humility. The Shoah was perhaps the greatest dose of collective *yissurim* we have ever suffered. Far from allowing it to push us to greater self-reliance and ever more aggressive assertiveness, we must let it lead us to a most profound humility—humility before G–d and humility before the image of G–d in every upright human being.

Herein, I believe, lies the antidote to the deep disunity that continues to afflict us so sorely.

The problem of our disunity across the one "great divide"—that which separates the heteronymous rule of G–d from the autonomous rule of humanity—runs very deep indeed. It is all but intractable, with no major change in sight. Even the very unity we all so desire is itself conceived differently by the two sides.

But what faces us today is not the case of new Judaism, which would inevitably have to lead to a split into separate peoples. Today's secularists or reformers are not akin to the Samaritans or the Sadducees or the early Christians or the Karaites. Nor are they, generally, outright assimilationists, who no longer take pride in being Jewish. Rather, they are compromisers who identify with the prevailing zeitgeist while still wanting also to remain distinct as Jews. Therefore, with a generous dose of humility and patience with each other—whereby we recognize things for what they are, realize the limits of our reaches, and refrain from aggressive or assertive agendas—we can still learn to live side by side in peace, bound together by overt familial solidarity, for the benefit of all. This should be the basis of a distinctly Jewish democracy, a democracy of humility.

If we can today derive from the undying memory of the Shoah the dual profound lessons of unity and humility, then we may yet ultimately find it truthfully within ourselves, all of us together, to sing a profoundly new *shirah,* the kind of "*hallel*" made possible only in the aftermath of suffering. In unity and humility, we may all of us yet proclaim together, with a whole heart, "*yitgadal v'yitkadash shemeih rabba*"! (may His great Name grow exalted and sanctified).

Part II

The Holocaust and the State of Israel

Is There Religious Meaning to the Rebirth of the State of Israel after the Shoah?

Shalom Ratzabi

The question posed in the title of this paper involves too many issues to be dealt with in one paper. I will therefore confine my discussion in the present essay to national religious Zionist thought as it has been manifested during the last century. The theme of this discussion is that although the greatest stream in the Zionist camp bases its outlook on traditional religious Zionist thought, since the 1960s and particularly since 1967, some religious thinkers have started to develop new concepts to determine the connection between Israel and the Shoah. In my view, these religious thinkers believed that Zionist thought had failed to face the totality of the Jewish experience since the Holocaust. This failure was revealed in the fact that the older forms of Zionist thought could not satisfy the religious feelings of the generation whose most formative experience was the Holocaust and the emergence of Israel, and particularly the sequence of these events—that is to say, the realization of the greatest expectations of the Jewish people, such as the ingathering of the exiles and the foundation of the sovereign state of Israel, which actually means the abolition of the "kingdom of bondage," and all of this in only three years after the most catastrophic event in the whole of Jewish history, the Shoah. As a consequence, in the first decade of the existence of the state of Israel, particularly during the phases of anxious expectation before the Six-Day War in 1967 and of the euphoria after Israel's victory that took hold of the whole Jewish people, religious thinkers and theologians began searching for new concepts to explain their religious experience.

Regarding the religious meaning of Israel, two main traditional approaches are prevalent in the religious Zionists' camp. One approach claims that the state of Israel is a human institution. That is, it is a state that has been established to solve existential, political, and other problems that threatened the Jewish people as a collective. Today we might infer that the fundamental premise of this stance is that it perceives in Israel an ordinary state. Consequently, we should treat Israel just as we treat any other modern state. Alternatively, there is the attitude of the major stream in the religious Zionist camp, which bases its Zionist worldview on Rabbi Kook's mystical national doctrine. Assuming that the messianic era is the goal of Judaism, Rabbi Kook identified Zionism with the core of Judaism. The reason for this identification is obvious. If the messianic era is the concrete aim that has shaped Jewish life, it is evident that Zionism, whose aims are the ingathering of the people of Israel and the reestablishment of a sovereign Jewish state in the Holy Land, is the modern embodiment of the messianic hope. This means that Zionism is not a secular ideology but the very heart of the Jewish religion. By adopting Rabbi Kook's mystical Zionist doctrine, this camp perceives the state of Israel as a holy instrument that has an important role in the messianic process.[1]

According to both of these approaches, there is not a unique connection between the rebirth of Israel and the Holocaust. Thus, for example, the first approach views the state of Israel as a response to the Shoah just as it is a response to other existential woes that tormented the Jewish people in exile. One of the pioneers of this position was Rabbi Reines.[2] Apologizing for cooperation with religious Jews (haredim) and nonreligious Jews (hiloniim), he argued that the Zionist movement comes to solve the Tzarat ha-yehudim ("the troubles of the Jews") and not the Tzarath ha-yahdut ("the troubles of Judaism"). This means that there is no necessary connection between Zionism as a political phenomenon and the cultural or religious-spiritual issues confronting the Jewish people. It is obvious that by adopting such a view we are unable to attach any religious significance to the state of Israel. Rather, as the culmination of Zionist activity, the state of Israel is an instrument intended to improve the capacity of the Jewish people to survive in a nonredeemed world. But it has no special religious meaning.

Alternately, according to the second attitude, which is based on Rabbi Kook's mystical teaching, the reborn state of Israel is charged with religious significance. Indeed, from this mystical perspective it is clear that Israel's very being has metaphysical significance. In fact, the state of Israel represents an important stage in the process of universal redemption, while the Shoah is one of the most tragic expressions of the unredeemed character of the world as it presently exists. But even as there is a religious connection between the rebirth of Israel after the Holocaust and the Holocaust itself, this linkage is not an exclusive connection. That is to say, the Shoah does not have any special significance. It has the same status as all other ordeals that have been the destiny of the people of Israel on their route from *galut* ("exile") to *geula* ("redemption"). The Shoah is only one in a chain of results that was caused by the nature of the unredeemed world.

Unfortunately, religious feelings and the very fact of the sequence that exists between the Shoah and the foundation of Israel do not permit the Shoah to be viewed by many as merely another common event. Many Jews with heightened religious sensitivities have felt that the two prevalent ultraorthodox attitudes toward the meaning of Israel did not do justice to the most important events, i.e., the Holocaust and the creation of the Jewish state, in recent Jewish history. As I have already mentioned, these feelings were expressed already in the first decade of Israel's existence and intensified during the period before and after the Six-Day War. As a result, some religious thinkers and theologians began searching for new conceptual models by which to explain recent and contemporary historical events within their existential religious experience.

And indeed, it is true that the two main ultraorthodox theological schemas cannot adequately deal with the existence of the state of Israel, nor can they cope with the intuited religious connection between the Shoah and the rebirth of Israel three years after the end of World War II. The reason for this inability is inherent in their nature, and particularly in the historical situation that caused their shaping. As mentioned above, these approaches are not new at all. They were shaped and articulated in the formative years of the national religious Zionist movement and then repeated without change during the Mandatory era and then maintained in the first decades of the sovereign state of Israel. In those years, and in the early decades of the Zionist movement, national religious thinkers like Rabbi Reines, Rabbi Kook, and others had to struggle with two difficulties. The first was the halakic problem, that is, how to justify cooperation between religious Jews (*haredim*) and nonreligious Jews (*hiloniim*). The second was a theological one: how to evaluate the relation between Zionism and the messianic idea.

Rabbi Reines solved these difficulties by putting Zionist activities on the level of the Jewish struggle for survival. Thus, he was able to treat Zionism as a national philanthropic enterprise. Doing so severed the connection

between Zionism and messianism. In addition, he redefined Jewish identity utilizing the general conception of *Amamut* ("peoplehood"), which
includes religious, ethical, historical, and biological components. Accordingly, the cooperation between *haredim* and *hiloniim* was justified on the
philanthropic and national level. Rabbi Kook resolved these difficulties by
recourse to a mystical outlook. From this perspective, Zionism was not a
new national idea that had been generated from an arsenal of nationalist
theories. Rather, Zionism was only a new and modern expression of the
messianic process, and, justifying cooperation with this process by means
of his mystical system, Kook offered a Hegelianlike argument regarding
the "cunning of reason." As Kook understood the historic situation, the
religious Zionists thought that they were involved in building a secular,
socialist, and democratic state, but in actuality they were God's tool for
completing the messianic process. Obviously, from this point of view the
state of Israel is placed beyond human judgment and ordinary halakic
concepts. "Eventually," as David Hartman has written, "who is to judge or
appreciate a messianic process, which is only God's enterprise?"[3]

The establishment of the state of Israel has created a new situation. Not
only Jewish history but also the self-understanding of the Jewish people
has been radically altered. The dramatic change in the self-understanding
of the Jewish people caused by the establishment of Israel is clearly indicated by the fact that the traditional theological concept *galut,* "exile," has
lost its principle significance. Within the framework of traditional Jewish
thought, *galut* exists on two levels: the metaphysical and the empirical.
These in turn were the basic notions that defined Jewish identity, destiny,
and history. However, with the foundation of the state of Israel, the concept of *galut* has lost its meaning—and this because almost every Jew can
now make *aliyah,* and if he or she chooses to live in another country, this
circumstance is a consequence of personal choice rather than historical or
theological necessity.

Furthermore, the existence of the state of Israel has generated a new
halakic agenda. So, for instance, from the halakic perspective the greatest
difficulty prior to the establishment of the state of Israel was whether it is
permitted to cooperate with nonreligious Jews. In the new reality, where
the state of Israel is a historical fact, that question has lost its relevance.

It seems clear enough that the rebirth of Israel and its existence have
created a new situation that requires reexamining both existing halakic
standards and theological and historical attitudes. And indeed we do find
a new attitude toward the state of Israel among modern religious thinkers

and even among the non-Zionist rabbis. So, for instance, Rabbi Avraham Vainffeld, a non-Zionist, has argued that we are standing before a changed reality when there is a state within our Holy Land. That means, he continued, that we are not facing a halakic question. We, the *haredi* community, were not asked if it was permitted to build the state or not. All we can do now, he said decisively, is to clarify our attitude toward this state and this reality that we have found ourselves confronted with. However, he summed up his decision by pointing out that we do not find in the Bible, the Talmud, or the teachings of the later sages laws that relate to the modern state, nor even a concept like the modern state, and therefore these older sources do not provide a basis on which we can decide whether or not to acknowledge the state.

The implication of this argument is that from the halakic perspective it is not worth wrestling with questions of the legitimacy of the state of Israel or with the problem of cooperation between religious and nonreligious Jews in the maintenance of the state of Israel. The state is a reality and the Jews must treat it as they treat other circumstances they find themselves confronted with. Nevertheless, the religious Jew has to manage his relation with the state on the basis of halakah.

The urgent question is, therefore, whether traditional religious Zionist thought is still relevant. As I hinted before, the previous theological discourse about the legitimacy of Zionism was dominated by the messianic idea. But if we come to examine the enormous Jewish rabbinical and philosophical literature, which was written after the Mishnah (circa 200 C.E.) and before the spread of the Lurianic Kabbalah (sixteenth century), we will find a different tendency with regard to the goal of Jewish life. It seems that the messianic idea as it was presented in this vast literature was mainly a postulate of belief, that is to say a tenet of creed. So we cannot find any commandment (*mitzvah*) or religious law (halakah) that was manipulated on the ground of the messianic idea. At most, we can point at customs whose purpose was to preserve historical Jewish memories and to strengthen the hope for returning to Zion and mending the kingdom of the world in the "kingdom of heaven."

Moreover, even Maimonides, who included the hope for the coming of the Messiah in his Thirteen Principles, did not regard the messianic era as the goal of Judaism. In the last chapter of his *Hilkhoth Melakhim*, which Maimonides devoted to the character of the messianic era, it is implicit that he saw in the Messiah's days an instrument that would create the best environment for the realization of the individual's religious task.

According to this view the goal of the commandments is to create the best social environment in which men and women can protect themselves and each other, can promote justice, and can prevent disturbance. But this aim is only a tool to achieve the highest religious end: to make it possible for all human beings to live lives so well ordered that they can turn their focus away from the matters of this world and dedicate themselves to the life of the intellect. Thus, in the messianic era all the needs of the individual Jew will be provided for and all of his desire will be stilled. In such conditions Jews will be able to devote all their forces, energy, and interests to their highest religious goal of pure intellectual contemplation.[4]

In my opinion the main failure of religious Zionism can be located here. That is to say, on the basis of traditional theological understandings, e.g., those of Maimonides, the State of Israel in general and its religious value in particular have no religious meaning, either as tools for improving the capacity of the Jewish people to survive or as a stage in the messianic process. So, for example, according to Rabbi Kook's mystical doctrine, especially as Rav Kook's son (R. Zvi Kook) and his followers elaborated it, the state of Israel as a messianic tool cannot receive religious meaning. After all, even the Messiah has no intrinsic value and is but an instrument to satisfy religious needs. The same conclusion may be derived from Rabbi Reines's thought. For him, Israel was founded to satisfy a practical political need, so Israel cannot be treated as having religious value.

It is evident to some religious thinkers, such as Emil Fackenheim, Eliezer Berkovits, and others, that if Israel had some dimensions of a religious significance, as indeed sensitive, religious Jews feel, it could requite them only on the basis of its religious functions or if it had been created as the product of religious impulses. So that which can give to a particular event a religious meaning is the free answer and intention. That is to say, the state of Israel may attain religious meaning mainly through the modes by which it improves Jewish religious life or eases the ways of realizing Jewish religious tasks. From this perspective, we can assume that it is not worth spending time on the question of the affinity between the state of Israel and the messianic idea. These considerations, which have become frequent since the sixties, and particularly since the Six-Day War, in the writings of theologians like Rabbi Soloveitchik, Rabbi Berkovits, Prof. D. Hartman, and E. Fackenheim, might be summarized in the generalization that we should return to the traditional Jewish religious line of thought. That means we must adopt the worldview that claims that the aim of Judaism exists in the Jewish people's commitment to their covenant with the God of history and of the world. Pursuant to this outlook the state of Israel must be appreciated through the halakic standards and its role in improving the Jewish people's capacity to actualize its covenant with God as a "nation of priests."

In this framework we can point to at least two major benefits that the state of Israel provides us with. The first benefit is linked to the halakic perspective. The state of Israel creates a new opportunity to broaden the scope of halakah and to renew halakic creativity. Given the complexity of Judaism as a religion that requires regulating the whole life of the Jew, it is obvious that only in Israel can a Jew fulfill this task. After all, according to the halakah the Jewish people must build a holy community. This means that the covenant with God not only includes commandments concerned with the spiritual life of the individual and his or her close environment but also involves commandments whose goal can be completed only if Jews take responsibility for the social, economic, and political aspects of life. Indeed, herein lies the most difficult challenge to contemporary orthodox Jewry.[5]

Besides this benefit, which is connected to matters of halakah, there is a second theological benefit of significance that needs to be understood. It is well known that Judaism encompasses, as Rabbi Soloveitchik put it, two covenants: the Covenant of Egypt and the Covenant of Sinai. The Jew must actualize his or her commitment to God not only in private life but also within the communal frame. Moreover, the Jew's contact with God is based on the life of the people of Israel as a whole. Regarding this dual covenant it is clear that even if the state of Israel is a democratic secular state, it has an important function in maintaining the Sinai covenant. Within the Sinai covenant we find many ceremonies, rituals, and religious laws (halakhot) whose aim is to strengthen the Egypt covenant, that is to say the covenant that is based on natural links such as biological descent and shared history.

Given these values, we can attribute to the reborn state of Israel a fundamental religious role in preserving the unique character and history of the Jewish people. According to this perspective the establishment of Israel after the Shoah must be viewed as a testimony to the determined will of the people of Israel to carry on their mission, even though there have been strong and violent controversies about the content of this mission. So, for example, we find thinkers such as Emil Fackenheim and Eliezer Berkovits who hold that the religious meaning of the rebirth of the state of Israel is connected with the commandment to remember (*mitzvat zachor*). That is to say, Jews must remember their history, which is directed by God. Thus Berkovits, in a manner similar to the way in which he related the existence of the state of Israel to the Holocaust, did not discuss the messianic era but, rather, emphasized that the recreation of a Jewish state by the people of Israel was a collective declaration of belief in the presence of God despite His "hiddenness" during the Holocaust.[6] Accordingly, for Berkovits, the most important aspect of the reestablishment of the state of Israel is that it serves as a *Petah tiqvah* ("a doorway of hope") to Israel's future.[7]

Here we can also begin to gain an understanding of how Fackenheim was able to see a link between Auschwitz and the Six-Day War.[8] Only on the basis of this connection, he argued, can we understand how a military victory was given a religious meaning. Moreover, and going still further, Fackenheim declared that even if there is no religious or historical explanation for the Shoah, we must not only discern a connection between the state of Israel and the Holocaust but must also act in such a way that this connection will be inevitable.[9]

In this regard it is interesting to note the gap that Fackenheim argued for between the messianic era and the more general concept of salvation. Fackenheim argues that an examination of Jewish history proves that "the most characteristic of all Jewish experience" is the experience of salvation, and this is the real aim of Jewish history.[10] Salvation, according to this understanding, is "the sudden removal of a radical threat—a removal so astonishing that the more it is explained the deeper the astonishment becomes."[11] Moreover, and necessarily, salvation is not related to the fate of individual souls but to the fate of the whole Jewish people and Judaism. That is to say, "This side of the end [= the salvation of the Jewish people] of history, it is not the Messianic event that, so is the hope, will remove from humanity as a whole the evils of poverty and injustice, hatred, and war."[12] To make this understanding of salvation clearer he points out the similarity between the splitting of the Red Sea and the Six-Day War.[13] We can, in other words, assume that it is possible to relate to the state of Israel in the same way that we relate to the other sorts of salvation that have occurred in Jewish history. That is to say, even without reference to the messianic idea we can charge the state of Israel with religious meaning in the context of the Jewish people's struggle for survival. So Fackenheim concludes vis-à-vis the establishment of the state of Israel after the Holocaust, "Salvation came once again to the Jewish people in our time, just as it did in previous times; this time, however, it came too late, and all that is new and unprecedented in the contemporary Jewish religious situation is due to this circumstance.[14]

In analyzing the religious ritual of *Yom Ha'atzmaut* (Israel Independence Day), Fackenheim employs the discrimination between the messianic idea and the idea of salvation in an interesting way. There is, he says, no doubt that there is a vast difference between the establishment of the state of Israel and the salvation that we celebrate on Passover, Hanukkah, and Purim. In each of the three last named events, "catastrophe was averted, if but at the last moment. The Jewish people were saved. Coming as it did when it did, the State of Israel could save only the survivors."[15] As a result of this consideration Fackenheim argues that the Jew who celebrates *Yom Ha'atzmaut* by reciting the prayer composed by the Israeli chief rabbinate describing the state of Israel as "the beginning of the growth of redemption" of the Jewish people is doing the correct thing.[16] But he added, "to celebrate *Yom Ha'Atzmaut* as we celebrate the festivals of redemption would be to give meaning to Auschwitz through the rebuilt Jerusalem, and this is impossible."[17] But if this is so, as Fackenheim himself recognizes, "Where is the religious meaning of Israel? What is the salvation [entailed by] the State of Israel?" If the state of Israel had not been established after the Holocaust we would have seen a flight from Judaism and the Jewish people that would "dwarf anything known as 'assimilation.'"[18] Moreover, he goes on,

> Who could blame them [the remainder of the Jewish people]? Not long ago the world was divided into one part bent on the murder of every available Jew, and another that did less than was possible to prevent it, to stop it, or at least to slow the process down . . . and by what monumental affront could anyone . . . actually lecture to Jews on the duty to remain with their Judaism? Or to bring up Jewish children.[19]

The state of Israel is the haven of the survivors. It cannot save the third of the Jewish people who were murdered in the Holocaust. So we cannot measure the state of Israel in the same way we measure the redemption at the Red Sea. Nevertheless, if we interpret the concept of salvation as meaning the removal of a radical threat, as Fackenheim did, then we can view the rebuilding of Israel as a legitimate type of salvation. Accordingly, Fackenheim contends that were it not for the creation of the state of Israel after the Holocaust the situation of the Jewish people would have been "one of total demoralization, of a complete failure."[20]

According to Fackenheim, we must attribute religious significance to the state of Israel. But, at the same time, we must bear in mind that this religious meaning does not have any connection with the messianic process. For Fackenheim, the only connection between the state of Israel and the messianic idea resides in the realm of hope. Discussing the intention and the meaning of the chief rabbinate's *Yom Ha-Atzmaut* prayer, Fackenheim pointed out that the prayer is a mixture of two traditional images, "the beginning of Redemption" and the "the growth of redemption."[21] And according to his understanding, this mixture of images is the consequence of the unique situation of the Jewish people after the Shoah. The chief rabbinate, as Fackenheim well understood, knew that there was no absolute guarantee that Israel could not be destroyed. However, the chief rabbi believed that it would never be destroyed. And, Fackenheim explains, "This is the commitment of every Israeli that does not leave the country, of every Jew who moves to it, and of the vast majority of Jews everywhere. All these vow to do all they can to prevent what could happen from happening." But, he goes on, the Jews could not have made such a commitment "without that great quality that is essential to Messianism, namely, hope."[22] During the Holocaust the messianic hope died, and only the establishment of the state of Israel has restored it.

The state of Israel thus represents a meaningful form of salvation. Indeed, even if it is a haven only to the survivors and to the whole of the Jewish people, it has a religious meaning because it enables the entire Jewish people, wherever they are, to keep alive their hope in a messianic future. Thus, when asked what would be the most important thing to do for Jews who were committed to Judaism but not prepared to move to Israel, he replied,

> I thought of the Jews for whom salvation had come too late, and that salvation might come too late again. I thought of hope, of post-Holocaust Jewish hope, and of the world's need of a Jewish testimony to hope. Then I replied to the young woman: Have one more child than you plan to have.[23]

Fackenheim claims that even from a halakic perspective we should agree that the rebuilding of Israel is the one and only solution to the Jewish situation after the Holocaust. Here he based his argument on Maimonides' advice in *Iggeret Ha-shmad (The Epistle on Apostasy)*. Maimonides advises a community that would risk death were it to attempt to live according to the Torah to avoid doing so. But he adds that a person who was forced to transgress the commandments is forbidden to remain in that place. He, claims Maimonides, must leave everything and "wander day and night, until he has found a place where a person can observe the commandments. The world is wide and large." This solution, argues Fackenheim, was solid counsel through the ages. However, during the Third Reich for the Jews the world was not "wide and large." Moreover, in the Nazi reign not even outright apostasy could save a Jew's life. So, Fackenheim concludes,

> The Rambam would therefore have been compelled to alter two interrelated teachings of his day: Jewish "servitude to foreign power" must come to an end, not in some unspecified future, but here and now; and what is needed to end it is not patience and waiting, and prayer only if it is accompanied by resolute action.[24]

The Orthodox rabbi and theologian David Hartman also takes a similar position. He recognizes that the establishment of the state of Israel created a new era in Jewish history and religion. He agrees that, as Irving Greenberg put it in a famous article,[25] the emergence of the state of Israel marked a revolutionary turn in the course of Jewish history and at the same time represented a turning point in the religious situation of Judaism. In the exile, one of the great tasks of the Jewish religion was to give dignity to the powerless. Moreover, the task of the religious Jew and of the Jewish community in the exile was limited to prayer and learning. In *galut* ("exile") God "became portable through having become embodied in the halakhic life of the community," and He was present in "the personal lives of pious Jews whose actions made God beloved of their fellows."[26] Alternatively, the establishment of the state of Israel allows the Jewish people to return to the original biblical meaning of the covenant, the covenantal existence. To understand what this means we must remember that according to Hartman the original covenant

> can be divided between moments when the reality of divinity is felt in a direct, personal way . . . and times when the focus of consciousness is on interpersonal, social, and political behavior, when the God-awareness recedes into the background and is felt as an organizing framework, but lacks the intensity of those *mitsvot* which express relational intimacy.[27]

Interpreting this complex notion, Hartman argues that the state of Israel is a tool that facilitates the restoration of the biblical covenant. After all, the meaning of this covenantal bond is that holiness has to be made real in the whole of one's life, and this means not only in the spiritual life but also in the political and economic realms as well. Therefore the state of Israel entails appreciation of political responsibility and enables the covenant to find its widest possible application to life.[28] On this ground Hartman has written that in the new situation that the establishment of Israel has created "no adequate solution for the development of Halakhah can be found without regaining an awareness of the wide range of values that inspired the development of this legal tradition."[29] This means, according to Hartman, that in our modern religious situation, which necessarily involves the political and economic spheres, we cannot rely only on the traditional halakic canon. We must learn how to listen to the voice of *mitzva* that is the revelatory category, which precedes halakic specification.[30] Hartman summarizes his view on this essential matter in this way:

> The rabbinical tradition taught us how to develop a spiritual culture in isolation from the world. Our task is to develop a sense of covenantal holiness reflecting Judaism as the total way of life of a political independent nation, but without fueling Jewish identity by appealing to Balam's dubious blessing: "There is a people that dwells apart / not reckoned among the nations." (Num. 23:9)[31]

We might infer that according to such a view there is no religious connection between the establishment of the state of Israel and the Holocaust. But there is religious meaning to the existence of Israel after the Holocaust. The meaning is to be found in the reentry of the Jewish people into the realm of history and in the Jewish people taking responsibility for Jewish existence and the enterprise that is involved in widening the covenant. On this basis we can understand Fackenheim's declaration: "Had a Jewish state not been founded then, it would be a mitzvah to do it."[32] Berkovits goes even further. Jewish history, he explains, did not begin in Auschwitz and did not end there; therefore, the continued existence of the people of Israel and the ingathering of the exiles in the state of Israel are a declaration of the presence of God in the world, even if He is hidden from us.[33] The religious meaning of the state of Israel is not rooted either in the state of Israel per se or in historical events. However, it devolves from the intention that the people of Israel attribute to the establishment of the state.

That is, the religious meaning of the state of Israel was born when nothing else could redeem Israel, and the state of Israel became the *Petah Tiqvah* ("the gate of hope") regarding the future of the Jewish people.[34] As for the connection between the historical experiences of the people of Israel today and the religious meaning of the state of Israel, Hartman wrote, "Israel is a powerful agency for the renewal of Jewish spirituality because it forces the individual Jew to use his or her historical tools. History can thereby become a shaping influence on a Jew's rediscovery of the depths of experience present in a life inspired by the Torah and Halakhah." And he added, even "if we have not yet revitalized the covenantal commitment in Israel this does not invalidate my argument."[35] There is an affinity between this view and Soloveitchik's thought. For as Rabbi Soloveitchik points out in his essay "Kol Dodi Dofek" Jewish identity is not defined exclusively by the Sinai covenant but also includes the Covenant of Egypt. Therefore one needs to see the various responses of religious Jewry to Israel as a sign that this Jewry grasps the land of *Eretz Israel* in normative halakic terms alone, rather than by participation in the yearning of past generations,[36] and that these emotions grow from identification with the wholeness of Jewish life and of Jewish society. This society was a traditional one, and its cravings were suffused with traditional values and expressed in inherited terms. But this focus on the Covenant of Egypt remains crucial and necessary.

We can conclude that this new theological trend claims that the religious meaning of any existential being or of any behavior is not of a natural, intrinsic kind, i.e., it is not included or inherent in their very existential being. Only the halakah can define something as a tool that helps one fulfill a religious purpose and only an activity inspired by religious demands and impulses can have religious meaning. Hence the individual and his or her religiosity are the center of the affair. But as Rabbi Soloveitchik demands in his treatise "*U-viqashtem mi-sham,*"[37] the individual and the community must achieve historical identification with the past and future of the people, with its fate and its destiny. In accordance with this point of view the rebirth of the state of Israel can receive a religious meaning only by providing an existential framework for the people of Israel. Following this line of thought Hartman has written, "It is not only the Holocaust that brought us back to Zion, but also, and more important, the eternal spirit of Sinai—the refusal to abandon our historical memories and destiny."[38] The value of any state, including the state of Israel, is only the value of a tool. So when we speak of the religious value of the state of Israel we must determine such value by measuring the degree to which the state of Israel facilitates fulfilling the obligations imposed by the Sinaitic covenant. At the same time, we can and must refuse to see the state of Israel as a component in the *messianic* process. Yet we must not ignore the fact that the state of Israel has created a necessary ground for renewed Jewish religiosity insofar as all Jews have become responsible for the total way of life in a land that anchors them in their historical roots. Ultimately the Jewish people can bear witness to their destiny as God's covenantal partner only in the state of Israel.

NOTES

1. About the implication of this worldview, see also A. Ravitsky, *Ha-qetz ha-megule u-medinat ha-yehudim* (Tel Aviv, 1993), 111–200.

2. On Rabbi Reines see E. Schweid, "Teologia leumit ziyonit bereshita," *Hashiva me-hadash* (Jerusalem, 1991), 245–81.

3. See also D. Hartman, *Conflicting Visions* (New York, 1990), 42–43.

4. See the last halakah in chapter 12 of the *Mishne Torah*.

5. Contemporary thinkers such as Eliezer Berkovits, David Hartman, and Yeshaya Leibowitz have devoted considerable thought to this issue. See, for instance, Berkovits, *Mashber ha-yahdut be-medinat ha-yahudim* (Jerusalem, 1987), 49–91; Y. Leibowitz, *Yahdut, am yahudi u-medinat Israel* (Heb.) (Tel Aviv, 1957), 98–229; and D. Hartman, "Widening the Scope of Covenantal Consciousness," *A Heart of Many Rooms: Celebrating the Many Voices within Judaism* (Woodstock, VT, 1999), 235–46.

6. E. Berkovits, *Emunah le-ahar ha-shoah* (Jerusalem, 1987), 121–20.

7. Ibid., 121.

8. See for example E. Fackenheim, "Jewish Faith and the Holocaust: A Fragment," *Commentary* (August 1968), 30–36.

9. E. Fackenheim, "The Holocaust and the State of Israel: Their Relation," *Encyclopaedia Judaica Yearbook* (Jerusalem, 1974), 152–57.

10. E. Fackenheim, *What Is Judaism? An Interpretation for the Present Age* (New York, 1997), 35.

11. Ibid.

12. Ibid.

13. Ibid.

14. Ibid., 36.

15. Ibid., 36–37.

16. Ibid., 36.

17. Ibid., 37; see also 267.

18. Ibid., 38.

19. Ibid.

20. Ibid.

21. Ibid., 268.

22. Ibid.

23. Ibid., 269.

24. Ibid., 40.

25. See also Irving Greenberg, "The Third Great Cycle in Jewish History," *Perspective* (New York, 1981).

26. D. Hartman, "The Challenge of Modern Israel to Traditional Judaism," *Conflicting Visions: Spiritual Possibilities of Modern Israel* (New York, 1990), 38.

27. Ibid., 37.

28. See for example ibid., 45.

29. D. Hartman, "Widening the Scope of Covenantal Consciousness," 242.

30. See ibid., 240–41, 242–43.

31. Ibid., 245.

32. E. Fackenheim, *What Is Judaism? An Interpretation for the Present Age,* 239.

33. E. Berkovits, *Emunah aharei ha-shoah* (Jerusalem, 1973), 120.

34. See ibid., 120–21.

35. D. Hartman, *Conflicting Visions,* 101.

36. See P. Peli, *Be-sod ha-yahis ve-ha-yahad* (Jerusalem, 1976), 417 on.

37. See J. B. Soloveitchik, *"U-viqashtem mi-sham,"* *Hadarom* (Tishri, 5739 [1978]).

38. D. Hartman, "Widening the Scope of Covenantal Consciousness," 262.

Chapter 12

The Concept of Exile as a Model for Dealing with the Holocaust

Yehoyada Amir

The issue of theodicy, which has been frequently examined from a variety of different perspectives, as in this volume, is only one aspect of the multi-faceted body of thought dealing with the Holocaust. Jews and Christians, in searching for a religious vocabulary with which to deal with this question, often express their distress and dismay with the words, "Where was God during the Holocaust?" One must not deprecate the significance and profundity of this question for any monotheistic faith that seeks to see the providential God of creation as good and benevolent. But the Holocaust raises a number of other, parallel questions, in no less acute a manner: Where was humanity at that time,[1] and what are we to understand, as descendants of the actual and potential victims, on the one hand, and as part of that humanity that facilitated and executed the Holocaust, on the other hand—about ourselves, about the limits of ethical power, and about the meaning of the struggle against racism, discrimination, and xenophobia? No less relevant is the question, what light does the Holocaust shed upon the prevalent egotistical worldviews that often justify ignoring the suffering, poverty, and injustice inflicted upon the other?

Questions about the role played by religion during that time likewise arise, in all their severity. In recent years we have witnessed the beginning of an awakening of conscience among various Christian churches regarding their own responsibility for the human suffering that reached its climax in the Holocaust. The Roman Catholic Church, under the leadership of John Paul II, has recently made several significant, positive steps in this direction.[2] It is still too early to say how far-reaching this process is and to what extent it will filter down from the church leadership to the levels of the ordinary believers. In any event, it is clear that, if the process will indeed mature to a clear and unequivocal awareness of the role played by the church in instilling both classical Jew-hatred and modern anti-Semitism and of its own sins during the Holocaust, this will necessarily be accompanied by extensive theological and ideational change among the various streams in Christianity. Such a change, without which recognition of the sins of anti-Semitism and of persecution of "infidels" as such is meaningless, will necessarily upset the very foundations of Christian belief and create a new kind of religious and cultural orientation. It is still too early to say whether the Holocaust will in fact serve as a point of departure for this process, which would mark a new and revolutionary stage in the history of Christianity and in the annals of the relationship between Judaism and Christianity.

One must add that we as Jews are not merely a passive party in this process, expressing expectations and raising demands. Such a new Christian orientation, if it truly does penetrate from the periphery to the mainstreams of the different churches, will also demand of us a new approach towards our Judaism and its different principles, particularly in relation to the election of the Jewish people and the dangers of arrogance and xenophobia inherent in it.[3] Such a new perspective will require a completely different Jewish understanding of the relationship between Judaism and Christianity and Islam—a perception based on a recognition of the relative truth of the different revelations, such as alluded to in Franz Rosenzweig's philosophy.[4] It is incumbent upon us to examine the similarities and differences in the basic structure of the three faiths, to confront the issue of how we can learn from the successes and failures of the two other faiths, and to ascertain in what areas we may be able to cooperate with progressive and humanistic forces within them.

It must be emphasized that, particularly in the Christian context, this examination goes far beyond that generally implied by the aspiration for interfaith dialogue and peaceful multicoexistence with persons of different faiths. The history of problematic relationships between Judaism and Christianity and the manner in which the Holocaust poses extremely difficult questions to Christianity and Christians is likely—in the event of such profound change—to illuminate in an intimate and singular way the relationship between the two faiths. Christianity, in seeking its own Jewish roots, presents a significant challenge for Judaism that seeks to shatter the walls of the mental ghetto in which it existed.

But even more meaningful in the Jewish context is the question of the manner in which Jewish religion functioned for its adherents. Did Jewish faith have the power to raise their spirits and invigorate them during the most horrible crisis a person can imagine? Or did it provide false hopes, misleading and blinding its believers? To what extent did Judaism succeed in granting meaning to suffering, in helping the persecuted to endure, and in giving them a sense of direction in tumultuous times? And to what extent did it sanctify the lives of Jews living after the Holocaust—Jews who are all in principle survivors, since the grim reaper intended to get them, or their parents or grandparents?

It is no accident that we do not deal overly much with these onerous questions. When we do so, it is usually most convenient for us to focus on denouncing (in itself properly) some of the ultra-Orthodox leadership, who abandoned their followers while making empty promises of imminent heavenly redemption. But this focus upon "beating the chests of others" more often than not serves as an excuse—one providing political and ideational gain—to avoid dealing in an authentic and honest way with the fundamental and painful religious and Jewish questions that emerge after the Holocaust. Such are, for example, the questions raised by Richard Rubenstein regarding the principled relationship between biblical monotheism and the concept of genocide.[5] It also makes it possible to ignore questions regarding the meaning of faith and the significance of Jewish existence in a world in which Holocaust and genocide are among the accepted and available modes of action in various situations of tension and conflict.[6]

All these are a few aspects of the fundamental question regarding the orientation a person may adopt after the Holocaust and through confrontation with the fact of its occurrence. How can one believe in God, in humanity, in culture, or for that matter in religion, after the Holocaust? From whence can the educator or the philosopher glean the measure of optimism necessary for working in the field of education to create a new generation of productive and constructive people? In what manner can we explain both the past and the traditional interpretations of the past to make them meaningful for ourselves? Does not the fact that genocide is now a real option for human behavior—one that has recurred in various forms in the twentieth century—signify a total break in human culture, philosophy, and religion? Is it not in a sense the "crooked that cannot be made straight"?

The aim of this essay is to examine the possibility of developing a number of linguistic tools that will enable us to ask and confront some of these questions, and to a certain extent also to perhaps arrive at some answers. I make no pretension of "explaining" the Holocaust to any degree or of offering a series of "morals." I am very skeptical whether the Holocaust even gives us the option to do so. It may well be that the only explanations we can expect are historical ones that do not automatically translate into the theological or philosophical realm. As for the "lessons" that are offered every so often, these need to be thoroughly examined to ascertain that they do not serve some political, religious, or other ideological interest, for which the Holocaust serves merely as a pretext. I prefer to explore the possibility of developing a vocabulary that will enable us to ask questions regarding the significance of our existence in view of the Holocaust and that will provide us with tools to examine what we are obligated to do as educators, as people of culture, and as Jews.

The Jewish thinker, in attempting to deal with this complex of questions while relating to the religious and national sources of his or her culture, encounters already at the onset of one's perusal the special place held by history or, to be more precise, the special place held by "historical memory"[7] in shaping Jewish religious and cultural consciousness. It is well known that Jewish tradition usually regards God first and foremost as the God of history and only thus as the God of creation. The recognition that He is "the Creator of heaven and earth" is anchored paradoxically in the notion of God as "the Lord of Abraham, Isaac, and Jacob" Who led the Israelites out of Egypt, the God Who "sees even the lowly" in our human society[8] and Who will in the future redeem us and to Whom we will return. This motive reappears many times throughout Jewish prayer. Thus, for example, the worshipper, in reaffirming the fundaments of faith in the *Shema,* passes naturally from the assertion that "all this is perfectly true" and that "He is the Lord of the universe" to acknowledging that "we are Israel His people" and that He has redeemed us throughout history from the hands of foes and enemies.[9] In the same manner the Sabbath, as mentioned in the Kiddush on Friday night, serves simultaneously as "a memorial of the Exodus" and "a memorial of creation," without any special spiritual or intellectual effort being required to bridge the two proclamations.

Many Jewish philosophers of the second half of the twentieth century felt that this unique manner in which we regard God and the relationship between the Jew and his or her God creates a problematic affecting our manner of dealing with the Holocaust. These thinkers—such as Emil

Fackenheim, Yosef Hayim Yerushalmi, Eliezer Berkowitz, Joseph B. Soloveitchik, Martin Buber, Eliezer Schweid, David Hartman, and Abraham
Joshua Heschel—express their conviction that the intensity of the trauma
caused by the Holocaust requires a deep reexamination of the fundamen-
tals of faith, because the Holocaust redefines history and thereby also the
significance of God's presence therein.

The only exception, who, so to speak, proves the rule, is Yeshayahu
Leibowitz. In his view, the difficulty lies in a basic misunderstanding of
the nature of Jewish religious faith. It does not in fact regard God as the
"Prince of History," just as it does not regard him as the purveyor of
humanity's needs. Faith in God deals only with *faith* itself and the consequent commitment to carry out the obligations of halakah. History, like
all other areas of culture and civilization, is solely a human deed and God
has no part in it. From these basic axioms, it follows that the terrifying
questions that arise in face of the Holocaust need not be addressed to religion at all, but rather to humanity alone, and especially towards secular
humanistic worldviews.

This removes not only the matter of theodicy but also the difficulty
involving the possibility of faith after the Holocaust. But a very heavy
price is paid. Leibowitz totally separates human reality, with its values, failures, and uncertainties, from the religious dimension of human existence.
The believer can continue to believe and to fulfill the precepts, but all content is removed from it apart for the compulsion to carry out his or her
religious obligations. What Leibowitz grasps as *"Torah lishema"* (Torah for
its own sake) is nothing other than religiosity knowingly detaching itself
from every sphere of human life—from a person's spiritual aspirations
and psychological needs. All of the aforementioned are abandoned to the
"secular" sphere, at the same time that "religion" does recognize the value
of this realm and does not grant it any significance.

Hence, it is not surprising that most of the Jewish thinkers of that
period based their struggles with the Holocaust on the abovementioned
notion of Jewish tradition that anchors the relationship between humanity and God first and foremost in the historical and sociological spheres
and on the perception of God's providence over humanity in general and
the Jewish people in particular. To be precise: not only the particular
Jewish dimension is regarded by this tradition as historic but also that of
humanity in general. Reading Genesis reveals that the universal level of the
biblical story is also more "historic" than it is "cosmological" and "cosmogenic." Alongside the cosmogenic story of creation we encounter an "his-

toric" tale that tells of humanity, of the divergence of the sexes, and of Adam and Eve's sin.[10] This tale, and not the first one, takes us until the Flood, whose cause is social-moral. It is in this context that the central category of this history is introduced: the first covenant between God and humankind.

As an etiological story, the book of Genesis describes the status of humanity and the condition of humankind as a result of the "historic" covenant between God and those who disembarked from Noah's ark. Thus, concrete humankind, whose forefather is Noah, is not only a direct continuation of the creation and of God's mastery over the universe; it derives from the unique relationship between God and the "righteous person" who found favor in His eyes. At the core lies the covenant with the descendents of this chosen person, a covenant entailing simultaneously both promise and imperative.

In a certain sense, a central content of this covenant is the suspension of the human responsibility for the cosmic dimension. Thus, the rhythm of the seasons serves as a symbol of the order of creation—and its conversion into a constant, which is not affected by the drama that takes place on the axis between humanity and God. Humanity is obligated to carry out a number of precepts and prohibitions, first and foremost of which is the prohibition against murder. God binds Himself to this covenant by promising that, regardless of humanity's deeds and the extent to which people respond to God's decree, the natural continuity will be maintained and humanity will never again be annihilated. This is a covenant between superior and inferior, in which, paradoxically enough, it is the superior party who binds Himself irrevocably while the inferior party remains free to decide whether or not to keep the covenant.

Of course, in Jewish historical memory this covenant usually takes only a secondary and vague place, being viewed as the background for the emergence of the second covenant, that between God and His people. This latter covenant is rooted in the family history of the patriarchs, and especially in the story of the Exodus. And, just as the covenant with Noah entails the negation of the option of a second flood, so too the "redemption" in the book of Exodus is regarded as changing the existential state of the nation in an essential way.[11] From here on the nation finds itself in a direct covenant with God; it is that human community that receives the Torah and is meant to obey its laws. As such, it is subject to unique laws of providence, which transcend the overall providence of God over history and its passage.

The biblical admonitions explicitly point to the parameters of the covenant, which in turn parallel to a great extent what we have found in the covenant with Noah: the nation is obligated to obey the laws of God but maintains the ability to disobey at any time,[12] whereas God cannot be released from the covenant. According to its dicta, God is supposed to punish the nation for its sins and reward them for its good deeds; according to these very same rules, He is supposed to assure that the punishment He confers upon the nation for its sins—one that might very well be harsh and cruel—will never reach the point of total annihilation of the people. If God were to allow His people to be effaced from the face of the earth, that would be a breach of the covenant.[13]

The Bible describes a wide range of punishments that are supposed to be conferred on the people for their sins, whether these appear in the context of a prophetic admonition and a warning[14] or in the context of explication of historic reality post factum. At the pinnacle of this list is exile, which serves as the counterpoint to the covenant and the liberation from Egypt. Exile, with all its horrors, is the decisive expression of the estrangement between the sinful nation and its God, an estrangement that is supposed to bring the nation to the brink of its destruction.

The primary significance of exile is explicated in Jewish tradition according to the basic liturgical formula, which gives significance to the nation's existential circumstances after the destruction of the Second Temple: "Because of our sins we have been exiled from our land." This formula not only embodies the orientation of the Jews and the possibilities available for dealing with their circumstances but also retains a deep level of hope and solace. The punishment imparted by God, Who promised that we would not be obliterated off the face of the earth and that in time He will return us to our land and rehabilitate our lives—such a punishment cannot be immeasurable. The end of exile *must* come. The moment must come when it will be announced that Zion "has received from the Lord double for all its sins."[15] The suffering must end. Redemption is only a question of time and of our deeds, be these mystical, religious-halakic, acute-messianic, or political-redemptive.

The Holocaust subjected this formula to a severe crisis. For many religious philosophers, its intensity and totality is too appalling for them to retain the customary formula of punishment and reward. It is true that some ultra-Orthodox circles tried to hold onto this conception despite everything, but for central elements of the Jewish religious world—Orthodox as well as non-Orthodox—a major fissure had occurred. Even the more moderate formulation of this idea—that God's actions never-theless embody punishment and reward though we cannot comprehend His ways—is seen as inadequate. The religious philosopher who feels thus finds himself or herself in need of another explanation—one that would offer meaning to the terrible reality, and solace and hope to the life that follows in its wake.

In attempting to do so, the religious philosopher requires alternative models, to be found buried in the treasure house of Jewish religious thought. He or she must discover existing models and augment the poten-tial inherent in others. The secular nationalist philosopher, who cannot relate to the formula "because of our sins" in its original sense, will find him- or herself burrowing in the same treasure house to examine the range of options that exist from the secular viewpoint. Such a thinker, too, will seek a rhetoric offering meaning to Jewish and human existence after the Holocaust. For both, a significant point of departure for the process might be found in a deeper consideration of the concept of exile.

The concept of exile, as developed in the Jewish tradition, presents diffi-culty to the discussant. On the one hand, it seems self-evident that exile, in the context of the Jewish people, refers to the situation of existence out-side the boundaries of the land of Israel, the loss of sovereignty over the land and dispersion among the nations. One can easily bring scores of citations from the Bible, from rabbinic and liturgical texts, and from the various strata of Jewish thought and halakah, to support this understand-ing of the concept. But closer investigation reveals that its full meaning is not exhausted with this explication and that there remains an additional, deeper level of meaning. Moreover, even the mundane level of this con-cept needs to be examined in light of this wider spiritual meaning.

In most strata of traditional Jewish thought, the meaning of exile is not exclusively, or even predominantly, the presence of an individual or of the people outside of its land or place of origin. Exile is always bound with a sense of helplessness in the face of external forces over which one has no control and which one is powerless to direct. In essence, exile is existence outside of what is considered the right place to live, under conditions con-sidered to be defective in their decisive dimensions. Exile means living in a world in need of redemption, healing, and completion. It is bound up with the awareness that a valuable potential, which fundamentally exists in reality, is not and cannot be fulfilled until this longed-for *tikkun* (mend-ing) takes place. Exile is defined by the consciousness that something fundamental in historical reality—and in many cases also in cosmic and divine reality—is essentially disrupted. It is always bound with yearning for the perfect reality that existed in the past and for the days "that will be renewed as in the past," in which the perfection of old that was damaged will be set aright.

The first exile described in the Bible, the expulsion from the Garden of Eden, was not explicitly identified as such, but there can be no mistake as to its nature. As an etiologic story explaining the meaning of the concrete human condition in which we live, this first "historical" tale presents human existence as one in which a dimension of exile is an inherent part. Humanity should have lived in the Garden of Eden—that is, in a reality in which people and their surroundings were in total and primeval harmony among themselves, with nature, and with God. But because of humanity's sin—however this may be defined—we were exiled from this existence and lost it. It is no wonder that different prophets describe the future redemption in terms that, explicitly or implicitly, suggest a return to the Garden of Eden. Thus, for example, Ezekiel prophesizes, with regard to the exile in Babylon, about the day in which all those who will see the land of Israel rebuilt will say, "This land that was desolate has become like the garden of Eden; and the waste and desolate and ruined cities are become fenced, and are inhabited."[16] The prophet of the return to Zion, in delineating the absolute change that will occur in the nature of the land upon its redemption, makes similar use of this motif, albeit in a literary and not in the literal sense: "and he will make her wilderness like Eden, and her desert like the garden of the Lord."[17]

This perception of the expulsion from Eden as exile is expressed in some of the most central exegetical works of Judaism. Thus, in *Genesis Rabba* Abba Bar Kahana describes the *Shekhinah* (Divine Presence) as being exiled from the land because of humanity's sins, primarily because of those of Adam: "The *Shekhinah* was to be found on earth. Because Adam sinned, it took off to the first heaven. Cain's sin brought it to the second . . . Egypt in the days of Abraham to the seventh."[18] In the Kabbalah, especially in that of Rabbi Moshe Cordovero and the Lurianic school, this motif is extensively and exhaustively developed. The sin of Eden is described there as a decisive stage in "the breaking of vessels" and in the general upheaval of the divine and cosmic reality.

Thus, cosmic and human reality are touched from the very outset by a fundamental breach and impairment requiring *tikkun* and alluding to the meaning of future redemption. The story of the Garden of Eden depicts human reality as a form of exile whose meaning, according to the literal sense of scripture, is disruption in the life of man and in the life of woman, as well as in the relationship between them. This is a life in which death and suffering, hierarchical rule, alienation from the land, etc., are all present. Thus, all of the above are not self-evident elements of human life but represent a fundamental disruption of the laws of nature.[19]

Moreover, just as the expulsion from the Garden of Eden is not inherently considered as geographical "exile" but rather as exile in principle and in essence, so too geographical uprooting may not be viewed as *Galut* at all. Thus, for example, Abraham, who is commanded to leave his country, his place of origin and his father's home,[20] is not presented as going into exile but rather as going to the land that is destined to become a homeland for himself and his offspring. Similarly, Jacob and his family, who go down to Egypt to save themselves from famine, are not described in Genesis as "émigrés." Even though Egypt is not their land and their residence there is supposed to be temporary, the situation doesn't depict a sense of exile, indigence, or rupture. Only in the book of Exodus, which describes how life in Egypt becomes one of slavery and relates the danger of annihilation that hovers over the nation, does the tale become the story of the archetypal exile. Thus, the subject of the covenant between God and the fathers is expressed here in terms of God extricating the nation from Egypt—an act that is considered as a "redemption" and release, one that will serve as a foundation for grasping the place of the people of Israel in history and the cognition of the covenant between them and their God.

The Bible thus posits two exiles at the very onset of human history and of national history. The former, human exile, defines the condition of human existence as one of present and continuous exile; the other, national exile, defines the reality of the existence of the nation as one in which exile was negated on our behalf by God. Jews who regard themselves as having been liberated from Egypt[21] consider themselves to have been delivered from exile, as people who, following a long and arduous journey, have reached the geographical and existential place that may be presumed to be their natural home.[22] The relation between these two exiles is complex. As a person, the Jew is in the same exilic situation as that experienced by the entire human race. But within this reality of exile, the individual Jew experiences, through the formative myth of his or her people and the ever-repeated ritual, the deliverance from the national exile. The life of the individual Jew is encountered with the presence of exile as well as its cancellation and the hope for full redemption.

Understandably, these initial definitions of the concept of exile serve merely as background for the principal confrontation dealing with the historical "primary experience" of the destruction of the First Temple and the Babylonian exile.[23] It is worth noting that in Jewish consciousness—as expressed in biblical literature and in its postbiblical transfiguration—the destruction of the Temple and the geographical exile from the land of Israel combine into a single reality of total crisis in the history of the nation and in the covenant between the nation and its God. When the poet of the book of Lamentations cries out, "Return us unto thee, O Lord, and we shall be turned,"[24] his words carry both a geographical and a theological meaning. The exile from Jerusalem and from the land of Israel is regarded as exile from God and loss of the sense of intimacy in the relationship between the nation and its Divine Creator. Against this light, the prophecies of consolation, which naturally bind the national redemption and the nation's return to Jerusalem and the Temple with a radical change in the cosmic reality, can be well understood. This change, as mentioned above, is often described as a symbolic return to paradise and the annulment of this primary "exile." Against this background, one may also understand that the return to Zion requires making a renewed covenant in the form of the pact decreed by the people returning from Babylonia.

One may rightly argue that this viewpoint—rooted in the traditional explication of the reality of the Babylonian exile—generated in later years the consciousness of exile expressed in postbiblical literature, which in practice relates to the reality that existed after the destruction of the Second Temple and of Jerusalem. Here too the destruction is often regarded as a type of "exile," despite the fact that in the historical reality of the first and second centuries C.E. it is difficult to find decisive elements of geographical exile from the land of Israel.[25] The inability to perform sacrificial services, the exile and dismantling of the Sanhedrin[26] (as these developments are described by the halakic tradition), and the so-called exile from the land of Israel—all these are regarded as interrelated with one another and as expressing the overall reality, bound up from now on in the concept of exile.

The Jew living in this reality feels himself or herself in exile, whether living in the land of Israel or outside its borders, and whether the center of Jewish existence in his or her time is in Israel or is developing elsewhere. For exile is simultaneously a cosmic and a historic condition. It is exile of humanity and exile of the *Shekhinah*. As the famous Talmudic saying has it, "They were exiled to Egypt—the *Shekhinah* was with them; they were exiled to Babylonia—the *Shekhinah* was with them; they were exiled to Eilam—the *Shekhinah* is with them."[27] It is clear that this saying relates not only to the remote past of previous exiles but first and foremost to the contemporary exile and thus to the contemporary situation of the *Shekhinah* in the world. The idea that God suffers and is exiled with His people expresses the sense that the physical exile—whether regarded as a concrete experience or as a theological projection from another reality—is only an external expression of a far deeper exile that exists in the world.

The consciousness of exile would seem to reach its fullest theological significance in the Talmudic dictum, "From the day of the destruction of the Temple, the Holy One blessed be He has naught but the four cubits of halakah in His world."[28] This is an intentionally paradoxical saying. The world is God's world; He created it and He rules it. Yet nevertheless, God has, in this world, only the limited confines of halakah. From everything else—culture and history, civilization and the beauty of nature—God Himself was, so to speak, exiled. In essence, the world no longer functions as God's world, and the *Shekhinah* is depicted as if it no longer has a place in it. Whether or not this situation is itself a result of the divine will and could be nullified at any moment, exile is no longer portrayed exclusively as an expression of God's rule over history and the punishment that he confers on the sinning people who are his partners in a steadfast covenant but also as a cosmic and theological malfunction, which can only be mended by redemption.

Of course, alongside this meaning of the concept of exile there exists in Jewish literature the earthly one as well, which regards exile as the uprooting of the people from the land of Israel, explained as a punishment for the people's sins. Moreover, only rarely is this view of exile as cosmic malfunction expressed in full measure. But our concern here is not with the high road of Jewish theology but rather with examining the potential concealed in byways that may seem marginal and insufficiently developed. When we pose ourselves the question as to how can one develop a religious language that will deal with the Holocaust and function in the place where the concept of "because of our sins" no longer works, it seems to me that an examination of this meaning of exile holds a certain measure of relevance.

First, it has already been observed that in its extreme, this perception of exile is expressed in the idea of *hester hapanim* (the hiding of God's face).[29] This idea is quite problematic. Detached from an overall context, it is of no great help in providing orientation to the faithful. As such, it only points to the fact that we have no tools to explain or to absorb reality. That is how it looks in the writings of the first philosopher to use this term with regard to the Holocaust, Martin Buber. The discussion of *hester panim* enabled him to note the problematics of the issue of faith after the Holocaust, and to develop a metaphoric rhetoric to express his stubborn attachment to dialogue and revelation. His use of the term does not "explain" or "give solace."[30]

However, in the overall context of the perception of exile, it might be assigned a far broader meaning. In order to comprehend this meaning, we must first note those factors that even before the Holocaust lessened the willingness to accept the biblical formula of punishment and reward, which until the modern era delineated the parameters of Jewish historical consciousness with no little success. These factors to a great extent determine the range of options available to both Jewish religious and nonreligious cultural thought in attempting to deal with the issue of the Holocaust today.

The complex of causes that brought about this weakening are related to the different meanings of the process of secularization and the new perspectives that they open to both secular and religious philosophy. It should be noted that the rise of historical consciousness and historicist views removes from this formula the very basis for its existence. Firstly, in order to retain the classic biblical view one's historical outlook must be decisively Judeocentric; it must ignore almost entirely the immanent context of historical developments beyond the bounds of the people of Israel, whether in the cultural, spiritual, economic, social, political, or strategic areas. Only within such a framework could the victory of Nebuchadnezzar, for example, be explained in the Bible as punishment for the sins of the people of Israel rather than as a stage in the development of the Babylonian empire. Only by almost totally ignoring the overall historic processes could the modern Jew view the reality that he or she encountered as being completely focused on the Jewish people and its destiny.[31] For many nineteenth-century philosophers such an option was nonexistent. The integration of Jews in the society and culture of the nations in which they lived made such a view of history ludicrous.

Secondly, the concept of history itself undergoes change. It is no longer "sacred history" in the traditional sense, but rather history that operates in accordance with human-cultural perspectives and the dynamics that govern human society and cultures. Even religious philosophers, who continue to regard this very occurrence as an expression of divine providence, can no longer subjugate their entire view to the protective and restrictive biblical framework of punishment and reward. Finally, it is clear that the development of historical research per se, which vastly increased our knowledge of decisive eras in the annals of the Jewish people, placed the biblical formula in a rather problematic light. It could continue to be regarded as a picturesque expression of the nation's consciousness, but it was no longer able to encompass the diverse and complex historic developments that took place in different periods of time.

Against this background, the radical changes that occurred in the explanation given for exile and its significance during the course of the modern era may be understood. Many thinkers from the latter half of the eighteenth century and during the nineteenth century tend to depict the situation of the Jewish people during the modern era in unmistakable terms: they refer to the end of exile and the beginning of a new era with clearly messianic characteristics. Emancipation, integration in general society, and the Enlightenment movement (*Haskalah*) are all considered signs of this process. This is not the place to elaborate in an attempt to prove this assertion. It is sufficient to note Moses Mendelssohn's "Vision of the Future," which neutralizes any sense of exile and which theoretically positions the Jew within the tapestry of normal, regular life that holds neither sense of dearth nor consciousness of any vital need of redemption.[32] To the same extent it is clear that to a neo-Orthodox philosopher such as Samson Raphael Hirsch, who advocated the idea of "Torah and *Derekh Eretz* ["worldliness"; i.e., Western culture]," God's presence in His world entails much more than the four cubits of halakah. Art, culture, the European national milieu, and scientific progress are all God's and an expression of His indwelling within humankind. In an even more striking manner, the cognizance of the end of exile is expressed in the Reform notion of the "Mission of Israel" and the awareness that the integration of Jews within the surrounding societies and cultures is the highest stage in the development of Jewish "ethical monotheism" and in the realization of its full universal potential.

This consciousness of the end of exile began to show signs of fissure long before the Holocaust due to various factors. First, one must mention the rise of modern anti-Semitism, which served not only as a catalyst for the development of Zionist thought but also as the source of a sense of estrangement, insecurity, and alienation for many Jews. For many Jewish thinkers and cultural figures—whether religious, nationalist, or assimilated—it awakened a feeling that the success of emancipation per se places the Jew in a situation of exile and alienation, even if this is not necessarily apparent in the external parameters of his or her life.

Within the Zionist context as well, the significant change that occurred in the understanding of the concept of exile needs to be stressed. In Zionism, particularly of the secular variety, a special emphasis was placed on the land and its settlement, an emphasis that suppressed the other traditional dimensions of the concept of exile. The Zionist Jew living in Israel does not at all consider him- or herself as living in exile, whereas the traditional Jew that lived in that same place certainly did, and governed his or her halakic and social life by this premise. The earthly context of exile also defined, of course, the earthly and very concrete context of "redemption."

In another sense, the overall change of atmosphere in the Western world contributed to challenging this sense of the end of exile. The concept of exile was internalized on much deeper levels of human thought and became one of the cornerstones of human consciousness, whether articulated explicitly or indirectly.[33] The understanding that one can be alienated from oneself and from one's surroundings even while living in the supposedly natural environment into which one was born and raised is of decisive significance for the manner in which we decipher human existence and give it meaning.[34]

Undoubtedly, all this is expressed inter alia in the far more limited willingness on the part of many artists, writers, and thinkers to continue to assign a classical religious interpretation to reality, to fully accept and to justify God's actions. Characteristic of this reality is Hayyim Nahman Bialik's profound and distraught reaction to the pogroms in Kishinev (1905). In his famous poem "*Al Hashechita*" ("On the Slaughter"), the poet expressed to its fullest his inner struggle for faith. He prays to "heavens," not knowing whether they contain a God and whether there is any "path" to Him, and this, while declaring that there is no longer prayer left on his lips. He sets a clear limit to his willingness to anticipate any action on the part of celestial justice, vigorously challenging heaven using insolent language.

Hence, even before the Holocaust the orientation of the modern Jew diverged in a number of directions. On the one hand, for many thinkers the classical biblical model of reward and punishment and of God directing history in response to the behavior of the people of Israel and the parameters of the covenant became very problematic. On the other hand, the consciousness of exile changed in different ways. In a certain sense, the modern Jew felt that exile was a category symbolizing a world that had passed with the destruction of the walls of the ghettos. The world is his or her own world, the culture is his or her own culture, and he or she is living in a free and well-ordered space. Even if the Jew fosters a hope for redemption, this is not necessarily connected to a sense that the present reality is essentially deficient. On the other hand, the twentieth-century Jew—like many contemporaries in other nations and cultures—may well feel that his or her own human condition is best expressed by such categories as exile, alienation, the "breaking of the vessels" (*shevirat kelim*) and "divine hiddenness" (*hester panim*). This fact finds expression in central trends of modern art, in major works of literature—particularly those written by the generation of World War I—in speculative philosophy, and in social movements.

The Holocaust constitutes the cruelest and most definitive essence of exile in its widest sense. It places humanity in an impotent position within a horror deriving from the fact that that which is good and represents the beautiful has been completely nullified, that fundamental values are shattered, and that within the world of the Holy One blessed be He, God is not even left with the four cubits of halakah intact. From the viewpoint of Jewish history, the Holocaust nullifies first and foremost the achievements of the emancipation and of the Jews' integration into society as citizens with equal rights. In the general human context, it places the values of humanism and the hopes for progress in a cruel and ludicrous light and "sanctifies" absolute evil. The Holocaust represents a world in which the remnants of goodness, beauty, and faithfulness struggle to survive while all the forces of destruction celebrate one long and murderous Walpurgis Night.

In this sense, the actual deportation to the ghettos and the transports to the concentration and death camps, as well as the death marches, are distinct symbols of an exile that has almost no redress. There is no place that can be considered a "safe haven," there is no normal reality, and no measure of sanity and human values can continue and evolve. The Nazis' different modes of action were meant to destroy all elements of normal human existence for the Jews and, in so doing, managed to destroy many foundations of human existence generally. Deceit as a basic device of human behavior, the all-encompassing pressure to ignore the suffering and humanity of the other, the unrestrained looting, of whose full extent we have only become aware in recent years, as well as the manner in which it pervaded so many societies—all of the above were explicit elements of the "breaking of vessels," of a return to chaos, so to speak—in other words, an almost total embodiment of exile in the fullest sense.

With what does such an outlook provide us? It certainly does not offer comfort, and it might even increase the sense of terror. For a person contemplating the Holocaust, the events that preceded it, and its results, such an outlook does not provide any point of solace—neither in the "classic" sense of theodicy nor in that of a promise that it will never happen again. The covenant of the rainbow no longer seems relevant at this point; not much is left of the promise never to "eradicate" the people of Israel either. However, viewing the Holocaust as the very acme and embodiment of exile may provide one with tools for understanding that may be relevant in another sense. Our question does not pertain to the manner of dealing with the Holocaust at the time of its occurrence but rather to how we deal with the memory of the Holocaust and its significance for future generations.

We have mentioned that exile, by its very nature, is essentially a deficient situation in which the positive potential concealed within the very foundation of reality is not realized. Exile is not a self-evident situation, but a result of destruction and catastrophe. Exile is always bound with expectations of redemption and an imperative to act towards redemption. All these may be of great significance in dealing with the Holocaust. We asked at the beginning of our essay from whence the educator and thinker can secure the necessary measure of optimism and faith for working in the field of education and culture. The category of exile may provide that measure, in that it defies cruel reality and maintains that it is not self-explanatory, that it does not necessarily represent all that is intrinsic in the human race, and that it is not destined to last forever. If the prophet is allowed to envision the dissolution of exile and the return to the "Garden of Eden," so, too, the educator may believe in mending the world—even if this seems, at first, impossible.

Zionism adopted the slogan, which as such entails a large measure of superficiality and even estrangement, "from Holocaust to Rebirth." It is easy and necessary to criticize this catch phrase, as many in Israel and the Diaspora have done. True, it embodies to a great extent the arrogance of the Zionist towards the Diaspora Jew who is perceived as not heeding the "warnings" and not joining the Zionist endeavor in time. It measures the immeasurable sacrifice of the victims and the survivors on the scale of establishing the state of Israel, regarding the latter as a compensation of sorts that counterbalances what took place. It too easily serves trends of politicizing the remembrance of the Holocaust.

Despite all these flaws, it contains a significant measure of truth. If we accept this slogan as expressing the awareness that the Holocaust is the extreme embodiment of exile, then we may consider it as pointing to the fact that dealing with the Holocaust must be bound with the attempt to deal with exile and to "nullify" it, insofar as human power is capable of doing such. The superficiality mentioned above only relates to the assumption that the establishment and thriving of a Jewish state are a full expression of such nullification of exile and the confrontation with it. But if we adopt a wider perspective on exile, such as that which stems from the sources we have cited, then our confrontation with it will also be infinitely deeper and more encompassing.

In this perspective, exile is seen as the rule of injustice in a world that ought to have been the world of the Holy One blessed be He. Hence, defeating exile is only possible by means of a constant and stubborn struggle with injustice, whether it be rendered to you or to others, whether it be done by yourself or by your political and cultural representatives, or by others. The same perspective reveals that exile is also concerned with the sense of alienation and disregard for another person's suffering, despite the fact that he or she too was created in the image of God. The struggle against exile is tantamount to the struggle against poverty, ignorance, and gratuitous suffering. The establishment of a Jewish state and the struggle for its character and ways may be a step in this direction, so long as we acknowledge that it is no more than a single limited step.

The Bible depicts both human and national existence as the result of exile and as a struggle to nullify that exile. This struggle is that which is signified by the term "redemption." The Holocaust forces us to look in the mirror and to see our world with all of its cruelty and with all of its potential for carnage and ruin. It does not enable us to feel other than in exile. But opposite this mirror one may also pose the decision to believe in the possibility of goodness, in the ability to redeem, and in the spiritual and religious significance of human history. Franz Rosenzweig, who lived and died before the Holocaust, asserted that, just as creation and revelation are the work of God, so is redemption the work of humanity. In the wake of the Holocaust this assertion seems even more essential. It does not mean that redemption will come. But it does mean that one must demand and seek—both in the religious and in the secular humanistic sense—that the redemption will come about. In this perspective, perhaps it is yet possible to believe again, despite everything, in God and in humanity, who act in history and who sanctify it.

NOTES

1. See, for example, the title of the book by the German writer Heinrich Böll, *Wo warst du Adam?* (Where Have You Been, Adam?). It is no coincidence that this discussion developed first of all in postwar Germany, but its applicability is not in the least limited to any one national or cultural group.

2. The tendency in various Jewish circles both in Israel and in the Diaspora to take petty inventory of this process is regrettable. Alongside just and substantial demands, such as refraining from canonizing Pope Pius XII, a certain broadness of mind and understanding of the complex contexts in which the Catholic Church is operating in this issue must be shown.

3. The demurral from the concept of the election of the Jewish people, or at least from the exclusive interpretation that places the Gentile as inferior to the Jew, is common to many modern philosophers. This demurral reached it climax in the thought of Mordecai Kaplan, who wished to totally eliminate expressions of this idea from the religious Jewish agenda. But even for a philosopher such as Rosenzweig, in whose philosophy the idea of the election plays a very central place, the concept serves to indicate a viewpoint of equal worth and necessary cooperation among the different faiths. It must be said that the idea of the "election of Israel," which devolved in Christianity to the idea of God's chosen people being embodied in the church, may turn out to be the source of much of the sanctified hatred of the other, of the readiness to ignore the other's religiosity and humanity, and of the capability not to empathize with the other or with his or her suffering.

4. In his book *Star of Redemption,* Rosenzweig develops the concept of "man's part in truth"—an idea that provides a basis for considering religious truth, as perceived by humanity, as a subjective expression of the ultimate objective truth. He demands of each person to "experience" his or her truth and to "look" at the other's truth and recognize it. While Rosenzweig develops this concept only as a basis for mutual recognition between Judaism and Christianity, in principle it may certainly be broadened to a wider interfaith context. I deal with this issue extensively in my paper, "Man's Part in Truth: On the Concept of Truth in *The Star of Redemption*" (Hebrew), in *Qolot Rabbim* (Many Voices), Rivka Schatz-Uffenheimer Memorial Volume, vol. 2, Rachel Elior & Joseph Dan (eds.) = *Mehkarei Yerushalayim be-mahshevet Yisrael*, vols. 12–13 (1996), 557–80.

5. Richard Rubenstein, *After Auschwitz; Radical Theology and Contemporary Judaism* (Indianapolis, 1966), 1–58, 243–64.

6. True, the Holocaust was not the first instance of genocide in the twentieth century, and there is room to conjecture that the ease with which the genocide of

1.5 million Armenians by the Turks during World War I was accepted served as a catalyst for the idea of the attempted total annihilation of the Jewish people on the part of the Nazis. All the same, it is clear that during the second half of the twentieth century, in the wake of the Holocaust, genocide and "ethnic purging" became reasonable modes of action in different situations of conflict, both in "Third World" countries and in the heart of Europe.

7. On the role of historical memory and its relation to historiography, see Yosef Haim Yerushalmi, *Zakhor: Jewish History and Jewish Memory* (Seattle, 1982).

8. Ps. 113:5–6.

9. Thus according to the formulation in the blessing of "redemption" in the Evening Prayer. The different formulae in the parallel blessing in the Morning Prayer point in a similar direction. Equally natural is the transition, in the *Nishmat* prayer recited on Shabbat and Festival mornings, from the awareness that "every living soul will bless your name, O God, our Lord" to the idea that we, the children of Israel, wish to thank Him for "all the thousands upon thousands and myriads of good times You have granted to our forefathers and to us: You redeemed us from Egypt," etc.

10. Gen. 1:1–2:3; 2:4–3:24.

11. See for example, Ex. 14:13: "For the Egyptians whom you see today you will never see again." The Bible doesn't view the fact that the Egyptians fail to disappear from the horizon of the Israelites as nonfulfillment of this covenant, since its concern is about radical change in the status of the Israelites and the relationship between themselves and Egypt, and not the actual presence of the Egyptians in the field of vision of the Israelites.

12. Latter-day philosophers such as Rabbi Judah Halevi thought that the nation cannot become completely evil. This view is not anchored in the biblical statements about the covenant and establishes an "ontological holiness" for the people of Israel, perhaps as a measure of consolation in light of the nation's downtrodden status in exile.

13. See Lev 26:44: "Yet for all that, when they are in the land of their enemies, I will not scorn them, neither will I abhor them so as to destroy them utterly and break my covenant with them; for I am the Lord their God."

14. See, e.g., Lev. 26:14–45; Deut. 28:15–69.

15. Isa. 40:2.

16. Ezek. 36:35.

17. Isa. 51:3

18. *Gen. Rab.* 19. 8 (ed. Theodor-Albeck, 176). The notion that seven heavens exist and that God's presence is found above the highest of those is very common in rabbinic and ancient Jewish mystical literature.

19. Maimonides proceeds in a similar direction, albeit in the context of a different worldview, in setting his commentary on the story of the Garden of Eden at the beginning of *The Guide of the Perplexed.* All human political existence,

including the need for law and for exhaustive treatment of human character and behavior, is no more than a consequence of the fact that human beings do not live the reality in which they were meant to. Lust and the human tendency to pursue bodily pleasures bring about "exile" from an existence in which humanity would realize its human intellectual potential to its fullest. See *Guide for the Perplexed* 1.1–2.

20. Gen. 12:1–3.

21. M. *Pesahim* 10.5.

22. See Martin Buber, *On Zion: The History of an Idea,* trans. S. Goodman (Bath, Eng., 1973), 1–29.

23. See Emil Fackenheim, *God's Presence in History* (New York, 1970), 8–30; Yosef Hayim Yerushalmi, *Zakhor: Jewish History and Jewish Memory.*

24. Lam. 5:21.

25. It is typical that the consciousness of exile is associated in classic rabbinic sources, as it is in modern Zionist historiography, with the destruction of the Second Temple and the Great Revolt, after which Jewish settlement continued to exist in every region of the land apart from Jerusalem itself, and not necessarily with the Bar Kokhba revolt, which resulted in the destruction of the Jewish settlement throughout the region of Judaea. In any event, even following the Bar Kokhba revolt, the land of Israel remained the center of Jewish existence, and, as we know, two generations later the Jewish center in the Galilee reached the height of its influence and growth.

26. See, for example, B.T. *Rosh Hashana* 31a–b.

27. B.T. *Megillah* 29a.

28. B.T. *Berakhot* 8a.

29. The motif of *hester panim,* according to which at the peak of God's punishments is the absence of His presence in history, is based on Deut. 31:18; Isa. 54:8. It is customary in rabbinic literature to refer to the story of Purim, in which God is not explicitly mentioned, as an example of *hester panim.* This interpretation is based on the similarity between the name Esther and the words in Deuteronomy, *haster astir.* See, e.g., B.T. *Hullin* 139b.

30. See Martin Buber, "The Dialogue between Heaven and Earth," *On Judaism* (New York, 1967), 221–25.

31. Nevertheless, the idea that the concept of punishment and reward is not unique to the people of Israel and that history involves the intertwining of the destinies of nations as a consequence of their actions already appears in the Bible. Thus, for example, in the Covenant between the Pieces, the fact that "the iniquity of the Amorite is not yet complete" (Gen. 15:16) and that therefore the land is not yet available for the nation that is to inherit it after them is used to explain the need for postponing the settlement of the Israelite nation on the land.

32. It is important to emphasize that all this does not necessarily apply to the way in which Mendelssohn understood the concrete reality in which he lived. To a

great extent it could be said that his vigilance with regard to the social value of equality and his unrealized aspiration to see Judaism as a full partner in the modeling of human society augmented his sense of exile.

33. See Natan Ofek, *Kafka vehakiyum hayehudi* (Kafka and Jewish Existence) (Jerusalem, 2002), 144–66.

34. It is worthwhile to reflect on the connection between this consciousness, which usually appears as an expression of the tragic state of humankind, and the motif of "for you are but resident strangers with me" (Lev. 25:23), which marks a central line within biblical thought.

Chapter 13

Is There a Theological Connection between the Holocaust and the Reestablishment of the State of Israel?

David Novak

Historical and Political Sequences

To see a connection between the Holocaust and the reestablishment of the state of Israel is inevitable when one looks at the historical facts. There is a virtual juxtaposition between January 1933, when Hitler and the Nazi regime came to power in Germany, and May 1948, when the independence of the state of Israel was declared. In the incredibly brief historical period of just fifteen and a half years, the Jewish people suffered its greatest tragedy ever and one of its greatest victories. Nevertheless, we must avoid the logical fallacy of post hoc ergo propter hoc, which assumes that mere temporal juxtaposition automatically signifies some necessary causal connection between an earlier event and a later one. Instead, the burden of proof is on those who assert that there is a deeper nexus within this temporal proximity, one that essentially links these two epoch-making events in the history of the Jews and, perhaps, in the history of Western civilization and the history of humankind.

In the secular and secularized world in which most contemporary Jews live and speak, the method most readily at hand for making an essential connection between historical events is political. In the case of the Holocaust and the reestablishment of the state of Israel, the connection is usually made by correlating political experience and political action. Many see the connection as a transition from passive Jewish impotence to active Jewish power. The Holocaust is the experience of Jewish impotence; the reestablishment of the state of Israel is the activation of Jewish power.

In terms of the experience of the Holocaust and the question of Jewish passivity, some quite recent scholarship has done much to dispel the impression that the six million Jewish victims of Nazi mass murder "went to the slaughter like lambs." Many Jews did not simply cooperate in their own destruction but bravely resisted as best they could despite the nearly impossible odds against them. Indeed, we need to learn much more about this resistance in order to properly honor the memory of those who can no longer speak of themselves or for themselves. Nevertheless, in terms of "suffering," both in the modern sense of enduring pain and in the earlier sense of being acted upon, for the Jewish people the Holocaust was far more what *happened to us* than what we were *able to do*. That is why attempts to fix any responsibility for the Holocaust on the Jews, whether by religious or secular thinkers, are regarded by most Jews (and by most fair-minded persons in general) as downright obscene.

It is not that everything done by every Jew at that time was right, but to fix any attention on what Jews may have done to cooperate with their own destruction, either before or during the Holocaust, deflects full moral judgment away from the Nazi murderers themselves by, in effect, "blaming the victim." (Aside from proven Jewish collaborators and informers who can and should be brought to human justice, whatever other sins were committed by Jewish victims either before or during the Holocaust are beyond the range of our judging and are best left to the Judge of the whole world and everything in it.) Thus the psychological fact that most Jews during the Holocaust did not accept what was being done to them does not dispel the political fact of our overwhelming weakness in relation to the power of the Nazis and their cohorts. Thank God the Allies defeated the Nazi regime on the battlefield. If not, all of us here today would likely be dead or never have been born. Nevertheless, as far as the Jews are concerned, those of us who survived did not defeat the Nazis; we just managed somehow or other to escape them. There is an enormous difference between being a refugee and being a victor. Later, we shall explore this point theologically.

Of course, at least two generations before the rise of Nazi genocide the Zionists, who rightly deserve credit for being the most direct cause of the existence of the state of Israel, advocated the idea of a Jewish state in the land of Israel as the solution to the so-called Jewish question (especially what came to be known as "*die Judenfrage in Europa*"). National sovereignty was intended to transform the Jewish people from a state of passive victimhood to one of active political responsibility. Nevertheless, the experience of radical Jewish vulnerability in the Holocaust became for many a necessary condition of the political claim on the Jewish people themselves and on the world at large for Jewish national sovereignty in the land of Israel. Due to our horrendous experience during the years 1933–1945, we Jews had, after Auschwitz, a powerful argument for a state of our own to protect us from anything like the Holocaust ever happening to us again.

There is no doubt that the experience of the Holocaust made Zionists out of all Jews except for a fringe on the (religious) Right and a fringe on the Left (both religious and secular). Along these lines, I remember quite vividly standing in the main plaza in Auschwitz in 1992 and hearing an Israeli general tell a group of Jewish high school students, in impassioned Hebrew (with simultaneous translation into Polish for the benefit of his Polish military hosts), that had there been an Israeli army in 1942–1945, the atrocities committed in that place would not have happened, there or anywhere. Of course, the truth of that claim, being pure supposition about the irretrievable past, is beyond ascertainment. Nevertheless, most Jews believe this would be true in the future were another Holocaust being planned, God forbid, anywhere else in the world. Apparently, enough of the political powers in the world (especially the United States and the Soviet Union) in 1947–1949 believed this too. Without the Holocaust, it is difficult to see how the Zionist claim for a sovereign Jewish state in the land of Israel could have been so internationally successful. Indeed, it is quite significant in terms of political rhetoric that when any important world leader comes for an official visit to Israel, he or she is taken for a highly publicized visit to Yad Vashem.

At the political level, this is as good an explanation as one could conceive of the connection between the Holocaust and the state of Israel. It has been the major political formulation of a raison d'être for a state containing deep internal divisions. (Whether it is still sufficient as a raison d'être when the memory of Jewish helplessness is receding further and further into the past is an issue that can only be resolved by those Jews who have chosen to be Israelis. We Diaspora Jews can only be nonvoting advisors.) The existence of the state of Israel as a political fact seems to be a stunning confirmation that despite our horrendous suffering in the Holocaust, the Jewish people has survived and has taken hold of its own life and future as never before. This reality has even developed into what can only be seen as a secular ritual these days, namely, highly organized tours for Jewish teenagers that begin with a trip to the killing fields in

Poland immediately followed by a direct flight to Israel. The very medium is the message. As we shall soon see, this political message quickly leads to theological interpretations.

Holocaust Theologies

What seems cogent at the political level becomes much more problematic at the theological level. Because it is much harder to think theologically than politically, for that very reason some Jews advocate that theological reflection on an issue as difficult as the Holocaust or the state of Israel, let alone on the connection of the two, be bracketed, even eliminated altogether. Isn't theological reflection arcane and thus a hopeless distraction from our real political needs here and now? Of course, that seems right if one conceives of "theology" as the type of "God-talk" (*theo-logia*) that deals with God-as-God-is-in-Godself, as was the case with Plato, Aristotle, and Plotinus, and some of the great Jewish thinkers they so heavily influenced. But if, as Spinoza so rightly recognized (however much we who have remained Jews differ with the ultimate conclusions he derives from that recognition), Jewish theology always concerns a theological-political realm, then Jewish thinkers cannot escape the theological component of Jewish politics any more than we can escape the political component of Jewish theology. That is because the most comprehensive and coherent idea of Jewish identity is that the Jews are a people involved in an everlasting covenant with God. (Thus, even Spinoza, who left the covenant as a Jew, had to argue on theological-political grounds that the claims of the covenant are indeed terminable. Yet, by so doing, he as much as those of us who have remained recognized the covenantal essence of the Jewish people to be Judaism.) Our theology, then, is about a national *relationship* between God and ourselves. How can anyone who precludes the covenantal dimension of Jewish life truly see any difference between Israel being a Jewish state and Israel being an Israeli state? Surely, without the Jewish past, of which the covenantal dimension is ubiquitous, can anyone think that a "Jewish" anything, much less a "Jewish state," would be historically cogent? Accordingly, Jewish political reflection has to become theological sooner or later.

The theological problem of connecting the Holocaust and the reestablishment of the state of Israel is that it is very hard to see how it was the same God who was involved in both events. That is the most serious challenge to Jewish monotheism presently imaginable. The historical jux-taposition of the two events raises two great theological questions. Regard-ing the Holocaust we ask, *where was God?* Regarding the reestablishment of the state of Israel, we ask, *how was God there?* Can the same God who seemed to have been so absent in the Holocaust suddenly become so pres-ent in the reestablishment of the state of Israel? Let us now look at the main theological explanations offered.

That intellectual coherence is not the same thing as intellectual satisfac-tion is shown by the theology of some Jews who propose what might well be the most explicit theology conceivable of the Holocaust and the state of Israel and their inner connection. We might call their thinking on the subject "pietistic," even though it is not shared by many *haredi* Jews. With chilling coherence, they argue that the Holocaust is God's punishment for the Jews having been seduced by the modern temptation to become part of the non-Jewish world, and the worst example of that temptation is Zionism. Like all modern ideologies, Zionism is a pseudo-messianism, albeit of a particularly Jewish sort, for them. They see Zionism as the arro-gant attempt to solve the ontological problem of the Jewish people by human political means rather than by waiting for the apocalyptic deliver-ance of the Jewish people (and with them the whole world) by God alone through His chosen messiah.

Truth be told, these pietists have a good deal of Jewish tradition behind their assertions. There is a whole strand of the tradition that assumes, in the words of the Talmud (*Berakhot* 5a), that "when a person sees suffering (*yisurin*) come upon him, let him carefully examine his deeds." Present suffering, especially Jewish suffering, is divine judgment for past sins. It is our warning to repent before it is too late. Certainly, even these pietists, in their denunciation of the Jewish people, do not exonerate the Nazi mur-derers. Nevertheless, their primary intention is to tell us where God was during the Holocaust: he was there as the avenger of the sins of the Jewish people. (Where and when God will avenge the sins committed against the Jewish people seems to be of less interest to them.)

As for the question of whether God was present in the reestablishment of the state of Israel, that is a question of human choice; it is a matter of human action rather than one of human experience. In that case, as the Talmud puts it, "everything is in the hands of God (*bi-yedei shamayim*) except the fear of God (*yir'at shamayim*)" (B.T. *Berakhot* 33b). Accord-ingly, the state of Israel is a human, not a divine, act. Regarding the Holo-caust as being ultimately a divine act, they want to justify the ways of God.

In the case of the state of Israel, conversely, they want to condemn the ways of humans. Thus they seem to want to echo Moses when he said to the people, "The Rock, His work is perfect, for all his ways are just (*mishpat*), a faithful God with no wrong, just and upright (*tsaddiq ve-yashar*) is he. Is corruption (*shehet*) his? No, it is the fault of his children, a generation crooked and twisted" (Deut. 32:4–5). In other words, following this strict logic, since the Jews were punished for their sin of Zionism by God through the Holocaust, they should expect further punishment, perhaps even worse than the Holocaust, for their sin of supporting Zionism's historical fruit: the state of Israel.

Turning their argument on its head, the American Jewish thinker Richard Rubenstein argued that if the Jews are innocent, then God is guilty. However, since it seems religiously impossible to have a relationship with such a guilty God, Rubenstein concludes that because of Auschwitz no relationship with the covenantal God is possible ever again. Better to have no God or an indifferent God than a guilty one, for him.

In this pietistic approach (and Rubenstein's exact inversion of it) we have an essentially theological explanation for our dual problem. In this view, monotheism has been preserved: it is the same recognizable God who was both at the Holocaust and at the reestablishment of the state of Israel. At the Holocaust, God was judge; at the reestablishment of the state of Israel God was giving a negative commandment, a warning (*azharah*). This negative commandment, for them, is usually located in the injunction in the Talmud that we "not rebel (*she-lo yimrodu*) against the nations of the world" (B.T. *Ketubot* 111a). Thus, for them, our task is to live under the political rule of the various nations of the world and not defy God's commandment by declaring our national sovereignty before the arrival of the Messiah and his reign over all the earth.

If we do not like this theology, we have two choices. First, we can use it to dismiss Jewish theology altogether as not only irrelevant to the present situation of the Jewish people but, even more so, a sadistic assault on our still-open Holocaust wounds and our newfound strength in the state of Israel. However, to do that is to lose our connection to classical Jewish theology as the most coherent explanation of Jewish historical-political identity and continuity. Second, we can critique this theological view theologically. And moving up from that critique, we can offer a better theological constitution of the inner connection of the two epoch-making events. Before that, however, we might look at a second theological approach, after which we can critique both approaches, looking for their strengths and weaknesses in order to reject the former and include the latter in a third, more adequate theology.

The second theological approach might be termed "religio-nationalist," even though many religious Zionists do not accept it. In diametric opposition to the pietistic approach, religio-nationalists regard the reestablishment of the state of Israel to be the most important religious imperative of our time. Furthermore, this imperative, for them, is not just the commandment to settle the land of Israel (*yishuv erets yisrael*) and make it habitable by Jews. Instead, the imperative to reestablish the Jewish state in the land of Israel is an imperative for Jews to actively bring about the reign of the Messiah. In this view, the messianic reality is a process that begins with the reestablishment of the state of Israel and is to culminate in the full messianic reign in the land of Israel and beyond. This view has found liturgical expression in the prayer composed in 1948 for the new state of Israel, which asks God to bless the state as "the beginning of the growth of our redemption" (*r'esheet tsemihat ge'ulateinu*). Thus the significance of the founding of the state is eschatological. It is the beginning of the end of history itself. At this final juncture of history Jews as Zionists are called upon by God to play a unique and central role.

One would think, though, that with this emphasis on the active role of Jews so newly franchised politically, the Holocaust would be an event to be forgotten as much as possible. After all, isn't the suffering of the Holocaust the very antithesis of what Jews are now being called upon to *do*? And, indeed, during much of the early period of the state, Zionist theory and teaching, both secular and religious, seemed to almost ignore the Holocaust. In fact, at this time it was often said that Zionists, and especially Israeli Zionists, were embarrassed by the Holocaust, for it seemed to be the epitome of the very Jewish political impotence that Zionism's project was supposed to get the Jews over once and for all. Nevertheless, with the large number of Holocaust survivors in Israel and the Diaspora whose memories and questions simply would not go away, the Holocaust and its significance for Jewish life and thought too would not go away. Add to that the continuing genocidal threats of Israel's Arab enemies (and non-Arab Muslim enemies like Iran and Pakistan), and one sees why the present still suggests to many Jews certain terrifying repetitions of past threats, threats that quickly turned into deadly realities. This was especially the case in 1967.

Because what many wanted to be forgotten would not be forgotten, the religio-nationalists had to include the Holocaust in their theological-messianic vision. They did this by basically redrawing the boundaries of their view of the messianic reality as a process. Whereas in the past, the beginning of this eschatological process was located in 1948, a new beginning for it is now located in 1933 with the rise to power of the Nazi regime, which planned all along the total extermination of the Jewish people. But how is all of this a divine plan? The answer given by some religio-nationalists is that the Jewish people *had* to suffer the Holocaust *in order* to be worthy of the state of Israel. The Holocaust, then, becomes the necessary price to be paid for the state of Israel so that its Jewish citizens and supporters may be in the vanguard of the emerging messianic process in history leading towards history's true goal: the "End of Days" (*ahareet hayamim*). Indeed, it could be said that in the pietistic view the dead of the Holocaust are a guilt offering (*qorban asham*) for the Jewish past, whereas in the religio-nationalist view the dead of the Holocaust are a burnt offering (*qorban olah*) for the Jewish future.

Messianic Theologies

One of the key differences between these two theologies of the connection of the Holocaust and the reestablishment of the state of Israel is the difference between their respective messianisms, both of which have plenty of precedent in the sources of Jewish theology. One might term these respective theological positions "extensive messianism" and "apocalyptic messianism."

In extensive messianism, a view best proposed by Maimonides, the reign of the Messiah is brought about by a Jewish ruler powerful enough to gather the Jewish exiles back to the land of Israel, reestablish a Torah government there, and rebuild the Temple in Jerusalem. Also, for Maimonides, this reestablishment of full Jewish sovereignty will have a political influence on the entire world. This messianism, then, requires a maximum of Jewish political activity in the world, which is to be centered in the land of Israel. It follows from this messianism that Jewish political subservience to any regime other than a Jewish one in the land of Israel, whether that subservience be from religious or secular motives, is the greatest Jewish sin at this juncture of history. It is not difficult to see why religio-nationalists are so fond of Maimonides' extensive messianism. It seems to provide a historical immanentism to justify the Jewish seizure of political power that they advocate theologically. Nevertheless, they seem to ignore the transcendent otherworldliness of Maimonides' doctrine of the world-beyond (*olam ha-ba*). Indeed, it is the world-beyond, not the messianic reign, which the Torah finally intends. For him, this is the true goal of all human life, and it is a goal that is clearly transpolitical.

In apocalyptic messianism, which has far richer resources in biblical and rabbinic teaching, the reign of the Messiah is not the culmination of a discernable process within history leading to its end. Instead, the coming of the Messiah is one event, and it will have no active preconditions on the part of any human being. There is no potential in the world for the coming of the Messiah. The Messiah is the object of Jewish hope, not the result of Jewish effort. The Messiah is transcendent, not in any way immanent. Intending as it does a transcendent object, Jewish messianic hope functions as a limit on the pretensions of this-worldly projects. It reminds Jews of the dangers of identifying with any totalizing schemes in the world, which claim to be able to generate the end of history from within historical resources at hand. For the pietists, this messianism entails a political quietism, namely, a willingness to live under the finite rule of the Gentiles rather than submit to the temptation of creating a Jewish utopia. The "Jewish problem" will only be solved by the consummating eschatological event, not by any historical process that can predict it or lead into it. Thus, instead of seeing the Holocaust as an example of lamentable Jewish passivity, the pietists see the Holocaust as God's terrifying response to the lamentable and condemnable Jewish arrogation of political power, which they could only use for evil purposes.

At the theological level, the options seem to be no messianism, extensive messianism, or apocalyptic messianism. However, before we make a choice from among these three options, we have to add a necessary component required for the assertion of one theological position over the other. That necessary component is the halakic implications of any theological position. The choice of one theological position over another might very well be, if not actually determined, then at least heavily conditioned by the fact that it implies a better halakic position than the alternatives, or that the alternatives imply a worse halakic position. This methodological point needs some explanation before I apply it.

Theology and Halakah

The relation between theology and halakah might well be clarified in the light of the Talmudic dialectic between the theoretical and the practical.

All the questions discussed in the Talmud (and related rabbinic literature) should be seen as normative questions. They are questions either of what one is to think or of what one is to do. Every prescribed thought has some practical implication; every prescribed act has some theoretical implication. Thus in a dispute evidently about what is to be done, the editors of the Talmud typically ask, *be-mai qa mipalgei?*—namely, what is the *distinction in principle*? Conversely, in a dispute evidently about what is to be thought (a difference in principle), the editors of the Talmud typically ask, *mai beineihu?*—namely, what is the *actual difference*? It can be shown that when one gets to the more abstract level of principles, these principles are theological ideas. And when one gets to the most concrete level of acts, one is dealing with the content of halakah, the mitzvot. No question is so concrete that it doesn't involve some thought; no question is so abstract that it doesn't involve some act.

That messianic theology has practical implications (indeed, practical explications) has been shown quite convincingly in the recent work of Professor Aviezer Ravitsky. In the case of the two types of messianic theology noted above, interestingly enough, we see dangerous practical implications. In fact, we see the very same practical implication coming out of both of them, and it is an implication that the proponents of these theologies draw themselves. The practical implication is one that causes great pain to the vast majority of the Jewish people, and greatest pain to the survivors of the Holocaust (*sh'ereet ha-pleitah*). Surely the greatest mitzvah now in relation to the Holocaust is to comfort the mourners, especially those who directly witnessed the murders and overall destruction of much of the most spiritually intense Jewish culture in the world. One of the main ways we comfort any mourner is to let him or her initiate the conversation, to tell his or her story, and to listen to that story without any interpretations of our own. In the case of the pietist theology, it says to the Jewish people (all of whom are survivors, however indirect our personal and familial connections to the murderous process actually are) that our sisters and brothers, mothers and fathers, wives and husbands, daughters and sons, all of them died *because of* their own sins or because of the sin of being part of the Jewish people who had been so taken in by Zionism. In the case of the religio-nationalist theology, it says to the Jewish people that six million Jews *had to die* in order for there to be a Jewish state in the land of Israel. It is hard to tell which answer is more morally offensive to Jews by Jewish moral criteria.

In the case of the pietists, we could question whether working for a Jewish state in the land of Israel is a sin. Furthermore, since the so-called prohibition against declaring Jewish political sovereignty is at most one *aggadic* opinion, one that is not codified by any of the accepted medieval *posqim,* how could it be the reason for God allowing mass murder as a punishment for it, even if one thinks this opinion is true? Isn't punishment supposed to be commensurate with the crime (*middah ke-neged middah*)? Here we see the enormous theological difference between asking God—even angrily asking God—to justify himself in the end, and providing a conclusive answer in the name of God here and now. One would think that proponents of an apocalyptic messianism would leave the revelation of the consequences of sin to the final messianic-redemptive revelation at the end of history, not within it. Instead, they use the Holocaust as a stick to beat down their theological opponents. If we assume with scripture and the rabbis that God is "the judge of all the earth who practices justice (*mishpat*)" (Gen. 18:25), then isn't this theology a blasphemous indictment of God himself?

In the case of the religio-nationalists, did the Jewish victims of the Holocaust (both those who died and those who survived) choose to be sacrificed for the sake of a Jewish state? And even if they chose what could only be designated a "suicide mission," could that be justified in the face of the halakic norms "one life is not set aside for another" (*ein dohin nefesh mipnei nafesh*) (B.T. *Ohalot* 7.6) and "your life takes precedence (*qodmim*) over the life of someone else" (B.T. *Baba Metsia* 62a)? If the lives of six million Jews, and the continuing pain suffered by all the survivors, is the price that had to be paid for a Jewish state in the cosmic economy, then the price is too high. The end result, however good, is not worth it, at least following this logic. Is it not a case of cosmic overcharge (*ona'ah*)?

The halakic-moral fault of both of these theologies is that they are guilty of verbal abuse, in this case theo*logical* abuse (*ona'at devarim*). As long as even one direct survivor of the Holocaust is still alive among us, any suggestion that his or her family and friends *had to die* because of something they did, or someone else did, or because they were means to an end they themselves could not be part of, is abusive in the extreme. The survivors are especially vulnerable to such abuse as witnessed, for example, by how deeply outraged they are by Holocaust denial. A good case can be made that as long as even one direct survivor is still among us, that person, and all of us who survived the Holocaust less directly, have the status of mourners (*avelim*), or perhaps orphans (*yetomim*). Accordingly, we may not present any explanation of the Holocaust that they could not possibly accept.

We can learn the immorality of such theological explanations of the Holocaust from the rebuke of God to the three "friends" of Job (Eliphaz, Bildad, and Zophar), who when they came to comfort him in his mourning condemned him instead. Thus when God says to them, "You have not spoken to Me correctly" (Job 42:7), Rashi elaborates, "You should have comforted him as Elihu did, but it was not enough that Job was in sorrow and suffering (*be-tsarato ve-yisurav*); you added rebellion (*pesha*) to your own sins by vexing him (*le-haqnito*)." It is important to note that the Hebrew text reads "*lo dibartem elei nekhonah,*" whereas Rashi interprets it to refer to the way the friends spoke to Job. Perhaps, we could say that Rashi understands *elei* as if it were written *alei*, that is, the way they spoke *about* God to Job, or it could mean that whatever we say or do to another human being is also said to God who hears all. "One who belittles a poor person (*lo'eg le-rash*) reviles his Maker" (Prov. 17:5; and see also B.T. *Berakhot* 18a). Also, Rashi's interpretation is consistent with the mention of this verse in the Talmud (B.T. *Baba Batra* 16b), when "Rava says that a person is not to be appeased at the time of his pain (*nitpas be-sha'at tsa'aro*)." And Maimonides says that the line (*shurah*) of those who come to comfort the mourners are to say to them, "may you be comforted by God" (*tenuhamu min ha-shamayim—Hilkhot Evel,* 13.2). Commenting on this, R. Abraham ibn Abi Zimra notes, "Their only obligation (*dvar shel hiyyuv*) is to comfort the mourner." Totalizing explanations, which the victims themselves would have hardly given, cannot possibly be comforting.

A Different Messianism

Despite the fact that many of the proponents of apocalyptic messianism are guilty of hatred of the Jewish people (*sin'at yisrael*), apocalyptic messianism need not lead in this direction at all. Apocalyptic messianism can also play an important role in Jewish political activity, such as the activity involved in the reestablishment of the state of Israel and its continued life and strength. Indeed, it can provide an important context for Jewish political activity, one that keeps it realistic and bound by Jewish moral criteria precisely because it deflects from any pseudo-messianic futurism. One might even say that apocalyptic messianism is the best sublimation of political fanaticism. On the other hand, extensive messianism can quickly turn into pseudo-messianism when its proponents are convinced that our own time is the beginning of the end time and that we are thus dispensed from the criteria of ordinary Jewish morality, in our dealings both with fellow Jews and with non-Jews (especially those who live under our control). Apocalyptic messianism keeps our attention in the present and focuses our minds on the needs of the present. In my mind, apocalyptic messianism, minus pseudo-messianic historical judgments, lends itself to an adequate theological connection between the Holocaust and the reestablishment of the state of Israel much better than the extensive messianism of the religio-nationalists. (On this point, I have learned much from the thought of the late Professor Yeshayahu Leibowitz.) It seems to be harder, if not impossible, for the religio-nationalists to express their messianism without at the same time seeing the Holocaust and its victims playing some sort of instrumental role in a cosmic drama.

The question is, how does our primary moral duty to comfort the mourners of Auschwitz and Buchenwald enable us to constitute a coherent theology that intends the same God both in the Holocaust and in the reestablishment of the state of Israel? Here again, we need to look to the halakah in order to get a practical handle on a theoretical issue. I would suggest that we look at the obligations of any survivor. "Rav Yehudah said in the name of Rav there are four people who must give thanks (*tsrikhin le-hodot*): those who went down to the sea, those who have gone into the wilderness, one who was sick and then was healed, and one who was imprisoned and was released" (B.T. *Berakhot* 54b). But what if some of these people do not want to thank God for being saved? Why not? Well, this reluctance, even refusal, could come from a sense of unworthiness. Perhaps they were saved but others with them were lost. Perhaps these survivors feel as if the wrong people were saved, that the truly righteous were lost, that the ones who really deserved to live in fact died. I have heard these feelings from some Holocaust survivors. Today we call it "survivor's guilt." It is like the position described in the Talmud of the person who would rather share his flask of water with his companion in the desert and die than drink it all himself and live. The reason given there is "let not one of them have to see the death of his fellow" (*al yir'eh ehad mehem be-meetato shel havero*) (*Baba Metsia* 62a).

Why God let one person live and another person, even many persons, die is a mystery. It should not be answered by any human being. It is on the messianic agenda of questions we may ask God in the end time. Theodicy is not only not called for; I think it is forbidden. God will justify himself in the world-yet-to-come (*olam ha-ba*). Also, it is obvious why the thanksgiving of the survivor is done more in sadness than in joy. Those whom I wanted to survive with me did not survive. They died horribly (*meetah meshunah*). Yet the commandment to live, not die, is not dependent on one's sense of his or her own worthiness. "The Torah was not given to the subservient angels" (*malakhei ha-sharet*—B.T. *Kiddushin* 54a). Indeed, the more authoritative opinion of Rabbi Akibah insists in the above Talmudic case that at the moment of survival one's own life takes precedence (*hayyekha qodmim*). One's obligation to live is greater than one's obligation to identify with the dead. One finds the opinion in the Talmud that no one can claim to be worthy to live (B.T. *Shabbat* 55a–b; Eruvin 13b). But that excuses no one from the duty to live, especially to live for the sake of the covenant. As the well-known hymn in the High Holy Day liturgy, *hine ka-homer,* puts it, "God, look to the covenant, not to our corrupt inclinations" (*la-berit habet v'al tefen la-yetser*).

Transposing this to the theological level, we need to separate our anger with God over the amount of death and suffering in the Holocaust from the judgment made by a number of contemporary Jewish theologians that the Holocaust falsifies the fundamental covenantal promise made by God to Israel. That promise, however, would only be falsified if either all the Jews had been destroyed, or the surviving Jews were so demoralized that they could not go on as Jews and thus were to commit religious and cultural suicide. But that judgment is not true; its converse has been verified in this world (*ha'olam ha-zeh*). Two-thirds of the Jewish people did survive and in many ways, most especially in the reestablishment of the state of Israel, the Jewish people has done much more than merely survive. That is true, and in the light of our obligation to comfort the mourners of the Holocaust, what greater comfort could we possibly give them than to demonstrate that truth to them in our own lives with them? The Holocaust must be judged to have been a failure, even though we can only have a Purim when a murderous plan never even got started. No new *yom tov* (holiday) can come out of that defeat of our enemies and their murderous plan.

But in the case of the reestablishment of the state of Israel we can have a *yom tov* and we can even say Hallel. Why, when many died at this time too? The answer, I think, is because we only escaped the Holocaust, and the defeat of the murderers only came through the hands of others. But in the case of *yom ha'atsma'ut* (Independence Day) we didn't just escape our enemies; we triumphed over them. God gave the victory to us. As such, *yom ha-zikaron* (Memorial Day) with its sadness need not trump *yom ha'atsma'ut* with its joy, which is unlike the way *yom ha-shoah* (Holocaust Remembrance Day) would trump the suggestion that there be a new

Purim of sorts to celebrate the liberation from the death camps in 1945. There is a difference in the way we thank God for having let us survive and the way we thank God for letting us triumph, but the God who saved us from Hitler and the God who gave us the state of Israel is neither a God whose covenant has been falsified nor a God whose final and unique messianic victory has yet come. We who are alive today still have more to thank God for than to contend with him about.

So, what is the theological connection between the Holocaust and the reestablishment of the state of Israel? If by "connection" one means some sort of causal relation, then there is none and there should be none, at least by theological criteria. If there were any such causal relation, then it would seem we would have to "thank" the Holocaust in one way or another for the blessing of the state of Israel. The state of Israel does not have to claim the Holocaust as its necessary precondition in any theologically cogent way.

Making a causal connection between any two events would have to be linear, one event coming after the other. But that is not the only type of relation. There are also analogical relations. Here the events are not viewed in any linear sequence; instead, they are viewed as having certain similarities. These similarities lie side by side, as it were; one is not prior or subsequent to the other. There is no case here of post hoc ergo propter hoc. The similarities are located in the very similar responses that are prescribed for those who have experienced either event. God is to be thanked now for our survival then. That salvation does not admit of any theodicy because the ways of God are mysterious. The ultimate secrets are yet to be revealed. "The secrets (ha-nistarot) are God's; for us and our children there is [only] doing all the words of this Torah, which are revealed (ha-niglot)" (Deut. 29:28). Any attempt to reveal now what is now to be hidden can only be destructive to ourselves and painfully abusive to others.

The Holocaust and the reestablishment of the state of Israel both pose great challenges to the Jewish people to remain faithful to the covenant. Each also poses a temptation: the Holocaust tempts us to believe we are so weak that the covenant and its responsibilities are beyond us; the reestablishment of the state of Israel tempts us to believe we are so strong that the covenant and its responsibilities are behind us. By tempering the fear of the Holocaust with the joy of the state of Israel, and by tempering the joy of the state of Israel with the fear of the Holocaust, we are able to speak to God and of God in the world, without presuming to speak for God or in place of God. That is the true task of Jewish theology at this juncture of history—nothing more and nothing less.

Chapter 14

The Holocaust and the State of Israel

A Historical View of Their Impact on and Meaning for the Understanding of the Behavior of Jewish Religious Movements

Dan Michman

History

In this conference the participants have debated the meaning of the Shoah (or Holocaust, *Churban,* Catastrophe) for the post-1945 Jewish religious world. The majority of the participants have tackled this problem from the point of view of traditional religious and/or modern philosophical thought. "Cold" historical aspects influencing the stands that have been taken were only partially taken into consideration. I would like to emphasize several historical aspects that, I believe, have had—and still have—a considerable impact on the behavior of the Jewish people in general and of the different religious movements in particular, and that consequently influence theological and other interpretations of the *Shoah and the state of Israel.*[1] Keeping in mind historical contexts is, in my eyes, important for the possibility of assessing the real relevance and acceptability of theological, overarching interpretations that relate to a historical event. On the other hand, it should be clear from the outset that the "historical language" has its own contours and modes of working and is different from the theological, philosophical, and midrashic "languages" that have been mentioned throughout this conference.

"Jewish" Dimensions of the Shoah

On the other hand, I deem the surveys presented and approaches pro-posed during our convening to be essential for future handling of the Shoah issue. If during the first two to three decades after 1945 most schol-ars of the Shoah were Jewish (acquainted with Jewish society and Jewish modes of living and patterns of thought), the present-day situation is very different. The "popularity" of the topic attracted and still attracts many researchers whose focus of interest is either "the perpetrator" or "the bystander" (a focus that is indeed important and results from the desire to cope with the past in non-Jewish societies). In this context the *Jewish* dimension of the Shoah is very often forgotten or not properly under-stood. Therefore, an increased effort to present the Jewish aspects, while integrating them in the findings of the ever growing body of Holocaust research, is in my eyes of the utmost importance.

Definitions of the Shoah

We tend to use the term "Shoah" as if we know precisely what we are speaking about. However, understandings of the term differ immensely among historians as well as among laypeople. Some use it to mean the wholesale extermination of the Jews; others to refer to one kind of geno-cide—not in the first place Jewish (and including also other persecutees of National Socialism); others to describe the German drive to erase Jewish-ness entirely—while other scholars use the term still differently. Different understandings impact, of course, on different periodizations (1932–1945, 1933–1945, 1935–1945, 1938–1945, 1939–1945, 1941–1944, 1933–1948, etc.) and different interpretations. This is not only the case for historians. In our prayer books too we'll find disagreement about the nature of the event. In the *Rinnat Yisrael* siddur, commonly used in Mizrahi (national-religious) circles, the *yizkor* (memorial prayer) mentions the dates 5700–5705 (Sep-tember 1939–May 1945). The Shoah is thus clearly linked to World War II and the invasion of Poland. But the fate of German Jewry in the 1930s is excluded, and when reciting this memorial prayer, we, as it were, do not remember the inflictions of that first period of Nazi rule. On the other hand, there is in many memorial prayers an uneven emphasis on the loss of Torah centers and religious leaders as compared to the loss of other, nonreligious treasures and segments of the Jewish world.

In this context I believe it also to be essential to mention that historical findings can put certain question marks behind popular statements. For instance, the nonlinear internal developments of Nazi anti-Jewish policies (known among experts as the intentionalist/functionalist debate) or the —even though marginal—exemptions (such as the exchanges of Jews for Germans in 1942 and 1945) should temper the tendency towards generalizations about the nature of Nazism.

The Post-1945 Period: The Context of Modern Jewish History

When making links between the Shoah and the state of Israel, one should keep in mind the developments of modern Jewish history. On the eve of the modern period Jewry knew no distinction and differentiation between religion and peoplehood—as expressed in *Megillat Ruth*: "Your people is my people and your God is my God." Modernity—the centralist state crushing the traditional Jewish community on the one hand, and emancipation integrating individual Jews in the body of the general society on the other hand—changed the situation abruptly. Since the era of Emancipation the decision to maintain Jewishness has become a personal one for every Jew, recurring at any moment. This was and still is the dilemma of the modern Jew: whether to belong to the Jewish entity at all, and if so, how to define Jewishness. First this gave rise to the tendency to define Judaism as religion only, thus enabling integration in local nations. Later on, vis-à-vis growing secularization among the Jews, the flourishing of national movements, and the rise of modern anti-Semitism (especially in Eastern Europe), the secular Jewish national concept emerged. This included Autonomism, Territorialism, and Zionism. But secularization also played a role in countries in which emancipation proceeded reasonably. If Judaism was now conceived as a religion only, how could one remain "Jewish" if he or she was nonbelieving? Thus a form of expressing Jewishness through philanthropy emerged during the second half of the nineteenth century. Additionally, the rise of modern politics and the repercussions of the Industrial Revolution affected Jewish society everywhere. Consequently Jews got involved in and split into many general or Jewish parties and movements. Consequently, on the eve of the Nazi period the Jewish world was disunited and lacking common purposes as never before. Zionism, even though of considerable importance, was a minority position.

The Holocaust changed this situation entirely. First, it physically erased the broad variety of movements and ideologies rivaling Zionism in Europe; second, the experience of persecution caused almost all Jews—inside and outside Europe—to acknowledge their being a people. Assimilation indeed continued also after 1945—but not as an ideology any more, only as practice. In this situation Zionism (and afterwards the state) became the dominant ideological force and in many aspects representative for all Jews in the postwar Jewish world. Thus, the Shoah was actually linked to the status of Zionism and the state.

The Religious Movements and Religious Interpretations

Two points—or factors—seem to me of the utmost importance: one of space, another of time. The first point (a) is the impact of physical annihilation on the balance among the different parts of world Jewry in general and within religious Jewry in particular, and on their nature. The second (b) is the demographical and material changes that have taken place since 1945, which currently provide movements with new perspectives.

Balance and Nature

The Holocaust actually (even if not entirely) destroyed the traditional spiritual bastions and the strongest demographic centers of organized Orthodoxy (Hassidut, Mitnaggedim, German neo-Orthodoxy, and the political parties representing them) and of European-type religious liberalism. The original crucible that forged all these movements, the beating heart, the site of pilgrimage, and the seat of the core of spiritual leadership had been uprooted. This had two consequences:

1. The remaining branches of Orthodox Jewry (in the United States, Eretz-Israel, and South America) that had formerly relied on the European "trunk" became, unwillingly, centers that had to assume the burdens of rehabilitation and continuation. That is, formerly "dependent" outposts suddenly became leading centers—a change of positions that had to be very demanding. For Progressive Judaism the balance changed so much that the prestigious European branch, which had started the movement and given it its most basic theological foundations (in the nineteenth century), evaporated entirely, while American Reform became the dominant

branch. Consequently Reform thus came to be seen everywhere as mainly "American" and not as a genuine worldwide Jewish phenomenon.

2. The change of positions happened and the need to rehabilitate Jewry had to be undertaken under conditions totally different from those preceding the Holocaust. First there was the demographic contraction that the wholesale murder had caused, and that had hit very hard on the religious centers; thus, in the immediate postwar period the proportion of religious Jews within world Jewry declined and the influence they could exert on general Jewish developments diminished. Moreover, leaders had perished and organizational infrastructures had collapsed. Second, rehabilitation—for which there were strong drives among *She'erit Hapletah*—took place in entirely different linguistic and cultural environments: in young, dynamic immigrant societies (the United States, Israel) with democratic and pioneering ideals, in which the dominant languages were demanding and assimilating (English, Hebrew). This would have a major impact on lifestyles (such as strengthening religious life through the modern media: "Dial-a-shiur," ArtScroll publications, Internet), actions (such as lobbying in the United States, political maneuvering and pressure in Israel, "public relations" and "buying power" regarding kosher products in both), and thinking of religious Jews. Therefore, rehabilitation (*Hadesh yameinu keqedem*) was in no place a genuine revival of and a return to the pre-Holocaust past, but always something new. But from this perspective, and through the filter of the Nazi catastrophe, nostalgia in the postwar religious world peaked. In *haredi* society (but also in writings of the Conservative movement in the United States) we can find an idealization of the prewar Eastern European *shtetl* (which had actually been declining and a place from which most Jews tried to escape), especially in educational literature. The Reform movement started to include songs in Yiddish in *haggadot* and ceremonies, a language banned in the past entirely from the official Reform horizon.

Changes since 1945

Historians of Jewish history still tend to periodize this history into major eras, finishing with the "modern period," which started somewhere at the end of the seventeenth century and continues until today. Some add a subdivision around the 1880s, thus splitting modern times into two (first, "Et Hadasha" and second, "Et Hadisha" or "Dorot Aharonim"). However, from the retrospective point of view of the beginning of the twenty-first century, it is quite clear that in the 1940s Jewry entered a new period.

This new (postmodern) period has been highly shaped by two foci of influence and reflection: the Holocaust and the establishment of the state of Israel. Their occurrence within one decade with only three years' buffering between them also made them interrelated in the eyes of many.[2] From the religious point of view the twin coins of *Hurban* (destruction) and *Tekuma* (rebirth) seemed to be properly applicable and represented a nexus. Indeed, the very fact of the establishment of Israel was undoubtedly very encouraging for the majority of remaining Jewry. Nevertheless, a religious question that remained was whether the *Tekuma* was *really* identical or could be allied with *Ge'ula*.

On this the views differed and differ. This conference also pays much attention to that issue. However, again I would like to draw attention to the fact that the interpretation of the historical data has been dependent both on former, pre-Holocaust views and on the physical post-Holocaust situation. As far as the last point is concerned, a subdivision of post-1945 Jewish history into two periods should also be applied: until the 1970s, and afterwards.

As most pre-Holocaust political movements competing with and rivaling Zionism in world Jewry were physically erased because of the wholesale murder, Zionism became the dominant force in the immediate post-1945 period. Moreover, from the point of view of the mid-1940s it seemed to most survivors in Europe and to Jews in untouched centers as if Zionism had been right before the catastrophe and that certainly it was the proper answer for the Jews in its wake.

Within the religious segment of Jewry this strengthened the position of religious Zionism very much—vis-à-vis the non- and anti-Zionists. One should remember that before the 1930s religious Zionism had been significantly weaker than the streams opposing it, its religious leaders had been mostly of a lesser stature, and it had been a beleaguered group within the religious camp. Religious Zionism's promotion thus resulted from the Holocaust and the success of Zionism in general. The bereavement in religious Zionism over the losses of Torah centers and relatives was deep, but compensation was found in the success of revival. This nexus between extreme poles—having fallen into a deep pit but afterwards being lifted to a summit—was to influence religious Zionist theology and activities for the next five decades.

Today many identify religious Zionism with the school of Rabbi Yitzhak Hacohen Kook, promoted by his successors at Yeshivat Mercaz Harav and culminating in *Gush Emunim*. However, in spite of Rav Kook being chief rabbi of Eretz Israel until his death in 1935, his approach was not the only and not even the dominant one in religious Zionism. The leading forces in religious Zionism in Eretz Israel were to be found in *Hapoel Hamizrahi*, which consisted of a more labor-oriented constituency. Among them the influence of Shahal (Shmuel Haim Landau) on the one hand and of Western (German) religious Zionism and the *Kibbutz Dati* (Religious Kibbutz movement) on the other were very strong. This meant that Zionism and the return to the land were interpreted as a laborious journey of pragmatic religious revival even if with redemptive aspects—but not as part of *the* final redemption as such. Simha Friedmann, one of the leading theoreticians of the *Kibbutz Dati*, stated after the establishment of the state that

> I do not ascribe religious weight and meaning to the state, as do some other, better Jews. . . . I see the State of Israel—whose establishment was a surprise, and for which we were unprepared—as a challenge calling upon us: "hic Rhodos hic salta." Meaning: You got a state—now it is your task to prove that you can be faithful Jews who observe the *mitzwot* in this state. . . . Prove yourselves now as more complete Jews.[3]

But in the wake of the Holocaust and the establishment of Israel the pragmatic approach dwindled in the religious-Zionist educational infrastructure (even though some of its representatives contributed to scholarly Holocaust research—such as Shaul Esh, Joseph Walk, Mordechai Eliav) and gave way to the messianic one, which saw the state as *Athalta dige'ula*, "*reshit tzemihat ge'ulatenu*" (the dawn of redemption).[4] For Rabbi Joseph Dov (Ber) Soloveitchik,

> In the midst of a nightmare replete with the atrocities of Majdanek, Treblinka, and Buchenwald, a night of gas chambers and crematoria, a night when God's visage was utterly absent . . . a night of endless searching and seeking of the Beloved [God]—on this very night the Beloved came forth. The Deity who conceals Himself in the hidden pavilion suddenly appeared and began to knock at the door of the tent where His oppressed, aggrieved beloved [the people of Israel] dwelled, lay writhing and convulsing on her bed in hellish agony. *Because of this banging at the door of the beloved, shrouded in grief, the State of Israel was born!*[5]

For Rabbi Zwi Yehuda Kook the Holocaust had been a tool by the *Hashgaha* (Providence) to cut off the ties that linked the Jews to the Diaspora.[6]

The apocalyptic tension between the Holocaust and rebirth, formed during the first subperiod of contemporary Jewish history, was reinforced during the 1950s in religious Zionism and was intensified after the Six-Day War. It was a driving force behind the growing involvement of religious Zionists in all spheres of life in Israel and exerted special influence on Israeli internal and external politics in the 1970s and 1980s.[7] It reached its peak in the beginning of the 1990s and contributed to the mood of despair that rose when confronted with Prime Minister Yitzhak Rabin's policies regarding the Palestinian issue—a political direction that was understood as undermining redemption.

Ultra-Orthodox (*haredi*) Jewry moved along a different path of development. During about three decades, the leaders of the major sections of this social segment did not provide a satisfying answer for the believers. Indeed, as Gershon Greenberg, Amos Goldberg, and others have shown, it is wrong to state that there was a complete silence within this community. A variety of religious responses were presented in the immediate wake of liberation, and also later on in popular publications.[8] However, these were all personal expressions, and no established explanation and justification received official backing and legitimization. Rabbi Chaim Yisrael Zimmerman wrote in 1947 that

> the main question today is that of the six million Jews who were killed in sanctification of God's name in Europe and elsewhere, by all conceivable manners of torture; it is an agonizing, depressing question that penetrates the depth of the heart and troubles every member of the Jewish people. . . . Even today, two years after the end of the World War, these questions have not ceased. But there is silence, no answer, no reply, no one to explain the actions of the Master of the Universe in order to silence the question without profaning the name of the Holy One, blessed be He.[9]

This authentic expression, which is verified by the literature at our disposal, refutes Eliezer Schweid's claim that

> the *haredi* movements responded to the challenges of the buckling of faith in God and religion during the Holocaust with answers that convinced their believers. Moreover: their answers fulfilled the main task of any theodicy: to obtain from the destruction a consoling truth which creates new energies of

faith and hope, and with it also a normative-observant path which rehabilitates religious modes of life after the destruction.[10]

A *historical* analysis will show that the process was the opposite. The religious responses during the Holocaust *did not console* the ultra-Orthodox, as pointed out by Rabbi Zimmerman. Many also turned their back on religion. The establishment of Israel undermined the position of the fervent anti-Zionist right wing of ultra-Orthodoxy even more.[11] At that time Reb Yoelish Teitelbaum of Satmar was the only one to openly oppose the state and see it as part of the same disaster as the Holocaust, both caused by Zionism:

> They are the reason for this awful cataclysm of the killing of six million Jews, and since then thousands more of Jews have been killed because of this impure idea of establishing a state by means of the sword and man's power before the time has come as fixed by the Blessed be He.[12]

This view was accepted by the Satmar Hasidim (and their allies, the *Naturei Karta* in Jerusalem)—but not in wider circles. (One has to take into account, too, that most of *haredi* society was much closer to Zionism in the 1950s than it is today: Rabbi Cahanman of the Ponivhez Yeshiva raised Israel's flag on *Yom Haatzmaut,* writers on the Holocaust such as Moshe Prager and Yehiel Granatstein cooperated with Yad Vashem, etc.).

However, several nucleae of devoted *haredi* believers cleaved to faith and observance while leaving the "big" questions open and postponing theological answers. They started with *practical* reconstruction and rehabilitation, both in Israel[13] and in the United States. The success of reviving an educational infrastructure, a demographic boom, and the agreement with Ben-Gurion on nonrecruiting of Yeshiva-*bachurim* (students) to the army, which created the "learning society" (as Menahem Friedman has called it)—all these developments that were made possible to a large extent thanks to the state of Israel, made the *haredi* segment of Jewish society after the 1970s (the second subperiod of contemporary Jewish history) strong and self-confident again. It is from that time onwards that interest in the *Churban* and activities regarding Holocaust remembrance became openly expressed and have peaked in all subgroups of *haredi* society, especially in Israel.[14] Most recently Ruth Lichtenstein has published what could be called the most authoritative *haredi* publication on the Holocaust—a publication that is informative as well as educational and commemorative. Three thousand copies were sold within six weeks![15] In many of these publications the general tendency is anti-Zionist, but according to my feeling the general mood towards Zionism and the state has somewhat tempered and is today at least less militant than it was some twenty years ago. Also an amazing "flirting" with established Zionist historiography can be discerned in this literature.[16]

Present-day *haredi* involvement in Holocaust issues can thus be explained as a result of renewed self-confidence, which itself is a result of the space and possibilities afforded by the state of Israel to this segment of Jewry. Never before in Jewish history have there been so many *yeshivot* and such a concentration of Torah scholars as in Israel today. Moreover, in the 1990s religious Zionism—the long-time rival of ultra-Orthodoxy—had to face a deepening crisis resulting from its splitting into subgroups, its losing grounds to *Shas*, and the affluence of many bourgeois religious Zionists, which caused them to prefer the general Israeli hedonic lifestyle over ideological struggles regarding *Eretz-Yisrael* (the land of Israel). Israeli society in general began to lose its cohesion and its dominant Zionist ethos (the first cracks appearing after the Yom Kippur war), and in the Diaspora assimilation and intermarriage made deep inroads in all other segments of Jewish society. Only from such a perspective and context could—and can—the theological explanation of the Holocaust and establishment of Israel be tackled with inner conviction from a *haredi* non- or anti-Zionist perspective.[17]

We should pay attention to a new dimension entering the podium: the rise of oriental *Harediyut* (*Shas*), with its own educational infrastructure, now makes this social and ideological movement increasingly involved in activities related to the Shoah, its interpretation, and the keeping of its memory. First expressions of this involvement, mostly to be found in weekly leaflets (*Parashat Shavua* [Torah portions of one week] leaflets), are fascinating and are waiting for scholarly analysis.

Conclusions

The Holocaust and the establishment of Israel were and remain major issues of reflection for all religious attitudes. One could even say that these issues have established themselves as a kind of battleground for ideological fights. The ways of interpretation differ and have gained or lost strength during the past fifty-five years according to social and geographic factors. The Torah tells us in the song of *Ha'azinu,*

Zechor yemot olam, binu shnot dor vador,
She'al avicha veyagedcha, zekeinecha veyomru lach (Deut 32:7)

—"your father and elders will tell you." It seems as if, regarding the Holocaust, the opposite will become the rule: not the fathers and elders, i.e., the survivors, will provide the theological interpretations, but the younger generations—whether we like it or not.

NOTES

1. Some of the following observations have been presented first in my survey, "The Impact of the Holocaust on Religious Jewry," in Y. Gutman and A. Saf (eds.), *Major Changes within the Jewish People in the Wake of the Holocaust* (Jerusalem, 1996), 659–707. For more on general definitions and problems of Holocaust historiography see my *Hashoa Vehikra, Hamsaga, Minuah Vesugyot Yesod* (Tel Aviv, 1998); now available in English, *Holocaust Historiography from a Jewish Perspective* (London, 2001).

2. See Y. Gorny, *Bein Auschwitz Lirushalayim* (Tel Aviv, 1998). The actual historical causality between the two is not as simple as is usually believed. See my article "The Causal Connection between the Holocaust and the Birth of Israel: Historiography between Myth and Reality," in D. Michman, *Holocaust Historiography from a Jewish Perspective* (London, 2001).

3. S. Friedmann, "Hesder hayahassim bein datiyim lehiloniyim," in J. and A. Tirosh (eds.), *Hatziyonut Hadatit Vehamedina* (Jerusalem, 1978), 280.

4. See also D. Schwartz, *Hatziyonut Hadatit bein Higayon Limshihiyut* (Tel Aviv, 1999), 91–96. My view differs from Schwartz's in that in his study pragmatic, western European religious Zionism is not represented.

5. J. D. Soloveitchik, "Shesh Defikot" (given on *Yom Ha'atzma'ut* 1956), cited in Tirosh, op. cit., 21.

6. Z. Y. Kook, *Lintivot Yisrael* I (Jerusalem, 1989), 136. See also other papers in this conference.

7. See also my article "'Ziyonut Datit'—Mabat Histori," in *Daf Shevu'I Milimudei Yesod. Hotza'a Meyuhedet Letziyun Yom Hasheloshim Lemoto Shel Rosh Hamemshala Yitzhak Rabin Z"l* (Ramat-Gan, 1995), 15–19.

8. G. Greenberg (compiler), *She'erit Hapletah Vehashoa: Reshimat Ma'amarim Usfarim al Hashkafot Be'inyenei Ha'emuna Hayehudit Le'ahar Sho'at Yehudei*

Eiropa (1944–1949) (Ramat-Gan, 1994); idem (compiler), *Hatzibbur Hadati Bayishuv Be'eretz-Yisrael Bitkufat Hashoa: Reshimat Pirsumim [Ma'amarim Usfarim] al Haskafot Be'inyenei Ha'emuna Hayehudit Vehashoa, 1938–1948* (Ramat-Gan, 1997); idem (compiler), *Ha'emuna Hayehudit Vehasho'a Bamahshava Hayehudit Be'artsot Haberit Bashanim, 1938–1948* (Ramat-Gan, 1999); and A. Goldberg, "Hashoah ba'itonut haharedit—bein zikkaron lehadhaka," *Yahadut Zemaneinu,* vols. 11–12 (1998), 155–206.

9. Ch. Y. Zimmerman, *Sefer Tamim Po'olo. She'elot Utshuvot Bidvar Hahashmada Ha'ayuma shel Shisha Milyon Hayehudim, Hashem Yinkom Damam* (Jerusalem, 1947), 4–5.

10. Schweid has tried to present this view in many publications. The quotation is from his article "Hashoa besof hame'ah ha'esrim minkudat mabat te'ologit umehkarit," *Mada'ei Hayahdut,* vol. 39 (1999), 37.

11. Today it is hard to imagine that the prevalent *haredi* attitudes in the 1950s were much more moderate than today. Ultra-Orthodox Jews were less separated in daily life, and those who were involved in Holocaust remembrance—Moshe Prager and Yehiel Granatstein, for instance—used to come to Yad Vashem, write for its bulletin, and work together with its staff.

12. Y. Teitelbaum, "Ma'amar Shalosh Shvuot," in idem, *Vayo'el Moshe* (New York, 1961), 140, 174, 175.

13. See M. Friedman, *Hahevra Haharedit* (Jerusalem, 1991).

14. See K. Kaplan, "Hahevra haharedit veyahasa lashoa—kri'a mehadash," *Alpayim,* vol. 17 (1999), 176–208.

15. Information given by R. Lichtenstein, March 27, 2000.

16. R. Lichtenstein, *Edut. Hurban Yahadut Eiropa* (Jerusalem, 2000). An analysis of this book and other recent writings is to be found in Kimmy Kaplan, "Many Lies Accumulated in History Books? The Holocaust in Ashkenazi *Haredi* Historical Consciousness in Israel," *Yad Vashem Studies,* vol. 29 (Jerusalem, 2001), 321–76.

17. See on these issues M. Verdiger, *Hashoa Kinkudat Mifneh Te'ologit* (Ramat-Gan, 1998).

Chapter 15

Theology and the Holocaust

The Presence of God and Divine Providence in
History from the Perspective of the Holocaust

Yosef Achituv

This essay will evaluate various explanations of the Holocaust offered by the religious Zionist circles. It is not concerned with a comparative analysis that would elicit some criterion for judging how "successful" these explanations are. Rather, it focuses on one single issue: God's presence and His providence in human history. It will dwell on the place this issue occupies in the "theology" of religious Zionism and will examine the extent of its durability in the face of the Holocaust. I will also inquire whether it has been weakened or undermined as a result of the trauma of the Holocaust and, in addition, will explore the ways in which the Holocaust is "exploited" for the purpose of strengthening the religious-Zionist identity. Finally, it will point at the process through which the religious Zionist conception that emerged from the Merkaz-ha-Rav school of thought lost its hold on religious Zionism, after dominating it for over twenty years, from the end of the 1960s to the mid-1980s. This development has given rise to two opposite trends. The first sharpens and reinforces the notion of the presence of God and His providence by associating it with a particular messianic faith and a mystification of Israeli nationalism, in conformity with the Merkaz-ha-Rav teaching. The second moderates this notion and shifts the emphasis to coping with the Holocaust on a human, ethical basis, in affinity with the nonillusionary theology that is claimed by modern Orthodox circles.

As is well known, the trauma of the Holocaust led many Jews to deny God and lose their faith. Many were forced to rebuild themselves and their world, a world devoid of God and Torah. Those who retained their faith

and were still clinging to the Torah and the mitzvot sought the "explanation" for the Holocaust, as well as the meaning it carried—however
unique and traumatic it was—within the framework of their religious
world. Their modes of reaction were not, and could not have been, fundamentally revolutionary. Neither those who were satisfied with an agnostic
approach nor those who preferred to keep quiet were able to create a completely new religious language. From their own religious tradition and
faith-oriented world they retrieved some points and anchors that made it
possible for them to survive as believing Jews, while shifting emphases and
reorganizing the religious priorities in their life. In other words, the most
they could do was to create a variant of religious language that was absorbed in the parameters of their own, traditional religious world.

History teaches us that seldom does reality uproot faith from the hearts
of those it slaps in the face. Whether consciously or unconsciously, the
believers mobilize all the interpretive options available to them in order to
come up with adequate interpretation of the conflicting reality that threatens their world. These things are true of the individual believer. They are
even more valid for a movement that invests tremendous efforts to recruit
the shapers of public opinion, the educational systems, and the agents of
cultural transmission for the purpose of inculcating and inseminating the
principles of its faith in its followers.[1] I assume that many of you would
acknowledge this point if you considered the powerful measures taken by
the ultra-Orthodox community in response to the Holocaust. Its intense
indoctrinating initiative, which found its expression in numerous publications and in the introduction of ultra-Orthodox narratives of the Holocaust, is well documented in some fascinating studies that have been
published in the last decades.

I would like to begin with some basic assumptions related to the issue of
the presence of God and His providence in history.

1. Side by side with the belief that God revealed Himself in front of all
Israel at least once in history, in the Sinaite revelation, there is also a traditional religious position that God reveals Himself through history. This
position is prevalent not only in Judaism but also in Christianity. According to the Christian version, the abject historical situation of the Jewish
people serves as an irrefutable proof that God abandoned His covenant
with the people of Israel and passed it on to those who are "Israel by
spirit." Down through the ages this very notion served to oppress and
humiliate the Jews. That is to say, whoever contemplates historical occur-

rences, at least the global ones, and is struck by the lowly, ignoble state of the Jewish people must see in it the hand of God, who speaks to us through history. In this way, the lessons taught by history fortify the Christian faith.

2. Paradoxically, another pervasive notion was that by contemplating history we come to realize that the people of Israel is not part of it. It is subject to different laws because it belongs to metahistory. This is one of the formulae that was offered to counter the Christian claim. What it suggests is that the very abject situation of the Jewish people attests to its covenant with God. The people of Israel has a "different account" with God precisely because it is the Chosen People. This approach left the belief in divine providence intact. It suggested that with respect to the people of Israel, divine providence operates in a unique way, with a different kind of intensity and on a different level from the workings of His universal providence. This belief has a long and continuous tradition. Down through the ages, it assumed various forms of religious discourse, in keeping with the changing conceptual systems. Yet, essentially it did not change at all. In its traditional formulation it goes back to the Talmudic saying, "Israel is immune from planetary influence." What this means is that the people of Israel is not governed by the celestial systems. These are the agents of God. It is He who governs the world and Israel is subject to His direct providence. "For the Lord's portion is his people; Jacob is the lot of His inheritance" (Deut. 32:9). R. Yehudah ben Asher, son of R. Asher ben Yehiel, who lived in the beginning of the fourteenth century, conveyed this idea eloquently, as follows:

> "Let us return to God for he has torn and he will heal us; he has smitten and he will bind up; after two days he will revive us: in the third day he will raise us up, and we shall live in his presence" (Hos. 6:1–2). These verses acknowledge that the punishments we suffer every day and the exile that empowers us are a matter of a profound intent and not just accidental or compelled by history. For if we trust in the blessed God in all our actions, He shall change history for us from bad to good. God forbid that we should believe in the stars, as the idolaters do, for then history will govern us and He will abandon us to the arbitrariness of the accidents. . . . For it is not the nature of heavenly spheres to drop rain over dry land and produce rain in its season and the like as a reward for observing the Torah and the mitzvot. The truth is that "Thine is the Kingdom O Lord" and the power over the upper worlds and everything below them. God is capable of changing Nature whether

positively or adversely. . . . All the more so that it is impossible for us to know His ways and how He administers the world.[2]

3. This notion recurs in a different language in various conceptual adjustments in the writings of various thinkers, ranging from R. Isaac Breuer of Agudat Israel to Franz Rosenzveig,[3] who both insisted that the people of Israel is governed by metahistorical laws. Rav Kook himself exploited the idea when he suggested that it was time for the Jewish people to resume its place in history. This was in the aftermath of the First World War, when Rav Kook was still under the innocent, euphoric impression that it was meant to be the last war on earth. He therefore proclaimed that it was now possible for the Jews to return to "world politics" and found a Jewish state.

4. Here is the place to mention that it is doubtful whether we can reckon Maimonides among those subscribing to this widespread view that God reveals Himself through history. In his *Mishneh Torah,* Maimonides states, "But how may one discover the way to love and fear Him? When man will reflect concerning His works, and His great and wonderful creatures, and will behold through them His wonderful, matchless, and infinite wisdom."[4] This statement makes no reference to the contemplation of human history. Furthermore, Maimonides' position on the issue of divine providence, as suggested in his *Guide to the Perplexed,* is far more simple. One may say that with respect to his point, he failed to make an imprint on Jewish theological thought as it developed in the course of time. In the last decade, however, some minor circles in religious Zionism invoked Maimonides in an attempt to provide religious legitimacy to their exceptional views.

5. In its extreme manifestation, this "modern deviation" suggests an awareness of the change that occurred in the traditional position in the response to "nonillusionary"[5] theology, on the one hand, and to modern notions about the nature of history and historical interpretation, on the other hand. The nonillusionary theological position corroborates the denial of any pretension to discover God through human history. Modern hermeneutics raises our awareness of the connection between the historian's system of beliefs, values, and ideology and his account of history, precise and well documented as it may be. Thus, the assumption that "the facts speak for themselves" is no longer held to be true.

For the purpose of our discussion, I am going to divide religious Zionism into three periods. The first lasted until the 1960s. During this period, religious Zionism was close in spirit to the ideals of the other pioneer movements in the Jewish *yishuv* (settlement in Palestine). This meant that, generally speaking, it perceived historical events as normal political processes. In the second period, from the 1960s up to the late 1980s, religious Zionism was dominated by the Merkaz-ha-Rav school of thought whose intensive notion of divine providence was based on a mystical perception of Israeli nationalism. This school of thought made its imprint on, and directly influenced, the educational systems of religious Zionism, such as the high school yeshivas, the *Hesder* yeshivas, and the *Ulpanot.* The third period, from the mid-1980s onward, is characterized by a weakening of this hegemony by a wider variety of religious Zionist ideologies and by the absorption of other, more moderate notions of divine providence.[6]

Religious Zionism is closely intertwined with the belief in the presence of God in history and His immanence. The term *Athalta di-Ge'ulah,* "the beginning of redemption," which has accompanied religious Zionism since its inception, was embraced by the precursors of Zionism as early as the beginning of the nineteenth century. It is infused with explicit mystical elements concerning the theurgic impact of normal human activity stimulated by *it'aruta di-le-tata,* the "arousal below," on *it'artua di-le-eila,* the corresponding "arousal on high." There is some misapprehension in exclusively associating this arousal with realistic acts of redemption. Thus, for Rabbi Kalisher, the clearest indication of the beginning of redemption was to be found in the land yielding its fruit. "There can be no more manifest sign of redemption than this," said R. Kalisher. About a hundred years later, in 1967, on the eve of Independence Day, R. Zvi Yehudah used almost the same words when he declared at the Merkaz-ha-Rav Yeshivah,

> The issues of redemption associated with Israel's Independence Day . . . are visible and explicit . . . they are explicitly stated in the Gemara. . . . There can be no more manifest sign of redemption than this. How can we recognize it? By the fact that the land of Israel produces fruit in abundance.[7]

This quasi-realistic account is nothing but a mystical formulation, no different in essence from the signs usually indicated by those who calculated the end of days and the advent of the Messiah.

This term, "the beginning of redemption," gave rise to the phrase "the beginning of the emergence of our redemption." The latter was introduced into the "Prayer for the Safety of the State" in recognition of its significance, and it is in current use within all religious Zionist circles.

On the face of it, religious Zionism has its own, exclusive linguistic and conceptual tools for "explaining" the Holocaust. Generally speaking, one can say that in religious Zionism, especially from the 1960s onward, there has been a marked tendency to separate the Holocaust from the divine system of reward and punishment. Instead of attributing the Holocaust to the divine settling of scores on account of the people's sins in the past, religious Zionism views the Holocaust as an advance payment in preparation for the future, for the redemption. This transformation of the notion of the Holocaust does not transcend the limits of traditional theodicy. It is a matter of change in emphasis. In the circles of religious Zionism, the presence of God and His providence is sharply and excessively reinforced by the attempts to trace the divine redemptive moves. Henceforth I will refer to this as "an intensive notion of providence."

In order to appreciate how exaggerated this conception is, we will find it interesting to compare it to the stand taken by Rabbi Hayyim David Ha-Levi[8] toward the Holocaust. Rabbi Ha-Levi was much interested in the philosophy of history. He defined the study of history as a mitzvah and tended to interpret historical and topical events in terms of his own notion of providence. He used the same approach to clarify the term "the beginning of redemption" and to explore the meaning of the Holocaust and its connection with the founding of the state of Israel.

For Rabbi Ha-Levi, however, the individual's freedom of choice is a primary constituting principle. Hence, although history has a direction and a purpose, it is not deterministic. Divine providence acts in history as a "hidden hand" that offers and opens to humans "a window of opportunities" for realizing the divine purpose in the domain of history. Humans have the right to either take advantage of this opportunity or let it slip away. R. Ha-Levi's confidence in the possibility of fulfilling the divine intentions through human history rests on the assumption that the long course of history guarantees the necessary accumulation of appropriate human decisions.

According to Rabbi Ha-Levi, some historical periods are more "crowded" in terms of the quantitative and qualitative opportunities that unfold before us. He was convinced that the ingathering of the exiles and the founding of the state of Israel were all part of the progress of world history. Nonetheless, he insisted on the contingency of these progressive moves. He held on to his contingent notion of history even after the Six-Day War. Like many others, he was elated by the unexpected victory and the liberation of the occupied territories of the land of Israel, including the temple mount.

R. Ha-Levi made a similar observation about the contingency of human history in reference to the period following the First World War and the Balfour Declaration. He even suggested that had the Jewish people extricated itself from the exile in those days and settled down in the land of Israel, the Holocaust would not have taken place. God does not interfere with the free choice of human beings.

After the Six-Day War, and due to a variety of factors, the preoccupation with the Holocaust gained momentum. The surging involvement with the Holocaust, in the Diaspora and Israel alike, has performed a constructive role in shaping the Jewish identity of many Jews, especially those who were psychologically and mentally alienated from the halakic way of life and the traditional Jewish culture. It is true that some interpret this phenomenon unfavorably. Many others share the view that it is quite possible for religious Zionism to build and shape Jewish identity without invoking the Holocaust.

Yet, if we examine the literature about the Holocaust that emerged from the circles of religious Zionism, we notice that it practically swelled following the Six-Day War and corresponding to the rising hegemony of the Merkaz-ha-Rav school of thought. Presumably, the "manifest miracle" of the victory won in the Six-Day War intensified the need to relate to the Holocaust in retrospect, while at the same time offering the opportunity to do so. In its powerful and unmatched impact, the "miraculous" victory heightened the psychological awareness of the divine workings of providence, and this entailed an instant awareness, in retrospect, of the connection between the Holocaust and national revival. The "manifest redemption" embodied in the triumphant Six-Day War has become more compelling than the fecundity of trees on the mountains of Israel. It should be noted that from a metaphysical-mystical viewpoint, the "manifest redemption" signified by the transformation of the soil is far superior because of the metaphysical standing of the land of Israel.[9] No wonder that the vigorous redemptive settlement activity, which was initiated mostly by the adherents of the Merkaz-ha-Rav teaching and *Gush Emunim,* began right after the Six-Day War.

Thus it is no coincidence that at that time there was a breakthrough in disseminating the mystical perception of Israeli nationalism, along with a detailed "providential" interpretation of the divine moves that leave their imprint on current reality. This perception originates in the teaching of R. Abraham Isaac Ha-Kohen Kook in the first decade after he settled in Israel. However, only after the Six-Day War, as a result of a concurrent combination of various factors, did this latent perception emerge from below the surface and make a striking impression.[10] From 1967 onwards, Rabbi Zvi Yehudah spoke of the Holocaust by using the startling image of a divine healing operation performed on the body of the nation in order to cut it off from the bonds of exile. Prof. Avi Ravitsky, who was the first to comment on this image, noted that Rabbi M. M. Shneurson has preceded R. Zvi Yehudah in using it, although he did not associate it with a divine purpose of redemption. In 1971, T. Aviner wrote—apparently expressing the view for the first time—as follows:[11]

> Once again we must mention that we are not speaking here of sin and retribution. . . . We only speak of the fact that the people of Israel was bonded with the Exile and it was necessary to sever these ties in a cruel way. . . . This is what my master and teacher, Rabbi Zvi Yehudah, said about this: "The truth is that all Israel, millions of individual Jews, form one single body, and when the time of redemption comes . . . , it is necessary to separate Israel from the exile against their will. It is then that the hand of God appears and performs a cruel operation, which brings about the separation and leads back to the land of Israel. . . . In fact . . . , the final act of severance, with all the traumatic convulsions it entails . . . signifies the light of the living and the revival of the holy people. . . . We are obligated to contemplate history, to consider the Word of God as revealed to us through the increasingly expanding channel of guidance provided by the great of Israel. . . . We must discern the 'sweetness' within the 'bitterness.' We must see the lights that emerged from the darkness. This light of the living is bound to intensify even as we continue to build our Holy Land and be rebuilt by it."[12]

Recently, my friend Yishai Rozen-Zvi has discussed this issue at length in a yet unpublished paper entitled "*Ha-Holeh ha-Medumeh*" [The Hypochondriac]. He shows that the transition from justifying the ways of God to justifying the Holocaust eventually led to a decatastrophization of the Holocaust. In this explanatory system, the Holocaust does not precede redemption but rather forms an integral part of it. Rozen-Zvi further demonstrates that this idea found its way to the circles of the Merkaz-ha-

Rav school of thought. It is taught in the yeshivas and is disseminated through the publication of books, such as R. Eliyahu Bazak's last work, *Medaber bi-Zedakah*.[13] It should be added that in the beginning of 1999, preparations were made to set up the Zvi Yisrael Institute for studying the Holocaust in the light of faith, according to the teaching of R. Zvi Yehudah ha-Koheh Kook. The institute is presently annexed to the Ateret Kohanim yeshiva in the old city of Jerusalem. Here is an excerpt from an interview with Rabbi Solomon Aviner that was conducted at that time:

> *R. Aviner*: We are ordained to study history out of faith.
>
> *Question*: What does it mean "out of faith?" Isn't history a sequence of objective facts? Where is the place of faith in this sequence?
>
> *R. Aviner*: It all depends on what approach we adopt to relate to the facts. The starting point is that "the city is governed by a Leader," that God did not abandon the land, that He is always with us, whether in the light or in the darkness. It is not that we observe the world and accordingly we come to conclusions about the Master of the world. On the contrary, out of our faith in the Master of the world we strive to understand what is happening in this world. We even try to understand a little about the Holocaust. . . .
>
> *Question*: And how did he [i.e., R. Zvi Yehudah] understand the Holocaust?
>
> *R. Aviner*: He did not explain it. He said that it was an enigma. Nonetheless, he elaborated a complete and profound system, which he himself summed up in a parable: "There is a house in the forest and it is surrounded by dangerous beasts. Mother is inside the house, preparing warm and tasty food for her child. Inside the house it is not as dangerous as outside. There is warm nourishing food. So mother calls her child to come inside. But the child refuses. He wants to play outside. Mother is concerned about her child and so she pulls him vigorously and drags him into the house. Now he is scratched and bruised. He is bleeding all over. Yet, he is alive."
>
> *Question*: Doesn't God have another way?
>
> *R. Aviner*: Our master, R. Zvi Yehudah, describes the Holocaust as a divine horrible operation designed to cut Israel off from the Exile. . . . The terrible destruction prepares the magnificent building. From the depth of impurity and wickedness the redeemed praise the Lord with a new song.

Once the Holocaust is explained in terms of this model of divine surgery, the intensive notion of providence is reinforced. Hence we can say that in the excerpt I quoted, the Holocaust serves to strengthen the religious Zionist conception fostered by the Merkaz-ha-Rav teaching.

As I've already indicated, during the last decade there occurred a complex inner development within religious Zionism. This development, for which various internal and external factors are responsible, is basically characterized by the decline of the hegemony of Merkaz-ha-Rav ideology and the rise of other ideological and religious trends. It seems plausible that the incentive to establish the Zvi Yisrael Institute came—among other things—in response to these opposite trends.

I will try to sum up those characteristics of the new trends that are relevant to this discussion. Note that by their very nature, these characteristics are diffusive rather than monolithic.

1. A contingent perception of historical events and a forecast of an open future.
2. Various concepts that moderate the intense notion of the actual role of providence in history, with the most extreme one completely denying any divine intervention in human activity and placing on humans full moral responsibility for their actions. Prof. Yeshayahu Leibowits conveyed this position in a pointed manner when he stated,

> I am saying it as strongly as I can, notwithstanding the pain this should cause to many people, among them myself, that I cannot attach any religious meaning to the Holocaust. . . . The Holocaust was a product of a particular reality of the world. . . . This is the fate of the helpless when they are in the hands of the wicked.

3. Treating secularism as a possible alternative for understating reality. This approach instantly rejects the redemptive messianic interpretation and the notion of divine providence. At the very least it requires a revision of traditional conventions.
4. Unwillingness to attribute to the rabbis a supreme knowledge of God and the Torah, the kind of knowledge that would enable them to explain the divine intentions underlying current historical and political moves.

In the course of a discussion I led with some members of the Religious Kibbutz Movement in preparation for this conference, I asked their opinion about the lessons of the Holocaust and whether they can point to any indications of them in the Religious Kibbutz Movement. Naturally, I got various answers, for the Religious Kibbutz Movement is not made of one piece. The following comments, however, are noteworthy: Relatively speaking, there is only a small number of written publications on this issue in the periodicals published by the religious kibbutzim. On the whole, however, this communal and ideological structure of the Religious Kibbutz Movement seems to reflect a general response to the Holocaust. This finds its expression in sensitivity to human rights; sensitivity to the use of aggressive force; a sense of duty with respect to the communal rehabilitation of the Jewish society; a principled willingness to take a critical stand towards the religious leadership; and the cultivation of modesty and humility with regard to the pretension to explain the Holocaust in religious terms.

NOTES

1. Prof. Dov Schwartz: "There is hardly any religious Zionist thinker that has changed his views as a result of the Holocaust," *Ha-Ziyyonut ha-Datit bein Higgayon li-Meshihiyyut* (Tel Aviv, 1999), 134.

2. *Responsa Zikhron Yehudah,* par. 91.

3. As he said, "Everything the Jew does, immediately leaps out of the temporal framework and becomes eternity." See Ephraim Meir, *Kokhav mi-Ya'akov,* chs. 5–6.

4. *Hilkhot Yesodei ha-Torah,* II, 2.

5. On the nonillusionary belief see my "One Hundred Years of Religious Zionism," in *Ha-Ziyyonut ha-Datit,* vol. 3, ed. Avi Sagi and Yedidia Stern (Ramat Gan, 2002), 17–29 (Hebrew). This paper was written by following in the footsteps of Prof. Eliezer Goldman. The nonillusionary belief denies the pretension that humans as such are capable of identifying God's intention with any measure of certainty. In addition, it removes from the concept of providence its ontological meaning and the pretension to provide a causal meaning to the course of events.

6. "Moderate concepts of providence" include a sequence represented by such figures and thinkers as R. Hayyim David Ha-Levi, Prof. E. E. Urbach, and Moshe Una, and up to Prof. Eliezer Goldman and Yeshayahu Leibovitz, who denied that the belief in providence had any empirical meaning. I disagree with Prof. Dov Schwartz, who excluded Goldman from the category of those worthy of being included in religious Zionism, and who stated that "Goldman's thought can no longer be labeled typical religious Zionist thought and it is doubtful whether it can be ascribed to any existing religious Zionist approach whatsoever." See Dov Schwartz (supra, note 1), 136.

7. See Avi Ravitsky, *Ha-Ketz ha-Meguleh u-Medinat ha-Yehudim: Meshihiyyut, Ziyyonut ve-Redicalism Dati be-Yisrael* (Tel Aviv, 1993), ch. 3, particularly 170–200.

8. The description of R. Ha-Levi's position is based on Zvi Zohar, "Sephardic Religious Thought in Israel: Aspects of the Theology of Rabbi Haim David Halevi," in *Critical Essays on Israeli Society, Religion, and Government,* ed. Kevin Avruch and Walter Zenner (Albany, 1997), 115–36.

9. According to the well-known words of R. Abba in B.T. *Sanhedrin* 98a, "There can be no more manifest sign of redemption than this, viz., what is said (Ezek. 36), 'But ye O mountains of Israel, ye shall shoot forth your branches, and yield your fruit to my people of Israel, for they are at hand to come.'"

10. See my lecture on religious Zionism, which was presented in the Van Lear Institute in honor of Prof. Eliezer Schweid's seventieth anniversary.

11. "Sho'ah u-Geulah," published in several publications from 1976 onwards. The excerpt I cited is taken from the collection *Emunah ba-Sho'ah,* based on a study day on the Jewish religious meaning of the Holocaust and published by the Ministry of Culture and Education, the Department of *Tarbut Toranit* (Jerusalem, 1980), 65–66.

12. Ibid., 67 ff.

13. (Jerusalem, 2000).

Chapter 16

Educational Implications of
Holocaust and Rebirth

Tova Ilan

I want to begin by acknowledging the humility demanded of me when we discuss such an explosive topic as the implications of the Holocaust and the establishment of the state of Israel for our spirituality and religious concepts.[1]

I am aware of the fact that great respect is due both to those who were killed and to those who survived. I know that when we deal with these topics, due to the magnitude of the questions and the doubts to which they lead, and due to the limitations of words and the means of communication, often silence is preferable to speech. I am well aware of the high quality of much that has been said and written on the topic. Indeed, it seems that everything has already been said. Please, therefore, see in my coming words the random thoughts of one whose questions are far more numerous than her answers.

In my brief remarks I will relate to two aspects of the subject that bear educational implications. For education is the field in which I have life-long experience and from which I come. I will ask two from among many questions, for the limitations of time do not permit more.

The first question will deal with "how"—that is to say, how we transmit our culture from generation to generation. Jewish culture is characterized, as is well known, as a culture of historic memory. How are we to remember and how are we to transmit the values that stem from the memories of the most recent events of our past?

The second subject will deal with educating towards and instilling religious faith in Orthodox society and will address the question of the proper characteristics of that faith after, and as a result of, the Holocaust. In addition, I will add a comment about the moral approaches that are required after the Holocaust. This question is magnified by the additional fact that we now have the responsibility that derives from our renewed sovereignty in our own land, the state of Israel.

I will maintain that our subject has implications for the halakah, and for a proper relationship between the halakah and ethics as we understand ethics today.

Only I am responsible for my comments. However, to some extent they are reflective of the prevalent mood and attitude in my community, the community of the Religious Kibbutz Movement, and within its periphery in that which is often called modern Orthodoxy.[2]

My following remarks are not the result of scientific research conducted within these communities. Nor are they the fruit of systematic philosophic thought. But it seems to me that they reflect a complex outlook of a community that merges conservative traditionalism with revolutionary creativity, a community of religious pathos and ethos. The members of this community prefer the traditional halakic component in their lives. At the same time they have internalized the concept of the "holy rebellion" that was, in their opinion, at the heart of the Zionist revolution. This understanding of the Zionist enterprise brought to it a type of religious charisma that enabled the creation of new halakic terms and concepts in various areas that were brought to the fore by the renewal of Jewish sovereignty.[3]

This complexity shaped people who were more autonomous, less dependent on the ideas and opinions of rabbis and religious and halakic deciders (*poskim*), people who were willing to question and doubt. These qualities were deepened and sharpened, due to the lessons of the Holocaust. This complexity was also due to a dual responsibility: on one hand nationalism, which is based on a commitment that each Jew can and should feel for each and every other Jew; and on the other hand, a universal responsibility, a responsibility to human harmony and to the realization of human potential.

These dual responsibilities were deepened in the wake both of the creation of the state as well as of the tragedy of the Holocaust. I hope that my comments will be expressive of this complex spiritual climate.

A Culture of Remembrance

The culture of remembrance of the Jewish people was never merely a passive one. We were not commanded just to remember the Exodus from Egypt. The living memory must be renewed during the Passover Seder every year. On that occasion each of us is commanded to view himself or herself as if he or she personally participated in the Exodus.

This stress carries an educational message that is fundamental to Jewish culture. We are commanded not only to remember the past but also to apply the moral conclusion to the present. "You shall not oppress a stranger, for you know the feelings of the stranger, having yourselves been strangers in the land of Egypt" (Ex. 23:9). This message is repeated in the Torah often and in various forms, more than any other of the commandments. The case is similar for other commandments of memory. We are commanded not only to recall the past but also to cause the remembrance to guide our behavior.

Two statements related to the Holocaust have become deeply imbedded in the Jewish collective consciousness:

(1) Remember! And don't forget!
(2) Never again!

As I mentioned before, in our culture the imperative to remember contains within it an active component. This enables us to counter the natural human tendency to put the past, especially the painful past, out of mind, to forget. The effort to preserve an event, especially within the cultural context of communal remembrance, requires a conscious effort to overcome human nature—forgetfulness. This effort must be intensified if we desire to include within the act of remembrance an active educational message, as in the example of the prohibition against wronging a stranger who lives in our midst, mentioned in connection with the Exodus from Egypt. The lessons that we learn from the Holocaust must include not only the one of shared Jewish fate but also the message of Jewish morality.

In an article written by Professor Charles Liebman in 1977[4] Liebman relates to the concept of "civil religion" in Israel and examines one facet of its belief system: those beliefs that are related to the Holocaust. There he stresses that beliefs can be expressed in a rationally conscious form, that is to say, in linguistic terms that can be expressed within a framework of theological and philosophic propositions—or in mythical structures. "Myth," according to his definition, "is a story which arouses strong emotions, which transmits the values of a society, and gives them added intensity. . . . The events themselves can be proven empirically. This is especially true, it would seem, of modern myths."

Liebman claims that the central myth of Israeli civil religion is the Holocaust. "The Holocaust shapes our national consciousness and the way in which we understand ourselves."[5] These myths, I would add, are powerful educational tools and have deep and far-reaching influence. Liebman analyzes the components of this myth. He points, in particular, to two of its fundamental premises: "It is well known that Esau hates Jacob" (*Sifrei Numbers* par. 69)—which serves as a symbol for the relationships between Jew and Gentile; and we are "a people that dwells apart" (Num. 23:9)—in the way that was fashioned by Yaacov Herzog in our time. These concepts constitute the symbols that are deeply imbedded in the culture of the people. These symbols rose to the surface anew, and with greater force, in the wake of the Holocaust, in both the religious and the nonreligious sectors of society.

Through the Holocaust, he claims, certain ruptures in the fabric of the relationships between Israel and the Diaspora, between Israelis and themselves, and between Israelis and their cultural heritage were healed. This healing, even though it is far from complete or perfect and indeed can never be expected to achieve perfection, expresses a distancing from Israeli civil religions of the past, such as the "religions" of Labor and Socialism.

In this new civil religion Yad Va'Shem is the central temple dedicated to the Holocaust, according to Liebman, a place that is secondary in importance only to the Western Wall. The wail of the sirens on the memorial days for the Holocaust and heroism—the Seventh of Nisan and on the Tenth of Tevet, and the ceremonies at official occasions—such as Memorial Day (for the fallen soldiers) and Independence Day—are all understood by Liebman as being the rites and rituals of this civil religion.

It is important to note that Liebman wrote his article in 1977, after the Yom Kippur War and before Saadat landed in Jerusalem. Since then, because of the processes involved in making peace with our neighbors, a desire has been born[6] to distance ourselves from the mindset that "the whole world is against us," or at least to blunt the sharpness of the emotions involved. All this is due to a desire to create a new framework for better relationships with the rest of the world.

This is to be understood within the framework of Israel's willingness to sacrifice in order to achieve peace with her neighbors. The result, however, is that there is danger that the ritual means of expression, of which Liebman spoke, will lose their force and their formative power.

Therefore it is necessary to create additional tools, through symbols and ceremonies, that will ensure the transmission of memory from generation to generation. We need tools whose symbolic power enables them to say more than that which is contained within them, and to link up with the "inner-I" of the individual. In order for such an experience to become an experience of the community, of the collective, it must contain within itself an educational message that demands activism and that is moral, that contains the imperative to battle human evil and every form of racism and aggression.

Such an experience must link up with the historic Jewish ethos of the past and must find expression in the family life of the Jewish home, as do the rest of the Jewish holidays and days of remembrance. Through these experiences, consciously and subconsciously, these messages will find their way into the hearts of future generations. It would seem to me that the design of days of remembrance and holidays that are related to the Holocaust and the establishment of the state have not yet achieved this level of sophistication.

It is important to remember that we still live the historic experiences through direct contact with that generation that lived and survived the events. The crystallization of clear and simple messages that will find their way into the Jewish home and into Jewish education is not yet possible. But as we face the future and plan for eternity, the design and fashioning of active memory still awaits our attention.

Religious Education—Faith Inculcation

On the subject of the transmission of historic memory to future generations, enough has been said. The present-day parent and teacher are required to fulfill their responsibilities in the here and now and do not have historic time before them. They cannot wait until a collective spirit or attitude, saturated with symbols and ceremonies, is crystallized. Therefore, being cognizant of the imperfection and possible shallowness of our present-day endeavors, we have no choice but to work on both planes: to work in the here and now through the educational process[7] while keeping a creative eye on eternity. The central question that the religious educator must ask is, what could possibly be the meaning of the ethos that we wish to transmit, after we have experienced the absurd and satanic totality of the powers of evil in the Holocaust?

Is it possible to educate to "faith" after the Holocaust? What is the message that we can pass on to our children?

Where was God during the Holocaust?

Where was the good and compassionate God "when our children cried in the shadow of the gallows"?

Is it possible to sanctify a sacrificial altar to which were led a million babes who had not sinned?

Is it possible to conceive of an image of God, the God of Israel, whose historic providence should function in such a way that the establishment of the state of Israel should necessitate the sacrifice of six million of His Jews?

I know that there are those who think that it is indeed possible and cite Rabbi Aviner's article, in the book *Faith after the Holocaust*, which presents prooftexts from scripture and rabbinical writings to that effect.[8] Similarly, one can ask, is it possible to educate about a Holocaust understood as a supposed punishment for sins that the Jewish people have supposedly committed, as is customary in certain ultra-Orthodox communities—a punishment for the sin of Zionism or for the sin of assimilation? Is it possible to explain the Holocaust in terms of a "divine plan" or in terms of the concepts of causality customary in religious discourse?

It is my opinion that we cannot. "And Aaron was silent" (Leviticus 10:3). Only the immense silence that expresses the absolute impossibility of human comprehension, only this silence is possible in my opinion. I am incapable of finding meaning or understanding in the greatest of traumas that has beset humanity and that has befallen the Jewish people.

In the contexts of the Holocaust and the establishment of the state of Israel—or any other context for that matter—there is no room for concepts that imply that the ways of God in history are comprehensible to human beings. There is no place for such concepts in the framework of religious education.[9] In the present context I even have difficulty with the classic concept of God's hidden face (*hester panim*, Ez. 39:23–24). I admit that I flee from an honest attempt to deal with the question of God's providence and theodicy. I prefer the formulation of Rabbi Soloveitchik in *The Man of Faith*. He deals with the problem of suffering and evil in the world and determines that

Judaism, with its realistic approach to man and the human condition in the real world, understood that evil cannot be covered up or hidden. . . . Evil is a fact that cannot be denied. There is evil, there is suffering and there is hellish and heinous pain in the world. He who wishes to delude himself by distracting his attention from the rent in the fabric of Being . . . is none other than a fool and a hallucinator.[10]

Because it is "impossible to overcome the monstrosity of evil through philosophic speculative thought," as he puts it, "man must not ask himself why suffering has befallen him, but rather, what is it that suffering requires of him to do." In another place he writes that "coping with evil is possible only through human actions. Neither to accept defeat with resignation, nor to accustom oneself to suffering; but rather to fight it." He goes on to write, "*Metaphysics* comes to justify evil or to deny its existence. *Ethics* has for its task the transformation of suffering from a foreign force which we encounter by chance into a unifying force."

On the basis of these ideas, Rabbi Soloveitchik formulated two new and distinctive concepts: the thematic halakah and the topical halakah. The thematic halakah is that which developed the metaphysics of suffering. The topical halakah, which is identical to what is commonly called "the halakah," refused to do so. It developed—*instead of a metaphysics of evil*—ethics. An ethics whose concern, in his terms, "is with the pathetic mood of suffering man, with the submersion of the pain in an all-encompassing awareness, in a broad response to suffering and crisis."[11]

His halakic ethics is founded upon various premises. First, evil does exist and it is indeed bad. Second, one must not assent to evil, compromise with it, nor be forgiving of its existence. The halakah urges us to actively fight evil by the use of all available means that God has given to us. God has called upon humanity to battle evil actively. Third, faith. As the rabbi explains, "Even if man should lose the battle, the topical Halacha always believed that in the future, at some distant date, evil will be vanquished and will vanish completely. Indeed this is a long war, an ongoing struggle, in the course of which one loses many a battle."[12]

There are those who criticized this third premise of Rabbi Soloveitchik and maintained that by using the term "faith" and by referring to its messianic component, he is returning to the language of metaphysics.[13] He himself mentioned[14] that "the topical Halacha cannot allow itself to ignore eschatology." It is true that the rabbi was not always consistent in the rejection of metaphysical explanations of human suffering. However, it seems to me that, as opposed to philosophy and theology, faith is not required to exhibit a logically coherent explanation or justification for God's actions.

These concepts, which have been magnified in the wake of the Holocaust and in the light of modern insights, have implications for education.

Our generation has witnessed the collapse of the "grand ideologies" as well as the retreat of science from the conceit that it will eventually be possible to explain all the phenomena of the universe with absolute certainty. Our generation has undergone the frustrating religious experience of "the disappearance of God" and the frustrating humanistic experience that humanity, that very humanity that was thought to be enlightened and cultured, has disappointed our expectations.

In the film *The Argument,* based on a story written by Chaim Grade and directed by Eli Cohen, we are told of two Jewish childhood friends who underwent the Holocaust and survived. They meet after many years, by chance, in Canada. One, an author and poet, is an atheist who zealously hurls his accusations at the God who was not there for the Jews in their hour of need during the Holocaust. The other, a rebbe in language and dress, clings desperately to the yeshiva and to Jewish tradition and defends his God and implores his friend to repent. For a full day they argue and are finally reconciled. It is a very powerful emotional drama that leaves you with a strong feeling *that they are both right.*

If you are a person committed to truth, you cannot but admit that the argument between faith in humanity and faith in God, in terms of who contributes more to the perfection of humanity and the world, remains undecided. And so, the claim that reality is characterized by a dialectic nature and that positive and negative meanings and implications of every value coexist, as proffered by my teacher, Professor Carl Frankenstein, was reinforced in my mind.

And so Yitzchak Greenberg and others who are of a like mind and who propose the notion that today, after the Holocaust, there is a need for a secularism that has within it a spark of holiness and a religiosity that is more secular are correct.[15] We must search out the dialectic, the complexity, and a sense of identity that is multifaceted and dynamic.

In the wake of the Holocaust we must be more humble and we must limit our truth claims. It would seem to me that we should prefer the concept of perfection (*tikkun*) as opposed to the concept of redemption (*geulah*).

I do not mean to say that we must completely forego the utopian messianic dream as a concept of that which is proper and should be, that towards which we must strive. But in our daily lives we have to settle for "small redemptions," for incremental progress and improvement. We have to be tolerant in our understanding of human diversity. Each individual shall live by the light of his or her own faith and belief. We must learn to understand and accept that the individual who chooses the kingship of God is wagering on this option not because of convincing rational arguments but due to an existential sense of identity, personal biography, and a deep personal need for meaning and commitment. Some will prefer the description of God as the Presence that was with us in the crematoria of Auschwitz, as opposed to the cold and alienated God who needs, as it were, our sacrifice in order to rule the world. And others, who choose a world without God, will make do with humanity, while maintaining a deep awareness of its limitations.

Both need to battle the evil that is to be found in every person and the evil that is in the world. Hopefully such an understanding can contribute to an awareness of Jewish kinship on one hand and the universal kinship of humanity on the other, without any sense of contradiction between them. Hopefully it will enable the establishment of communal frameworks for positive creative activity. Hopefully it will contribute to a sense of solidarity among people who are aware of their differences but also understand that the "other" is in reality part of "me."

The upshot of this is that the dichotomous and polarized categories of thought to which we have grown accustomed must change. Faith education must change direction. Instead of a language in which absolute concepts are rife, we have a need for a language of doubt, which will include a humanism that is neither naive nor aggressive. Two basic experiences must join in a unity of contradiction. This implies that Jewish education after the Holocaust needs new symbols and a new hermeneutic for ancient ones.

I am aware of the difficulty and the degree of abstraction that is necessary to translate this approach, which is so complex, into education. In practice the principles have to be transformed into a language fitting for the different ages and different levels of education. But first the educator must internalize the basic principles and only then search for his or her method of implementation. In truth, so I believe, such an approach will find the path to hearts, even if it is difficult for the digestion.

One more thing: we see in the existence and well-being of the state of Israel the "beginning of our redemption." The state of Israel has to be the long arm that will defend all Jews wherever they may be and wherever they are persecuted because of their Jewish identity. The experience of the Holocaust has sensitized us to the precariousness of Jewish survival. The memory of the Holocaust has deepened our awareness of the need for the maintenance of a powerful defense force to protect us and to defend our country.

In addition, the memory of the Holocaust must tell us something about the mode of Jewish existence and temporal power. Power is necessary in order to prevent another Holocaust from taking place. But we are aware of the fact that power can also be destructive. We must be constantly aware of the ethical limitations on the use of force and of the thin line that separates the defensive use of force on one hand and the power of the aggressor on the other. We must stress this subject in the educational process. But even here the dialectic and the oscillation between its two poles require an educational system geared to an understanding and an awareness of complexity.

And in conclusion, the memory of the Holocaust and the miracle of the establishment of the state of Israel are fundamental religious experiences that must stimulate halakic creativity. There is a pressing need to correct imbalances in the status of the stranger, the Gentile, women, and all those who are weak in our society. We must reformulate in a more sensitive way the concept of our being a "chosen people." We need a different approach to the Gentile. We need a halakic activism that educates towards justice and charity in relation to the problems and challenges of our generation. We need a halakic activism that expresses our ethical sensitivity, which has been sharpened in the wake of the Holocaust.

In summation: faith-oriented education in our generation, a generation that has experienced the Holocaust and the establishment of the state of Israel, should not concern itself with the transmission of a metaphysical or theological message that seeks to explain God's providence.

This is a huge task and we cannot conceivably complete it. But to paraphrase the sages of the Talmud (M. Avot 2), the work is not upon us to finish, but we are not free to desist from it.

NOTES

1. During the preparations for this conference a meeting was held at the offices of the Religious Kibbutz Movement in which a number of members of the Religious Kibbutz Movement participated. We discussed the questions that were to be raised at the conference and tried to develop a common approach. The meeting

was opened by Mr. Amos Goldberg, who deals with the research on the Shoah at the Yad Va'Shem Memorial. I thank him and the members of the movement for their participation and for their views and comments. I am especially indebted to Mr. Goldberg, who introduced me to new insights and understandings as well as to the relevant bibliography.

2. In the course of the meeting mentioned in note 1, it became clear that it is not possible to speak in the name of the community of the Religious Kibbutz Movement. There is no uniformity of ideas among its members in relation to the subjects with which I deal here. A very broad range of theological/belief concepts as well as political/social stances is represented within this community; and the multiplicity of positions continues to increase. This is why I have preferred to speak in terms of attitudes and mood that create, I think, a certain spiritual climate, although it cannot be measured scientifically. I would hope that I am being reflective of this climate. It is important to note that some of the communities, some of the senior kibbutzim of the Religious Kibbutz Movement, were established by refugees from Nazism and the Holocaust. The question of how to institutionalize the memory of the Shoah was dealt with intensively by these kibbutzim and their members. The stories of those people and their absorption into the kibbutzim during the days of the existential struggle of the War of Independence are worthy of independent research.

3. See Aryeh Fishman's book *Between Religion and Ideology: Judaism and Modernization in the Religious Kibbutz* (Jerusalem, 1990).

4. The article appeared in a revised form in *Tfuzot Israel* (1978).

5. From a quotation cited by Liebman taken from a communiqué sent to all officers in the IDF (Israel Defense Forces).

6. This phenomenon is especially characteristic of "leftist" factions in Israel. But it is possible to observe a similar and parallel phenomenon in the Diaspora.

7. In his article "The Expulsion from Spain and the Holocaust," which appeared in the journal *2000*, no. 3 (5751), Professor Eliezer Schweid raises the educational question as to whether it is possible to educate and construct a common Jewish identity purely on the basis of traumas, destruction, and satanic evil. The same question was raised at the Education Committee of the Religious Kibbutz Movement. Because of it, for a long time we refused to send our youth on "the Holocaust tour" of Poland. The fact that Hitler and his legions sought to destroy us might, so it was claimed, produce an effect the very opposite of that which we desire. It might spawn a desire to escape one's Jewish identity.

It is necessary to educate on the basis of positive values and the Jewish heritage, values and a heritage that contain the challenges within themselves and that can generate excitement. Or at least it was so claimed. Despite the truth of this claim, today our students do go to Poland. And we cannot deny that the powerful experience, when supported with proper and exacting preparation, leaves an immense impression on their creativity, both written and oral, arouses them to search for their roots, and encourages them to take moral positions. Such results have no parallel in any other educational activity. Professor Schweid, it seems, referred to the sectors of the population where all sense of identity with Judaism is based only on the Holocaust, which surely isn't true of education in the Religious Kibbutz Movement. Even so it is possible to learn from this of the strength and impact of the experience gained from the visit to Poland on the students.

8. See Rabbi Shlomo Chaim HaCohen Aviner's article "Holocaust and Redemption" in the anthology *Faith after the Shoah: An Investigation of the Jewish Religious Meaning of the Holocaust* (Jerusalem, 5718) (Heb.), published by the Religious Culture branch of the Ministry of Education. See footnote 1 of that article, wherein you will find a bibliography of articles and books that maintain similar positions. Most of them originate from the "Marcaz Harav" sector of religious Zionism.

9. One must distinguish between a search for an explanation on our part today and in retrospect, on one hand, and the search for a meaningful explanation of God's judgment that was conducted at the time of the events themselves, on the other. It is fitting and proper to draw the attention of students to texts that were written within the blood and fire of the Holocaust itself. See for example an analysis of Hasidic texts written during the Holocaust in the article of Dr. Pesach Schindler in *Faith after the Shoah* (see note 8 above). Such texts give rise to great amazement at the depth of the faith and the psychological fortitude that is expressed within them. But no comparison can be made between a call from the depth of anguish on one hand, and theological analysis after the fact, today, on the other.

10. "Kol Dodi Dofek" in *The Man of Faith* (Jerusalem, 5731), 67 (Heb.). Notwithstanding this statement of Rabbi Soloveitchik here, in *The Man of Faith*, 77–78, he calls the Holocaust "a phenomenon of the hiding of God's face"—and he categorizes it theologically as a phenomenon of the chaos at the onset of creation. Although we do not have the key to the question why, the establishment of the state of Israel, in his opinion, reflects the return of God to active providence. (See "Chapters in the Thought of the Rav," 30, and the relevant discussion in the work of Mrs. Zivan listed in the following note.)

11. The quotations are all taken from a lecture by Rabbi Soloveitchik entitled "On Mental Health" delivered in 1961 (the 28th of Kislev, 5722) within the framework of a seminar on "Religion and Mental Health." His comments were not published among the writings of the rabbi and were accidentally discovered by Professor Avi Sagi. The article is now available in David Shatz (ed.), *Out of the Whirlwind* (Hoboken, 2003), 86–115.

Some of the ideas contained therein were already mentioned in an abbreviated and nebulous way in "Kol Dodi Dofek." I became aware of them through reading the doctoral dissertation by Mrs. Gili Zivan that deals, among other things, with the thought of Rabbi Soloveitchik. See her Ph.D. thesis entitled *Hagut Yehudit*

Orthodoxit Nokhah Olam Post-Moderni (Bar Ilam University, Ramat Gan, 2000). The ideas pertaining to the "question of evil" appear in the first chapter of her work. Mrs. Zivan there provides an additional bibliography dealing with the same question of suffering and evil in postmodern Jewish theology.

12. The entire discussion, including the last quotation, is taken from the aforementioned lecture "On Mental Health" (see note 11 above). See especially pp. 18–20 thereof. Rabbi Soloveitchik derives the halakic position concerning evil and suffering from the opinion of the halakah vis-à-vis medicine and doctors: "And he shall cure" (Ex. 21:19), which is taken to mean that humanity is commanded to actively intervene in order to extirpate evil. All of the above, as was mentioned, is taken from the work of Mrs. Gili Zivan.

13. See Mrs. Zivan's discussion on the topic in her doctorate (note 11 above).

14. In his lecture "On Mental Health" (see note 11 above) and in this context.

15. Irving Greenberg, in *Perspectives: Auschwitz, Beginning of a New Era—Reflections on the Holocaust,* edited by Eva Fleisher, published by CLAL, New York (no date), chapter 7. The entire article is of great importance. This particular chapter deals with religion and secularism after the Holocaust.

About the Contributors

Yosef Achituv is Research Fellow at the Shalom Hartman Institute in Jerusalem and teaches Talmud and Jewish Philosophy in the Kibbutz Hadati Yeshiva and in the Yaacov Herzog Center for Jewish Studies, both located in Kibbutz Ein Tzurim. He received an honorary doctorate from Bar-Ilan University on 18 May 2004, in recognition of his contributions to religious Zionism and the Religious Kibbutz Movement, and his impact on Israel's developing Jewish, Zionist, and democratic character. He is author of *Al Gvul Hatmura* (On the Cusp of Change)—a study of contemporary Jewish meanings—and has published over 150 articles in the field of contemporary Jewish thought.

Yehoyada Amir is Professor of Modern Jewish Thought and Director of the Israel Rabbinic Program at Hebrew Union College in Jerusalem. He is the author of the recently published book *Da'at Ma'amina: iyunim bemishnato shel Franz Rosenzweig* [Reason out of Faith: The Philosophy of Franz Rosenzweig]. Dr. Amir focuses his research on nineteenth- and twentieth-century Jewish philosophy.

Ester Farbstein is head of the Rab-Abeles Center for Holocaust Researches and Studies at Jerusalem College, Jerusalem, Israel, and is an Academic Advisor and Lecturer at the Teachers' Continuing Education Center of Holocaust Instruction, Mercaz Beth Jacob, Jerusalem. Ms. Farbstein received her M.A. magna cum laude at the Institute of Contemporary Jewry, Hebrew University, Jerusalem. Her publications include *Diaries and Memoirs as a Historical Source: The Diary and Memoirs of a Rabbi at the "Konin House of Bondage"*; and *"Beseter Ra'am" ("Hidden Thunder"): Perspectives on Faith, Theology, and Leadership during the Holocaust.*

Gershon Greenberg is Professor of Jewish Studies and Philosophy at American University in Washington, D.C. He is author of three definitive bibliographies on religious thought and the Holocaust, as well as *The Holy*

Land in American Religious Thought: 1620–1948. In addition, he has published a large number of papers on modern Jewish thought with a special emphasis on the Orthodox religious responses to the Holocaust.

Warren Zev Harvey is Professor of Jewish Philosophy at the Hebrew University. Among his many publications are *Physics and Metaphysics in Hasdai Crescas*; (editor), *Studies on a Rabbinic Family: the de Botons*; and *Hasdai Crescas's Critique of the Theory of the Acquired Intellect*.

Tova Ilan is President of the Yaacov Herzog Center for Jewish Studies, which she cofounded in 1988. She chairs the Meimad council and is a member of numerous steering committees. Her recent publications include *One Hundred Years of Zionism*; *The Kibbutz: The Experiment That Hasn't Failed—Indeed?*; *An Examination of the Path of the Religious Kibbutz Today*; *Educating to Jewish Identity in the Diaspora*; *Ben-Gurion and His Attitude to Jewish Culture*; *Do We Want Kindness?*; and *Teaching Civics on the Ulpan to Immigrants from the USSR*.

Rabbi Shmuel Jakobovits is Chairman of *URA Kevode,* the Charedi [ultra-Orthodox] Association for Clarification of Contemporary Jewish Issues.

Steven T. Katz, the editor of this volume, is Professor of Jewish Studies and Director of the Elie Wiesel Center for Judaic Studies at Boston University. Among his publications are *Post-Holocaust Dialogues*; *Historicism, the Holocaust, and Zionism*; and *The Holocaust in Historical Context,* vol. 1. Volume 2 of this project is now in preparation at Oxford University Press. Among his other distinctions, he was awarded the Lucas Prize by the University of Tübingen in 1999.

Dan Michman is Professor of Holocaust Studies at Bar Ilan University and Director of Research at the Yad Vashem Institute in Jerusalem. Among his many publications are *Holocaust Historiography, a Jewish Perspective: Conceptualizations, Terminology, Approaches, and Fundamental Issues*; *Ha-Shoah* [The Holocaust]; and *Katastrofa evropei˜skogo evrei˜stva* [The European Catastrophe].

David Novak is Professor of Jewish Studies and Philosophy and Director of the Jewish Studies Program at the University of Toronto. His long list of publications includes *Covenantal Rights: A Study in Jewish Political Theory*; *Jewish-Christian Relations in a Secular Age*; and *Natural Law in Judaism*.

Shalom Ratzabi is Professor of Jewish History at Tel Aviv University. He is the editor of the journal *Zionism* and has published widely on Zionism, modern Orthodoxy, and trends in modern Judaism.

Michael Rosenak is Professor Emeritus of Jewish Philosophy and Education at the Hebrew University. Among his many important books are *Tsarikh 'iyun: masoret u-modernah ba-hinukh ha-Yehudi bi-zemanenu* [*More Study Needed: Tradition and Modernity in Contemporary Jewish Education*]; *Tree of Life, Tree of Knowledge: Conversations with the Torah*; and *Abiding Challenges: Research Perspectives on Jewish Education: Studies in Memory of Mordechai Bar-Lev*.

Shalom Rosenberg is Professor of Jewish Philosophy at the Hebrew University of Jerusalem. Among his many publications are '*Ets ha-da'at Tov ve-ra*' [The Tree of Good and Evil]; *Ha-Kuzari*; and *Parashat Shela? meraglim u-ma'pilim*.

Eliezer Schweid is Professor Emeritus at the Hebrew University of Jerusalem. He has published many influential books on Jewish thought in the modern era. Among them are *Toldot Filosofyat ha-dat ha-Yehudit ba-zeman he-hadash* [The Holocaust of Modern Jewish Philosophy]; *The Jewish Experience of Time: Philosophical Dimensions of the Jewish Holy Days*; and *Wrestling Until Day-Break: Searching for Meaning in the Thinking of the Holocaust*.

Joseph A. Turner is Professor of Jewish Studies at the Jewish Theological Seminary School in Jerusalem. He has published widely in the area of modern Jewish thought. His *Faith and Humanism: An Investigation of Franz Rosensweig's Religious Philosophy* was copublished by HaKibbutz Hameuchad in 2001.

Index of Names

Aaron, 112, 117, 292
Abraham, 29, 116, 127–28, 146, 149–50, 172, 229, 234–35
Abramsky, R. Yehezkel, 185
Achituv, Yosef, 275
Adam, 231, 234
Ahad Ha'am (Asher Zir Ginsburg), 75
Ahronson, Rabbi Joshua M., 178, 180, 188
Akiva, R., 74, 115, 164, 172, 261
Amiel, Mosheh Avigador, 133, 136, 143
Amir, Yehoyada, 226
Amital, R. Yehudah, 102
Amram, 181
Arendt, Hannah, 92–94, 200–201
Aristotle, 70–72, 251
Asher, R. Yehuda ben, 277
Ashkenazi, Shemuel Yaffe, 134
Ashlag, R. Yehuda, 152
Atiyah, Mordekhai, 134–35, 138, 152–53
Attar, R. Hayim Ibn, 138
Auerbach, Rabbi Hayyim Yehuda Leib, 189
Aviner, R. Solomon, 283, 292
Aviner, T., 282
Ayer, Alfred J., 17, 27
Azariah, 149, 170

Baal Shem Tov (Israel Ben Eliezer), 150
Bacharach, Yair Hayim, 141
Bakon, Hayim David, 147, 150
Barth, Karl, 15
Bauer, Yehuda, 93
Bazak, R. Eliyahu, 283
Benjamin, 115
Berkovits, Eliezer, 1, 29, 32, 35–41, 45, 150, 163–64, 171, 216–18, 230
Bettelheim, Bruno, 92–93
Bialik, Hayyim Nahman, 240
Bildad, 259
Blaykher, Moshe, 147, 154

Bloch, Avraham Yitshak, 141
Botschko, R. Eliyahu, 139
Boyaner, R., 146
Brazovsky, R. Shalom Noah, 145–46, 150–51
Breuer, R. Isaac, 278
Buber, Martin, 21, 23–26, 230, 238
Buzaglo, Shalom, 135, 152

Cain, 127, 234
Chanman, R., 271
Chief Rabbi Sirlowy, 187
Cohen, Arthur A., 40–48
Cohen, Eli, 294
Cohen, Herman, 69, 73–75, 195–96
Cordovero, R. Moshe, 234
Czoka, Pagiel, 1

Daniel, 170–72, 204–5
David, 49
Davids, R. Aaron Issachar, 187
Deuteronomy, 95, 121, 140, 142–43, 145
Druckman, Hayim, 154

Ecclesiastes, 116
Eckardt, A. Roy, 48
Ehrenreich, R. Shlomo Zalman, 111–13, 115, 117–18, 122, 126, 133–34, 136, 141, 143–44
Eichmann, Adolf, 92–93, 200
Elberg, R. Simha, 127–29, 144, 148, 151
Eleazar, 134–35
Eliav, R. Mordechai, 269
Elihu, 259
Elijah, 26, 29
Eliphaz, 259
Emden, R. Ya'akov, 139
Ephraim of Suldikov, 111
Esau, 113–14, 123, 134, 145, 290
Esh, Shaul, 269
Eve, 231

305

Index of Places